# 50% OFF Online GED Prep Course!

Dear Customer,

We consider it an honor and a privilege that you chose our GED Study Guide. As a way of showing our appreciation and to help us better serve you, we have partnered with Mometrix Test Preparation to offer **50% off their online GED Prep Course.** Many GED courses are needlessly expensive and don't deliver enough value. With their course, you get access to the best GED prep material, and you only pay half price.

**Mometrix has structured their online course to perfectly complement your printed study guide.** The GED Prep Course contains **in-depth lessons** that cover all the most important topics, **300+ video reviews** that explain difficult concepts, **over 1000 practice questions** to ensure you feel prepared, and **digital flashcards**, so you can fit some studying in while you're on the go.

## Online GED Prep Course

### Topics Covered:

- Reasoning Through Language Arts
  - *Reading Comprehension*
  - *Critical Thinking*
  - *Writing*
- Mathematical Reasoning
  - *Number Operations*
  - *Algebra, Functions, and Patterns*
  - *Measurement and Geometry*
- Science
  - *Physical Science*
  - *Earth and Space Science*
- Social Studies
  - *History and Government*
  - *Economics*

### Course Features:

- GED Study Guide
  - Get content that complements our best-selling study guide.
- 3 Full-Length Practice Tests
  - With over 1000 practice questions, you can test yourself again and again.
- Mobile Friendly
  - If you need to study on-the-go, the course is easily accessible from your mobile device.
- GED Flashcards
  - The course includes a flashcard mode consisting of over 400 content cards to help you study.

To receive this discount, simply head to their website: mometrix.com/university/ged or simply scan this QR code with your smartphone. At the checkout page, enter the discount code: **TPBGED50**

If you have any questions or concerns, please don't hesitate to contact Mometrix at universityhelp@mometrix.com.

SCAN HERE

D1716336

# FREE Test Taking Tips DVD Offer

To help us better serve you, we have developed a Test Taking Tips DVD that we would like to give you for FREE. **This DVD covers world-class test taking tips that you can use to be even more successful when you are taking your test.**

All that we ask is that you email us your feedback about your study guide. Please let us know what you thought about it – whether that is good, bad or indifferent.

To get your **FREE Test Taking Tips DVD**, email freedvd@studyguideteam.com with "FREE DVD" in the subject line and the following information in the body of the email:

      a. The title of your study guide.

      b. Your product rating on a scale of 1-5, with 5 being the highest rating.

      c. Your feedback about the study guide. What did you think of it?

      d. Your full name and shipping address to send your free DVD.

If you have any questions or concerns, please don't hesitate to contact us at freedvd@studyguideteam.com.

Thanks again!

# GED Study Guide
# 2022 & 2023 All Subjects

GED Test Prep Book with 2 Practice Exams
[7th Edition]

Joshua Rueda

Copyright © 2021 by TPB Publishing

All rights reserved. No part of this publication may be reproduced, distributed, or transmitted in any form or by any means, including photocopying, recording, or other electronic or mechanical methods, without the prior written permission of the publisher, except in the case of brief quotations embodied in critical reviews and certain other noncommercial uses permitted by copyright law.

Written and edited by TPB Publishing.

TPB Publishing is not associated with or endorsed by any official testing organization. TPB Publishing is a publisher of unofficial educational products. All test and organization names are trademarks of their respective owners. Content in this book is included for utilitarian purposes only and does not constitute an endorsement by TPB Publishing of any particular point of view.

Interested in buying more than 10 copies of our product? Contact us about bulk discounts:
bulkorders@studyguideteam.com

ISBN 13: 9781637757673
ISBN 10: 1637757670

# Table of Contents

Test Prep Books!!!

# Quick Overview

As you draw closer to taking your exam, effective preparation becomes more and more important. Thankfully, you have this study guide to help you get ready. Use this guide to help keep your studying on track and refer to it often.

This study guide contains several key sections that will help you be successful on your exam. The guide contains tips for what you should do the night before and the day of the test. Also included are test-taking tips. Knowing the right information is not always enough. Many well-prepared test takers struggle with exams. These tips will help equip you to accurately read, assess, and answer test questions.

A large part of the guide is devoted to showing you what content to expect on the exam and to helping you better understand that content. In this guide are practice test questions so that you can see how well you have grasped the content. Then, answer explanations are provided so that you can understand why you missed certain questions.

Don't try to cram the night before you take your exam. This is not a wise strategy for a few reasons. First, your retention of the information will be low. Your time would be better used by reviewing information you already know rather than trying to learn a lot of new information. Second, you will likely become stressed as you try to gain a large amount of knowledge in a short amount of time. Third, you will be depriving yourself of sleep. So be sure to go to bed at a reasonable time the night before. Being well-rested helps you focus and remain calm.

Be sure to eat a substantial breakfast the morning of the exam. If you are taking the exam in the afternoon, be sure to have a good lunch as well. Being hungry is distracting and can make it difficult to focus. You have hopefully spent lots of time preparing for the exam. Don't let an empty stomach get in the way of success!

When travelling to the testing center, leave earlier than needed. That way, you have a buffer in case you experience any delays. This will help you remain calm and will keep you from missing your appointment time at the testing center.

Be sure to pace yourself during the exam. Don't try to rush through the exam. There is no need to risk performing poorly on the exam just so you can leave the testing center early. Allow yourself to use all of the allotted time if needed.

Remain positive while taking the exam even if you feel like you are performing poorly. Thinking about the content you should have mastered will not help you perform better on the exam.

Once the exam is complete, take some time to relax. Even if you feel that you need to take the exam again, you will be well served by some down time before you begin studying again. It's often easier to convince yourself to study if you know that it will come with a reward!

# Test-Taking Strategies

### 1. Predicting the Answer

When you feel confident in your preparation for a multiple-choice test, try predicting the answer before reading the answer choices. This is especially useful on questions that test objective factual knowledge. By predicting the answer before reading the available choices, you eliminate the possibility that you will be distracted or led astray by an incorrect answer choice. You will feel more confident in your selection if you read the question, predict the answer, and then find your prediction among the answer choices. After using this strategy, be sure to still read all of the answer choices carefully and completely. If you feel unprepared, you should not attempt to predict the answers. This would be a waste of time and an opportunity for your mind to wander in the wrong direction.

### 2. Reading the Whole Question

Too often, test takers scan a multiple-choice question, recognize a few familiar words, and immediately jump to the answer choices. Test authors are aware of this common impatience, and they will sometimes prey upon it. For instance, a test author might subtly turn the question into a negative, or he or she might redirect the focus of the question right at the end. The only way to avoid falling into these traps is to read the entirety of the question carefully before reading the answer choices.

### 3. Looking for Wrong Answers

Long and complicated multiple-choice questions can be intimidating. One way to simplify a difficult multiple-choice question is to eliminate all of the answer choices that are clearly wrong. In most sets of answers, there will be at least one selection that can be dismissed right away. If the test is administered on paper, the test taker could draw a line through it to indicate that it may be ignored; otherwise, the test taker will have to perform this operation mentally or on scratch paper. In either case, once the obviously incorrect answers have been eliminated, the remaining choices may be considered. Sometimes identifying the clearly wrong answers will give the test taker some information about the correct answer. For instance, if one of the remaining answer choices is a direct opposite of one of the eliminated answer choices, it may well be the correct answer. The opposite of obviously wrong is obviously right! Of course, this is not always the case. Some answers are obviously incorrect simply because they are irrelevant to the question being asked. Still, identifying and eliminating some incorrect answer choices is a good way to simplify a multiple-choice question.

### 4. Don't Overanalyze

Anxious test takers often overanalyze questions. When you are nervous, your brain will often run wild, causing you to make associations and discover clues that don't actually exist. If you feel that this may be a problem for you, do whatever you can to slow down during the test. Try taking a deep breath or counting to ten. As you read and consider the question, restrict yourself to the particular words used by the author. Avoid thought tangents about what the author *really* meant, or what he or she was *trying* to say. The only things that matter on a multiple-choice test are the words that are actually in the question. You must avoid reading too much into a multiple-choice question, or supposing that the writer meant something other than what he or she wrote.

## 5. No Need for Panic

It is wise to learn as many strategies as possible before taking a multiple-choice test, but it is likely that you will come across a few questions for which you simply don't know the answer. In this situation, avoid panicking. Because most multiple-choice tests include dozens of questions, the relative value of a single wrong answer is small. As much as possible, you should compartmentalize each question on a multiple-choice test. In other words, you should not allow your feelings about one question to affect your success on the others. When you find a question that you either don't understand or don't know how to answer, just take a deep breath and do your best. Read the entire question slowly and carefully. Try rephrasing the question a couple of different ways. Then, read all of the answer choices carefully. After eliminating obviously wrong answers, make a selection and move on to the next question.

## 6. Confusing Answer Choices

When working on a difficult multiple-choice question, there may be a tendency to focus on the answer choices that are the easiest to understand. Many people, whether consciously or not, gravitate to the answer choices that require the least concentration, knowledge, and memory. This is a mistake. When you come across an answer choice that is confusing, you should give it extra attention. A question might be confusing because you do not know the subject matter to which it refers. If this is the case, don't eliminate the answer before you have affirmatively settled on another. When you come across an answer choice of this type, set it aside as you look at the remaining choices. If you can confidently assert that one of the other choices is correct, you can leave the confusing answer aside. Otherwise, you will need to take a moment to try to better understand the confusing answer choice. Rephrasing is one way to tease out the sense of a confusing answer choice.

## 7. Your First Instinct

Many people struggle with multiple-choice tests because they overthink the questions. If you have studied sufficiently for the test, you should be prepared to trust your first instinct once you have carefully and completely read the question and all of the answer choices. There is a great deal of research suggesting that the mind can come to the correct conclusion very quickly once it has obtained all of the relevant information. At times, it may seem to you as if your intuition is working faster even than your reasoning mind. This may in fact be true. The knowledge you obtain while studying may be retrieved from your subconscious before you have a chance to work out the associations that support it. Verify your instinct by working out the reasons that it should be trusted.

## 8. Key Words

Many test takers struggle with multiple-choice questions because they have poor reading comprehension skills. Quickly reading and understanding a multiple-choice question requires a mixture of skill and experience. To help with this, try jotting down a few key words and phrases on a piece of scrap paper. Doing this concentrates the process of reading and forces the mind to weigh the relative importance of the question's parts. In selecting words and phrases to write down, the test taker thinks about the question more deeply and carefully. This is especially true for multiple-choice questions that are preceded by a long prompt.

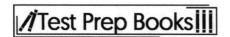 

## 9. Subtle Negatives

One of the oldest tricks in the multiple-choice test writer's book is to subtly reverse the meaning of a question with a word like *not* or *except*. If you are not paying attention to each word in the question, you can easily be led astray by this trick. For instance, a common question format is, "Which of the following is...?" Obviously, if the question instead is, "Which of the following is not...?," then the answer will be quite different. Even worse, the test makers are aware of the potential for this mistake and will include one answer choice that would be correct if the question were not negated or reversed. A test taker who misses the reversal will find what he or she believes to be a correct answer and will be so confident that he or she will fail to reread the question and discover the original error. The only way to avoid this is to practice a wide variety of multiple-choice questions and to pay close attention to each and every word.

## 10. Reading Every Answer Choice

It may seem obvious, but you should always read every one of the answer choices! Too many test takers fall into the habit of scanning the question and assuming that they understand the question because they recognize a few key words. From there, they pick the first answer choice that answers the question they believe they have read. Test takers who read all of the answer choices might discover that one of the latter answer choices is actually *more* correct. Moreover, reading all of the answer choices can remind you of facts related to the question that can help you arrive at the correct answer. Sometimes, a misstatement or incorrect detail in one of the latter answer choices will trigger your memory of the subject and will enable you to find the right answer. Failing to read all of the answer choices is like not reading all of the items on a restaurant menu: you might miss out on the perfect choice.

## 11. Spot the Hedges

One of the keys to success on multiple-choice tests is paying close attention to every word. This is never truer than with words like almost, most, some, and sometimes. These words are called "hedges" because they indicate that a statement is not totally true or not true in every place and time. An absolute statement will contain no hedges, but in many subjects, the answers are not always straightforward or absolute. There are always exceptions to the rules in these subjects. For this reason, you should favor those multiple-choice questions that contain hedging language. The presence of qualifying words indicates that the author is taking special care with their words, which is certainly important when composing the right answer. After all, there are many ways to be wrong, but there is only one way to be right! For this reason, it is wise to avoid answers that are absolute when taking a multiple-choice test. An absolute answer is one that says things are either all one way or all another. They often include words like *every*, *always*, *best*, and *never*. If you are taking a multiple-choice test in a subject that doesn't lend itself to absolute answers, be on your guard if you see any of these words.

## 12. Long Answers

In many subject areas, the answers are not simple. As already mentioned, the right answer often requires hedges. Another common feature of the answers to a complex or subjective question are qualifying clauses, which are groups of words that subtly modify the meaning of the sentence. If the question or answer choice describes a rule to which there are exceptions or the subject matter is complicated, ambiguous, or confusing, the correct answer will require many words in order to be expressed clearly and accurately. In essence, you should not be deterred by answer choices that seem excessively long. Oftentimes, the author of the text will not be able to write the correct answer without

offering some qualifications and modifications. Your job is to read the answer choices thoroughly and completely and to select the one that most accurately and precisely answers the question.

## 13. Restating to Understand

Sometimes, a question on a multiple-choice test is difficult not because of what it asks but because of how it is written. If this is the case, restate the question or answer choice in different words. This process serves a couple of important purposes. First, it forces you to concentrate on the core of the question. In order to rephrase the question accurately, you have to understand it well. Rephrasing the question will concentrate your mind on the key words and ideas. Second, it will present the information to your mind in a fresh way. This process may trigger your memory and render some useful scrap of information picked up while studying.

## 14. True Statements

Sometimes an answer choice will be true in itself, but it does not answer the question. This is one of the main reasons why it is essential to read the question carefully and completely before proceeding to the answer choices. Too often, test takers skip ahead to the answer choices and look for true statements. Having found one of these, they are content to select it without reference to the question above. Obviously, this provides an easy way for test makers to play tricks. The savvy test taker will always read the entire question before turning to the answer choices. Then, having settled on a correct answer choice, he or she will refer to the original question and ensure that the selected answer is relevant. The mistake of choosing a correct-but-irrelevant answer choice is especially common on questions related to specific pieces of objective knowledge. A prepared test taker will have a wealth of factual knowledge at their disposal, and should not be careless in its application.

## 15. No Patterns

One of the more dangerous ideas that circulates about multiple-choice tests is that the correct answers tend to fall into patterns. These erroneous ideas range from a belief that B and C are the most common right answers, to the idea that an unprepared test-taker should answer "A-B-A-C-A-D-A-B-A." It cannot be emphasized enough that pattern-seeking of this type is exactly the WRONG way to approach a multiple-choice test. To begin with, it is highly unlikely that the test maker will plot the correct answers according to some predetermined pattern. The questions are scrambled and delivered in a random order. Furthermore, even if the test maker was following a pattern in the assignation of correct answers, there is no reason why the test taker would know which pattern he or she was using. Any attempt to discern a pattern in the answer choices is a waste of time and a distraction from the real work of taking the test. A test taker would be much better served by extra preparation before the test than by reliance on a pattern in the answers.

# FREE DVD OFFER

Don't forget that doing well on your exam includes both understanding the test content and understanding how to use what you know to do well on the test. We offer a completely FREE Test Taking Tips DVD that covers world class test taking tips that you can use to be even more successful when you are taking your test.

All that we ask is that you email us your feedback about your study guide. To get your **FREE Test Taking Tips DVD**, email freedvd@studyguideteam.com with "FREE DVD" in the subject line and the following information in the body of the email:

- The title of your study guide.
- Your product rating on a scale of 1-5, with 5 being the highest rating.
- Your feedback about the study guide. What did you think of it?
- Your full name and shipping address to send your free DVD.

# Introduction to the GED Exam

## Function of the Test

The General Education Development (GED) test is an exam developed and administered by the GED Testing Service, a joint venture of the American Council on Education and Pearson VUE. The GED offers those without a high school diploma the chance to earn a high school equivalency credential by evaluating their knowledge of core high school subjects.

GED test takers represent a wide age group with diverse goals. Generally, the GED is appropriate for people who did not graduate from high school but who wish to pursue advancement in their career and/or education. According to MyGED, approximately 98% of U.S. colleges and universities accept a GED as the equivalent of a high school diploma (other schools may require additional preparation courses in addition to a passing GED score in order to be considered for admission). Over 20 million adults have earned GED credentials, and the latest reported pass rates for the 2014 GED are around 60%.

## Test Administration

GED tests are widely offered throughout the United States and Canada, although jurisdictions (state, province, etc.) may vary in terms of things like pricing, scheduling, and test rules. For international students and US military, international testing options are also available. Official GED Testing Centers are often operated by community colleges, adult education centers, and local school boards; GED Testing Service offers a comprehensive search of nearby test centers.

Keeping in mind that rules may vary between jurisdictions, all tests are administered in-person and taken on a computer. Tests are scheduled throughout the year; candidates should refer to their local testing centers for available test times. Candidates may take one of the four subject tests in an administration, or multiple (up to all four). Generally, test takers are able to take any test module three times without any restrictions on retesting. However, after three failed attempts, the candidate must wait a minimum of 60 days to retake the test. GED testing centers can also offer accommodations for students with disabilities, such as additional test time or Braille format tests. Test takers can request these accommodations when they register for an account on GED.com; approvals occur on an individual basis and typically take 30 days to receive.

## Test Format

The GED consists of four sections, or modules: Mathematical Reasoning, Science, Social Studies, and Reasoning Through Language Arts. As mentioned, although the complete test is offered together, it is not necessary to take all four modules on one day. Note that for the Mathematical Reasoning section, a formula sheet will be provided. Test subjects vary in length. The following chart provides information about the sections:

| Subject | Time | Topics |
|---|---|---|
| Mathematical Reasoning | 115 minutes | Basic Math, Geometry, Basic Algebra, Graphs and Functions |
| Science | 90 minutes | Reading for Meaning, Designing and Interpreting Science Experiments, Using Numbers and Graphs in Science |
| Social Studies | 70 minutes | Reading for Meaning, Analyzing Historical Events and Arguments, Using Numbers and Graphs in Social Studies |
| Reasoning Through Language Arts | 150 minutes | Reading for Meaning, Identifying and Creating Arguments, Grammar and Language |

A ten-minute break is given between each module.

On the testing day, test takers are not permitted to eat, drink, smoke, or use their cell phones during the test. Test takers are permitted to bring a handheld calculator (TI-30XS Multiview Scientific Calculator) to the test; testing centers will not provide handheld calculators, although an on-screen calculator will be available on the computer. Students will also be provided with three erasable note boards to use during the test.

## Scoring

Because the GED is now a computer-based test, scores will be available on MyGED within 24 hours of completing the test. The four modules of the GED are scored on a scale of 100–200. In order to earn high school equivalency, it is necessary to achieve a passing score on all of the four modules, and scores cannot be made up between modules—that is, a high score on one subject cannot be used to compensate for a low score on another subject. Scores are divided into four ranges:

1. A score lower than 145 points earns a score of "Not Passing." It is necessary to retake the test to earn high school equivalency.

2. A score at or higher than 145 points earns "GED Passing Score/High School Equivalency."

3. A score of 165-175 is deemed "GED College Ready." This designation advises colleges and universities that the test taker is ready to begin a degree program without further placement testing or preparation courses (policies vary among schools).

4. A score over 175 earns the test taker "GED College Ready + Credit." For some institutions, a score at this level allows the GED graduate to earn college credit for certain courses (policies vary among schools).

Test takers are encouraged to check what scores are required for admission by the colleges they intend to apply to, as some schools may seek scores that differ than the typical requisite 145. In 2017, the average scores of all test takers (including those who did not pass) were 154 for Science, 153 for Social Studies, 152 for Reasoning in Language Arts, and 150 for Math.

# Study Prep Plan for the GED Exam

**1**    **Schedule** - Use one of our study schedules below or come up with one of your own.

**2**    **Relax** - Test anxiety can hurt even the best students. There are many ways to reduce stress. Find the one that works best for you.

**3**    **Execute** - Once you have a good plan in place, be sure to stick to it.

## One Week Study Schedule

| Day 1 | Basic Math and Geometry |
|---|---|
| Day 2 | Basic Algebra, Graphs, and Functions |
| Day 3 | Reading Comprehension |
| Day 4 | Science |
| Day 5 | Social Studies |
| Day 6 | Practice Test #1 and Practice Test #2 |
| Day 7 | Take Your Exam! |

## Two Week Study Schedule

| Day 1 | Basic Math | Day 8 | Numbers, Graphs and Science Questions |
|---|---|---|---|
| Day 2 | Geometry | Day 9 | Reading for Meaning in Social Studies |
| Day 3 | Basic Algebra | Day 10 | Historical Events and Arguments |
| Day 4 | Graphs and Functions | Day 11 | Using Numbers and Graphics in Social Studies |
| Day 5 | Reading Comprehension and Arguments | Day 12 | Practice Test #1 |
| Day 6 | Grammar and Language | Day 13 | Practice Test #2 |
| Day 7 | Reading in Science and Designing Experiments | Day 14 | Take Your Exam! |

## One Month Study Schedule

| | | | | | |
|---|---|---|---|---|---|
| Day 1 | Basic Math | Day 11 | GED Science Questions | Day 21 | Review Grammar and Language |
| Day 2 | Geometry | Day 12 | Reading for Meaning in Social Studies | Day 22 | Review Reading for Meaning in Science |
| Day 3 | Basic Algebra | Day 13 | Analyzing Historical Events and Arguments | Day 23 | Review Science Experiments |
| Day 4 | Graphs and Functions | Day 14 | Using Numbers and Graphics in Social Studies | Day 24 | Review Numbers and Graphics in Science |
| Day 5 | Reading for Meaning in ELA | Day 15 | Practice Test #1 | Day 25 | Review GED Science Questions |
| Day 6 | Identifying and Creating Arguments | Day 16 | Review Answers | Day 26 | Review Reading for Meaning in Social Studies |
| Day 7 | Grammar and Language | Day 17 | Review Geometry | Day 27 | Review Analyzing Historical Events and Arguments |
| Day 8 | Reading for Meaning in Science | Day 18 | Review Algebra | Day 28 | Review Numbers and Graphics in Social Studies |
| Day 9 | Designing and Interpreting Science Experiments | Day 19 | Review Graphs and Functions | Day 29 | Practice Test #2 |
| Day 10 | Using Numbers and Graphics in Science | Day 20 | Review Creating Arguments | Day 30 | Take Your Exam! |

# Mathematical Reasoning

## Basic Math

Numbers usually serve as an adjective representing a quantity of objects. They function as placeholders for a value. Numbers can be better understood by their type and related characteristics.

### Definitions

A few definitions:

**Whole numbers:** describes a set of numbers that does not contain any fractions or decimals. The set of whole numbers includes zero.

> Example: 0, 1, 2, 3, 4, 189, 293 are all whole numbers.

**Integers:** describes whole numbers and their negative counterparts. (Zero does not have a negative counterpart here. Instead, zero is its own negative.)

> Example: -1, -2, -3, -4, -5, 0, 1, 2, 3, 4, 5 are all integers.

-1, -2, -3, -4, -5 are considered negative integers, and 1, 2, 3, 4, 5 are considered positive integers.

**Absolute value:** describes the value of a number regardless of its sign. The symbol for absolute value is | |.

> Example: The absolute value of 24 is 24 or $|24| = 24$.

The absolute value of -693 is 693 or $|-693| = 693$.

**Even numbers:** describes any number that can be divided by 2 evenly, meaning the answer has no decimal or remainder portion.

> Example: 2, 4, 9082, -2, -16, -504 are all considered even numbers, because they can be divided by 2, without leaving a remainder or forming a decimal. It does not matter whether the number is positive or negative.

**Odd numbers:** describes any number that does not divide evenly by 2.

> Example: 1, 21, 541, 3003, -9, -63, -1257 are all considered odd numbers, because they cannot be divided by 2 without a remainder or a decimal.

**Prime numbers:** describes a number that is only evenly divisible, resulting in no remainder or decimal, by 1 and itself.

> Example: 2, 3, 7, 13, 113 are all considered prime numbers because each can only be evenly divided by 1 and itself.

**Composite numbers:** describes a positive integer that is formed by multiplying two smaller integers together. Composite numbers can be divided evenly by numbers other than 1 or itself.

Example: 9, 24, 66, 2348, 10002 are all considered composite numbers because they are the result of multiplying two smaller integers together. In particular, these are all divisible by 2.

**Decimals:** designated by a decimal point which indicates that what follows the point is a value that is less than 1 and is added to the integer number preceding the decimal point. The digit immediately following the decimal point is in the tenths place, the digit following the tenths place is in the hundredths place, and so on.

For example, the decimal number 1.735 has a value greater than 1 but less than 2. The 7 represents seven tenths of the unit 1 (0.7 or $\frac{7}{10}$); the 3 represents three hundredths of 1 (0.03 or $\frac{3}{100}$); and the 5 represents five thousandths of 1 (0.005 or $\frac{5}{1000}$).

**Real numbers:** describes rational numbers and irrational numbers.

**Rational numbers:** describes any number that can be expressed as a fraction, with a non-zero denominator. Since any integer can be written with 1 in the denominator without changing its value, all integers are considered rational numbers. Every rational number has a decimal expression that terminates or repeats. That is, any rational number either will have a countable number of nonzero digits or will end with an ellipsis or a bar (3.6666... or $3.\overline{6}$) to depict repeating decimal digits. Some examples of rational numbers include 12, -3.54, $110.\overline{256}$, $\frac{-35}{10}$, and $4.\overline{7}$.

**Irrational numbers:** describes numbers that cannot be written as a finite decimal. Pi ($\pi$) is considered to be an irrational number because its decimal portion is unending or a non-repeating decimal. The most common irrational number is $\pi$, which has an endless and non-repeating decimal, but there are other well-known irrational numbers like $e$ and $\sqrt{2}$.

## Basic Addition and Subtraction

### Addition

Addition is the combination of two numbers so their quantities are added together cumulatively. The sign for an addition operation is the + symbol. For example, 9 + 6 = 15. The 9 and 6 combine to achieve a cumulative value, called a **sum**.

Addition holds the **commutative property**, which means that the order of the numbers numbers in an addition equation can be switched without altering the result. The formula for the commutative property is a + b = b + a. Let's look at a few examples to see how the commutative property works:

$$7 = 3 + 4 = 4 + 3 = 7$$

$$20 = 12 + 8 = 8 + 12 = 20$$

Addition also holds the **associative property**, which means that the grouping of numbers doesn't matter in an addition problem. In other words, the presence or absence of parentheses is irrelevant. The formula for the associative property is (a + b) + c = a + (b + c). Here are some examples of the associative property at work:

$$30 = (6 + 14) + 10 = 6 + (14 + 10) = 30$$

$$35 = 8 + (2 + 25) = (8 + 2) + 25 = 35$$

There are set columns for addition: ones, tens, hundreds, thousands, ten-thousands, hundred-thousands, millions, and so on. To add how many units there are total, each column needs to be combined, starting from the right, or the ones column.

| THOUSANDS | HUNDREDS | TENS | ONES |
|-----------|----------|------|------|

Every 10 units in the ones column equals one in the tens column, and every 10 units in the tens column equals one in the hundreds column, and so on.

Example: The number 5432 has 2 ones, 3 tens, 4 hundreds, and 5 thousands. The number 371 has 3 hundreds, 7 tens and 1 one. To combine, or add, these two numbers, simply add up how many units of each column exist. The best way to do this is by lining up the columns:

$$
\begin{array}{r}
5\ 4\ 3\ 2 \\
+\quad 3\ 7\ 1 \\
\hline
\end{array}
$$

The ones column adds 2 + 1 for a total (sum) of 3.

The tens column adds 3 + 7 for a total of 10; since 10 of that unit was collected, add 1 to the hundreds column to denote the total in the next column:

$$
\begin{array}{r}
1\quad\quad \\
5\ 4\ 3\ 2 \\
+\quad 3\ 7\ 1 \\
\hline
0\ 3 \\
\end{array}
$$

When adding the hundreds column, this extra 1 needs to be combined, so it would be the sum of 4, 3, and 1.

$$4 + 3 + 1 = 8$$

The last, or thousands, column listed would be the sum of 5. Since there are no other numbers in this column, that is the final total.

The answer would look as follows:

$$
\begin{array}{r}
5\ 4\ 3\ 2 \\
+\quad 3\ 7\ 1 \\
\hline
5\ 8\ 0\ 3 \\
\end{array}
$$

### Example
Find the sum of 9,734 and 895.

Set up the problem:

$$
\begin{array}{r}
9\ 7\ 3\ 4 \\
+\quad 8\ 9\ 5 \\
\hline
\end{array}
$$

Total the columns:

$$
\begin{array}{r}
9\;7\;3\;4 \\
+\quad\; 8\;9\;5 \\
\hline
1\;0\;6\;2\;9
\end{array}
$$

In this example, another column (ten-thousands) is added to the left of the thousands column, to denote a carryover of 10 units in the thousands column. The final sum is 10,629.

When adding using all negative integers, the total is negative. The integers are simply added together and the negative symbol is tacked on.

$$(-12) + (-435) = -447$$

## Subtraction

Subtraction is taking away one number from another, so their quantities are reduced. The sign designating a subtraction operation is the − symbol, and the result is called the **difference**. For example, 9 - 6 = 3. The number *6* detracts from the number *9* to reach the difference *3*.

Unlike addition, subtraction follows neither the commutative nor associative properties. The order and grouping in subtraction impact the result.

$$15 = 22 - 7 \neq 7 - 22 = -15$$

$$3 = (10 - 5) - 2 \neq 10 - (5 - 2) = 7$$

When working through subtraction problems involving larger numbers, it's necessary to regroup the numbers. Let's work through a practice problem using regrouping:

$$
\begin{array}{r}
3\;2\;5 \\
-\;\;7\;7 \\
\hline
\end{array}
$$

Here, it is clear that the ones and tens columns for 77 are greater than the ones and tens columns for 325. To subtract this number, borrow from the tens and hundreds columns. When borrowing from a column, subtracting 1 from the lender column will add 10 to the borrower column:

$$
\begin{array}{ccccccc}
3\text{-}1 & 10\text{+}2\text{-}1 & 10\text{+}5 & & 2 & 11 & 15 \\
-\quad & 7 & 7 & = - & & 7 & 7 \\
\hline
& & & & 2 & 4 & 8
\end{array}
$$

After ensuring that each digit in the top row is greater than the digit in the corresponding bottom row, subtraction can proceed as normal, and the answer is found to be 248.

## Addition and Subtraction with Negative Integers

When adding mixed-sign integers, determine which integer has the larger absolute value. Absolute value is the distance of a number from zero on the number line. Absolute value is indicated by these symbols: | |.

Take this equation for example:

$$12 + (-435)$$

The absolute value of each of the numbers is as follows:

$$|12| = 12$$

$$|-435| = 435$$

Since -435 is the larger integer, the final number will have its sign. In this case, that sign is negative. Now, subtract the smaller integer from the larger one. If you work out the equation, it will look like this:

$$12 + (-435) = -423$$

Mathematically, the equation looks like the one above, but practically speaking you will be doing it like this:

$$435 - 12 = 423$$

(then add the negative sign)

When using subtraction with negative integers, every unmarked integer is assumed to have a positive sign unless it is clearly marked as a negative integer. Subtracting an integer is the same as adding a negative integer.

Example:
-3 - 4
-3 + (-4)
-3 + (-4) = -7

Subtracting a negative integer is the same as adding a positive integer.

Example
-3 - (-4)
-3 + 4
-3 + 4 = 1

## Multiplication of Whole Numbers

Multiplication involves adding together multiple copies of a number. It is indicated by an × symbol or a number immediately outside of a parenthesis. For example:

$$5(8 - 2)$$

The two numbers being multiplied together are called **factors**, and their result is called a **product**. For example, $9 \times 6 = 54$. This can be shown alternatively by expansion of either the 9 or the 6:

$$9 \times 6 = 9 + 9 + 9 + 9 + 9 + 9 = 54$$

$$9 \times 6 = 6 + 6 + 6 + 6 + 6 + 6 + 6 + 6 + 6 = 54$$

Like addition, multiplication holds the commutative and associative properties:

$$115 = 23 \times 5 = 5 \times 23 = 115$$

$$84 = 3 \times (7 \times 4) = (3 \times 7) \times 4 = 84$$

Multiplication also follows the **distributive property**, which allows the multiplication to be distributed through parentheses. The formula for distribution is $a \times (b + c) = ab + ac$. This is clear after the examples:

$$45 = 5 \times 9 = 5(3 + 6) = (5 \times 3) + (5 \times 6) = 15 + 30 = 45$$

$$20 = 4 \times 5 = 4(10 - 5) = (4 \times 10) - (4 \times 5) = 40 - 20 = 20$$

For larger-number multiplication, how the numbers are lined up can ease the process. It is simplest to put the number with the most digits on top and the number with fewer digits on the bottom. If they have the same number of digits, select one for the top and one for the bottom. Line up the problem, and begin by multiplying the far-right column on the top and the far-right column on the bottom. If the answer to a column is more than 9, the ones place digit will be written below that column and the tens place digit will carry to the top of the next column to be added after those digits are multiplied. Write the answer below that column. Move to the next column to the left on the top, and multiply it by the same far-right column on the bottom. Keep moving to the left one column at a time on the top number until the end.

## Example
Multiply 37 × 8

Line up the numbers, placing the one with the most digits on top.

$$
\begin{array}{r}
3\ 7 \\
\times \quad 8 \\
\hline
\end{array}
$$

Multiply the far-right column on the top with the far-right column on the bottom (7 x 8). Write the answer, 56, as below: The ones value, 6, gets recorded, the tens value, 5, is carried.

```
      +5
      3 7
   X    8
        6
```

Move to the next column left on the top number and multiply with the far-right bottom (3 x 8). Remember to add any carry over after multiplying: 3 x 8 = 24, 24 + 5 = 29. Since there are no more digits on top, write the entire number below.

```
      +5
      3 7
   X    8
      2 9 6
```

The solution is 296.

If there is more than one column to the bottom number, move to the row below the first strand of answers, mark a zero in the far-right column, and then begin the multiplication process again with the far-right column on top and the second column from the right on the bottom. For each digit in the bottom number, there will be a row of answers, each padded with the respective number of zeros on the right. Finally, add up all of the answer rows for one total number.

Example: Multiply $512 \times 36$.

Line up the numbers (the one with the most digits on top) to multiply.

Begin with the right column on top and the right column on bottom ($2 \times 6$).

```
      5 1 2
   X    3 6
```

Move one column left on top and multiply by the far-right column on the bottom ($1 \times 6$). Add the carry over after multiplying: $1 \times 6 = 6, 6 + 1 = 7$.

```
        +1
      5 1 2
   x    3 6
        7 2
```

Move one column left on top and multiply by the far-right column on the bottom ($5 \times 6$). Since this is the last digit on top, write the whole answer below.

```
      5 1 2
   X    3 6
    3 0 7 2
```

Now move on to the second column on the bottom number. Starting on the far-right column on the top, repeat this pattern for the next number left on the bottom (2 × 3). Write the answers below the first line of answers; remember to begin with a zero placeholder on the far right.

```
        5 1 2
    X     3 6
    3 0 7 2
          6 0
```

Continue the pattern (1 × 3).

```
        5 1 2
    X     3 6
    3 0 7 2
        3 6 0
```

Since this is the last digit on top, write the whole answer below.

```
        5 1 2
    x     3 6
    3 0 7 2
  1 5 3 6 0
```

Now add the answer rows together. Pay attention to ensure they are aligned correctly.

```
        5 1 2
    x     3 6
    3 0 7 2
  1 5 3 6 0
  1 8 4 3 2
```

The solution is 18,432.

## Division of Whole Numbers

Division and multiplication are inverses of each other in the same way that addition and subtraction are opposites. The signs designating a division operation are the ÷ and / symbols. In division, the second number divides into the first.

The number before the division sign is called the **dividend** or, if expressed as a fraction, the **numerator**. For example, in $a \div b$, $a$ is the dividend, while in $\frac{a}{b}$, $a$ is the numerator.

The number after the division sign is called the **divisor** or, if expressed as a fraction, the **denominator.** For example, in $a \div b$, $b$ is the divisor, while in $\frac{a}{b}$, $b$ is the denominator.

Like subtraction, division doesn't follow the commutative property, as it matters which number comes before the division sign, and division doesn't follow the associative or distributive properties for the same reason. For example:

$$\frac{3}{2} = 9 \div 6 \neq 6 \div 9 = \frac{2}{3}$$

$$2 = 10 \div 5 = (30 \div 3) \div 5 \neq 30 \div (3 \div 5) = 30 \div \frac{3}{5} = 50$$

$$25 = 20 + 5 = (40 \div 2) + (40 \div 8) \neq 40 \div (2 + 8) = 40 \div 10 = 4$$

The answer to a division problem is called the **quotient.** If a divisor doesn't divide into a dividend an integer number of times, whatever is left over is termed the **remainder.** The remainder can be further divided out into decimal form by using long division; however, this doesn't always give a quotient with a finite number of decimal places, so the remainder can also be expressed as a fraction over the original divisor.

## Example
Divide 1050/42 or 1050 ÷ 42.

Set up the problem with the denominator being divided into the numerator.

$$42\overline{)1050}$$

Check for divisibility into the first unit of the numerator, 1.

42 cannot go into 1, so add on the next unit in the denominator, 0.

42 cannot go into 10, so add on the next unit in the denominator, 5.

42 can be divided into 105 two times. Write the 2 over the 5 in 105 and multiply 42 x 2. Write the 84 under 105 for subtraction and note the remainder, 21 is less than 42.

$$
\begin{array}{r}
2\phantom{00} \\
42\overline{)1050} \\
-84\phantom{0} \\
\hline
21\phantom{0}
\end{array}
$$

Drop the next digit in the numerator down to the remainder (making 21 into 210) to create a number 42 can divide into. 42 divides into 210 five times. Write the 5 over the 0 and multiply 42 × 5.

$$
\begin{array}{r}
25\phantom{0} \\
42\overline{)1050} \\
-84\phantom{0} \\
\hline
210
\end{array}
$$

Write the 210 under 210 for subtraction. The remainder is 0.

```
        2 5
4 2|1 0 5 0
  - 8 4
    2 1 0
  - 2 1 0
          0
```

The solution is 25.

<u>Example</u>
Divide 375/4 or 375 ÷ 4.

Set up the problem.

```
4|3 7 5
```

4 cannot divide into 3, so add the next unit from the numerator, 7. 4 divides into 37 nine times, so write the 9 above the 7. Multiply $4 \times 9 = 36$. Write the 36 under the 37 for subtraction. The remainder is 1 (1 is less than 4).

```
        9
4|3 7 5
- 3 6
      1
```

Drop the next digit in the numerator, 5, making the remainder 15. 4 divides into 15, three times, so write the 3 above the 5. Multiply $4 \times 3$. Write the 12 under the 15 for subtraction, remainder is 3 (3 is less than 4).

```
        9 3
4|3 7 5
- 3 6
    1 5
  - 1 2
        3
```

The solution is 93 remainder 3 or 93 ¾ (the remainder can be written over the original denominator).

## Decimals

Decimals mark the division between the whole portion and the fractional (or decimal) portion of a number. For example, 3.15 has 3 in the whole portion and 15 in the fractional or decimal portion. A number such as 645 is all whole, but there is still a decimal place. The decimal place in 645 is to the right of the 5, but usually not written, since there is no fractional or decimal portion to this number. The same number can be written as 645.0 or 645.00 or 645.000, etc. The position of the decimal place can change the entire value of a number, and impact a calculation. In the United States, the decimal place is used

when representing money. You'll often be asked to round to a certain decimal place. Here is a review of some basic decimal **place value** names:

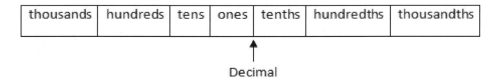

The number 12,302.2 would be read as "twelve thousand, three hundred two and two-tenths."

In the United States, a period denotes the decimal place; however, some countries use a comma. The comma is used in the United States to separate thousands, millions, and so on.

To round to the nearest whole number (eliminating the decimal portion), the example would become 12,302. For rounding, go to the number that is one place to the right of what you are rounding to. If the number is 0 through 4, there will be no change. For numbers 5 through 9, round up to the next whole number.

Example
Round 6,423.7 to the ones place.

Since the tenths place is the position to the right of the ones place, we use that number to determine if we round up or not. In this case, the 3 is in the ones place and the 7 is in the tenths place. (6,42<u>3</u>.7)

The 7 in the tenths place means we round the 3 up, so the final number will be 6,424.0

Example
Round 542.88 to the nearest tens

Since the ones place is the position to the right of the tens, we use that number to determine if we round up or not. In this case, the 4 is in the tens place and the 2 is in the ones place (5<u>4</u>2.88).

The 2 in the ones place means we do not round the 4 up, so the final number will be 540.00

Note: Everything to the right of the rounded position goes to 0 as a placeholder.

Example: Say you wanted to post an advertisement to sell a used vehicle for $2000.00. However, when typing the price, you accidentally moved the decimal over one place to the left. Now the asking price appears as $200.00. This difference of a factor of 10 is dramatic. As numbers get bigger or smaller, the impact of this mistake becomes more pronounced. If you were looking to sell a condo for $1,000,000.00, but made an error and moved the decimal place to the left one position, the price posts at $100,000.00. A mistake of a factor of 10 cost $900,000.00.

In dividing by 10, you move the decimal one position to the left, making a smaller number than the original. If multiplying by 10, move the decimal one position to the right, making a larger number than the original.

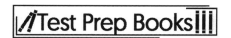

## Example
Divide 100 by 10 or 100 ÷ 10.

Move the decimal one place to the left, so the result is a smaller number than the original.

$$100 \div 10 = 10$$

## Example
Divide 1.0 by 10 or 1.0 ÷ 10.

Move the decimal one place to the left, so the result is a smaller number than the original.

$$1.0 \div 10 = 0.1$$

## Example
Multiply 100 by 10 or 100 x 10.

Move the decimal one place to the right, so the result is a larger number than the original.

$$100 \times 10 = 1000$$

## Example
Multiply 0.1 by 10 or 0.1 x 10.

Move the decimal one place to the right, so the result is a larger number than the original.

$$0.1 \times 10 = 1.0$$

## Prefixes

Moving the decimal place to the left or to the right illustrates multiplying or dividing by factors of 10. The metric system of units for measurement utilizes factors of 10 as displayed in the following table:

| kilo | 1000 units |
|------|------------|
| hecto | 100 units |
| deca | 10 units |
| base unit | |
| deci | 0.1 units |
| centi | 0.01 units |
| milli | 0.001 units |

It is important to have the ability to quickly manipulate by 10 according to prefixes for units.

Example: How many milliliters are in 5 liters of saline solution?

There are 1000 milliliters for every 1 liter. If we have 5 liters, it would be $5 \times 1000 = 5000$ mL

You may also count the zeros and which side of the decimal place they are on: 1000 has three zeroes to the left of the decimal, so insert three zeroes between the 5 and the decimal, or move the decimal place over three places to the right, for your answer of 5000 mL.

## Example
How many kilograms are in 4.8 grams?

There is 1 gram for every 0.001 kilograms. Since there is one-thousandth of a kilogram for each gram, that means divide by 1000, or move the decimal to the left by 3 places – 1 place for each 0. So, the result would be 0.0048 kg.

For quick conversions, move the decimal place the set number of spaces left or right to match the column/slot, as depicted below.

To convert from one prefix to another to the left or right of the base unit (follow the arrow to the left or right), move the decimal place the number of columns/slots as counted.

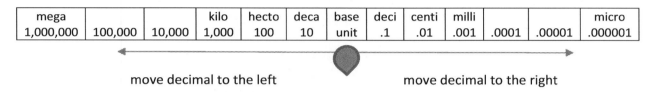

| mega | | | kilo | hecto | deca | base | deci | centi | milli | | | micro |
|---|---|---|---|---|---|---|---|---|---|---|---|---|
| 1,000,000 | 100,000 | 10,000 | 1,000 | 100 | 10 | unit | .1 | .01 | .001 | .0001 | .00001 | .000001 |

move decimal to the left　　　move decimal to the right

## Example
How many centiliters are in 4.7 kiloliters?

To convert a number with a unit prefixed as kilo into a unit prefixed as centi, move across five columns to the right, meaning move the decimal place five places to the right.

$$4.7 \text{ kL} = 470,000 \text{ cL}$$

## Example
How many liters are in 30 microliters?

Start with the unit marked micro and count the columns moving to the left until you reach the base unit for liters. Be sure to count the blank columns, as they are important placeholders. There are six columns from micro to the base unit moving to the left, so move the decimal place six places to the left.

$$30 \text{ mL} = 0.000030 \text{ L}$$

## Decimal Addition

Addition with decimals is done the same way as regular addition. All numbers could have decimals, but are often removed if the numbers to the right of the decimal are zeros. Line up numbers at the decimal place.

Example: Add $345.89 + 23.54$

Line the numbers up at the decimal place and add.

$$
\begin{array}{r}
3\ 4\ 5\ .\ 8\ 9 \\
+\quad\ \ 2\ 3\ .\ 5\ 4 \\
\hline
3\ 6\ 9\ .\ 4\ 3
\end{array}
$$

## Decimal Subtraction

Subtraction with decimals is done the same way as regular subtraction.

Example: Subtract 345.89 − 23.54

Line the numbers up at the decimal place and subtract.

$$
\begin{array}{r}
3\ 4\ 5\ .\ 8\ 9 \\
-\quad\ \ 2\ 3\ .\ 5\ 4 \\
\hline
3\ 2\ 2\ .\ 3\ 5
\end{array}
$$

## Decimal Multiplication

The simplest way to handle multiplication with decimals is to calculate the multiplication problem pretending the decimals are not there, then count how many decimal places there are in the original problem. Use that total to place the decimal the same number of places over, counting from right to left.

Example: Multiply 42.33 × 3.3

Line the numbers up and multiply, pretending there are no decimals.

$$
\begin{array}{r}
4\ 2\ 3\ 3 \\
\times\quad\ \ \ 3\ 3 \\
\hline
1\ 2\ 6\ 9\ 9 \\
1\ 2\ 6\ 9\ 9\ 0 \\
\hline
1\ 3\ 9\ 6\ 8\ 9
\end{array}
$$

Now look at the original problem and count how many decimal places were removed. Two decimal places were removed from 42.33 to get 4233, and one decimal place from 3.3 to get 33. Removed were $2 + 1 = 3$ decimal places. Place the decimal three places from the right of the number 139689. The answer is 139.689.

Another way to think of this is that when you move the decimal in the original numbers, it is like multiplying by 10. To put the decimals back, you need to divide the number by 10 the same amount of times you multiplied. It would still be three times for the above solution.

Example: Multiply 0.03 × 1.22

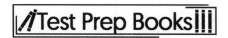
Line the numbers up and multiply, pretending there are no decimals. The zeroes in front of the 3 are unnecessary, so take them out for now.

$$\begin{array}{r} 1\ 2\ 2 \\ \times\qquad 3 \\ \hline 3\ 6\ 6 \end{array}$$

Look at the original problem and count how many decimals places were removed, or how many times each number was multiplied by 10. The 1.22 moved two places (or multiplied by 10 twice), as did 0.03. That is $2 + 2 = 4$ decimal places removed. Count that number, from right to left of the number 366, and place the decimal. The result is 0.0366.

## Decimal Division

Division with decimals is simplest when you eliminate some of the decimal places. Since you divide the bottom number of a fraction into the top, or divide the denominator into the numerator, the bottom number dictates the movement of the decimals. The goal is to remove the decimals from the denominator and mirror that movement in the numerator. You do not need the numerator to be decimal free, however. Divide as you would normally.

Example
Divide 4.21/0.2 or $4.21 \div 0.2$

Move the decimal over one place to the right in the denominator, making 0.2 simply 2. Move the decimal in the numerator, 4.21, over the same amount, so it is now 42.1.

$$0.2\overline{)4.21}$$

Becomes

$$2\overline{)42.1}$$

Divide.

$$\begin{array}{r} 21.05 \\ 2\overline{)42.10} \end{array}$$

The answer is 21.05 with the correct decimal placement. In decimal division, move the decimal the same amount for both numerator and denominator. There is no need to adjust anything after the problem is completed.

## Fractions

A fraction is an equation that represents a part of a whole but can also be used to present ratios or division problems. An example of a fraction is $\frac{x}{y}$. In this example, x is called the **numerator**, while y is the **denominator**. The numerator represents the number of parts, and the denominator is the total number

of parts. They are separated by a line or slash, known as a **fraction bar**. In simple fractions, the numerator and denominator can be nearly any integer. However, the denominator of a fraction can never be zero because dividing by zero is a function that is undefined.

Imagine that an apple pie has been baked for a holiday party, and the full pie has eight slices. After the party, there are five slices left. How could the amount of the pie that remains be expressed as a fraction? The numerator is 5 since there are 5 pieces left, and the denominator is 8 since there were eight total slices in the whole pie. Thus, expressed as a fraction, the leftover pie totals $\frac{5}{8}$ of the original amount.

Fractions come in three different varieties: proper fractions, improper fractions, and mixed numbers. **Proper fractions** have a numerator less than the denominator, such as $\frac{3}{8}$, but **improper fractions** have a numerator greater than the denominator, such as $\frac{15}{8}$. **Mixed numbers** combine a whole number with a proper fraction, such as $3\frac{1}{2}$. Any mixed number can be written as an improper fraction by multiplying the integer by the denominator, adding the product to the value of the numerator, and dividing the sum by the original denominator. For example:

$$3\frac{1}{2} = \frac{3 \times 2 + 1}{2} = \frac{7}{2}$$

Whole numbers can also be converted into fractions by placing the whole number as the numerator and making the denominator 1. For example, $3 = \frac{3}{1}$.

One of the most fundamental concepts of fractions is their ability to be manipulated by multiplication or division. This is possible since $\frac{n}{n} = 1$ for any non-zero integer. As a result, multiplying or dividing by $\frac{n}{n}$ will not alter the original fraction since any number multiplied or divided by 1 doesn't change the value of that number. Fractions of the same value are known as equivalent fractions. For example, $\frac{2}{4}, \frac{4}{8}, \frac{50}{100}$, and $\frac{75}{150}$ are equivalent, as they all equal $\frac{1}{2}$.

Although many equivalent fractions exist, they are easier to compare and interpret when reduced or simplified. The numerator and denominator of a simple fraction will have no factors in common other than 1. When reducing or simplifying fractions, divide the numerator and denominator by the **greatest common factor**. A simple strategy is to divide the numerator and denominator by low numbers, like 2, 3, or 5 until arriving at a simple fraction, but the same thing could be achieved by determining the greatest common factor for both the numerator and denominator and dividing each by it. Using the first method is preferable when both the numerator and denominator are even, end in 5, or are obviously a multiple of another number. However, if no numbers seem to work, it will be necessary to factor the numerator and denominator to find the GCF. Let's look at examples:

1) Simplify the fraction $\frac{6}{8}$:

Dividing the numerator and denominator by 2 results in $\frac{3}{4}$, which is a simple fraction.

2) Simplify the fraction $\frac{12}{36}$:

Dividing the numerator and denominator by 2 leaves $\frac{6}{18}$. This isn't a simple fraction, as both the numerator and denominator have factors in common. Dividing each by 3 results in $\frac{2}{6}$, but this can be further simplified by dividing by 2 to get $\frac{1}{3}$. This is the simplest fraction, as the numerator is 1. In cases like this, multiple division operations can be avoided by determining the greatest common factor between the numerator and denominator.

3) Simplify the fraction $\frac{18}{54}$ by dividing by the greatest common factor:

First, determine the factors for the numerator and denominator. The factors of 18 are 1, 2, 3, 6, 9, and 18. The factors of 54 are 1, 2, 3, 6, 9, 18, 27, and 54. Thus, the greatest common factor is 18. Dividing both the numerator and denominator by 18 leaves $\frac{1}{3}$, which is the simplest fraction. This method takes slightly more work, but it definitively arrives at the simplest fraction.

## Operations with Fractions

### Multiplication of Fractions

Of the four basic operations that can be performed on fractions, the one that involves the least amount of work is multiplication. To multiply two fractions, simply multiply the numerators together, multiply the denominators together, and place the products of each as a fraction. Whole numbers and mixed numbers can also be expressed as a fraction, as described above, to multiply with a fraction. Let's work through a couple of examples.

$$1) \frac{2}{5} \times \frac{3}{4} = \frac{6}{20} = \frac{3}{10}$$

$$2) \frac{4}{9} \times \frac{7}{11} = \frac{28}{99}$$

### Division of Fractions

Dividing fractions is similar to multiplication with one key difference. To divide fractions, flip the numerator and denominator of the second fraction, and then proceed as if it were a multiplication problem:

$$1) \frac{7}{8} \div \frac{4}{5} = \frac{7}{8} \times \frac{5}{4} = \frac{35}{32}$$

$$2) \frac{5}{9} \div \frac{1}{3} = \frac{5}{9} \times \frac{3}{1} = \frac{15}{9} = \frac{5}{3}$$

### Addition and Subtraction of Fractions

Addition and subtraction require more steps than multiplication and division, as these operations require the fractions to have the same denominator, also called a **common denominator**. It is always possible to find a common denominator by multiplying the denominators. However, when the denominators are large numbers, this method is unwieldy, especially if the answer must be provided in its simplest form. Thus, it's beneficial to find the **least common denominator** of the fractions—the least common denominator is incidentally also the least common multiple.

Once equivalent fractions have been found with common denominators, simply add or subtract the numerators to arrive at the answer:

1) $\frac{1}{2} + \frac{3}{4} = \frac{2}{4} + \frac{3}{4} = \frac{5}{4}$

2) $\frac{3}{12} + \frac{11}{20} = \frac{15}{60} + \frac{33}{60} = \frac{48}{60} = \frac{4}{5}$

3) $\frac{7}{9} - \frac{4}{15} = \frac{35}{45} - \frac{12}{45} = \frac{23}{45}$

4) $\frac{5}{6} - \frac{7}{18} = \frac{15}{18} - \frac{7}{18} = \frac{8}{18} = \frac{4}{9}$

## Changing Fractions to Decimals

To change a fraction into a decimal, divide the denominator into the numerator until there are no remainders. There may be repeating decimals, so rounding is often acceptable. A straight line above the repeating portion denotes that the decimal repeats.

Example
Express 4/5 as a decimal.

Set up the division problem.

$$5\overline{)4}$$

5 does not go into 4, so place the decimal and add a zero.

$$5\overline{)4.0}$$

5 goes into 40 eight times. There is no remainder.

$$\begin{array}{r} 0.8 \\ 5\overline{)4.0} \\ -4.0 \\ \hline 0 \end{array}$$

The solution is 0.8.

Example
Express 33 1/3 as a decimal.

Since the whole portion of the number is known, set it aside to calculate the decimal from the fraction portion.

Set up the division problem.

$$3\overline{)1}$$

3 does not go into 1, so place the decimal and add zeros. 3 goes into 10 three times.

$$\begin{array}{r} 0.3 \\ 3\overline{\smash{)}1.0} \end{array}$$

This will repeat with a remainder of 1.

$$\begin{array}{r} 0.333 \\ 3\overline{\smash{)}1.000} \\ \underline{-9} \\ 10 \\ \underline{-9} \\ 10 \end{array}$$

So, we will place a line over the 3 to denote the repetition. The solution is written $33.\overline{3}$.

## Changing Decimals to Fractions

To change decimals to fractions, place the decimal portion of the number, the numerator, over the respective place value, the denominator, then reduce, if possible.

<u>Example</u>
Express 0.25 as a fraction.

This is read as twenty-five hundredths, so put 25 over 100. Then reduce to find the solution.

$$\frac{25}{100} = \frac{1}{4}$$

<u>Example</u>
Express 0.455 as a fraction

This is read as four hundred fifty-five thousandths, so put 455 over 1000. Then reduce to find the solution.

$$\frac{455}{1000} = \frac{91}{200}$$

There are two types of problems that commonly involve percentages. The first is to calculate some percentage of a given quantity, where you convert the percentage to a decimal, and multiply the quantity by that decimal. Secondly, you are given a quantity and told it is a fixed percent of an unknown quantity. In this case, convert to a decimal, then divide the given quantity by that decimal.

<u>Example</u>
What is 30% of 760?

Convert the percent into a useable number. "Of" means to multiply.

$$30\% = 0.30$$

Set up the problem based on the givens, and solve.

$$0.30 \times 760 = 228$$

## Example

8.4 is 20% of what number?

Convert the percent into a useable number.

$$20\% = 0.20$$

The given number is a percent of the answer needed, so divide the given number by this decimal rather than multiplying it.

$$\frac{8.4}{0.20} = 42$$

## Ratios and Proportions

### Ratios

**Ratios** are used to show the relationship between two quantities. The ratio of oranges to apples in the grocery store may be 3 to 2. That means that for every 3 oranges, there are 2 apples. This comparison can be expanded to represent the actual number of oranges and apples, such as 36 oranges to 24 apples. Another example may be the number of boys to girls in a math class. If the ratio of boys to girls is given as 2 to 5, that means there are 2 boys to every 5 girls in the class. Ratios can also be compared if the units in each ratio are the same. The ratio of boys to girls in the math class can be compared to the ratio of boys to girls in a science class by stating which ratio is higher and which is lower.

**Rates** are used to compare two quantities with different units. *Unit rates* are the simplest form of rate. With **unit rates**, the denominator in the comparison of two units is one. For example, if someone can type at a rate of 1000 words in 5 minutes, then their unit rate for typing is $\frac{1000}{5} = 200$ words in one minute or 200 words per minute. Any rate can be converted into a unit rate by dividing to make the denominator one. 1000 words in 5 minutes has been converted into the unit rate of 200 words per minute.

Ratios and rates can be used together to convert rates into different units. For example, if someone is driving 50 kilometers per hour, that rate can be converted into miles per hour by using a ratio known as the **conversion factor.** Since the given value contains kilometers and the final answer needs to be in miles, the ratio relating miles to kilometers needs to be used. There are 0.62 miles in 1 kilometer. This, written as a ratio and in fraction form, is $\frac{0.62 \ miles}{1 \ km}$. To convert 50km/hour into miles per hour, the following conversion needs to be set up:

$$\frac{50 \ km}{hour} * \frac{0.62 \ miles}{1 \ km} = 31 \ miles \ per \ hour$$

The ratio between two similar geometric figures is called the **scale factor.** For example, a problem may depict two similar triangles, A and B. The scale factor from the smaller triangle A to the larger triangle B is given as 2 because the length of the corresponding side of the larger triangle, 16, is twice the corresponding side on the smaller triangle, 8. This scale factor can also be used to find the value of a missing side, $x$, in triangle A. Since the scale factor from the smaller triangle (A) to larger one (B) is 2, the

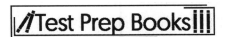 

larger corresponding side in triangle B (given as 25) can be divided by 2 to find the missing side in A ($x = 12.5$). The scale factor can also be represented in the equation $2A = B$ because two times the lengths of A gives the corresponding lengths of B. This is the idea behind similar triangles.

## Proportions

Much like a scale factor can be written using an equation like $2A = B$, a **relationship** is represented by the equation $Y = kX$. X and Y are proportional because as values of X increase, the values of Y also increase. A relationship that is inversely proportional can be represented by the equation $Y = \frac{k}{X}$, where the value of $Y$ decreases as the value of $X$ increases and vice versa.

Proportional reasoning can be used to solve problems involving ratios, percentages, and averages. Ratios can be used in setting up proportions and solving them to find unknowns. For example, if a student completes an average of 10 pages of math homework in 3 nights, how long would it take the student to complete 22 pages? Both ratios can be written as fractions. The second ratio would contain the unknown.

The following proportion represents this problem, where x is the unknown number of nights:

$$\frac{10 \; pages}{3 \; nights} = \frac{22 \; pages}{x \; nights}$$

Solving this proportion entails cross-multiplying (multiplying both sets of numbers that are diagonally across and setting them equal to each other) and results in the following equation: $10x = 22 * 3$. Simplifying and solving for $x$ results in the exact solution: $x = 6.6 \; nights$. The result would be rounded up to 7 because the homework would actually be completed on the 7th night.

The following problem uses ratios involving percentages:

If 20% of the class is girls and 30 students are in the class, how many girls are in the class?

To set up this problem, it is helpful to use the common proportion: $\frac{\%}{100} = \frac{is}{of}$. Within the proportion, % is the percentage of girls, 100 is the total percentage of the class, *is* is the number of girls, and *of* is the total number of students in the class. Most percentage problems can be written using this language. To solve this problem, the proportion should be set up as $\frac{20}{100} = \frac{x}{30}$ and then solved for x. Cross-multiplying results in the equation $20 * 30 = 100x$, which results in the solution $x = 6$. There are 6 girls in the class.

Problems involving volume, length, and other units can also be solved using ratios. For example, A problem may ask for the volume of a cone that has a radius, $r = 7m$ and a height, $h = 16m$. Referring to the formulas provided on the test, the volume of a cone is given as: $V = \pi r^2 \frac{h}{3}$, where r is the radius, and h is the height. Plugging $r = 7$ and $h = 16$ into the formula, the following is obtained:

$$V = \pi (7^2) \frac{16}{3}$$

Therefore, the volume of the cone is found to be approximately 821m³. Sometimes, answers in different units are sought. If this problem wanted the answer in liters, 821m³ would need to be converted.

Using the equivalence statement 1m³ = 1000L, the following ratio would be used to solve for liters:

$$821\text{m}^3 * \frac{1000L}{1m^3}$$

Cubic meters in the numerator and denominator cancel each other out, and the answer is converted to 821,000 liters, or $8.21 * 10^5$ L.

Other conversions can also be made between different given and final units. If the temperature in a pool is 30°C, what is the temperature of the pool in degrees Fahrenheit? To convert these units, an equation is used relating Celsius to Fahrenheit. The following equation is used:

$$T_{°F} = 1.8T_{°C} + 32$$

Plugging in the given temperature and solving the equation for T yields the result:

$$T_{°F} = 1.8(30) + 32 = 86°F$$

Both units in the metric system and U.S. customary system are widely used.

Here are some more examples of how to solve for proportions:

1) $\frac{75\%}{90\%} = \frac{25\%}{x}$

To solve for $x$, the fractions must be cross multiplied: ($75\%x = 90\% \times 25\%$). To make things easier, let's convert the percentages to decimals: ($0.9 \times 0.25 = 0.225 = 0.75x$). To get rid of $x$'s coefficient, each side must be divided by that same coefficient to get the answer $x = 0.3$. The question could ask for the answer as a percentage or fraction in lowest terms, which are 30% and $\frac{3}{10}$, respectively.

2) $\frac{x}{12} = \frac{30}{96}$

Cross-multiply: $96x = 30 \times 12$

Multiply: $96x = 360$

Divide: $x = 360 \div 96$

Answer: $x = 3.75$

3) $\frac{0.5}{3} = \frac{x}{6}$

Cross-multiply: $3x = 0.5 \times 6$

Multiply: $3x = 3$

Divide: $x = 3 \div 3$

Answer: $x = 1$

You may have noticed there's a faster way to arrive at the answer. If there is an obvious operation being performed on the proportion, the same operation can be used on the other side of the proportion to solve for $x$. For example, in the first practice problem, 75% became 25% when divided by 3, and upon

doing the same to 90%, the correct answer of 30% would have been found with much less legwork. However, these questions aren't always so intuitive, so it's a good idea to work through the steps, even if the answer seems apparent from the outset.

## Percentages

Think of percentages as fractions with a denominator of 100. In fact, **percentage** means "per hundred." Problems often require converting numbers from percentages, fractions, and decimals. The following explains how to work through those conversions.

## Conversions

*Decimals and Percentages*: Since a percentage is based on "per hundred," decimals and percentages can be converted by multiplying or dividing by 100. Practically speaking, this always amounts to moving the decimal point two places to the right or left, depending on the conversion. To convert a percentage to a decimal, move the decimal point two places to the left and remove the % sign. To convert a decimal to a percentage, move the decimal point two places to the right and add a "%" sign. Here are some examples:

65% = 0.65
0.33 = 33%
0.215 = 21.5%
99.99% = 0.9999
500% = 5.00
7.55 = 755%

*Fractions and Percentages*: Remember that a percentage is a number per one hundred. So, a percentage can be converted to a fraction by making the number in the percentage the numerator and putting 100 as the denominator:

$$43\% = \frac{43}{100}$$

$$97\% = \frac{97}{100}$$

$$4.7\% = \frac{47}{1000}$$

Note in the last example, that the decimal can be removed by going from 100 to 1,000, because it's accomplished by multiplying the numerator and denominator by 10.

Note that the percent symbol (%) kind of looks like a 0, a 1, and another 0. So, think of a percentage like 54% as 54 over 100. Note that it's often good to simplify a fraction into the smallest possible numbers. So, 54/100 would then become 27/50:

$$\frac{54}{100} \div \frac{2}{2} = \frac{27}{50}$$

To convert a fraction to a percent, follow the same logic. If the fraction happens to have 100 in the denominator, you're in luck. Just take the numerator and add a percent symbol:

$$\frac{28}{100} = 28\%$$

Another option is to make the denominator equal to 100. Be sure to multiply the numerator and the denominator by the same number. For example:

$$\frac{3}{20} \times \frac{5}{5} = \frac{15}{100}$$

$$\frac{15}{100} = 15\%$$

If neither of those strategies work, divide the numerator by the denominator to get a decimal:

$$\frac{9}{12} = 0.75$$

Then convert the decimal to a percentage:

$$0.75 = 75\%$$

## Percent Formula

The percent formula looks like this:

$$\frac{part}{whole} = \frac{\%}{100}$$

After numbers are plugged in, multiply the diagonal numbers and then divide by the remaining one. It works every time.

So, when a question asks what percent 5 is of 10. You plug the numbers in:

$$\frac{5}{10} = \frac{\%}{100}$$

Multiply the diagonal numbers:

$$5 \times 100 = 500$$

Divide by the remaining number:

$$\frac{500}{10} = 50\%$$

The percent formula can be applied in a number of different circumstances by plugging in the numbers appropriately.

## Fractions and Decimals in Order

A rational number is any number that can be written as a fraction or ratio. Within the set of rational numbers, several subsets exist that are referenced throughout the mathematics topics. Counting numbers are the first numbers learned as a child. Counting numbers consist of 1,2,3,4, and so on. Whole numbers include all counting numbers and zero (0,1,2,3,4,…). Integers include counting numbers, their opposites, and zero (…,-3,-2,-1,0,1,2,3,…). Rational numbers are inclusive of integers, fractions, and decimals that terminate, or end (1.7, 0.04213) or repeat (0.136$\bar{5}$).

Placing numbers in an order in which they are listed from smallest to largest is known as **ordering**. Ordering numbers properly can help in the comparison of different quantities of items.

When comparing two numbers to determine if they are equal or if one is greater than the other, it is best to look at the digit furthest to the left of the decimal place (or the first value of the decomposed numbers). If this first digit of each number being compared is equal in place value, then move one digit to the right to conduct a similar comparison. Continue this process until it can be determined that both numbers are equal or a difference is found, showing that one number is greater than the other. If a number is greater than the other number it is being compared to, a symbol such as > (greater than) or < (less than) can be utilized to show this comparison. It is important to remember that the "open mouth" of the symbol should be nearest the larger number.

For example:

1,023,100 compared to 1,023,000

First, compare the digit farthest to the left. Both are decomposed to 1,000,000, so this place is equal.

Next, move one place to right on both numbers being compared. This number is zero for both numbers, so move on to the next number to the right. The first number decomposes to 20,000, while the second decomposes to 20,000. These numbers are also equal, so move one more place to the right. The first number decomposes to 3,000, as does the second number, so they are equal again. Moving one place to the right, the first number decomposes to 100, while the second number is zero. Since 100 is greater than zero, the first number is greater than the second. This is expressed using the greater than symbol:

1,023,100 > 1,023,000 because 1,023,100 is greater than 1,023,000 (Note that the "open mouth" of the symbol is nearest to 1,023,100).

Notice the > symbol in the above comparison. When values are the same, the equals sign (=) is used. However, when values are unequal, or an **inequality** exists, the relationship is denoted by various inequality symbols. These symbols describe in what way the values are unequal. A value could be greater than (>); less than (<); greater than or equal to (≥); or less than or equal to (≤) another value. The statement "five times a number added to forty is more than sixty-five" can be expressed as $5x + 40 > 65$. Common words and phrases that express inequalities are:

| Symbol | Phrase |
|---|---|
| < | is under, is below, smaller than, beneath |
| > | is above, is over, bigger than, exceeds |
| ≤ | no more than, at most, maximum |
| ≥ | no less than, at least, minimum |

Another way to compare whole numbers with many digits is to use place value. In each number to be compared, it is necessary to find the highest place value in which the numbers differ and to compare the value within that place value. For example, 4,523,345 < 4,532,456 because of the values in the ten thousands place.

## Comparing and Ordering Decimals

To compare decimals and order them by their value, utilize a method similar to that of ordering large numbers.

The main difference is where the comparison will start. Assuming that any numbers to left of the decimal point are equal, the next numbers to be compared are those immediately to the right of the decimal point. If those are equal, then move on to compare the values in the next decimal place to the right.

For example:

Which number is greater, 12.35 or 12.38?

Check that the values to the left of the decimal point are equal:

$$12 = 12$$

Next, compare the values of the decimal place to the right of the decimal:

$$12.3 = 12.3$$

Those are also equal in value.

Finally, compare the value of the numbers in the next decimal place to the right on both numbers:

$$12.3\textbf{5} \text{ and } 12.3\textbf{8}$$

Here the 5 is less than the 8, so the final way to express this inequality is:

$$12.35 < 12.38$$

Comparing decimals is regularly exemplified with money because the "cents" portion of money ends in the hundredths place. When paying for gasoline or meals in restaurants, and even in bank accounts, if enough errors are made when calculating numbers to the hundredths place, they can add up to dollars and larger amounts of money over time.

Number lines can also be used to compare decimals. Tick marks can be placed within two whole numbers on the number line that represent tenths, hundredths, etc. Each number being compared can then be plotted. The value farthest to the right on the number line is the largest.

## Comparing Fractions

To compare fractions with either the same **numerator** (top number) or same **denominator** (bottom number), it is easiest to visualize the fractions with a model.

For example, which is larger, $\frac{1}{3}$ or $\frac{1}{4}$? Both numbers have the same numerator, but a different denominator. In order to demonstrate the difference, shade the amounts on a pie chart split into the number of pieces represented by the denominator.

The first pie chart represents $\frac{1}{3}$, a larger shaded portion, and is therefore a larger fraction than the second pie chart representing $\frac{1}{4}$.

If two fractions have the same denominator (or are split into the same number of pieces), the fraction with the larger numerator is the larger fraction, as seen below in the comparison of $\frac{1}{3}$ and $\frac{2}{3}$:

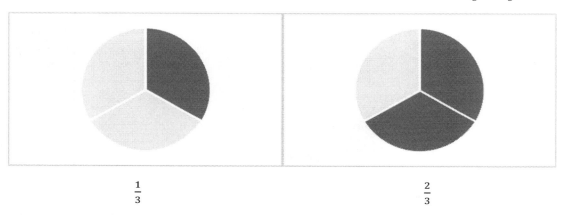

$$\frac{1}{3} \qquad\qquad\qquad\qquad \frac{2}{3}$$

A **unit fraction** is one in which the numerator is 1 ($\frac{1}{2}, \frac{1}{3}, \frac{1}{8}, \frac{1}{20}$, etc.). The denominator indicates the number of equal pieces that the whole is divided into. The greater the number of pieces, the smaller each piece will be. Therefore, the greater the denominator of a unit fraction, the smaller it is in value. Unit fractions can also be compared by converting them to decimals. For example, $\frac{1}{2} = 0.5$, $\frac{1}{3} = 0.\overline{3}$, $\frac{1}{8} = 0.125$, $\frac{1}{20} = 0.05$, etc.

Comparing two fractions with different denominators can be difficult if attempting to guess at how much each represents. Using a number line, blocks, or just finding a common denominator with which to compare the two fractions makes this task easier.

For example, compare the fractions $\frac{3}{4}$ and $\frac{5}{8}$.

The number line method of comparison involves splitting one number line evenly into 4 sections, and the second number line evenly into 8 sections total, as follows:

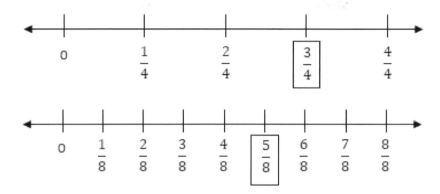

Here it can be observed that $\frac{3}{4}$ is greater than $\frac{5}{8}$, so the comparison is written as $\frac{3}{4} > \frac{5}{8}$.

This could also be shown by finding a common denominator for both fractions, so that they could be compared. First, list out factors of 4: 4, 8, 12, 16.

Then, list out factors of 8: 8, 16, 24.

Both share a common factor of 8, so they can be written in terms of 8 portions. In order for $\frac{3}{4}$ to be written in terms of 8, both the numerator and denominator must be multiplied by 2, thus forming the new fraction $\frac{6}{8}$. Now the two fractions can be compared.

Because both have the same denominator, the numerator will show the comparison.

$$\frac{6}{8} > \frac{5}{8}$$

## Ordering Numbers

Whether the question asks to order the numbers from greatest to least or least to greatest, the crux of the question is the same—convert the numbers into a common format. Generally, it's easiest to write the numbers as whole numbers and decimals so they can be placed on a number line. Follow these examples to understand this strategy.

1) Order the following rational numbers from greatest to least:

$$\sqrt{36}, 0.65, 78\%, \frac{3}{4}, 7, 90\%, \frac{5}{2}$$

Of the seven numbers, the whole number (7) and decimal (0.65) are already in an accessible form, so concentrate on the other five.

First, the square root of 36 equals 6. (If the test asks for the root of a non-perfect root, determine which two whole numbers the root lies between.) Next, convert the percentages to decimals. A percentage

means "per hundred," so this conversion requires moving the decimal point two places to the left, leaving 0.78 and 0.9. Lastly, evaluate the fractions:

$$\frac{3}{4} = \frac{75}{100} = 0.75$$

$$\frac{5}{2} = 2\frac{1}{2} = 2.5$$

Now, the only step left is to list the numbers in the request order:

$$7, \sqrt{36}, \frac{5}{2}, 90\%, 78\%, \frac{3}{4}, 0.65$$

2) Order the following rational numbers from least to greatest:

$$2.5, \sqrt{9}, -10.5, 0.853, 175\%, \sqrt{4}, \frac{4}{5}$$

$$\sqrt{9} = 3$$

$$175\% = 1.75$$

$$\sqrt{4} = 2$$

$$\frac{4}{5} = 0.8$$

From least to greatest, the answer is: $-10.5, \frac{4}{5}, 0.853, 175\%, \sqrt{4}, 2.5, \sqrt{9}$

It is not possible to give similar relationships between two complex numbers $a + ib$ and $c + id$. This is because the real numbers cannot be identified with the complex numbers, and there is no form of comparison between the two. However, given any polynomial equation, its solutions can be solved in the complex field. If the zeros are real, they can be written as $a + i \times 0$; if they are complex, they can be written as $a + ib$; and if they are imaginary, they can be written as $ib$.

## Multiples and Factors

**Multiples** of a given number are found by taking that number and multiplying it by any other whole number. For example, 3 is a factor of 6, 9, and 12. Therefore, 6, 9, and 12 are multiples of 3. The multiples of any number are an infinite list. For example, the multiples of 5 are 5, 10, 15, 20, and so on. This list continues without end. A list of multiples is used in finding the **least common multiple**, or LCM, for fractions when a common denominator is needed. The denominators are written down and their multiples listed until a common number is found in both lists. This common number is the LCM.

The **factors** of a number are all integers that can be multiplied by another integer to produce the given number. For example, 2 is multiplied by 3 to produce 6. Therefore, 2 and 3 are both factors of 6. Similarly, $1 \times 6 = 6$ and $2 \times 3 = 6$, so 1, 2, 3, and 6 are all factors of 6. Another way to explain a factor is to say that a given number divides evenly by each of its factors to produce an integer. For example, 6 does not divide evenly by 5. Therefore, 5 is not a factor of 6.

**Prime factorization** breaks down each factor of a whole number until only prime numbers remain. All composite numbers can be factored into prime numbers. For example, the prime factors of 12 are 2, 2, and:

$$3 \ (2 \times 2 \times 3 = 12)$$

To produce the prime factors of a number, the number is factored, and any composite numbers are continuously factored until the result is the product of prime factors only. A **factor tree**, such as the one below, is helpful when exploring this concept.

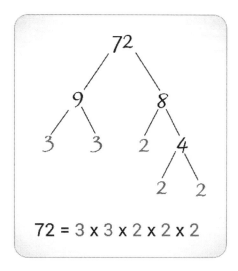

## Simplifying Exponents

**Exponents** are used in mathematics to express a number or variable multiplied by itself a certain number of times. For example, $x^3$ means $x$ is multiplied by itself three times. In this expression, x is called the **base,** and 3 is the **exponent.** Exponents can be used in more complex problems when they contain fractions and negative numbers.

**Fractional exponents** can be explained by looking first at the inverse of exponents, which are **roots.** Given the expression $x^2$, the square root can be taken, $\sqrt{x^2}$, cancelling out the 2 and leaving x by itself, if $x$ is positive. Cancellation occurs because $\sqrt{x}$ can be written with exponents, instead of roots, as $x^{\frac{1}{2}}$. The numerator of 1 is the exponent, and the denominator of 2 is called the root (which is why it's referred to as **square root**). Taking the square root of $x^2$ is the same as raising it to the $\frac{1}{2}$ power. Written out in mathematical form, it takes the following progression:

$$\sqrt{x^2} = (x^2)^{\frac{1}{2}} = x$$

From properties of exponents:

$$2 \times \frac{1}{2} = 1$$

is the actual exponent of $x$. Another example can be seen with $x^{\frac{4}{7}}$. The variable $x$, raised to four-sevenths, is equal to the seventh root of $x$ to the fourth power: $\sqrt[7]{x^4}$. In general,

$$x^{\frac{1}{n}} = \sqrt[n]{x}$$

and

$$x^{\frac{m}{n}} = \sqrt[n]{x^m}$$

**Negative exponents** also involve fractions. Whereas $y^3$ can also be rewritten as $\frac{y^3}{1}$, $y^{-3}$ can be rewritten as $\frac{1}{y^3}$. A negative exponent means the exponential expression must be moved to the opposite spot in a fraction to make the exponent positive. If the negative appears in the numerator, it moves to the denominator. If the negative appears in the denominator, it is moved to the numerator. In general, $a^{-n} = \frac{1}{a^n}$, and $a^{-n}$ and $a^n$ are reciprocals.

Take, for example, the following expression:

$$\frac{a^{-4}b^2}{c^{-5}}$$

Since $a$ is raised to the negative fourth power, it can be moved to the denominator. Since $c$ is raised to the negative fifth power, it can be moved to the numerator. The $b$ variable is raised to the positive second power, so it does not move.

The simplified expression is as follows:

$$\frac{b^2c^5}{a^4}$$

In mathematical expressions containing exponents and other operations, the order of operations must be followed. **PEMDAS** states that exponents are calculated after any parenthesis and grouping symbols but before any multiplication, division, addition, and subtraction.

There are a few rules for working with exponents. For any numbers $a, b, m, n$, the following hold true:

$$a^1 = a$$

$$1^a = 1$$

$$a^0 = 1$$

$$a^m \times a^n = a^{m+n}$$

$$a^m \div a^n = a^{m-n}$$

$$(a^m)^n = a^{m \times n}$$

$$(a \times b)^m = a^m \times b^m$$

$$(a \div b)^m = a^m \div b^m$$

Any number, including a fraction, can be an exponent. The same rules apply.

## Distance Between Numbers on a Number Line

Aside from zero, numbers can be either positive or negative. The sign for a positive number is the plus sign or the + symbol, while the sign for a negative number is the minus sign or the − symbol. If a number has no designation, then it's assumed to be positive.

Both positive and negative numbers are valued according to their distance from zero. Both +3 and -3 can be considered using the following number line:

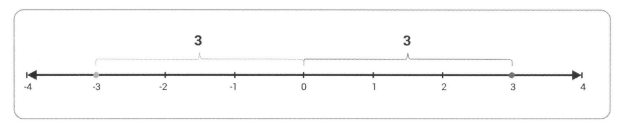

Both 3 and -3 are three spaces from zero. The distance from zero is called its **absolute value**. Thus, both -3 and 3 have an absolute value of 3 since they're both three spaces away from zero.

An absolute number is written by placing | | around the number. So, |3| and |−3| both equal 3, as that's their common absolute value.

## Implications for Addition and Subtraction

For addition, if all numbers are either positive or negative, they are simply added together. For example, $4 + 4 = 8$ and $-4 + -4 = -8$. However, things get tricky when some of the numbers are negative, and some are positive.

For example, with $6 + (-4)$, the first step is to take the absolute values of the numbers, which are 6 and 4. Second, the smaller value is subtracted from the larger. The equation becomes $6 - 4 = 2$. Third, the sign of the original larger number is placed on the sum. Here, 6 is the larger number, and it's positive, so the sum is 2.

Here's an example where the negative number has a larger absolute value: $(-6) + 4$. The first two steps are the same as the example above. However, on the third step, the negative sign must be placed on the sum, because the absolute value of (-6) is greater than 4. Thus, $-6 + 4 = -2$.

The absolute value of numbers implies that subtraction can be thought of as flipping the sign of the number following the subtraction sign and simply adding the two numbers. This means that subtracting a negative number will, in fact, be adding the positive absolute value of the negative number.

Here are some examples:

$$-6 - 4 = -6 + -4 = -10$$

$$3 - -6 = 3 + 6 = 9$$

$$-3 - 2 = -3 + -2 = -5$$

## Implications for Multiplication and Division

For multiplication and division, if both numbers are positive, then the product or quotient is always positive. If both numbers are negative, then the product or quotient is also positive. However, if the numbers have opposite signs, the product or quotient is always negative.

Simply put, the product in multiplication and quotient in division is always positive, unless the numbers have opposing signs, in which case it's negative. Here are some examples:

$$(-6) \times (-5) = 30$$

$$(-50) \div 10 = -5$$

$$8 \times |-7| = 56$$

$$(-48) \div (-6) = 8$$

If there are more than two numbers in a multiplication or division problem, then whether the product or quotient is positive or negative depends on the number of negative numbers in the problem. If there is an odd number of negatives, then the product or quotient is negative. If there is an even number of negative numbers, then the result is positive.

Here are some examples:

$$(-6) \times 5 \times (-2) \times (-4) = -240$$

$$(-6) \times 5 \times 2 \times (-4) = 240$$

## Properties of Operations

Properties of operations exist to make calculations easier and solve problems for missing values. The following table summarizes commonly used properties of real numbers.

| Property | Addition | Multiplication |
|---|---|---|
| Commutative | $a + b = b + a$ | $a \times b = b \times a$ |
| Associative | $(a + b) + c = a + (b + c)$ | $(a \times b) \times c = a \times (b \times c)$ |
| Identity | $a + 0 = a; 0 + a = a$ | $a \times 1 = a; 1 \times a = a$ |
| Inverse | $a + (-a) = 0$ | $a \times \dfrac{1}{a} = 1; a \neq 0$ |
| Distributive | $a(b + c) = ab + ac$ | |

The **commutative property of addition** states that the order in which numbers are added does not change the sum. Similarly, the **commutative property of multiplication** states that the order in which

numbers are multiplied does not change the product. The **associative property of addition** and **multiplication** state that the grouping of numbers being added or multiplied does not change the sum or product, respectively. The commutative and associative properties are useful for performing calculations. For example, $(47 + 25) + 3$ is equivalent to $(47 + 3) + 25$, which is easier to calculate.

The **identity property of addition** states that adding zero to any number does not change its value. The **identity property of multiplication** states that multiplying a number by one does not change its value. The **inverse property of addition** states that the sum of a number and its opposite equals zero. Opposites are numbers that are the same with different signs (ex. 5 and -5; $-\frac{1}{2}$ and $\frac{1}{2}$). The **inverse property of multiplication** states that the product of a number (other than zero) and its reciprocal equals one. **Reciprocal numbers** have numerators and denominators that are inverted (ex. $\frac{2}{5}$ and $\frac{5}{2}$). Inverse properties are useful for canceling quantities to find missing values (see algebra content). For example, $a + 7 = 12$ is solved by adding the inverse of $7(-7)$ to both sides in order to isolate $a$.

The **distributive property** states that multiplying a sum (or difference) by a number produces the same result as multiplying each value in the sum (or difference) by the number and adding (or subtracting) the products. Consider the following scenario: You are buying three tickets for a baseball game. Each ticket costs $18. You are also charged a fee of $2 per ticket for purchasing the tickets online. The cost is calculated:

$$3 \times 18 + 3 \times 2$$

Using the distributive property, the cost can also be calculated $3(18 + 2)$.

## Squares, Square Roots, Cubes, and Cube Roots

A **root** is a different way to write an exponent when the exponent is the reciprocal of a whole number. We use the **radical** symbol to write this in the following way:

$$\sqrt[n]{a} = a^{\frac{1}{n}}$$

This quantity is called the *n-th* **root** of $a$. The $n$ is called the **index** of the radical.

Note that if the *n*-th root of $a$ is multiplied by itself $n$ times, the result will just be $a$. If no number $n$ is written by the radical, it is assumed that $n$ is 2: $\sqrt{5} = 5^{\frac{1}{2}}$. The special case of the 2$^{nd}$ root is called the **square root,** and the third root is called the **cube root**.

A **perfect square** is a whole number that is the square of another whole number. For example, 16 and 64 are perfect squares because 16 is the square of 4, and 64 is the square of 8.

## Undefined Expressions

Expressions can be undefined when they involve dividing by zero or having a zero denominator. In simple fractions, the numerator and denominator can be nearly any integer. However, the denominator of a fraction can never be zero because dividing by zero is a function that is undefined. Trying to take the square root of a negative number also yields an undefined result.

## Unit Rates

Unit rate word problems will ask you to calculate the rate or quantity of something in a different value. For example, a problem might say that a car drove a certain number of miles in a certain number of minutes and then ask how many miles per hour the car was traveling. These questions involve solving proportions. Consider the following examples:

1) Alexandra made $96 during the first 3 hours of her shift as a temporary worker at a law office. She will continue to earn money at this rate until she finishes in 5 more hours. How much does Alexandra make per hour? How much will Alexandra have made at the end of the day?

This problem can be solved in two ways. The first is to set up a proportion, as the rate of pay is constant. The second is to determine her hourly rate, multiply the 5 hours by that rate, and then add the $96.

To set up a proportion, put the money already earned over the hours already worked on one side of an equation. The other side has $x$ over 8 hours (the total hours worked in the day). It looks like this:

$$\frac{96}{3} = \frac{x}{8}$$

Now, cross-multiply to get $768 = 3x$. To get $x$, divide by 3, which leaves $x = 256$. Alternatively, as $x$ is the numerator of one of the proportions, multiplying by its denominator will reduce the solution by one step. Thus, Alexandra will make $256 at the end of the day. To calculate her hourly rate, divide the total by 8, giving $32 per hour.

Alternatively, it is possible to figure out the hourly rate by dividing $96 by 3 hours to get $32 per hour. Now her total pay can be figured by multiplying $32 per hour by 8 hours, which comes out to $256.

2) Jonathan is reading a novel. So far, he has read 215 of the 335 total pages. It takes Jonathan 25 minutes to read 10 pages, and the rate is constant. How long does it take Jonathan to read one page? How much longer will it take him to finish the novel? Express the answer in time.

To calculate how long it takes Jonathan to read one page, divide the 25 minutes by 10 pages to determine the page per minute rate. Thus, it takes 2.5 minutes to read one page.

Jonathan must read 120 more pages to complete the novel. (This is calculated by subtracting the pages already read from the total.) Now, multiply his rate per page by the number of pages. Thus:

$$12 \times 2.5 = 300$$

Expressed in time, 300 minutes is equal to 5 hours.

3) At a hotel, $\frac{4}{5}$ of the 120 rooms are booked for Saturday. On Sunday, $\frac{3}{4}$ of the rooms are booked. On which day are more of the rooms booked, and by how many more?

The first step is to calculate the number of rooms booked for each day. Do this by multiplying the fraction of the rooms booked by the total number of rooms.

Saturday: $\frac{4}{5} \times 120 = \frac{4}{5} \times \frac{120}{1} = \frac{480}{5} = 96$ rooms

Sunday: $\frac{3}{4} \times 120 = \frac{3}{4} \times \frac{120}{1} = \frac{360}{4} = 90$ rooms

Thus, more rooms were booked on Saturday by 6 rooms.

4) In a veterinary hospital, the veterinarian-to-pet ratio is 1:9. The ratio is always constant. If there are 45 pets in the hospital, how many veterinarians are currently in the veterinary hospital?

Set up a proportion to solve for the number of veterinarians: $\frac{1}{9} = \frac{x}{45}$

Cross-multiplying results in $9x = 45$, which works out to 5 veterinarians.

Alternatively, as there are always 9 times as many pets as veterinarians, it is possible to divide the number of pets (45) by 9. This also arrives at the correct answer of 5 veterinarians.

5) At a general practice law firm, 30% of the lawyers work solely on tort cases. If 9 lawyers work solely on tort cases, how many lawyers work at the firm?

First, solve for the total number of lawyers working at the firm, which will be represented here with $x$. The problem states that 9 lawyers work solely on torts cases, and they make up 30% of the total lawyers at the firm. Thus, 30% multiplied by the total, $x$, will equal 9. Written as equation, this is: $30\% \times x = 9$.

It's easier to deal with the equation after converting the percentage to a decimal, leaving $0.3x = 9$. Thus:

$$x = \frac{9}{0.3} = 30$$

lawyers working at the firm.

6) Xavier was hospitalized with pneumonia. He was originally given 35mg of antibiotics. Later, after his condition continued to worsen, Xavier's dosage was increased to 60mg. What was the percent increase of the antibiotics? Round the percentage to the nearest tenth.

An increase or decrease in percentage can be calculated by dividing the difference in amounts by the original amount and multiplying by 100. Written as an equation, the formula is:

$$\frac{new\ quantity\ -\ old\ quantity}{old\ quantity} \times 100$$

Here, the question states that the dosage was increased from 35mg to 60mg, so these are plugged into the formula to find the percentage increase.

$$\frac{60 - 35}{35} \times 100 = \frac{25}{35} \times 100 = .7142 \times 100 = 71.4\%$$

## Objects at Scale

Scale drawings are used in designs to model the actual measurements of a real-world object. For example, the blueprint of a house might indicate that it is drawn at a scale of 3 inches to 8 feet. Given one value and asked to determine the width of the house, a proportion should be set up to solve the problem. Given the scale of 3in:8ft and a blueprint width of 1 ft (12 in.), to find the actual width of the building, the proportion $\frac{3}{8} = \frac{12}{x}$ should be used. This results in an actual width of 32 ft.

The ratio between two similar geometric figures is called the **scale factor**. For example, a problem may depict two similar triangles, A and B. The scale factor from the smaller triangle A to the larger triangle B is given as 2 because the length of the corresponding side of the larger triangle, 16, is twice the corresponding side on the smaller triangle, 8. This scale factor can also be used to find the value of a missing side, $x$, in triangle A. Since the scale factor from the smaller triangle (A) to larger one (B) is 2, the larger corresponding side in triangle B (given as 25) can be divided by 2 to find the missing side in A ($x$ = 12.5). The scale factor can also be represented in the equation $2A = B$ because two times the lengths of A gives the corresponding lengths of B. This is the idea behind similar triangles.

## Multiple-Step Problems that Use Ratios, Proportions, and Percentages

### Solving Real-World Problems Involving Ratios and Rates of Change

**Ratios** are used to show the relationship between two quantities. The ratio of oranges to apples in the grocery store may be 3 to 2. That means that for every 3 oranges, there are 2 apples. This comparison can be expanded to represent the actual number of oranges and apples, such as 36 oranges to 24 apples. Another example may be the number of boys to girls in a math class. If the ratio of boys to girls is given as 2 to 5, that means there are 2 boys to every 5 girls in the class. Ratios can also be compared if the units in each ratio are the same. The ratio of boys to girls in the math class can be compared to the ratio of boys to girls in a science class by stating which ratio is higher and which is lower.

Rates are used to compare two quantities with different units. **Unit rates** are the simplest form of rate. With unit rates, the denominator in the comparison of two units is one. For example, if someone can type at a rate of 1000 words in 5 minutes, then their unit rate for typing is $\frac{1000}{5} = 200$ words in one minute or 200 words per minute. Any rate can be converted into a unit rate by dividing to make the denominator one. 1000 words in 5 minutes has been converted into the unit rate of 200 words per minute.

Ratios and rates can be used together to convert rates into different units. For example, if someone is driving 50 kilometers per hour, that rate can be converted into miles per hour by using a ratio known as the **conversion factor**. Since the given value contains kilometers and the final answer needs to be in miles, the ratio relating miles to kilometers needs to be used. There are 0.62 miles in 1 kilometer. This, written as a ratio and in fraction form, is $\frac{0.62\ miles}{1\ km}$. To convert 50km/hour into miles per hour, the following conversion needs to be set up:

$$\frac{50\ km}{hour} \times \frac{0.62\ miles}{1\ km} = 31\ miles\ per\ hour$$

When dealing with word problems, there is no fixed series of steps to follow, but there are some general guidelines to use. It is important that the quantity to be found is identified. Then, it can be determined how the given values can be used and manipulated to find the final answer.

Example: Jana wants to travel to visit Alice, who lives one hundred and fifty miles away. If she can drive at fifty miles per hour, how long will her trip take?

The quantity to find is the *time* of the trip. The time of a trip is given by the distance to travel divided by the speed to be traveled. The problem determines that the distance is one hundred and fifty miles, while the speed is fifty miles per hour. Thus, 150 divided by 50 is $150 \div 50 = 3$. Because *miles* and *miles per hour* are the units being divided, the miles cancel out. The result is 3 hours.

Example: Bernard wishes to paint a wall that measures twenty feet wide by eight feet high. It costs ten cents to paint one square foot. How much money will Bernard need for paint?

The final quantity to compute is the *cost* to paint the wall. This will be ten cents ($0.10) for each square foot of area needed to paint. The area to be painted is unknown, but the dimensions of the wall are given; thus, it can be calculated.

The dimensions of the wall are 20 feet wide and 8 feet high. Since the area of a rectangle is length multiplied by width, the area of the wall is:

$$8 \times 20 = 160 \; square \; feet$$

Multiplying $0.1 \times 160$ yields $16 as the cost of the paint.

## Solving Real-World Problems Involving Proportions

Much like a scale factor can be written using an equation like $2A = B$, a **relationship** is represented by the equation $Y = kX$. $X$ and $Y$ are proportional because as values of $X$ increase, the values of $Y$ also increase. A relationship that is inversely proportional can be represented by the equation $Y = \frac{k}{X}$, where the value of $Y$ decreases as the value of $X$ increases and vice versa.

Proportional reasoning can be used to solve problems involving ratios, percentages, and averages. Ratios can be used in setting up proportions and solving them to find unknowns. For example, if a student completes an average of 10 pages of math homework in 3 nights, how long would it take the student to complete 22 pages? Both ratios can be written as fractions. The second ratio would contain the unknown.

The following proportion represents this problem, where x is the unknown number of nights:

$$\frac{10 \; pages}{3 \; nights} = \frac{22 \; pages}{x \; nights}$$

Solving this proportion entails cross-multiplying and results in the following equation: $10x = 22 \times 3$. Simplifying and solving for $x$ results in the exact solution: $x = 6.6 \; nights$. The result would be rounded up to 7 because the homework would actually be completed on the 7th night.

The following problem uses ratios involving percentages:

If 20% of the class is girls and 30 students are in the class, how many girls are in the class?

To set up this problem, it is helpful to use the common proportion: $\frac{\%}{100} = \frac{is}{of}$. Within the proportion, % is the percentage of girls, 100 is the total percentage of the class, *is* is the number of girls, and *of* is the total number of students in the class. Most percentage problems can be written using this language. To

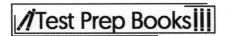

solve this problem, the proportion should be set up as $\frac{20}{100} = \frac{x}{30}$, and then solved for x. Cross-multiplying results in the equation $20 \times 30 = 100x$, which results in the solution $x = 6$. There are 6 girls in the class.

Problems involving volume, length, and other units can also be solved using ratios. For example, a problem may ask for the volume of a cone to be found that has a radius:

$$r = 7m$$

and a height:

$$h = 16m$$

Referring to the formulas provided on the test, the volume of a cone is given as:

$$V = \pi r^2 \frac{h}{3}$$

where r is the radius, and h is the height. Plugging $r = 7$ and $h = 16$ into the formula, the following is obtained:

$$V = \pi (7^2) \frac{16}{3}$$

Therefore, volume of the cone is found to be $821 m^3$. Sometimes, answers in different units are sought. If this problem wanted the answer in liters, $821 m^3$ would need to be converted. Using the equivalence statement $1m^3 = 1000L$, the following ratio would be used to solve for liters:

$$821 m^3 \times \frac{1000L}{1m^3}$$

Cubic meters in the numerator and denominator cancel each other out, and the answer is converted to 821,000 liters, or $8.21 \times 10^5$ L.

Other conversions can also be made between different given and final units. If the temperature in a pool is 30°C, what is the temperature of the pool in degrees Fahrenheit? To convert these units, an equation is used relating Celsius to Fahrenheit. The following equation is used:

$$T_{°F} = 1.8 T_{°C} + 32$$

Plugging in the given temperature and solving the equation for T yields the result:

$$T_{°F} = 1.8(30) + 32 = 86°F$$

Units in both the metric system and U.S. customary system are widely used.

Here are some more examples of how to solve for proportions:

1) $\frac{75\%}{90\%} = \frac{25\%}{x}$

To solve for $x$, the fractions must be cross multiplied:

$$(75\%x = 90\% \times 25\%)$$

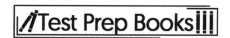

To make things easier, let's convert the percentages to decimals:

$$(0.9 \times 0.25 = 0.225 = 0.75x)$$

To get rid of $x$'s coefficient, each side must be divided by that same coefficient to get the answer $x = 0.3$. The question could ask for the answer as a percentage or fraction in lowest terms, which are 30% and $\frac{3}{10}$, respectively.

2) $\frac{x}{12} = \frac{30}{96}$

Cross-multiply: $96x = 30 \times 12$

Multiply: $96x = 360$

Divide: $x = 360 \div 96$

Answer: $x = 3.75$

3) $\frac{0.5}{3} = \frac{x}{6}$

Cross-multiply: $3x = 0.5 \times 6$

Multiply: $3x = 3$

Divide: $x = 3 \div 3$

Answer: $x = 1$

You may have noticed there's a faster way to arrive at the answer. If there is an obvious operation being performed on the proportion, the same operation can be used on the other side of the proportion to solve for $x$. For example, in the first practice problem, 75% became 25% when divided by 3, and upon doing the same to 90%, the correct answer of 30% would have been found with much less legwork. However, these questions aren't always so intuitive, so it's a good idea to work through the steps, even if the answer seems apparent from the outset.

## Solving Real-World Problems Involving Percentages

Questions dealing with percentages can be difficult when they are phrased as word problems. These word problems almost always come in three varieties. The first type will ask to find what percentage of some number will equal another number. The second asks to determine what number is some percentage of another given number. The third will ask what number another number is a given percentage of.

One of the most important parts of correctly answering percentage word problems is to identify the numerator and the denominator. This fraction can then be converted into a percentage, as described above.

The following word problem shows how to make this conversion:

A department store carries several different types of footwear. The store is currently selling 8 athletic shoes, 7 dress shoes, and 5 sandals. What percentage of the store's footwear are sandals?

First, calculate what serves as the **whole**, as this will be the denominator. How many total pieces of footwear does the store sell? The store sells 20 different types ($8\ athletic + 7\ dress + 5\ sandals$).

Second, what footwear type is the question specifically asking about? Sandals. Thus, 5 is the numerator.

Third, the resultant fraction must be expressed as a percentage. The first two steps indicate that $\frac{5}{20}$ of the footwear pieces are sandals. This fraction must now be converted into a percentage:

$$\frac{5}{20} \times \frac{5}{5} = \frac{25}{100} = 25\%$$

# Geometry

## Side Lengths of Shapes When Given the Area or Perimeter

The **perimeter** of a polygon is the distance around the outside of the two-dimensional figure or the sum of the lengths of all the sides. Perimeter is a one-dimensional measurement and is therefore expressed in linear units such as centimeters (*cm*), feet (*ft*), and miles (*mi*). The perimeter (*P*) of a figure can be calculated by adding together each of the sides.

Properties of certain polygons allow that the perimeter may be obtained by using formulas. A regular polygon is one in which all sides have equal length and all interior angles have equal measures, such as a square and an equilateral triangle. To find the perimeter of a regular polygon, the length of one side is multiplied by the number of sides.

A rectangle consists of two sides called the length (*l*), which have equal measures, and two sides called the width (*w*), which have equal measures. Therefore, the perimeter (*P*) of a rectangle can be expressed as:

$$P = l + l + w + w$$

This can be simplified to produce the following formula to find the perimeter of a rectangle:

$$P = 2l + 2w \text{ or } P = 2(l + w)$$

Consider the following problem:

The total perimeter of a rectangular garden is 36m. If the length of each side is 12m, what is the width?

The formula for the perimeter of a rectangle is $P = 2l + 2w$, where P is the perimeter, L is the length, and W is the width. The first step is to substitute all of the data into the formula:

$$36 = 2(12) + 2w$$

Simplify by multiplying $2 \times 12$:

$$36 = 24 + 2w$$

Simplify this further by subtracting 24 on each side, which gives:

$$36 - 24 = 24 - 24 + 2w$$

$$12 = 2w$$

Divide by 2:

$$6 = w$$

The width is 6m. Remember to test this answer by substituting this value into the original formula:

$$36 = 2(12) + 2(6)$$

The perimeter of a square is measured by adding together all of the sides. Since a square has four equal sides, its perimeter can be calculated by multiplying the length of one side by 4. Thus, the formula is $P = 4 \times s$, where $s$ equals one side. For example, the following square has side lengths of 5 meters:

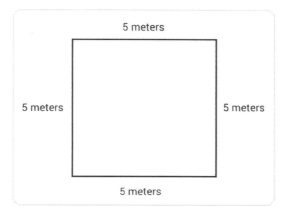

The perimeter is 20 meters because 4 times 5 is 20.

A triangle's perimeter is measured by adding together the three sides, so the formula is $P = a + b + c$, where $a, b$, and $c$ are the values of the three sides. The area is calculated by multiplying the length of the base times the height times ½, so the formula is:

$$A = \frac{1}{2} \times b \times h = \frac{bh}{2}$$

The base is the bottom of the triangle, and the height is the distance from the base to the peak. If a problem asks to calculate the area of a triangle, it will provide the base and height.

Missing side lengths can be determined using subtraction. For example, if you are told that a triangle has a perimeter of 34 inches and that one side is 12 inches, another side is 16 inches, and the third side is unknown, you can calculate the length of that unknown side by setting up the following subtraction problem:

$$34\ inches = 12\ inches + 16\ inches + x$$

$$34\ inches = 28\ inches + x$$

$$6\ inches = x$$

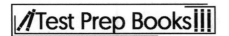
Therefore, the missing side length is 6 inches.

## Area and Perimeter of Two-Dimensional Shapes

As mentioned, the **perimeter** of a polygon is the distance around the outside of the two-dimensional figure. Perimeter is a one-dimensional measurement and is therefore expressed in linear units such as centimeters (*cm*), feet (*ft*), and miles (*mi*). The perimeter (*P*) of a figure can be calculated by adding together each of the sides.

The **area** of a polygon is the number of square units needed to cover the interior region of the figure. Area is a two-dimensional measurement. Therefore, area is expressed in square units, such as square centimeters ($cm^2$), square feet ($ft^2$), or square miles ($mi^2$). Regarding the area of a rectangle with sides of length *x* and *y*, the area is given by *xy*. For a triangle with a base of length *b* and a height of length *h*, the area is $\frac{1}{2}bh$. To find the area (*A*) of a parallelogram, the length of the base (*b*) is multiplied by the length of the height:

$$(h) \rightarrow A = b \times h$$

Similar to triangles, the height of the parallelogram is measured from one base to the other at a 90° angle (or perpendicular).

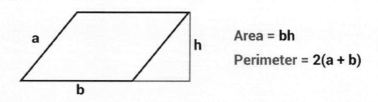

The area of a trapezoid can be calculated using the formula:

$$A = \frac{1}{2} \times h(b_1 + b_2)$$

where *h* is the height, and $b_1$ and $b_2$ are the parallel bases of the trapezoid.

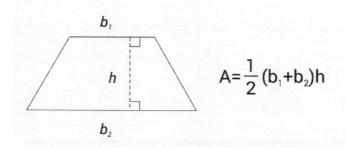

The area of a regular polygon can be determined by using its perimeter and the length of the **apothem**. The apothem is a line from the center of the regular polygon to any of its sides at a right angle. (Note that the perimeter of a regular polygon can be determined given the length of only one side.) The formula for the area (A) of a regular polygon is

$$A = \frac{1}{2} \times a \times P$$

where $a$ is the length of the apothem, and $P$ is the perimeter of the figure. Consider the following regular pentagon:

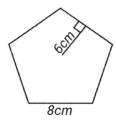

To find the area, the perimeter (P) is calculated first:

$$8cm \times 5 \rightarrow P = 40cm$$

Then the perimeter and the apothem are used to find the area (A):

$$A = \frac{1}{2} \times a \times P$$

$$A = \frac{1}{2} \times (6cm) \times (40cm)$$

$$A = 120cm^2$$

Note that the unit is:

$$cm^2 \rightarrow cm \times cm = cm^2$$

The area of irregular polygons is found by decomposing, or breaking apart, the figure into smaller shapes. When the area of the smaller shapes is determined, the area of the smaller shapes will produce the area of the original figure when added together. Consider the example below:

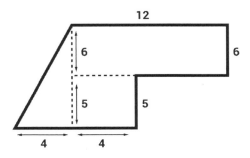

The irregular polygon is decomposed into two rectangles and a triangle. The area of the large rectangle:

$$(A = l \times w \rightarrow A = 12 \times 6)$$

is 72 square units. The area of the small rectangle is 20 square units:

$$A = 4 \times 5$$

The area of the triangle:

$$A = \frac{1}{2} \times b \times h$$

$$A = \frac{1}{2} \times 4 \times 11$$

22 square units

The sum of the areas of these figures produces the total area of the original polygon:

$$A = 72 + 20 + 22$$

$$A = 114 \text{ square units}$$

The perimeter ($P$) of the figure below is calculated by:

$$P = 9m + 5m + 4m + 6m + 8m \rightarrow P = 32\ m$$

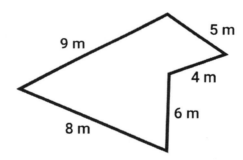

## Area, Circumference, Radius, and Diameter of a Circle

A **circle** can be defined as the set of all points that are the same distance (known as the **radius**, $r$) from a single point (known as the **center** of the circle). The center has coordinates $(h, k)$, and any point on the circle can be labelled with coordinates $(x, y)$.

A circle's perimeter—also known as its circumference—is measured by multiplying the diameter (the straight line measured from one end to the direct opposite end of the circle) by $\pi$, so the formula is $\pi \times d$. This is sometimes expressed by the formula $C = 2 \times \pi \times r$, where $r$ is the radius of the circle. These formulas are equivalent, as the radius equals half of the diameter.

The area of a circle is calculated through the formula $A = \pi \times r^2$. The test will indicate either to leave the answer with $\pi$ attached or to calculate to the nearest decimal place, which means multiplying by 3.14 for $\pi$.

Given two points on the circumference of a circle, the path along the circle between those points is called an **arc** of the circle. For example, the arc between *B* and *C* is denoted by a thinner line:

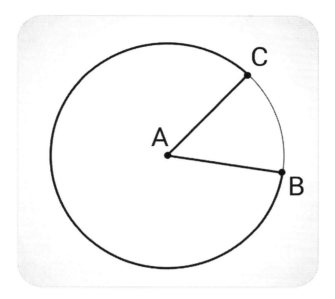

The length of the path along an arc is called the **arc length**. If the circle has radius *r*, then the arc length is given by multiplying the measure of the angle in radians by the radius of the circle.

## Pythagorean Theorem

The Pythagorean theorem is an important concept in geometry. It states that for right triangles, the sum of the squares of the two shorter sides will be equal to the square of the longest side (also called the **hypotenuse**). The longest side will always be the side opposite to the 90° angle. If this side is called *c*, and the other two sides are *a* and *b*, then the Pythagorean theorem states that:

$$c^2 = a^2 + b^2$$

Since lengths are always positive, this also can be written as:

$$c = \sqrt{a^2 + b^2}$$

A diagram to show the parts of a triangle using the Pythagorean theorem is below.

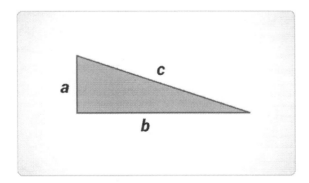

As an example of the theorem, suppose that Shirley has a rectangular field that is 5 feet wide and 12 feet long, and she wants to split it in half using a fence that goes from one corner to the opposite corner. How long will this fence need to be? To figure this out, note that this makes the field into two right triangles, whose hypotenuse will be the fence dividing it in half. Therefore, the fence length will be given by

$$\sqrt{5^2 + 12^2} = \sqrt{169} = 13 \text{ feet long}$$

## Volume and Surface Area of Three-Dimensional Shapes

Geometry in three dimensions is similar to geometry in two dimensions. The main new feature is that three points now define a unique **plane** that passes through each of them. Three-dimensional objects can be made by putting together two-dimensional figures in different surfaces. Below, some of the possible three-dimensional figures will be provided, along with formulas for their volumes and surface areas.

**Volume** is the measurement of how much space an object occupies, like how much space is in the cube. Volume questions will ask how much of something is needed to completely fill the object. The most common surface area and volume questions deal with spheres, cubes, and rectangular prisms.

**Surface area** of a three-dimensional figure refers to the number of square units needed to cover the entire surface of the figure. This concept is similar to using wrapping paper to completely cover the outside of a box. For example, if a triangular pyramid has a surface area of 17 square inches (written $17in^2$), it will take 17 squares, each with sides one inch in length, to cover the entire surface of the pyramid. Surface area is also measured in square units.

A **rectangular prism** is a box whose sides are all rectangles meeting at 90° angles. Such a box has three dimensions: length, width, and height. If the length is $x$, the width is $y$, and the height is $z$, then the volume is given by $V = xyz$.

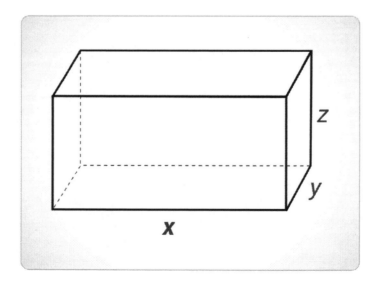

The **surface area** will be given by computing the surface area of each rectangle and adding them together. There is a total of six rectangles. Two of them have sides of length $x$ and $y$, two have sides of length $y$ and $z$, and two have sides of length $x$ and $z$. Therefore, the total surface area will be given by:

$$SA = 2xy + 2yz + 2xz$$

A **cube** is a special type of rectangular solid in which its length, width, and height are the same. If this length is $s$, then the formula for the volume of a cube is $V = s \times s \times s$. The surface area of a cube is $SA = 6s^2$.

A **rectangular pyramid** is a figure with a rectangular base and four triangular sides that meet at a single vertex. If the rectangle has sides of length $x$ and $y$, then the volume will be given by $V = \frac{1}{3}xyh$.

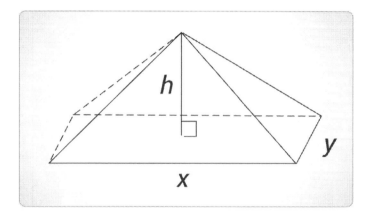

Many three-dimensional figures (solid figures) can be represented by nets consisting of rectangles and triangles. The surface area of such solids can be determined by adding the areas of each of its faces and bases. Finding the surface area using this method requires calculating the areas of rectangles and triangles.

Consider the following triangular prism, which is represented by a net consisting of two triangles and three rectangles.

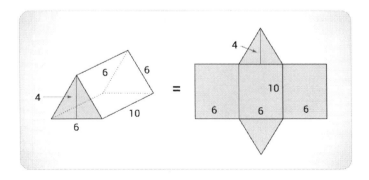

The surface area of the prism can be determined by adding the areas of each of its faces and bases. The surface area (*SA*) = area of triangle + area of triangle + area of rectangle + area of rectangle + area of rectangle.

$$SA = \left(\frac{1}{2} \times b \times h\right) + \left(\frac{1}{2} \times b \times h\right) + (l \times w) + (l \times w) + (l \times w)$$

$$SA = \left(\frac{1}{2} \times 6 \times 4\right) + \left(\frac{1}{2} \times 6 \times 4\right) + (6 \times 10) + (6 \times 10) + (6 \times 10)$$

$$SA = (12) + (12) + (60) + (60) + (60)$$

$$SA = 204 \; square \; units$$

A **sphere** is a set of points all of which are equidistant from some central point. It is like a circle, but in three dimensions. The volume of a sphere of radius *r* is given by:

$$V = \frac{4}{3}\pi r^3$$

The surface area is given by $A = 4\pi r^2$.

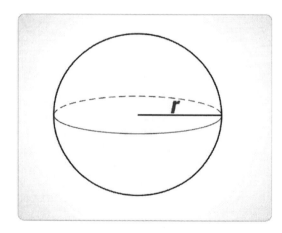

The volume of a **cylinder** is then found by adding a third dimension onto the circle. Volume of a cylinder is calculated by multiplying the area of the base (which is a circle) by the height of the cylinder. Doing so results in the equation $V = \pi r^2 h$. The volume of a **cone** is $\frac{1}{3}$ of the volume of a cylinder. Therefore, the formula for the volume of a **cone** is:

$$\frac{1}{3}\pi r^2 h$$

## Solving Three-Dimensional Problems

Three-dimensional objects can be simplified into related two-dimensional shapes to solve problems. This simplification can make problem-solving a much easier experience. An isometric representation of a three-dimensional object can be completed so that important properties (e.g., shape, relationships of faces and surfaces) are noted. Edges and vertices can be translated into two-dimensional objects as well.

For example, below is a three-dimensional object that's been partitioned into two-dimensional representations of its faces:

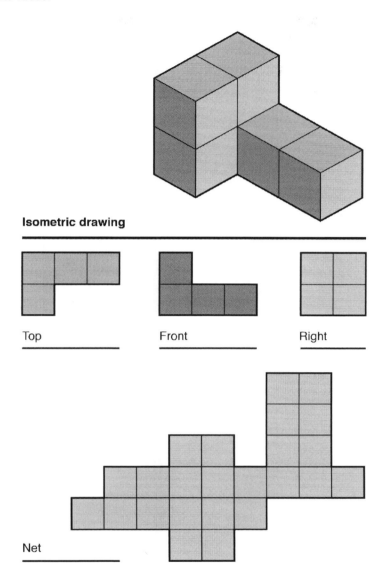

The net represents the sum of the three different faces. Depending on the problem, using a smaller portion of the given shape may be helpful, by simplifying the steps necessary to solve.

Many objects in the real world consist of three-dimensional shapes such as prisms, cylinders, and spheres. Surface area problems involve quantifying the outside area of such a three-dimensional object, and volume problems involve quantifying how much space the object takes up. Surface area of a prism is the sum of the areas, which is simplified into $SA = 2A + Bh$, where $A$ is the area of the base, $B$ is the perimeter of the base, and $h$ is the height of the prism. The volume of the same prism is $V = Ah$. The surface area of a cylinder is equal to the sum of the areas of each end and the side, which is:

$$SA = 2\pi rh + 2\pi r^2$$

An example when one of these formulas should be used would be when calculating how much paint is needed for the outside of a house. In this scenario, surface area must be used. The sum of all individual areas of each side of the house must be found. Also, when calculating how much water a cylindrical tank can hold, a volume formula is used. Therefore, the amount of water that a cylindrical tank that is 8 feet tall with a radius of 3 feet is:

$$\pi \times 3^2 \times 8 = 226.1 \text{ cubic feet}$$

The formula used to calculate the volume of a cone is $\frac{1}{3}\pi r^2 h$. In a real-life example where the radius of a cone is 2 meters and the height of a cone is 5 meters, the volume of the cone is calculated by utilizing the formula:

$$\frac{1}{3}\pi 2^2 \times 5$$

After substituting 3.14 for $\pi$, the volume is 20.9 $m^3$.

## Graphical Data Including Graphs, Tables, and More

A set of data can be visually displayed in various forms allowing for quick identification of characteristics of the set. **Histograms**, such as the one shown below, display the number of data points (vertical axis) that fall into given intervals (horizontal axis) across the range of the set. The histogram below displays the heights of black cherry trees in a certain city park. Each rectangle represents the number of trees with heights between a given five-point span. For example, the furthest bar to the right indicates that two trees are between 85 and 90 feet. Histograms can describe the center, spread, shape, and any unusual characteristics of a data set.

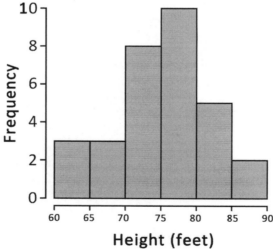

A **box plot**, also called a **box-and-whisker plot**, divides the data points into four groups and displays the five-number summary for the set as well as any outliers. The five-number summary consists of:

- The lower extreme: the lowest value that is not an outlier
- The higher extreme: the highest value that is not an outlier

- The median of the set: also referred to as the second quartile or $Q_2$
- The first quartile or $Q_1$: the median of values below $Q_2$
- The third quartile or $Q_3$: the median of values above $Q_2$

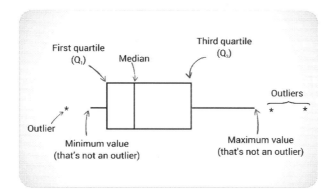

Suppose the box plot displays IQ scores for $12^{th}$ grade students at a given school. The five-number summary of the data consists of: lower extreme (67); upper extreme (127); $Q_2$ or median (100); $Q_1$ (91); $Q_3$ (108); and outliers (135 and 140). Although all data points are not known from the plot, the points are divided into four quartiles each, including 25% of the data points. Therefore, 25% of students scored between 67 and 91, 25% scored between 91 and 100, 25% scored between 100 and 108, and 25% scored between 108 and 127. These percentages include the normal values for the set and exclude the outliers. This information is useful when comparing a given score with the rest of the scores in the set.

A **scatter plot** is a mathematical diagram that visually displays the relationship or connection between two variables. The independent variable is placed on the *x*-axis, or horizontal axis, and the dependent variable is placed on the *y*-axis, or vertical axis. When visually examining the points on the graph, if the points model a linear relationship, or if a line of best-fit can be drawn through the points with the points relatively close on either side, then a correlation exists. If the line of best-fit has a positive slope (rises from left to right), then the variables have a positive correlation. If the line of best-fit has a negative slope (falls from left to right), then the variables have a negative correlation. If a line of best-fit cannot be drawn, then no correlation exists. A positive or negative correlation can be categorized as strong or weak, depending on how closely the points are graphed around the line of best-fit.

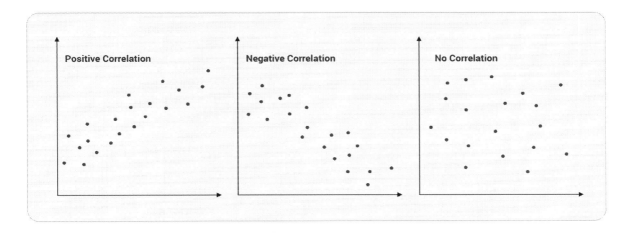

Like a scatter plot, a **line graph** compares variables that change continuously, typically over time. Paired data values (ordered pair) are plotted on a coordinate grid with the *x*- and *y*-axis representing the variables. A line is drawn from each point to the next, going from left to right. The line graph below displays cell phone use for given years (two variables) for men, women, and both sexes (three data sets).

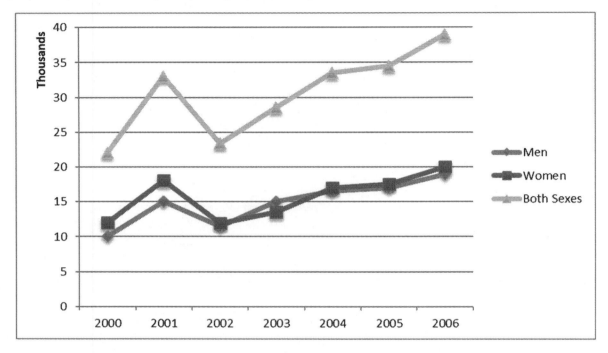

A **line plot**, also called **dot plot**, displays the frequency of data (numerical values) on a number line. To construct a line plot, a number line is used that includes all unique data values. It is marked with x's or dots above the value the number of times that the value occurs in the data set.

### % Conformance to Goal

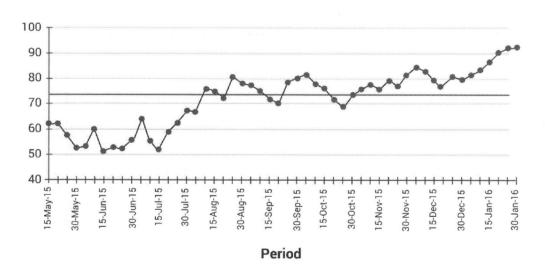

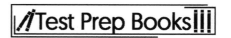

A **bar graph** is a diagram in which the quantity of items within a specific classification is represented by the height of a rectangle. Each type of classification is represented by a rectangle of equal width. Here is an example of a bar graph:

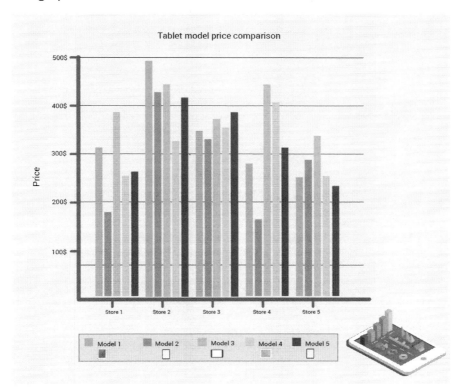

A **circle graph**, also called a **pie chart**, shows categorical data with each category representing a percentage of the whole data set. To make a circle graph, the percent of the data set for each category must be determined. To do so, the frequency of the category is divided by the total number of data points and converted to a percent. For example, if 80 people were asked what their favorite sport is and 20 responded basketball, basketball makes up 25% of the data ($\frac{20}{80} = 0.25 = 25\%$). Each category in a data set is represented by a slice of the circle proportionate to its percentage of the whole.

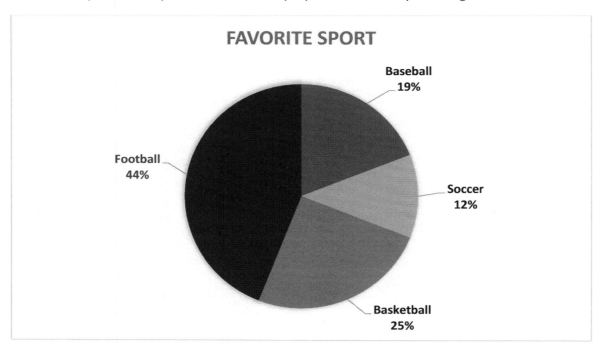

A **stem-and-leaf plot** is a method of displaying sets of data by organizing numbers by their stems (usually the tens digit) and different leaf values (usually the ones digit).

For example, to organize a number of movie critic's ratings, as listed below, a stem-and-leaf plot could be utilized to display the information in a more condensed manner.

Movie critic scores: 47, 52, 56, 59, 61, 64, 66, 68, 68, 70, 73, 75, 79, 81, 83, 85, 86, 88, 88, 89, 90, 90, 91, 93, 94, 96, 96, 99.

|   | **Movie Ratings** |
|---|---|
| **4** | 7 |
| **5** | 2 6 9 |
| **6** | 1 4 6 8 8 |
| **7** | 0 3 5 9 |
| **8** | 1 3 5 6 8 8 9 |
| **9** | 0 0 1 3 4 6 6 9 |

**Key**      6 | 1  represents 61

Looking at this stem and leaf plot, it is easy to ascertain key features of the data set. For example, what is the range of the data in the stem-and-leaf plot?

Using this method, it is easier to visualize the distribution of the scores and answer the question pertaining to the range of scores, which is $99 - 47 = 52$.

A **tally chart** is a diagram in which tally marks are utilized to represent data. Tally marks are a means of showing a quantity of objects within a specific classification. Here is an example of a tally chart:

| Number of days with rain | Number of weeks |
|---|---|
| 0 | II |
| 1 | IIII |
| 2 | IIII |
| 3 | IIII |
| 4 | IIII IIII IIII IIII |
| 5 | IIII I |
| 6 | IIII I |
| 7 | IIII |

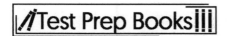 

Data is often recorded using fractions, such as half a mile, and understanding fractions is critical because of their popular use in real-world applications. Also, it is extremely important to label values with their units when using data. For example, regarding length, the number 2 is meaningless unless it is attached to a unit. Writing 2 cm shows that the number refers to the length of an object.

## Mean, Median, Mode, and Range

Suppose that $X$ is a set of data points $(x_1, x_2, x_3, \ldots x_n)$ and some description of the general properties of this data need to be found.

The first property that can be defined for this set of data is the **mean**. To find the mean, add up all the data points, then divide by the total number of data points. This can be expressed using **summation notation** as:

$$\bar{X} = \frac{x_1 + x_2 + x_3 + \cdots + x_n}{n} = \frac{1}{n}\sum_{i=1}^{n} x_i$$

For example, suppose that in a class of 10 students, the scores on a test were 50, 60, 65, 65, 75, 80, 85, 85, 90, 100. Therefore, the average test score will be:

$$\frac{1}{10}(50 + 60 + 65 + 65 + 75 + 80 + 85 + 85 + 90 + 100) = 75.5$$

The mean is a useful number if the distribution of data is normal (more on this later), which roughly means that the frequency of different outcomes has a single peak and is roughly equally distributed on both sides of that peak. However, it is less useful in some cases where the data might be split or where there are some outliers. **Outliers** are data points that are far from the rest of the data. For example, suppose there are 10 executives and 90 employees at a company. The executives make $1000 per hour, and the employees make $10 per hour.

Therefore, the average pay rate will be:

$$\frac{\$1000 \times 10 + \$10 \times 90}{100} = \$109 \text{ per hour}$$

In this case, this average is not very descriptive since it's not close to the actual pay of the executives or the employees.

Another useful measurement is the **median**. In a data set $X$ consisting of data points $x_1, x_2, x_3, \ldots x_n$, the median is the point in the middle. The middle refers to the point where half the data comes before it and half comes after, when the data is recorded in numerical order. If $n$ is odd, then the median is:

$$x_{\frac{n+1}{2}}$$

If $n$ is even, it is defined as $\frac{1}{2}\left(x_{\frac{n}{2}} + x_{\frac{n}{2}+1}\right)$, the mean of the two data points closest to the middle of the data points. In the previous example of test scores, the two middle points are 75 and 80. Since there is no single point, the average of these two scores needs to be found. The average is:

$$\frac{75 + 80}{2} = 77.5$$

The median is generally a good value to use if there are a few outliers in the data. It prevents those outliers from affecting the "middle" value as much as when using the mean.

One additional measure to define for *X* is the **mode**. This is the data point that appears more frequently. If two or more data points all tie for the most frequent appearance, then each of them is considered a mode. In the case of the test scores, where the numbers were 50, 60, 65, 65, 75, 80, 85, 85, 90, 100, there are two modes: 65 and 85.

Since an outlier is a data point that is far from most of the other data points in a data set, this means an outlier also is any point that is far from the median of the data set. The outliers can have a substantial effect on the mean of a data set but usually do not change the median or mode, or do not change them by a large quantity. For example, consider the data set (3, 5, 6, 6, 6, 8). This has a median of 6 and a mode of 6, with a mean of $\frac{34}{6} \approx 5.67$. Now, suppose a new data point of 1000 is added so that the data set is now (3, 5, 6, 6, 6, 8, 1000). The median and mode, which are both still 6, remain unchanged. However, the average is now $\frac{1034}{7}$, which is approximately 147.7. In this case, the median and mode will be better descriptions for most of the data points.

Outliers in a given data set are sometimes the result of an error by the experimenter, but oftentimes, they are perfectly valid data points that must be taken into consideration.

The **first quartile** of a set of data *X* refers to the largest value from the first ¼ of the data points. In practice, there are sometimes slightly different definitions that can be used, such as the median of the first half of the data points (excluding the median itself if there are an odd number of data points). The term also has a slightly different use: when it is said that a data point lies in the first quartile, it means it is less than or equal to the median of the first half of the data points. Conversely, if it lies *at* the first quartile, then it is equal to the first quartile.

When it is said that a data point lies in the **second quartile**, it means it is between the first quartile and the median.

The **third quartile** refers to data that lies between ½ and ¾ of the way through the data set. Again, there are various methods for defining this precisely, but the simplest way is to include all of the data that lie between the median and the median of the top half of the data.

Data that lies in the **fourth quartile** refers to all of the data above the third quartile.

**Percentiles** may be defined in a similar manner to quartiles. Generally, this is defined in the following manner:

If a data point lies *in* the n-th percentile, this means it lies in the range of the first *n*% of the data.

If a data point lies *at* the *n*-th percentile, then it means that *n*% of the data lies below this data point.

Given a data set *X* consisting of data points $(x_1, x_2, x_3, \ldots x_n)$, the **variance of X** is defined to be:

$$\frac{\sum_{i=1}^{n}(x_i - \bar{X})^2}{n}$$

This means that the variance of *X* is the average of the squares of the differences between each data point and the mean of *X*. In the formula, $\bar{X}$ is the mean of the values in the data set, and $x_i$ represents

each individual value in the data set. The sigma notation indicates that the sum should be found with $n$ being the number of values to add together. $i = 1$ means that the values should begin with the first value.

Given a data set $X$ consisting of data points $(x_1, x_2, x_3, \ldots x_n)$, the **standard deviation of X** is defined to be

$$s_x = \sqrt{\frac{\sum_{i=1}^{n}(x_i - \bar{X})^2}{n}}$$

In other words, the standard deviation is the square root of the variance.

Both the variance and the standard deviation are measures of how much the data tend to be spread out. When the standard deviation is low, the data points are mostly clustered around the mean. When the standard deviation is high, this generally indicates that the data are quite spread out, or else that there are a few substantial outliers.

As a simple example, compute the standard deviation for the data set (1, 3, 3, 5). First, compute the mean, which will be:

$$\frac{1 + 3 + 3 + 5}{4} = \frac{12}{4} = 3$$

Now, find the variance of $X$ with the formula:

$$\sum_{i=1}^{4}(x_i - \bar{X})^2 = (1 - 3)^2 + (3 - 3)^2 + (3 - 3)^2 + (5 - 3)^2$$

$$-2^2 + 0^2 + 0^2 + 2^2 = 8$$

Therefore, the variance is $\frac{8}{4} = 2$. Taking the square root, the standard deviation will be $\sqrt{2}$.

Note that the standard deviation only depends upon the mean, not upon the median or mode(s). Generally, if there are multiple modes that are far apart from one another, the standard deviation will be high. A high standard deviation does not always mean there are multiple modes, however.

## Describing a Set of Data

A set of data can be described in terms of its center, spread, shape and any unusual features. The center of a data set can be measured by its mean, median, or mode. The spread of a data set refers to how far the data points are from the center (mean or median). The spread can be measured by the range or the quartiles and interquartile range. A data set with all its data points clustered around the center will have a small spread. A data set covering a wide range of values will have a large spread.

When a data set is displayed as a **histogram** or frequency distribution plot, the shape indicates if a sample is normally distributed, symmetrical, or has measures of skewness or kurtosis. When graphed, a data set with a **normal distribution** will resemble a bell curve.

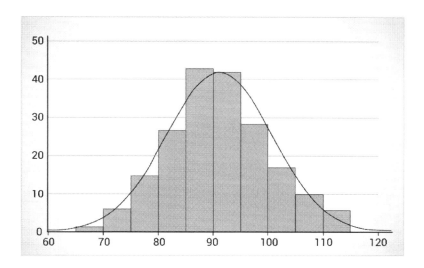

If the data set is symmetrical, each half of the graph when divided at the center is a mirror image of the other. If the graph has fewer data points to the right, the data is **skewed right**. If it has fewer data points to the left, the data is **skewed left**.

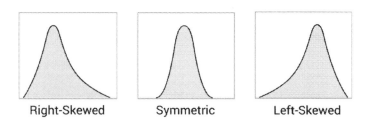

Right-Skewed          Symmetric          Left-Skewed

**Kurtosis** is a measure of whether the data is heavy-tailed with a high number of outliers, or light-tailed with a low number of outliers.

A description of a data set should include any unusual features such as gaps or outliers. A **gap** is a span within the range of the data set containing no data points. An **outlier** is a data point with a value either extremely large or extremely small when compared to the other values in the set.

## Counting Techniques

The **addition rule** for probabilities states that the probability of A or B happening is:

$$P(A \cup B) = P(A) + P(B) - P(A \cap B)$$

Note that the subtraction of $P(A \cap B)$ must be performed, or else it would result in double counting any outcomes that lie in both A and in B. For example, suppose that a 20-sided die is being rolled. Fred bets that the outcome will be greater than 10, while Helen bets that it will be greater than 4 but less than 15. What is the probability that at least one of them is correct?

We apply the rule:

$$P(A \cup B) = P(A) + P(B) - P(A \cap B)$$

where $A$ is that outcome $x$ is in the range $x > 10$, and $B$ is that outcome $x$ is in the range $4 < x < 15$.

$$P(A) = 10 \times \frac{1}{20} = \frac{1}{2}$$

$$P(B) = 10 \times \frac{1}{20} = \frac{1}{2}$$

$P(A \cap B)$ can be computed by noting that $A \cap B$ means the outcome $x$ is in the range $10 < x < 15$, so

$$P(A \cap B) = 4 \times \frac{1}{20} = \frac{1}{5}$$

Therefore:

$$P(A \cup B) = P(A) + P(B) - P(A \cap B)$$

$$\frac{1}{2} + \frac{1}{2} - \frac{1}{5} = \frac{4}{5}$$

Note that in this particular example, we could also have directly reasoned about the set of possible outcomes $A \cup B$, by noting that this would mean that $x$ must be in the range $5 \leq x$. However, this is not always the case, depending on the given information.

The **multiplication rule** for probabilities states the probability of $A$ and $B$ both happening is:

$$P(A \cap B) = P(A)P(B|A)$$

As an example, suppose that when Jamie wears black pants, there is a ½ probability that she wears a black shirt as well, and that she wears black pants ¾ of the time. What is the probability that she is wearing both a black shirt and black pants?

To figure this, use the above formula, where $A$ will be "Jamie is wearing black pants," while $B$ will be "Jamie is wearing a black shirt." It is known that $P(A)$ is ¾. It is also known that $P(B|A) = \frac{1}{2}$. Multiplying the two, the probability that she is wearing both black pants and a black shirt is:

$$P(A)P(B|A) = \frac{3}{4} \times \frac{1}{2} = \frac{3}{8}$$

## Probability of an Event

Given a set of possible outcomes $X$, a **probability distribution** of $X$ is a function that assigns a probability to each possible outcome. If the outcomes are $(x_1, x_2, x_3, \ldots x_n)$, and the probability distribution is $p$, then the following rules are applied.

- $0 \leq p(x_i) \leq 1$, for any i.

- $\sum_{i=1}^{n} p(x_i) = 1$.

In other words, the probability of a given outcome must be between zero and 1, while the total probability must be 1.

If $p(x_i)$ is constant, then this is called a **uniform probability distribution**, and $p(x_i) = \frac{1}{n}$. For example, on a six-sided die, the probability of each of the six outcomes will be $\frac{1}{6}$.

If seeking the probability of an outcome occurring in some specific range $A$ of possible outcomes, written $P(A)$, add up the probabilities for each outcome in that range. For example, consider a six-sided die, and figure the probability of getting a 3 or lower when it is rolled. The possible rolls are 1, 2, 3, 4, 5, and 6. So, to get a 3 or lower, a roll of 1, 2, or 3 must be completed. The probabilities of each of these is $\frac{1}{6}$, so add these to get:

$$p(1) + p(2) + p(3) = \frac{1}{6} + \frac{1}{6} + \frac{1}{6} = \frac{1}{2}$$

An outcome occasionally lies within some range of possibilities $B$, and the probability that the outcomes also lie within some set of possibilities $A$ needs to be figured. This is called a **conditional probability**. It is written as $P(A|B)$, which is read "the probability of $A$ given $B$." The general formula for computing conditional probabilities is:

$$P(A|B) = \frac{P(A \cap B)}{P(B)}$$

However, when dealing with uniform probability distributions, simplify this a bit. Write $|A|$ to indicate the number of outcomes in $A$. Then, for uniform probability distributions, write:

$$P(A|B) = \frac{|A \cap B|}{|B|}$$

(recall that $A \cap B$ means "$A$ intersect $B$," and consists of all of the outcomes that lie in both $A$ and $B$)

This means that all possible outcomes do not need to be known. To see why this formula works, suppose that the set of outcomes $X$ is $(x_1, x_2, x_3, \dots x_n)$, so that $|X| = n$. Then, for a uniform probability distribution:

$$P(A) = \frac{|A|}{n}$$

However, this means:

$$(A|B) = \frac{P(A \cap B)}{P(B)} = \frac{\frac{|A \cap B|}{n}}{\frac{|B|}{n}} = \frac{|A \cap B|}{|B|}$$

since the $n$'s cancel out.

For example, suppose a die is rolled, and it is known that it will land between 1 and 4. However, how many sides the die has is unknown. Figure the probability that the die is rolled higher than 2. To figure this, $P(3)$ or $P(4)$ does not need to be determined, or any of the other probabilities, since it is known

that a fair die has a uniform probability distribution. Therefore, apply the formula $\frac{|A \cap B|}{|B|}$. So, in this case $B$ is (1, 2, 3, 4) and $A \cap B$ is (3, 4). Therefore:

$$\frac{|A \cap B|}{|B|} = \frac{2}{4} = \frac{1}{2}$$

Conditional probability is an important concept because, in many situations, the likelihood of one outcome can differ radically depending on how something else comes out. The probability of passing a test given that one has studied all of the material is generally much higher than the probability of passing a test given that one has not studied at all. The probability of a person having heart trouble is much lower if that person exercises regularly. The probability that a college student will graduate is higher when their SAT scores are higher, and so on. For this reason, there are many people who are interested in conditional probabilities.

Note that in some practical situations, changing the order of the conditional probabilities can make the outcome very different. For example, the probability that a person with heart trouble has exercised regularly is quite different than the probability that a person who exercises regularly will have heart trouble. The probability of a person receiving a military-only award, given that he or she is or was a soldier, is generally not very high, but the probability that a person being or having been a soldier, given that he or she received a military-only award, is 1.

However, in some cases, the outcomes do not influence one another this way. If the probability of $A$ is the same regardless of whether $B$ is given; that is, if $P(A|B) = P(A)$, then $A$ and $B$ are considered **independent**. In this case:

$$P(A|B) = \frac{P(A \cap B)}{P(B)} = P(A)$$

So:

$$P(A \cap B) = P(A)P(B)$$

In fact, if $P(A \cap B) = P(A)P(B)$, it can be determined that $P(A|B) = P(A)$ and $P(A|B) = P(B)$ by working backward. Therefore, $B$ is also independent of $A$.

An example of something being independent can be seen in rolling dice. In this case, consider a red die and a green die. It is expected that when the dice are rolled, the outcome of the green die should not depend in any way on the outcome of the red die. Or, to take another example, if the same die is rolled repeatedly, then the next number rolled should not depend on which numbers have been rolled previously. Similarly, if a coin is flipped, then the next flip's outcome does not depend on the outcomes of previous flips.

This can sometimes be counter-intuitive, since when rolling a die or flipping a coin, there can be a streak of surprising results. If, however, it is known that the die or coin is fair, then these results are just the result of the fact that over long periods of time, it is very likely that some unlikely streaks of outcomes will occur. Therefore, avoid making the mistake of thinking that when considering a series of independent outcomes, a particular outcome is "due to happen" simply because a surprising series of outcomes has already been seen.

There is a second type of common mistake that people tend to make when reasoning about statistical outcomes: the idea that when something of low probability happens, this is surprising. It would be surprising that something with low probability happened after just one attempt. However, with so much happening all at once, it is easy to see at least something happen in a way that seems to have a very low probability. In fact, a lottery is a good example. The odds of winning a lottery are very small, but the odds that somebody wins the lottery each week are actually fairly high. Therefore, no one should be surprised when some low probability things happen.

A **simple event** consists of only one outcome. The most popular simple event is flipping a coin, which results in either heads or tails. A **compound event** results in more than one outcome and consists of more than one simple event. An example of a compound event is flipping a coin while tossing a die. The result is either heads or tails on the coin and a number from one to six on the die. The probability of a simple event is calculated by dividing the number of possible outcomes by the total number of outcomes. Therefore, the probability of obtaining heads on a coin is $\frac{1}{2}$, and the probability of rolling a 6 on a die is $\frac{1}{6}$. The probability of compound events is calculated using the basic idea of the probability of simple events. If the two events are independent, the probability of one outcome is equal to the product of the probabilities of each simple event. For example, the probability of obtaining heads on a coin and rolling a 6 is equal to:

$$\frac{1}{2} \times \frac{1}{6} = \frac{1}{12}$$

The probability of either A or B occurring is equal to the sum of the probabilities minus the probability that both A and B will occur. Therefore, the probability of obtaining either heads on a coin or rolling a 6 on a die is:

$$\frac{1}{2} + \frac{1}{6} - \frac{1}{12} = \frac{7}{12}$$

The two events aren't mutually exclusive because they can happen at the same time. If two events are mutually exclusive, and the probability of both events occurring at the same time is zero, the probability of event A or B occurring equals the sum of both probabilities. An example of calculating the probability of two mutually exclusive events is determining the probability of pulling a king or a queen from a deck of cards. The two events cannot occur at the same time.

# *Basic Algebra*

## Adding, Subtracting, Multiplying, and Factoring Linear Expressions

Algebraic expressions look similar to equations, but they do not include the equal sign. Algebraic expressions are comprised of numbers, variables, and mathematical operations. Some examples of algebraic expressions are:

$$8x + 7y - 12z$$

$$3a^2$$

$$5x^3 - 4y^4$$

Algebraic expressions consist of variables, numbers, and operations. A term of an expression is any combination of numbers and/or variables, and terms are separated by addition and subtraction. For example, the expression:

$$5x^2 - 3xy + 4y - 2$$

consists of 4 terms: $5x^2$, $-3xy$, $4y$, and $-2$. Note that each term includes its given sign (+ or −). The variable part of a term is a letter that represents an unknown quantity. The coefficient of a term is the number by which the variable is multiplied. For the term $4y$, the variable is $y$, and the coefficient is 4. Terms are identified by the power (or exponent) of its variable.

A number without a variable is referred to as a constant. If the variable is to the first power ($x^1$ or simply $x$), it is referred to as a linear term. A term with a variable to the second power ($x^2$) is quadratic, and a term to the third power ($x^3$) is cubic. Consider the expression:

$$x^3 + 3x - 1$$

The constant is -1. The linear term is $3x$. There is no quadratic term. The cubic term is $x^3$.

An algebraic expression can also be classified by how many terms exist in the expression. Any like terms should be combined before classifying. A monomial is an expression consisting of only one term. Examples of monomials are: 17, $2x$, and $-5ab^2$. A binomial is an expression consisting of two terms separated by addition or subtraction. Examples include $2x - 4$ and $-3y^2 + 2y$. A trinomial consists of 3 terms. For example:

$$5x^2 - 2x + 1$$

is a trinomial.

Algebraic expressions and equations can be used to represent real-life situations and model the behavior of different variables. For example, $2x + 5$ could represent the cost to play games at an arcade. In this case, 5 represents the price of admission to the arcade, and 2 represents the cost of each game played. To calculate the total cost, use the number of games played for $x$, multiply it by 2, and add 5.

## Adding and Subtracting Linear Algebraic Expressions

An algebraic expression is simplified by combining like terms. A term is a number, variable, or product of a number and variables separated by addition and subtraction. For the algebraic expression:

$$3x^2 - 4x + 5 - 5x^2 + x - 3$$

the terms are $3x^2$, $-4x$, 5, $-5x^2$, $x$, and $-3$. Like terms have the same variables raised to the same powers (exponents). The like terms for the previous example are $3x^2$ and $-5x^2$, $-4x$ and $x$, 5 and $-3$. To combine like terms, the coefficients (numerical factor of the term including sign) are added, and the variables and their powers are kept the same. Note that if a coefficient is not written, it is an implied coefficient of 1 ($x = 1x$). The previous example will simplify to:

$$-2x^2 - 3x + 2$$

When adding or subtracting algebraic expressions, each expression is written in parenthesis. The negative sign is distributed when necessary, and like terms are combined. Consider the following:

$$add\ 2a + 5b - 2\ to\ a - 2b + 8c - 4$$

The sum is set as follows:

$$(a - 2b + 8c - 4) + (2a + 5b - 2)$$

In front of each set of parentheses is an implied positive one, which, when distributed, does not change any of the terms. Therefore, the parentheses are dropped and like terms are combined:

$$a - 2b + 8c - 4 + 2a + 5b - 2$$

$$3a + 3b + 8c - 6$$

Consider the following problem:

$$Subtract\ 2a + 5b - 2\ from\ a - 2b + 8c - 4$$

The difference is set as follows:

$$(a - 2b + 8c - 4) - (2a + 5b - 2)$$

The implied one in front of the first set of parentheses will not change those four terms. However, distributing the implied -1 in front of the second set of parentheses will change the sign of each of those three terms:

$$a - 2b + 8c - 4 - 2a - 5b + 2$$

Combining like terms yields the simplified expression:

$$-a - 7b + 8c - 2$$

## Distributive Property
The **distributive property** states that multiplying a sum (or difference) by a number produces the same result as multiplying each value in the sum (or difference) by the number and adding (or subtracting) the products. Using mathematical symbols, the distributive property states:

$$a(b + c) = ab + ac$$

The expression $4(3 + 2)$ is simplified using the order of operations. Simplifying inside the parenthesis first produces $4 \times 5$, which equals 20. The expression $4(3 + 2)$ can also be simplified using the distributive property:

$$4(3 + 2)$$

$$4 \times 3 + 4 \times 2$$

$$12 + 8$$

$$20$$

Consider the following example: $4(3x - 2)$. The expression cannot be simplified inside the parenthesis because $3x$ and -2 are not like terms and therefore cannot be combined. However, the expression can be simplified by using the distributive property and multiplying each term inside of the parenthesis by the term outside of the parenthesis: $12x - 8$. The resulting equivalent expression contains no like terms, so it cannot be further simplified.

Consider the expression:

$$(3x + 2y + 1) - (5x - 3) + 2(3y + 4)$$

Again, there are no like terms, but the distributive property is used to simplify the expression. Note there is an implied one in front of the first set of parentheses and an implied -1 in front of the second set of parentheses. Distributing the 1, -1, and 2 produces:

$$1(3x) + 1(2y) + 1(1) - 1(5x) - 1(-3) + 2(3y) + 2(4)$$

$$3x + 2y + 1 - 5x + 3 + 6y + 8$$

This expression contains like terms that are combined to produce the simplified expression:

$$-2x + 8y + 12$$

Algebraic expressions are tested to be equivalent by choosing values for the variables and evaluating both expressions. For example, $4(3x - 2)$ and $12x - 8$ are tested by substituting 3 for the variable $x$ and calculating to determine if equivalent values result.

## Evaluating Algebraic Expressions

To evaluate the expression, the given values for the variables are substituted (or replaced), and the expression is simplified using the order of operations. Parenthesis should be used when substituting. Consider the following: Evaluate $a - 2b + ab$ for $a = 3$ and $b = -1$. To evaluate, any variable $a$ is replaced with 3 and any variable $b$ with -1, producing:

$$(3) - 2(-1) + (3)(-1)$$

Next, the order of operations is used to calculate the value of the expression, which is 2.

Let's try two more.

Evaluate:

$$\frac{1}{2}x^2 - 3$$

$$x = 4$$

The first step is to substitute in 4 for $x$ in the expression:

$$\frac{1}{2}(4)^2 - 3$$

Then, the order of operations is used to simplify.

The exponent comes first, $\frac{1}{2}(16) - 3$, then the multiplication $8 - 3$, and then, after subtraction, the solution is 5.

Evaluate:

$$4|5 - x| + 2y$$

$$x = 4$$

$$y = -3$$

The first step is to substitute 4 in for *x* and -3 in for *y* in the expression:

$$4|5 - 4| + 2(-3)$$

Then, the absolute value expression is simplified, which is:

$$|5 - 4| = |1| = 1$$

The expression is:

$$4(1) + 2(-3)$$

which can be simplified using the order of operations.

First is the multiplication, $4 + (-6)$; then addition yields an answer of -2.

## Creating Algebraic Expressions

A linear expression is a statement about an unknown quantity expressed in mathematical symbols. The statement "five times a number added to forty" can be expressed as $5x + 40$. A linear equation is a statement in which two expressions (at least one containing a variable) are equal to each other. The statement "five times a number added to forty is equal to ten" can be expressed as:

$$5x + 40 = 10$$

Real world scenarios can also be expressed mathematically. Suppose a job pays its employees $300 per week and $40 for each sale made. The weekly pay is represented by the expression $40x + 300$ where *x* is the number of sales made during the week.

Consider the following scenario: Bob had $20 and Tom had $4. After selling 4 ice cream cones to Bob, Tom has as much money as Bob. The cost of an ice cream cone is an unknown quantity and can be represented by a variable (*x*). The amount of money Bob has after his purchase is four times the cost of an ice cream cone subtracted from his original:

$$\$20 \rightarrow 20 - 4x$$

The amount of money Tom has after his sale is four times the cost of an ice cream cone added to his original:

$$\$4 \rightarrow 4x + 4$$

After the sale, the amount of money that Bob and Tom have is equal:

$$20 - 4x = 4x + 4$$

## Adding, Subtracting, Multiplying, Dividing, and Factoring Polynomials

An expression of the form $ax^n$, where $n$ is a non-negative integer, is called a **monomial** because it contains one term. A sum of monomials is called a **polynomial**. For example, $-4x^3 + x$ is a polynomial, while $5x^7$ is a monomial. A function equal to a polynomial is called a **polynomial function**.

The monomials in a polynomial are also called the **terms** of the polynomial.

The constants that precede the variables are called **coefficients**.

The highest value of the exponent of $x$ in a polynomial is called the **degree** of the polynomial. So, $-4x^3 + x$ has a degree of 3, while:

$$-2x^5 + x^3 + 4x + 1$$

has a degree of 5. When multiplying polynomials, the degree of the result will be the sum of the degrees of the two polynomials being multiplied.

Addition and subtraction operations can be performed on polynomials with like terms. **Like terms** refers to terms that have the same variable and exponent. The two following polynomials can be added together by collecting like terms:

$$(x^2 + 3x - 4) + (4x^2 - 7x + 8)$$

The $x^2$ terms can be added as:

$$x^2 + 4x^2 = 5x^2$$

The $x$ terms can be added as:

$$3x + -7x = -4x$$

and the constants can be added as $-4 + 8 = 4$.

The following expression is the result of the addition:

$$5x^2 - 4x + 4$$

Let's try another:

$$(-2x^5 + x^3 + 4x + 1) + (-4x^3 + x)$$

$$-2x^5 + (1 - 4)x^3 + (4 + 1)x + 1$$

$$-2x^5 - 3x^3 + 5x + 1$$

Likewise, subtraction of polynomials is performed by subtracting coefficients of like powers of $x$. So:

$$(-2x^5 + x^3 + 4x + 1) - (-4x^3 + x)$$

$$-2x^5 + (1 + 4)x^3 + (4 - 1)x + 1$$

$$-2x^5 + 5x^3 + 3x + 1$$

To multiply two polynomials, multiply each term of the first polynomial by each term of the second polynomial and add the results. For example:

$$(4x^2 + x)(-x^3 + x)$$

$$4x^2(-x^3) + 4x^2(x) + x(-x^3) + x(x)$$

$$-4x^5 + 4x^3 - x^4 + x^2$$

In the case where each polynomial has two terms, like in this example, some students find it helpful to remember this as multiplying the First terms, then the Outer terms, then the Inner terms, and finally the Last terms, with the mnemonic FOIL. For longer polynomials, the multiplication process is the same, but there will be, of course, more terms, and there is no common mnemonic to remember each combination.

Factors for polynomials are similar to factors for integers—they are numbers, variables, or polynomials that, when multiplied together, give a product equal to the polynomial in question. One polynomial is a factor of a second polynomial if the second polynomial can be obtained from the first by multiplying by a third polynomial.

$$6x^6 + 13x^4 + 6x^2$$

can be obtained by multiplying together:

$$(3x^4 + 2x^2)(2x^2 + 3)$$

This means:

$$2x^2 + 3$$

and

$$3x^4 + 2x^2$$

are factors of:

$$6x^6 + 13x^4 + 6x^2$$

In general, finding the factors of a polynomial can be tricky. However, there are a few types of polynomials that can be factored in a straightforward way.

If a certain monomial is in each term of a polynomial, it can be factored out. There are several common forms polynomials take, which if you recognize, you can solve. The first example is a perfect square trinomial. To factor this polynomial, first expand the middle term of the expression:

$$x^2 + 2xy + y^2$$

$$x^2 + xy + xy + y^2$$

Factor out a common term in each half of the expression (in this case $x$ from the left and $y$ from the right):

$$x(x + y) + y(x + y)$$

Then the same can be done again, treating $(x + y)$ as the common factor:

$$(x + y)(x + y) = (x + y)^2$$

Therefore, the formula for this polynomial is:

$$x^2 + 2xy + y^2 = (x + y)^2$$

Next is another example of a perfect square trinomial. The process is the similar, but notice the difference in sign:

$$x^2 - 2xy + y^2$$

$$x^2 - xy - xy + y^2$$

Factor out the common term on each side:

$$x(x - y) - y(x - y)$$

Factoring out the common term again:

$$(x - y)(x - y) = (x - y)^2$$

Thus:

$$x^2 - 2xy + y^2 = (x - y)^2$$

The next is known as a difference of squares. This process is effectively the reverse of binomial multiplication:

$$x^2 - y^2$$

$$x^2 - xy + xy - y^2$$

$$x(x - y) + y(x - y)$$

$$(x + y)(x - y)$$

Therefore:

$$x^2 - y^2 = (x + y)(x - y)$$

The following two polynomials are known as the sum or difference of cubes. These are special polynomials that take the form of $x^3 + y^3$ or $x^3 - y^3$. The following formula factors the sum of cubes:

$$x^3 + y^3 = (x + y)(x^2 - xy + y^2)$$

Next is the difference of cubes, but note the change in sign. The formulas for both are similar, but the order of signs for factoring the sum or difference of cubes can be remembered by using the acronym SOAP, which stands for "same, opposite, always positive." The first sign is the same as the sign in the first expression, the second is opposite, and the third is always positive. The next formula factors the difference of cubes:

$$x^3 - y^3 = (x - y)(x^2 + xy + y^2)$$

The following two examples are expansions of cubed binomials. Similarly, these polynomials always follow a pattern:

$$x^3 + 3x^2y + 3xy^2 + y^3 = (x + y)^3$$

$$x^3 - 3x^2y + 3xy^2 - y^3 = (x - y)^3$$

These rules can be used in many combinations with one another. For example, the expression $3x^3 - 24$ has a common factor of 3, which becomes:

$$3(x^3 - 8)$$

A difference of cubes still remains which can then be factored out:

$$3(x - 2)(x^2 + 2x + 4)$$

There are no other terms to be pulled out, so this expression is completely factored.

When factoring polynomials, a good strategy is to multiply the factors to check the result. Let's try another example:

$$4x^3 + 16x^2$$

Both sides of the expression can be divided by 4, and both contain $x^2$, because $4x^3$ can be thought of as $4x^2(x)$, so the common term can simply be factored out:

$$4x^2(x + 4)$$

It sometimes can be necessary to rewrite the polynomial in some clever way before applying the above rules. Consider the problem of factoring $x^4 - 1$. This does not immediately look like any of the previous polynomials. However, it's possible to think of this polynomial as:

$$x^4 - 1 = (x^2)^2 - (1^2)^2$$

and now it can be treated as a difference of squares to simplify this:

$$(x^2)^2 - (1^2)^2$$

$$(x^2)^2 - x^2 1^2 + x^2 1^2 - (1^2)^2$$

$$x^2(x^2 - 1^2) + 1^2(x^2 - 1^2)$$

$$(x^2 + 1^2)(x^2 - 1^2)$$

$$(x^2 + 1)(x^2 - 1)$$

## Creating Polynomials from Written Descriptions

Polynomials that represent mathematical or real-world problems can also be created from written descriptions, much like algebraic expressions. For example, polynomials might be created when working with formulas. Formulas are mathematical expressions that define the value of one quantity, given the value of one or more different quantities. Formulas look like equations because they contain variables, numbers, operators, and an equal sign. All formulas are equations, but not all equations are formulas. A formula must have more than one variable. For example, $2x + 7 = y$ is an equation and a formula (it relates the unknown quantities x and y). However, $2x + 7 = 3$ is an equation but not a formula (it only expresses the value of the unknown quantity x).

Formulas are typically written with one variable alone (or isolated) on one side of the equal sign. This variable can be thought of as the **subject** in that the formula is stating the value of the subject in terms of the relationship between the other variables. Consider the distance formula:

$$distance = rate \times time$$

or

$$d = rt$$

The value of the subject variable d (distance) is the product of the variable r and t (rate and time). Given the rate and time, the distance traveled can easily be determined by substituting the values into the formula and evaluating.

The formula $P = 2l + 2w$ expresses how to calculate the perimeter of a rectangle (P) given its length (l) and width (w). To find the perimeter of a rectangle with a length of 3ft and a width of 2ft, these values are substituted into the formula for l and w:

$$P = 2(3ft) + 2(2ft)$$

Following the order of operations, the perimeter is determined to be 10ft. When working with formulas such as these, including units is an important step.

Given a formula expressed in terms of one variable, the formula can be manipulated to express the relationship in terms of any other variable. In other words, the formula can be rearranged to change which variable is the *subject*. To solve for a variable of interest by manipulating a formula, the equation may be solved as if all other variables were numbers. The same steps for solving are followed, leaving operations in terms of the variables instead of calculating numerical values. For the formula $P = 2l + 2w$, the perimeter is the subject expressed in terms of the length and width. To write a formula to

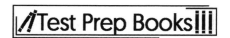
calculate the width of a rectangle, given its length and perimeter, the previous formula relating the three variables is solved for the variable *w*. If *P* and *l* were numerical values, this is a two-step linear equation solved by subtraction and division. To solve the equation $P = 2l + 2w$ for *w*, 2*l* is first subtracted from both sides:

$$P - 2l = 2w$$

Then both sides are divided by 2:

$$\frac{P - 2l}{2} = w$$

Test questions may involve creating a polynomial based on a formula. For example, using the perimeter of a rectangle formula, a problem may ask for the perimeter of a rectangle with a length of $2x + 12$ and a width of $x + 1$. Using the formula $P = 2l + 2w$, the perimeter would then be:

$$P = 2(2x + 12) + 2(x + 1)$$

This equals:

$$4x + 24 + 2x + 2 = 6x + 26$$

The area of the same rectangle, which uses the formula $A = l \times w$, would be:

$$A = (2x + 12)(x + 1)$$

$$2x^2 + 2x + 12x + 12$$

$$2x^2 + 14x + 12$$

## Adding, Subtracting, Multiplying, Dividing Rational Expressions

A fraction, or ratio, wherein each part is a polynomial, defines **rational expressions**. Some examples include:

$$\frac{2x + 6}{x}$$

$$\frac{1}{x^2 - 4x + 8}$$

and

$$\frac{z^2}{x + 5}$$

Exponents on the variables are restricted to whole numbers, which means roots and negative exponents are not included in rational expressions.

Rational expressions can be transformed by factoring. For example, the expression:

$$\frac{x^2 - 5x + 6}{(x - 3)}$$

can be rewritten by factoring the numerator to obtain:

$$\frac{(x-3)(x-2)}{(x-3)}$$

Therefore, the common binomial $(x-3)$ can cancel so that the simplified expression is:

$$\frac{(x-2)}{1} = (x-2)$$

Additionally, other rational expressions can be rewritten to take on different forms. Some may be factorable in themselves, while others can be transformed through arithmetic operations. Rational expressions are closed under addition, subtraction, multiplication, and division by a nonzero expression. **Closed** means that if any one of these operations is performed on a rational expression, the result will still be a rational expression. The set of all real numbers is another example of a set closed under all four operations.

Adding and subtracting rational expressions is based on the same concepts as adding and subtracting simple fractions. For both concepts, the denominators must be the same for the operation to take place. For example, here are two rational expressions:

$$\frac{x^3 - 4}{(x-3)} + \frac{x+8}{(x-3)}$$

Since the denominators are both $(x-3)$, the numerators can be combined by collecting like terms to form:

$$\frac{x^3 + x + 4}{(x-3)}$$

If the denominators are different, they need to be made common (the same) by using the **Least Common Denominator (LCD)**. Each denominator needs to be factored, and the LCD contains each factor that appears in any one denominator the greatest number of times it appears in any denominator. The original expressions need to be multiplied by a form of 1 such as $\frac{5}{5}$ or $\frac{x-2}{x-2}$, which will turn each denominator into the LCD. This process is like adding fractions with unlike denominators. It is also important when working with rational expressions to define what value of the variable makes the denominator zero. For this particular value, the expression is undefined.

Multiplication of rational expressions is performed like multiplication of fractions. The numerators are multiplied; then, the denominators are multiplied. The final fraction is then simplified. The expressions are simplified by factoring and cancelling out common terms. In the following example, the numerator of the second expression can be factored first to simplify the expression before multiplying:

$$\frac{x^2}{(x-4)} \times \frac{x^2 - x - 12}{2}$$

$$\frac{x^2}{(x-4)} \times \frac{(x-4)(x+3)}{2}$$

The $(x - 4)$ on the top and bottom cancel out:

$$\frac{x^2}{1} \times \frac{(x + 3)}{2}$$

Then multiplication is performed, resulting in:

$$\frac{x^3 + 3x^2}{2}$$

Dividing rational expressions is similar to the division of fractions, where division turns into multiplying by a reciprocal. Thus, the following expression can be rewritten as a multiplication problem:

$$\frac{x^2 - 3x + 7}{x - 4} \div \frac{x^2 - 5x + 3}{x - 4}$$

$$\frac{x^2 - 3x + 7}{x - 4} \times \frac{x - 4}{x^2 - 5x + 3}$$

The $x - 4$ cancels out, leaving:

$$\frac{x^2 - 3x + 7}{x^2 - 5x + 3}$$

The final answers should always be completely simplified. If a function is composed of a rational expression, the zeros of the graph can be found from setting the polynomial in the numerator as equal to zero and solving. The values that make the denominator equal to zero will either exist on the graph as a **hole** or a **vertical asymptote**.

A **complex fraction** is a fraction in which the numerator and denominator are themselves fractions, of the form:

$$\frac{\left(\frac{a}{b}\right)}{\left(\frac{c}{d}\right)}$$

These can be simplified by following the usual rules for the order of operations, or by remembering that dividing one fraction by another is the same as multiplying by the reciprocal of the divisor. This means that any complex fraction can be rewritten using the following form:

$$\frac{\left(\frac{a}{b}\right)}{\left(\frac{c}{d}\right)} = \frac{a}{b} \times \frac{d}{c}$$

The following problem is an example of solving a complex fraction:

$$\frac{\left(\frac{5}{4}\right)}{\left(\frac{3}{8}\right)} = \frac{5}{4} \times \frac{8}{3} = \frac{40}{12} = \frac{10}{3}$$

## Writing an Expression from a Written Description

When expressing a verbal or written statement mathematically, it is vital to understand words or phrases that can be represented with symbols. The following are examples:

| Symbol | Phrase |
|---|---|
| + | Added to; increased by; sum of; more than |
| − | Decreased by; difference between; less than; take away |
| × | Multiplied by; 3(4,5…) times as large; product of |
| ÷ | Divided by; quotient of; half (third, etc.) of |
| = | Is; the same as; results in; as much as; equal to |
| x,t,n, etc. | A number; unknown quantity; value of; variable |

Addition and subtraction are **inverse operations**. Adding a number and then subtracting the same number will cancel each other out, resulting in the original number, and vice versa. For example:

$$8 + 7 - 7 = 8$$

and

$$137 - 100 + 100 = 137$$

Similarly, multiplication and division are inverse operations. Therefore, multiplying by a number and then dividing by the same number results in the original number, and vice versa. For example:

$$8 \times 2 \div 2 = 8$$

and

$$12 \div 4 \times 4 = 12$$

Inverse operations are used to work backwards to solve problems. In the case that 7 and a number add to 18, the inverse operation of subtraction is used to find the unknown value ($18 - 7 = 11$). If a school's entire 4th grade was divided evenly into 3 classes each with 22 students, the inverse operation of multiplication is used to determine the total students in the grade ($22 \times 3 = 66$).

Recall that a rational expression is a fraction where the numerator and denominator are both polynomials.

Some examples of rational expressions include the following:

$$\frac{4x^3y^5}{3z^4}$$

$$\frac{4x^3 + 3x}{x^2}$$

and

$$\frac{x^2 + 7x + 10}{x + 2}$$

Since these refer to expressions and not equations, they can be simplified but not solved. Using the rules of exponents and roots, some rational expressions with monomials can be simplified. Other rational expressions such as the last example:

$$\frac{x^2 + 7x + 10}{x + 2}$$

take more steps to be simplified. First, the polynomial on top can be factored from:

$$x^2 + 7x + 10$$

into

$$(x + 5)(x + 2)$$

Then the common factors can be canceled, and the expression can be simplified to $(x + 5)$.

Consider this problem as an example of using rational expressions. Reggie wants to lay sod in his rectangular backyard. The length of the yard is given by the expression $4x + 2$, and the width is unknown. The area of the yard is $20x + 10$. Reggie needs to find the width of the yard. Knowing that the area of a rectangle is length multiplied by width, an expression can be written to find the width:

$$\frac{20x + 10}{4x + 2}$$

area divided by length. Simplifying this expression by factoring out 10 on the top and 2 on the bottom leads to this expression:

$$\frac{10(2x + 1)}{2(2x + 1)}$$

By cancelling out the $2x + 1$, that results in $\frac{10}{2} = 5$. The width of the yard is found to be 5 by simplifying a rational expression.

## Using Linear Equations to Solve Real-World Problems

Linear relationships describe the way two quantities change with respect to each other. The relationship is defined as linear because a line is produced if all the sets of corresponding values are graphed on a coordinate grid. When expressing the linear relationship as an equation, the equation is often written in the form $y = mx + b$ (slope-intercept form) where $m$ and $b$ are numerical values and $x$ and $y$ are variables (for example, $y = 5x + 10$). Given a linear equation and the value of either variable ($x$ or $y$), the value of the other variable can be determined.

Imagine the following problem: The sum of a number and 5 is equal to -8 times the number.

To find this unknown number, a simple equation can be written to represent the problem. Key words such as difference, equal, and times are used to form the following equation with one variable:

$$n + 5 = -8n$$

When solving for $n$, opposite operations are used. First, $n$ is subtracted from $-8n$ across the equals sign, resulting in $5 = -9n$. Then, -9 is divided on both sides, leaving $n = -\frac{5}{9}$. This solution can be graphed on the number line with a dot as shown below:

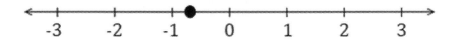

Suppose a teacher is grading a test containing 20 questions with 5 points given for each correct answer, adding a curve of 10 points to each test. This linear relationship can be expressed as the equation:

$$y = 5x + 10$$

where $x$ represents the number of correct answers, and $y$ represents the test score. To determine the score of a test with a given number of correct answers, the number of correct answers is substituted into the equation for $x$ and evaluated. For example, for 10 correct answers, 10 is substituted for $x$:

$$y = 5(10) + 10 \rightarrow y = 60$$

Therefore, 10 correct answers will result in a score of 60. The number of correct answers needed to obtain a certain score can also be determined. To determine the number of correct answers needed to score a 90, 90 is substituted for $y$ in the equation ($y$ represents the test score) and solved:

$$90 = 5x + 10 \rightarrow 80 = 5x \rightarrow 16 = x$$

Therefore, 16 correct answers are needed to score a 90.

Linear relationships may be represented by a table of 2 corresponding values. Certain tables may determine the relationship between the values and predict other corresponding sets. Consider the table below, which displays the money in a checking account that charges a monthly fee:

| Month | 0 | 1 | 2 | 3 | 4 |
|---|---|---|---|---|---|
| Balance | $210 | $195 | $180 | $165 | $150 |

An examination of the values reveals that the account loses $15 every month (the month increases by one and the balance decreases by 15). This information can be used to predict future values. To determine what the value will be in month 6, the pattern can be continued, and it can be concluded that the balance will be $120. To determine which month the balance will be $0, $210 is divided by $15 (since the balance decreases $15 every month), resulting in month 14.

## Solving a System of Two Linear Equations

A **system of equations** is a group of equations that have the same variables or unknowns. These equations can be linear, but they are not always so. Finding a solution to a system of equations means finding the values of the variables that satisfy each equation. For a linear system of two equations and two variables, there could be a single solution, no solution, or infinitely many solutions.

A single solution occurs when there is one value for $x$ and y that satisfies the system. This would be shown on the graph where the lines cross at exactly one point. When there is no solution, the lines are parallel and do not ever cross. With infinitely many solutions, the equations may look different, but they

are the same line. One equation will be a multiple of the other, and on the graph, they lie on top of each other.

The process of elimination can be used to solve a system of equations. For example, the following equations make up a system:

$$x + 3y = 10 \text{ and } 2x - 5y = 9$$

Immediately adding these equations does not eliminate a variable, but it is possible to change the first equation by multiplying the whole equation by $-2$. This changes the first equation to

$$-2x - 6y = -20$$

The equations can be then added to obtain $-11y = -11$. Solving for $y$ yields $y = 1$. To find the rest of the solution, 1 can be substituted in for $y$ in either original equation to find the value of $x = 7$. The solution to the system is (7, 1) because it makes both equations true, and it is the point in which the lines intersect. If the system is **dependent**—having infinitely many solutions—then both variables will cancel out when the elimination method is used, resulting in an equation that is true for many values of $x$ and $y$. Since the system is dependent, both equations can be simplified to the same equation or line.

A system can also be solved using **substitution.** This involves solving one equation for a variable and then plugging that solved equation into the other equation in the system. For example:

$$x - y = -2$$

and

$$3x + 2y = 9$$

can be solved using substitution. The first equation can be solved for $x$, where $x = -2 + y$. Then it can be plugged into the other equation:

$$3(-2 + y) + 2y = 9$$

Solving for $y$ yields:

$$-6 + 3y + 2y = 9$$

That shows that $y = 3$. If $y = 3$, then $x = 1$.

This solution can be checked by plugging in these values for the variables in each equation to see if it makes a true statement.

Finally, a solution to a system of equations can be found graphically. The solution to a linear system is the point or points where the lines cross. The values of x and y represent the coordinates $(x, y)$ where the lines intersect. Using the same system of equations as above, they can be solved for $y$ to put them in slope-intercept form, $y = mx + b$.

These equations become:

$$y = x + 2$$

and

$$y = -\frac{3}{2}x + 4.5$$

The slope is the coefficient of $x$, and the y-intercept is the constant value.

This system with the solution is shown below:

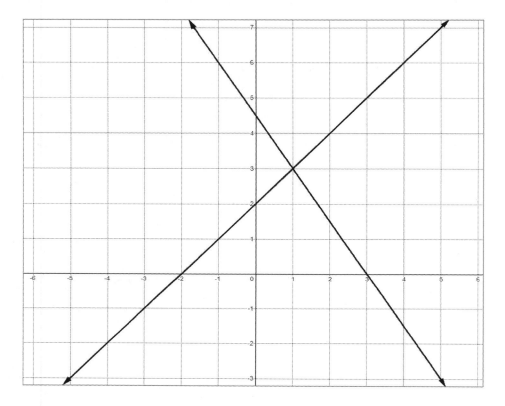

If the lines intersect, the point of intersection is the solution to the system. Every point on a line represents an ordered pair that makes its equation true. The ordered pair represented by this point of intersection lies on both lines and therefore makes both equations true. This ordered pair should be checked by substituting its values into both of the original equations of the system. Note that given a system of equations and an ordered pair, the ordered pair can be determined to be a solution or not by checking it in both equations.

If, when graphed, the lines representing the equations of a system do not intersect, then the two lines are parallel to each other or they are the same exact line. Parallel lines extend in the same direction without ever meeting. A system consisting of parallel lines has no solution. If the equations for a system represent the same exact line, then every point on the line is a solution to the system. In this case, there would be an infinite number of solutions. A system consisting of intersecting lines is referred to as independent; a system consisting of parallel lines is referred to as inconsistent; and a system consisting of coinciding lines is referred to as dependent.

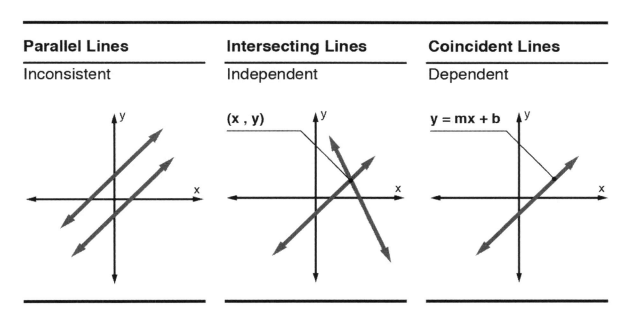

| **Parallel Lines** | **Intersecting Lines** | **Coincident Lines** |
|---|---|---|
| Inconsistent | Independent | Dependent |

Matrices can also be used to solve systems of linear equations. Specifically, for systems, the coefficients of the linear equations in standard form are the entries in the matrix. Using the same system of linear equations as above, $x - y = -2$ and $3x + 2y = 9$, the matrix to represent the system is:

$$\begin{bmatrix} 1 & -1 \\ 3 & 2 \end{bmatrix} \begin{bmatrix} x \\ y \end{bmatrix} = \begin{bmatrix} -2 \\ 9 \end{bmatrix}$$

To solve this system using matrices, the inverse matrix must be found. For a general $2 \times 2$ matrix:

$$\begin{bmatrix} a & b \\ c & d \end{bmatrix}$$

The inverse matrix is found by the expression:

$$\frac{1}{ad - bc} \begin{bmatrix} d & -b \\ -c & a \end{bmatrix}$$

The inverse matrix for the system given above is:

$$\frac{1}{2 - -3} \begin{bmatrix} 2 & 1 \\ -3 & 1 \end{bmatrix} = \frac{1}{5} \begin{bmatrix} 2 & 1 \\ -3 & 1 \end{bmatrix}$$

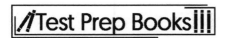
The next step in solving is to multiply this identity matrix by the system matrix above. This is given by the following equation:

$$\frac{1}{5}\begin{bmatrix} 2 & 1 \\ -3 & 1 \end{bmatrix}\begin{bmatrix} 1 & -1 \\ 3 & 2 \end{bmatrix}\begin{bmatrix} x \\ y \end{bmatrix} = \begin{bmatrix} 2 & 1 \\ -3 & 1 \end{bmatrix}\begin{bmatrix} -2 \\ 9 \end{bmatrix}\frac{1}{5}$$

which simplifies to

$$\frac{1}{5}\begin{bmatrix} 5 & 0 \\ 0 & 5 \end{bmatrix}\begin{bmatrix} x \\ y \end{bmatrix} = \frac{1}{5}\begin{bmatrix} 5 \\ 15 \end{bmatrix}$$

Solving for the solution matrix, the answer is:

$$\begin{bmatrix} 1 & 0 \\ 0 & 1 \end{bmatrix}\begin{bmatrix} x \\ y \end{bmatrix} = \begin{bmatrix} 1 \\ 3 \end{bmatrix}$$

Since the first matrix is the identity matrix, the solution is $x = 1$ and $y = 3$.

Finding solutions to systems of equations is essentially finding what values of the variables make both equations true. It is finding the input value that yields the same output value in both equations. For functions $g(x)$ and $f(x)$, the equation $g(x) = f(x)$ means the output values are being set equal to each other. Solving for the value of $x$ means finding the $x$-coordinate that gives the same output in both functions.

For example:

$$f(x) = x + 2$$

and

$$g(x) = -3x + 10$$

is a system of equations. Setting $f(x) = g(x)$ yields the equation:

$$x + 2 = -3x + 10$$

Solving for $x$, gives the $x$-coordinate $x = 2$ where the two lines cross. This value can also be found by using a table or a graph. On a table, both equations can be given the same inputs, and the outputs can be recorded to find the point(s) where the lines cross. Any method of solving finds the same solution, but some methods are more appropriate for some systems of equations than others.

## Solving Inequalities and Graphing the Answer on a Number Line

Linear inequalities and linear equations are both comparisons of two algebraic expressions. However, unlike equations in which the expressions are equal to each other, linear inequalities compare expressions that are unequal. Linear equations typically have one value for the variable that makes the

statement true. Linear inequalities generally have an infinite number of values that make the statement true.

If a problem were to say, "The sum of a number and 5 is greater than -8 times the number," then an inequality would be used instead of an equation. Using key words again, *greater than* is represented by the symbol >. The inequality"

$$n + 5 > -8n$$

can be solved using the same techniques, resulting in:

$$n < -\frac{5}{9}$$

The only time solving an inequality differs from solving an equation is when a negative number is either multiplied by or divided by each side of the inequality. The sign must be switched in this case. For this example, the graph of the solution changes to the following graph because the solution represents all real numbers less than $-\frac{5}{9}$. Not included in this solution is $-\frac{5}{9}$ because it is a *less than* symbol, not *equal to*.

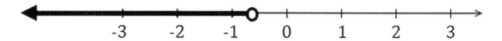

When solving a linear inequality, the solution is the set of all numbers that makes the statement true. The inequality $x + 2 \geq 6$ has a solution set of 4 and every number greater than 4 (4.0001, 5, 12, 107, etc.). Adding 2 to 4 or any number greater than 4 would result in a value that is greater than or equal to 6. Therefore, $x \geq 4$ would be the solution set.

Solution sets for linear inequalities often will be displayed using a number line. If a value is included in the set ($\geq$ or $\leq$), there is a shaded dot placed on that value and an arrow extending in the direction of the solutions. For a variable > or $\geq$ a number, the arrow would point right on the number line (the direction where the numbers increase); and if a variable is < or $\leq$ a number, the arrow would point left (where the numbers decrease). If the value is not included in the set (> or <), an open circle on that value would be used with an arrow in the appropriate direction.

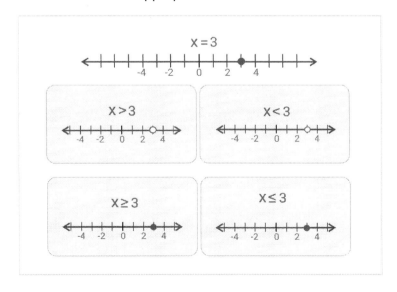

Students may be asked to write a linear inequality given a graph of its solution set. To do so, they should identify whether the value is included (shaded dot or open circle) and the direction in which the arrow is pointing.

In order to algebraically solve a linear inequality, the same steps should be followed as in solving a linear equation. The inequality symbol stays the same for all operations EXCEPT when multiplying or dividing by a negative number. If multiplying or dividing by a negative number while solving an inequality, the relationship reverses (the sign flips). Multiplying or dividing by a positive does not change the relationship, so the sign stays the same. In other words, $>$ switches to $<$ and vice versa. An example is shown below:

Solve $-2(x + 4) \leq 22$ for the value of $x$.

First, distribute -2 to the binomial by multiplying:

$$-2x - 8 \leq 22$$

Next, add 8 to both sides to isolate the variable:

$$-2x \leq 30$$

Divide both sides by -2 to solve for $x$:

$$x \geq -15$$

With a single equation in two variables, the solutions are limited only by the situation the equation represents. When two equations or inequalities are used, more constraints are added. For example, in a system of linear equations, there is often—although not always—only one answer. The point of intersection of two lines is the solution. For a system of inequalities, there are infinitely many answers.

The intersection of two solution sets gives the solution set of the system of inequalities. In the following graph, the darker shaded region is where two inequalities overlap. Any set of $x$ and $y$ found in that region satisfies both inequalities. The line with the positive slope is solid, meaning the values on that line are included in the solution.

The line with the negative slope is dotted, so the coordinates on that line are not included.

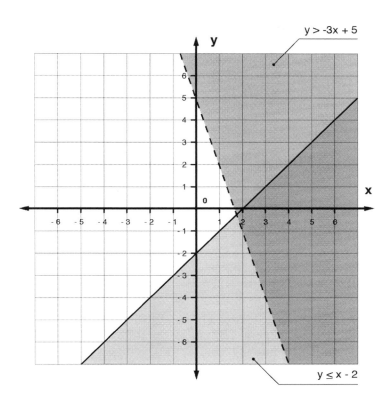

## Quadratic Equations with One Variable

A **quadratic equation** can be written in the form:

$$y = ax^2 + bx + c$$

The u-shaped graph of a quadratic equation is called a **parabola**. The graph can either open up or open down (upside down u). The graph is symmetric about a vertical line, called the **axis of symmetry**. Corresponding points on the parabola are directly across from each other (same *y*-value) and are the same distance from the axis of symmetry (on either side). The axis of symmetry intersects the parabola at its **vertex**. The *y*-value of the vertex represents the minimum or maximum value of the function. If the graph opens up, the value of *a* in its equation is positive, and the vertex represents the minimum of the

function. If the graph opens down, the value of *a* in its equation is negative, and the vertex represents the maximum of the function.

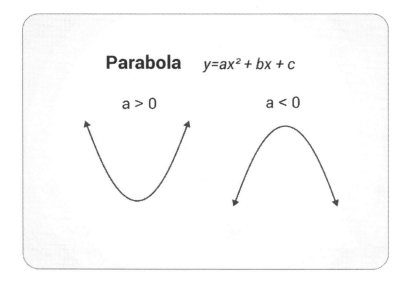

**Parabola** $y = ax^2 + bx + c$

a > 0                          a < 0

For a quadratic equation where the value of *a* is positive, as the inputs increase, the outputs increase until a certain value (maximum of the function) is reached. As inputs increase past the value that corresponds with the maximum output, the relationship reverses, and the outputs decrease. For a quadratic equation where *a* is negative, as the inputs increase, the outputs (1) decrease, (2) reach a maximum, and (3) then increase.

Consider a ball thrown straight up into the air. As time passes, the height of the ball increases until it reaches its maximum height. After reaching the maximum height, as time increases, the height of the ball decreases (it is falling toward the ground). This relationship can be expressed as a quadratic equation where time is the input (*x*), and the height of the ball is the output (*y*).

Equations with one variable (linear equations) can be solved using the addition principle and multiplication principle. If $a = b$, then $a + c = b + c$, and $ac = bc$. Given the equation"

$$2x - 3 = 5x + 7$$

the first step is to combine the variable terms and the constant terms. Using the principles, expressions can be added and subtracted onto and off both sides of the equals sign, so the equation turns into $-10 = 3x$. Dividing by 3 on both sides through the multiplication principle with $c = \frac{1}{3}$ results in the final answer of $x = \frac{-10}{3}$.

However, this same process cannot be used to solve nonlinear equations, including quadratic equations. Quadratic equations have a higher degree than linear ones (2 versus 1) and are not solved by simply using opposite operations. When an equation has a degree of 2, completing the square is an option. For example, the quadratic equation:

$$x^2 - 6x + 2 = 0$$

can be rewritten by completing the square. The goal of completing the square is to get the equation into the form:

$$(x - p)^2 = q$$

Using the example, the constant term 2 first needs to be moved over to the opposite side by subtracting. Then, the square can be completed by adding 9 to both sides, which is the square of half of the coefficient of the middle term $-6x$. The current equation is:

$$x^2 - 6x + 9 = 7$$

The left side can be factored into a square of a binomial, resulting in:

$$(x - 3)^2 = 7$$

To solve for $x$, the square root of both sides should be taken, resulting in:

$$(x - 3) = \pm\sqrt{7}$$

and

$$x = 3 \pm \sqrt{7}$$

Other ways of solving quadratic equations include graphing, factoring, and using the quadratic formula. The equation:

$$y = x^2 - 4x + 3$$

can be graphed on the coordinate plane, and the solutions can be observed where it crosses the x-axis. The graph will be a parabola that opens up with two solutions at 1 and 3.

If quadratic equations take the form $ax^2 - b = 0$, then the equation can be solved by adding $b$ to both sides and dividing by $a$ to get:

$$x^2 = \frac{b}{a} \text{ or } x = \pm\sqrt{\frac{b}{a}}$$

Note that this is actually two separate solutions, unless $b$ happens to be 0.

If a quadratic equation has no constant—so that it takes the form:

$$ax^2 + bx = 0$$

then the $x$ can be factored out to get

$$x(ax + b) = 0$$

Then, the solutions are $x = 0$, together with the solutions to

$$ax + b = 0$$

Both factors $x$ and $(ax + b)$ can be set equal to zero to solve for $x$ because one of those values must be zero for their product to equal zero. For an equation $ab = 0$ to be true, either $a = 0$, or $b = 0$.

A given quadratic equation:

$$x^2 + bx + c$$

can be factored into:

$$(x + A)(x + B)$$

where $A + B = b$, and $AB = c$. Finding the values of A and B can take time, but such a pair of numbers can be found by guessing and checking. Looking at the positive and negative factors for $c$ offers a good starting point.

For example, in:

$$x^2 - 5x + 6$$

the factors of 6 are 1, 2, and 3. Now, $(-2)(-3) = 6$, and $-2 - 3 = -5$. In general, however, this may not work, in which case another approach may need to be used.

A quadratic equation of the form:

$$x^2 + 2xb + b^2 = 0$$

can be factored into $(x + b)^2 = 0$. Similarly

$$x^2 - 2xy + y^2 = 0$$

factors into $(x - y)^2 = 0$.

The first method of completing the square can be used in finding the second method, the quadratic formula. It can be used to solve any quadratic equation. This formula may be the longest method for solving quadratic equations and is commonly used as a last resort after other methods are ruled out.

It can be helpful in memorizing the formula to see where it comes from, so here are the steps involved.

The most general form for a quadratic equation is:

$$ax^2 + bx + c = 0$$

First, dividing both sides by $a$ leaves us with:

$$x^2 + \frac{b}{a}x + \frac{c}{a} = 0$$

To complete the square on the left-hand side, c/a can be subtracted on both sides to get:

$$x^2 + \frac{b}{a}x = -\frac{c}{a}$$

$(\frac{b}{2a})^2$ is then added to both sides.

This gives:

$$x^2 + \frac{b}{a}x + (\frac{b}{2a})^2 = (\frac{b}{2a})^2 - \frac{c}{a}$$

The left can now be factored and the right-hand side simplified to give:

$$(x + \frac{b}{2a})^2 = \frac{b^2 - 4ac}{4a}$$

Taking the square roots gives:

$$x + \frac{b}{2a} = \pm\frac{\sqrt{b^2 - 4ac}}{2a}$$

Solving for x yields the quadratic formula:

$$x = \frac{-b \pm \sqrt{b^2 - 4ac}}{2a}$$

It isn't necessary to remember how to get this formula but memorizing the formula itself is the goal.

If an equation involves taking a root, then the first step is to move the root to one side of the equation and everything else to the other side. That way, both sides can be raised to the index of the radical in order to remove it, and solving the equation can continue.

# *Graphs and Functions*

## Locating Points and Graphing Equations

The coordinate plane, sometimes referred to as the Cartesian plane, is a two-dimensional surface consisting of a horizontal and a vertical number line. The horizontal number line is referred to as the *x*-axis, and the vertical number line is referred to as the *y*-axis. The *x*-axis and *y*-axis intersect (or cross) at a point called the origin. At the origin, the value of the *x*-axis is zero, and the value of the *y*-axis is zero. The coordinate plane identifies the exact location of a point that is plotted on the two-dimensional surface. Like a map, the location of all points on the plane are in relation to the origin. Along the *x*-axis (horizontal line), numbers to the right of the origin are positive and increasing in value (1,2,3, . . .) and to the left of the origin numbers are negative and decreasing in value (-1,-2,-3, . . .). Along the *y*-axis (vertical line), numbers above the origin are positive and increasing in value and numbers below the origin are negative and decreasing in value.

The *x*- and *y*-axis divide the coordinate plane into four sections. These sections are referred to as quadrant one, quadrant two, quadrant three, and quadrant four, and are often written with Roman numerals I, II, III, and IV.

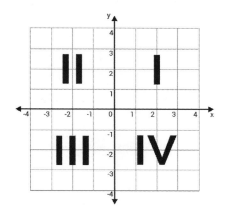

The upper right section is Quadrant I and consists of points with positive *x*-values and positive *y*-values. The upper left section is Quadrant II and consists of points with negative *x*-values and positive *y*-values. The bottom left section is Quadrant III and consists of points with negative *x*-values and negative *y*-values. The bottom right section is Quadrant IV and consists of points with positive *x*-values and negative *y*-values.

## Graphing in the Coordinate Plane

The coordinate plane represents a representation of real-world space, and any point within the plane can be defined by a set of **coordinates** (x, y). The coordinates consist of two numbers, x and y, which represent a position on each number line. The coordinates can also be referred to as an **ordered pair,** and (0, 0) is the ordered pair known as the **vertex,** or the origin, the point in which the axes intersect.

Here is an example of the coordinate plane with a point plotted:

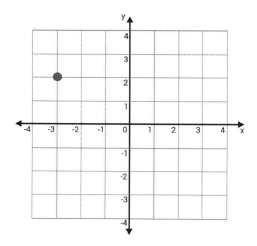

In order to plot a point on the coordinate plane, each coordinate must be considered individually. The value of x represents how many units away from the vertex the point lies on the x-axis. The value of y represents the number of units away from the vertex that the point lies on the y-axis.

For example, given the ordered pair (5, 4), the x-coordinate, 5, is the distance from the origin along the x-axis, and the y-coordinate, 4, is the distance from the origin along the y-axis. This is determined by counting 5 units to the right from (0, 0) along the x-axis and then counting 4 units up from that point, to reach the point where $x = 5$ and $y = 4$. In order to graph the single point, the point should be marked there with a dot and labeled as (5, 4). Every point on the plane has its own ordered pair.

## Graphing on the Coordinate Plane Using Mathematical Problems, Tables, and Patterns

Data can be recorded using a coordinate plane. Graphs are utilized frequently in real-world applications and can be seen in many facets of everyday life. A relationship can exist between the x- and y-coordinates that are plotted on a graph, and those values can represent a set of data that can be listed in a table. Going back and forth between the table and the graph is an important concept and defining the relationship between the variables is the key that links the data to a real-life application.

For example, temperature increases during a summer day. The x-coordinate can be used to represent hours in the day, and the y-coordinate can be used to represent the temperature in degrees. The graph would show the temperature at each hour of the day. Time is almost always plotted on the x-axis, and utilizing different units on each axis, if necessary, is important. Labeling the axes with units is also important.

Within the first quadrant of the coordinate plane, both the x and y values are positive. Most real-world problems can be plotted in this quadrant because most real-world quantities, such as time and distance, are positive. Consider the following table of values:

| X | Y |
|---|---|
| 1 | 2 |
| 2 | 4 |
| 3 | 6 |
| 4 | 8 |

Each row gives a coordinate pair. For example, the first row gives the coordinates (1,2). Each x-value tells you how far to move from the origin, the point (0,0), to the right, and each y-value tells you how far to move up from the origin.

Here is the graph of the points listed above in the table in addition to the origin:

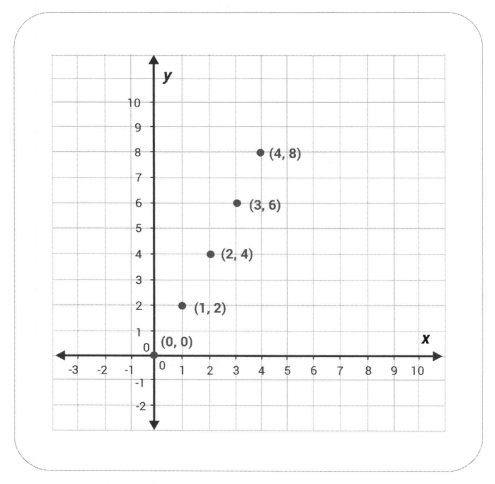

Notice that each *y*-value is found by doubling the *x*-value that forms the other portion of its coordinate pair.

## Determining the Slope of a Line from a Graph, Equation, or Table

**Rate of change** for any line calculates the steepness of the line over a given interval. Rate of change is also known as the **slope** or rise/run. The slope of a linear function is given by the change in *y* divided by the change in *x*. So, the formula looks like this:

$$slope = \frac{y_2 - y_1}{x_2 - x_1}$$

In the graph below, two points are plotted. The first has the coordinates of (0, 1), and the second point is (2, 3). Remember that the x coordinate is always placed first in coordinate pairs. Work from left to right when identifying coordinates. Thus, the point on the left is point 1 (0, 1), and the point on the right is point 2 (2, 3).

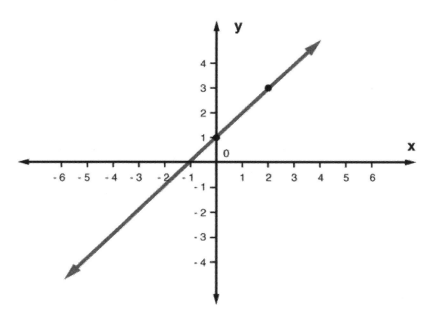

Now we need to just plug those numbers into the equation:

$$slope = \frac{3-1}{2-0}$$

$$slope = \frac{2}{2}$$

$$slope = 1$$

This means that for every increase of 1 for x, y also increased by 1. You can see this in the line. When x equaled 0, y equaled 1, and when x was increased to 1, y equaled 2.

Slope can be thought of as determining the rise over run:

$$slope = \frac{rise}{run}$$

The rise being the change vertically on the y axis and the run being the change horizontally on the x axis.

## Proportional Relationships for Equations and Graphs

The rate of change for a linear function is constant and can be determined based on a few representations. One method is to place the equation in slope-intercept form: $y = mx + b$. Thus, $m$ is the slope, and $b$ is the y-intercept. In the graph below, the equation is $y = x + 1$, where the slope is 1 and the $y$-intercept is 1. For every vertical change of 1 unit, there is a horizontal change of 1 unit.

The $x$-intercept is -1, which is the point where the line crosses the $x$-axis:

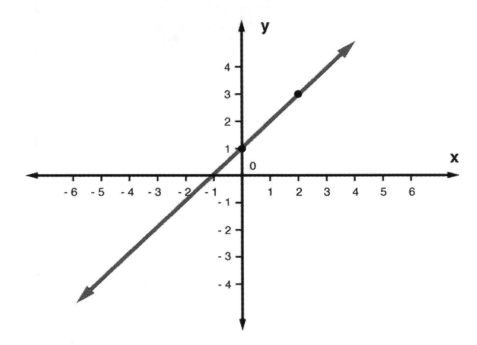

Let's look at an example of a proportional, or linear relationship, seen in the real world.

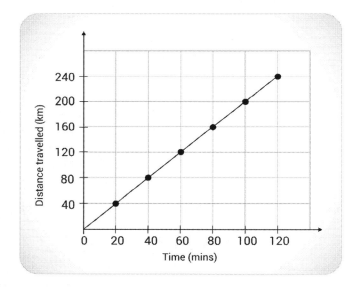

The graph above represents the relationship between distance traveled and time. To find the distance traveled in 80 minutes, the mark for 80 minutes is located at the bottom of the graph. By following this mark directly up on the graph, the corresponding point for 80 minutes is directly across from the 160 kilometer mark. This information indicates that the distance travelled in 80 minutes is 160 kilometers. To predict information not displayed on the graph, the way in which the variables change with respect to one another is determined. In this case, distance increases by 40 kilometers as time increases by 20 minutes. This information can be used to continue the data in the graph or convert the values to a table.

Let's try another example. Jim owns a car wash and charges $40 per car. The rent for the facility is $350 per month. An equation can be written to relate the number of cars Jim cleans to the money he makes per month. Let $x$ represent the number of cars and $y$ represent the profit Jim makes each month from the car wash. The equation $y = 40x - 350$ can be used to show Jim's profit or loss. Since this equation has two variables, the coordinate plane can be used to show the relationship and predict profit or loss for Jim. The following graph shows that Jim must wash at least nine cars to pay the rent, where $x = 9$. Anything nine cars and above yield a profit shown in the value on the y-axis.

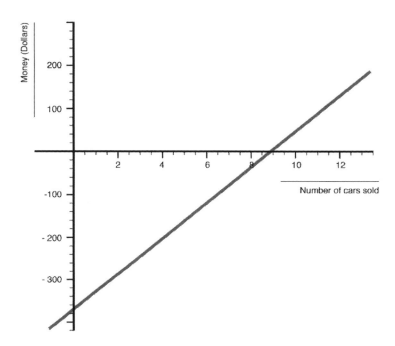

Formulas with two variables are equations used to represent a specific relationship. For example, the formula $d = rt$ represents the relationship between distance, rate, and time. If Bob travels at a rate of 35 miles per hour on his road trip from Westminster to Seneca, the formula $d = 35t$ can be used to represent his distance traveled in a specific length of time. Formulas can also be used to show different roles of the variables, transformed without any given numbers. Solving for $r$, the formula becomes $\frac{d}{t} = r$. The $t$ is moved over by division so that **rate** is a function of distance and time.

## Features of Graphs and Tables for Linear and Nonlinear Relationships

As mentioned, linear relationships describe the way two quantities change with respect to each other. The relationship is defined as linear because a line is produced if all the sets of corresponding values are graphed on a coordinate grid. When expressing the linear relationship as an equation, the equation is often written in the form $y = mx + b$ (**slope-intercept form**) where $m$ and $b$ are numerical values and $x$ and $y$ are variables (for example, $y = 5x + 10$). The slope is the coefficient of $x$, and the y-intercept is the constant value. The slope of the line containing the same two points is:

$$m = \frac{y_2 - y_1}{x_2 - x_1}$$

and is also equal to rise/run. Given a linear equation and the value of either variable ($x$ or $y$), the value of the other variable can be determined.

With polynomial functions such as quadratics, the x-intercepts represent zeros of the function. Finding the **zeros of polynomial functions** is the same process as finding the solutions of polynomial equations. These are the points at which the graph of the function crosses the x-axis. In the following quadratic equation, factoring the binomial leads to finding the zeros of the function:

$$x^2 - 5x + 6 = y$$

This equations factors into

$$(x - 3)(x - 2) = y$$

where 2 and 3 are found to be the zeros of the function when y is set equal to zero. The zeros of any function are the x-values where the graph of the function on the coordinate plane crosses the x-axis, which is the same as an x-intercept.

## Selecting an Equation that Best Represents a Graph

Three common functions used to model different relationships between quantities are linear, quadratic, and exponential functions. **Linear functions** are the simplest of the three, and the independent variable $x$ has an exponent of 1. Written in the most common form:

$$y = mx + b$$

the coefficient of $x$ indicates how fast the function grows at a constant rate, and the $b$-value denotes the starting point. A **quadratic function** has an exponent of 2 on the independent variable $x$. Standard form for this type of function is:

$$y = ax^2 + bx + c$$

and the graph is a parabola. These type functions grow at a changing rate. An **exponential function** has an independent variable in the exponent $y = ab^x$. The graph of these types of functions is described as **growth** or **decay**, based on whether the **base**, $b$, is greater than or less than 1. These functions are different from quadratic functions because the base stays constant. A common base is base $e$.

The following three functions model a linear, quadratic, and exponential function respectively: $y = 2x$, $y = x^2$, and $y = 2^x$. Their graphs are shown below. The first graph, modeling the linear function, shows that the growth is constant over each interval. With a horizontal change of 1, the vertical change is 2. It models constant positive growth. The second graph shows the quadratic function, which is a curve that is symmetric across the y-axis. The growth is not constant, but the change is mirrored over the axis. The last graph models the exponential function, where the horizontal change of 1 yields a vertical change that increases more and more with each iteration of horizontal change. The exponential graph gets very close to the $x$-axis, but never touches it, meaning there is an asymptote there. The y-value can never be zero because the base of 2 can never be raised to an input value that yields an output of zero.

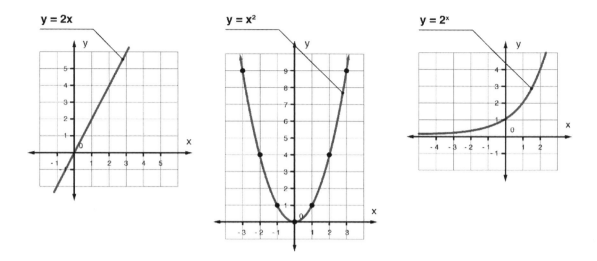

## Determining the Graphical Properties and Sketch a Graph Given an Equation

### Graphing a Linear Function

The process for graphing a line depends on the form in which its equation is written: slope-intercept form or standard form.

When an equation is written in slope-intercept form, $y = mx + b$, $m$ represents the slope of the line and $b$ represents the y-intercept. The y-intercept is the value of $y$ when $x = 0$ and the point at which the graph of the line crosses the y-axis. The slope is the rate of change between the variables, expressed as a fraction. The fraction expresses the change in $y$ compared to the change in $x$. If the slope is an integer, it should be written as a fraction with a denominator of 1. For example, 5 would be written as $\frac{5}{1}$.

To graph a line given an equation in slope-intercept form, the y-intercept should first be plotted. For example, to graph:

$$y = -\frac{2}{3}x + 7$$

the y-intercept of 7 would be plotted on the y-axis (vertical axis) at the point (0, 7). Next, the slope would be used to determine a second point for the line. Note that all that is necessary to graph a line is two points on that line. The slope will indicate how to get from one point on the line to another. The slope expresses vertical change ($y$) compared to horizontal change ($x$) and therefore is sometimes referred to as $\frac{rise}{run}$. The numerator indicates the change in the $y$ value (move up for positive integers and move down for negative integers), and the denominator indicates the change in the $x$ value. For the previous example, using the slope of $-\frac{2}{3}$, from the first point at the y-intercept, the second point should be found by counting down 2 and to the right 3. This point would be located at (3, 5).

When an equation is written in standard form, $Ax + By = C$, it is easy to identify the $x$- and y-intercepts for the graph of the line. Just as the y-intercept is the point at which the line intercepts the y-axis, the $x$-

intercept is the point at which the line intercepts the *x*-axis. At the *y*-intercept, $x = 0$; and at the *x*-intercept, $y = 0$. Given an equation in standard form, $x = 0$ should be used to find the *y*-intercept. Likewise, $y = 0$ should be used to find the *x*-intercept. For example, to graph $3x + 2y = 6$, 0 for *y* results in $3x + 2(0) = 6$. Solving for *y* yields $x = 2$; therefore, an ordered pair for the line is (2, 0). Substituting 0 for *x* results in $3(0) + 2y = 6$. Solving for *y* yields $y = 3$; therefore, an ordered pair for the line is (0, 3). The two ordered pairs (the *x*- and *y*-intercepts) can be plotted, and a straight line through them can be constructed.

**T - chart**

| x | y |
|---|---|
| 0 | 3 |
| 2 | 0 |

**Intercepts**

x - intercept : (2,0)

y - intercept : (0,3)

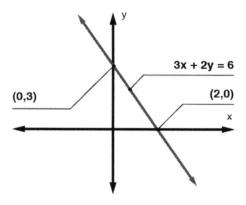

## Graphing a Quadratic Function
The standard form of a quadratic function is:

$$y = ax^2 + bx + c$$

The graph of a quadratic function is a u-shaped (or upside-down u) curve, called a parabola, which is symmetric about a vertical line (axis of symmetry). To graph a parabola, its vertex (high or low point for the curve) and at least two points on each side of the axis of symmetry need to be determined.

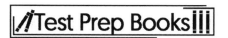
Given a quadratic function in standard form, the axis of symmetry for its graph is the line $x = -\frac{b}{2a}$. The vertex for the parabola has an $x$-coordinate of $-\frac{b}{2a}$. To find the $y$-coordinate for the vertex, the calculated $x$-coordinate needs to be substituted. To complete the graph, two different $x$-values need to be selected and substituted into the quadratic function to obtain the corresponding $y$-values. This will give two points on the parabola. These two points and the axis of symmetry are used to determine the two points corresponding to these. The corresponding points are the same distance from the axis of symmetry (on the other side) and contain the same $y$-coordinate. Plotting the vertex and four other points on the parabola allows for constructing the curve.

## Quadratic Function

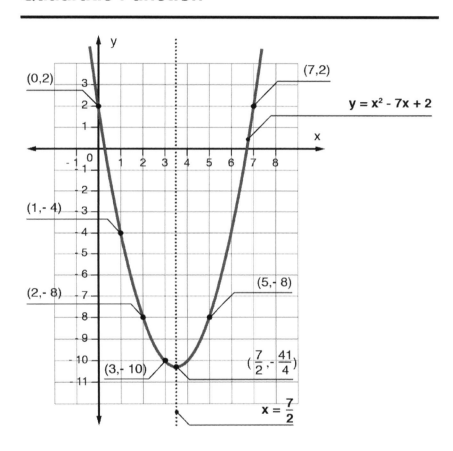

### Graphing an Exponential Function

Exponential functions have a general form of:

$$y = a \times b^x$$

The graph of an exponential function is a curve that slopes upward or downward from left to right. The graph approaches a line, called an asymptote, as $x$ or $y$ increases or decreases. To graph the curve for an exponential function, $x$-values are selected and then substituted into the function to obtain the corresponding *y*-values. A general rule of thumb is to select three negative values, zero, and three positive values. Plotting the seven points on the graph for an exponential function should allow for constructing a smooth curve through them.

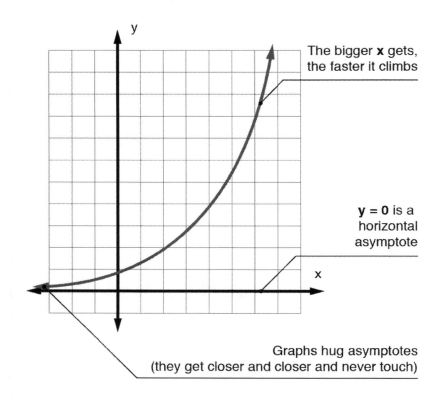

The bigger **x** gets, the faster it climbs

**y = 0** is a horizontal asymptote

Graphs hug asymptotes (they get closer and closer and never touch)

### Equation of a Line from the Slope and a Point on a Line

The point-slope form of a line:

$$y - y_1 = m(x - x_1)$$

is used to write an equation when given an ordered pair (point on the equation's graph) for the function and its rate of change (slope of the line). The values for the slope, *m*, and the point ($x_1$, $y_1$) are substituted into the point-slope form to obtain the equation of the line. A line with a slope of 3 and an ordered pair (4, -2) would have an equation:

$$y - (-2) = 3(x - 4)$$

If a question specifies that the equation be written in slope-intercept form, the equation should be manipulated to isolate *y*:

Solve: $y - (-2) = 3(x - 4)$

Distribute: $y + 2 = 3x - 12$

Subtract 2 from both sides: $y = 3x - 14$

## Equation of a Line from Two Points

Given two ordered pairs for a function, $(x_1, y_1)$ and $(x_2, y_2)$, it is possible to determine the rate of change between the variables (slope of the line). To calculate the slope of the line, m, the values for the ordered pairs should be substituted into the formula:

$$m = \frac{y_2 - y_1}{x_2 - x_1}$$

The expression is substituted to obtain a whole number or fraction for the slope. Once the slope is calculated, the slope and either of the ordered pairs should be substituted into the point-slope form to obtain the equation of the line.

## Using Slope of a Line

Two lines are parallel if they have the same slope and a different intercept. Two lines are **perpendicular** if the product of their slope equals -1. Parallel lines never intersect unless they are the same line, and perpendicular lines intersect at a right angle. If two lines aren't parallel, they must intersect at one point. If lines do cross, they're labeled as **intersecting lines** because they "intersect" at one point. If they intersect at more than one point, they're the same line. Determining equations of lines based on properties of parallel and perpendicular lines appears in word problems. To find an equation of a line, both the slope and a point the line goes through are necessary. Therefore, if an equation of a line is needed that's parallel to a given line and runs through a specified point, the slope of the given line and the point are plugged into the point-slope form of an equation of a line. Secondly, if an equation of a line is needed that's perpendicular to a given line running through a specified point, the negative reciprocal of the slope of the given line and the point are plugged into the **point-slope form**. Also, if the point of intersection of two lines is known, that point will be used to solve the set of equations. Therefore, to solve a system of equations, the point of intersection must be found. If a set of two equations with two unknown variables has no solution, the lines are parallel.

The **Parallel Postulate** states that if two parallel lines are cut by a transversal, then the corresponding angles are equal. Here is a picture that highlights this postulate:

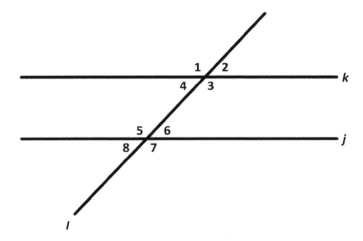

Because lines *k* and *i* are parallel, when cut by transversal *l*, angles 1 and 5 are equal, angles 2 and 6 are equal, angles 4 and 8 are equal, and angles 3 and 7 are equal. Note that angles 1 and 2, 3 and 4, 5 and 6, and 7 and 8 add up to 180 degrees.

This statement is equivalent to the **Alternate Interior Angle Theorem**, which states that when two parallel lines are cut by a transversal, the resultant interior angles are congruent. In the picture above, angles 3 and 5 are congruent, and angles 4 and 6 are congruent.

The Parallel Postulate or the Alternate Interior Angle Theorem can be used to find the missing angles in the following picture:

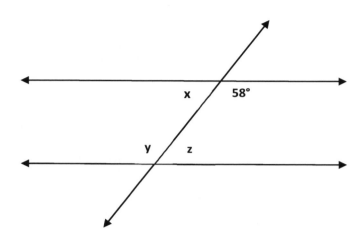

Assuming that the lines are parallel, angle x is found to be 122 degrees. Angle x and the 58-degree angle add up to 180 degrees. The Alternate Interior Angle Theorem states that angle y is equal to 58 degrees. Also, angles y and z add up to 180 degrees, so angle z is 122 degrees. Note that angles x and z are also alternate interior angles, so their equivalence can be used to find angle z as well.

An equivalent statement to the Parallel Postulate is that the sum of all angles in a triangle is 180 degrees. Therefore, given any triangle, if two angles are known, the third can be found accordingly.

### Functions Shown in Different Ways

First, it's important to understand the definition of a **relation**. Given two variables, x and y, which stand for unknown numbers, a **relation** between x and y is an object that splits all of the pairs (x, y) into those for which the relation is true and those for which it is false. For example, consider the relation of $x^2 = y^2$. This relationship is true for the pair (1, 1) and for the pair (-2, 2), but false for (2, 3). Another example of a relation is $x \leq y$. This is true whenever x is less than or equal to y.

A **function** is a special kind of relation where, for each value of x, there is only a single value of y that satisfies the relation. So, $x^2 = y^2$ is *not* a function because in this case, if x is 1, y can be either 1 or -1: the pair (1, 1) and (1, -1) both satisfy the relation. More generally, for this relation, any pair of the form $(a, \pm a)$ will satisfy it. On the other hand, consider the following relation:

$$y = x^2 + 1$$

This is a function because for each value of x, there is a unique value of y that satisfies the relation. Notice, however, there are multiple values of x that give us the same value of y. This is perfectly acceptable for a function. Therefore, y is a function of x.

To determine if a relation is a function, check to see if every x value has a unique corresponding y value.

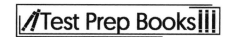

A function can be viewed as an object that has $x$ as its input and outputs a unique $y$-value. It is sometimes convenient to express this using **function notation**, where the function itself is given a name, often $f$. To emphasize that $f$ takes $x$ as its input, the function is written as $f(x)$. In the above example, the equation could be rewritten as:

$$f(x) = x^2 + 1$$

To write the value that a function yields for some specific value of $x$, that value is put in place of $x$ in the function notation. For example, $f(3)$ means the value that the function outputs when the input value is 3. If:

$$f(x) = x^2 + 1$$

then:

$$f(3) = 3^2 + 1 = 10$$

Another example of a function would be:

$$f(x) = 4x + 4$$

read "$f$ of $x$ is equal to four times $x$ plus four." In this example, the input would be $x$ and the output would be f(x). Ordered pairs would be represented as (x, f(x)). To find the output for an input value of 3, 3 would be substituted for $x$ into the function as follows:

$$f(3) = 4(3) + 4$$

resulting in $f(3) = 16$. Therefore, the ordered pair:

$$(3, f(3)) = (3, 16)$$

Note f(x) is a function of $x$ denoted by $f$. Functions of $x$ could be named g(x), read "$g$ of $x$"; p(x), read "$p$ of $x$"; etc.

As an example, the following function is in function notation:

$$f(x) = 3x - 4$$

The $f(x)$ represents the output value for an input of $x$. If $x = 2$, the equation becomes:

$$f(2) = 3(2) - 4 = 6 - 4 = 2$$

The input of 2 yields an output of 2, forming the ordered pair $(2, 2)$. The following set of ordered pairs corresponds to the given function: $(2, 2), (0, -4), (-2, -10)$. The set of all possible inputs of a function is its **domain**, and all possible outputs is called the **range**. By definition, each member of the domain is paired with only one member of the range.

Functions can also be defined recursively. In this form, they are not defined explicitly in terms of variables. Instead, they are defined using previously-evaluated function outputs, starting with either $f(0)$ or $f(1)$. An example of a recursively-defined function is:

$$f(1) = 2, f(n) = 2f(n - 1) + 2n, n > 1$$

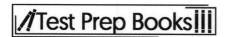

The domain of this function is the set of all integers.

A function can also be viewed as a table of pairs (*x, y*), which lists the value for *y* for each possible value of *x*.

## Functions in Tables and Graphs

The domain and range of a function can be found by observing a table. The table below shows the input values $x = -2$ to $x = 2$ for the function:

$$f(x) = x^2 - 3$$

The range, or output, for these inputs results in a minimum of $-3$. On each side of $x = 0$, the numbers increase, showing that the range is all real numbers greater than or equal to $-3$.

| x (domain/input) | y (range/output) |
|---|---|
| -2 | 1 |
| -1 | -2 |
| 0 | -3 |
| -1 | -2 |
| 2 | 1 |

## Determining the Domain and Range from a Given Graph of a Function

The domain and range of a function can also be found visually by its plot on the coordinate plane. In the function:

$$f(x) = x^2 - 3$$

for example, the domain is all real numbers because the parabola can stretch infinitely far left and right with no restrictions. This means that any input value from the real number system will yield an output in the real number system. For the range, the inequality $y \geq -3$ would be used to describe the possible output values because the parabola has a minimum at $y = -3$. This means there will not be any real output values less than $-3$ because $-3$ is the lowest value the function reaches on the y-axis.

## Determining the Domain and Range of a Given Function

The set of all possible values for *x* in $f(x)$ is called the **domain** of the function, and the set of all possible outputs is called the **range** of the function. Note that usually the domain is assumed to be all real numbers, except those for which the expression for $f(x)$ is not defined, unless the problem specifies otherwise. An example of how a function might not be defined is in the case of:

$$f(x) = \frac{1}{x + 1}$$

which is not defined when $x = -1$ (which would require dividing by zero). Therefore, in this case the domain would be all real numbers except $x = -1$.

## Interpreting Domain and Range in Real-World Settings

A function can be built from the information given in a situation. For example, the relationship between the money paid for a gym membership and the number of months that someone has been a member

can be described through a function. If the one-time membership fee is $40 and the monthly fee is $30, then the function can be written:

$$f(x) = 30x + 40$$

The $x$-value represents the number of months the person has been part of the gym, while the output is the total money paid for the membership. The table below shows this relationship. It is a representation of the function because the initial cost is $40 and the cost increases each month by $30.

| x (months) | f(x) (money paid to gym) |
|---|---|
| 0 | 40 |
| 1 | 70 |
| 2 | 100 |
| 3 | 130 |

In this situation, the domain of the function is real numbers greater than or equal to zero because it represents the number of months that a membership is held. We aren't told if the gym prorates memberships for partial months (if you join 10 days into a month, for example). If not, the domain would only be whole numbers plus zero, since there's a meaningful data point of $40, as a fee for joining. The range is real numbers greater than or equal to 40, because the range represents the total cost of the gym membership. Because there is a one-time fee of $40, the cost of carrying a membership will never be less than $40, so this is the minimum value.

When working through any word problem, the domain and range of the function should be considered in terms of the real-world context that the function models. For example, considering the above function for the cost of a gym membership, it would be nonsensical to include negative numbers in either the domain or range because there can't be negative months that someone holds a membership and similarly, the gym isn't going to pay a person for months prior to becoming a member. Therefore, while the function to model the situation (defined as $f(x) = 30x + 40$) theoretically could result in a true mathematical statement if negative values of are inputted, this would not make sense in the real-world context for which the function applies. Therefore, defining the domain as whole numbers and the range as all real numbers greater than or equal to 40 is important.

## Evaluating Functions

To evaluate functions, plug in the given value everywhere the variable appears in the expression for the function. For example, find $f(-2)$ where:

$$f(x) = 2x^2 - \frac{4}{x}$$

To complete the problem, plug in -2 in the following way:

$$f(-2) = 2(-2)^2 - \frac{4}{-2}$$

$$2 \times 4 + 2$$

$$8 + 2 = 10$$

# Practice Questions

1. The graph of which function has an $x$-intercept of $-2$?
   a. $y = 2x - 3$
   b. $y = 4x + 2$
   c. $y = x^2 + 5x + 6$
   d. $y = -\frac{1}{2} \times 2^x$

2. The table below displays the number of three-year-olds at Kids First Daycare who are potty-trained and those who still wear diapers.

|  | Potty-trained | Wear diapers |  |
|---|---|---|---|
| **Boys** | 26 | 22 | 48 |
| **Girls** | 34 | 18 | 52 |
|  | 60 | 40 |  |

What is the probability of a three-year-old girl from the school being potty-trained?
   a. 52%
   b. 34%
   c. 65%
   d. 57%

3. A rectangle was formed out of pipe cleaner. Its length was $\frac{1}{2}$ feet and its width was $\frac{11}{2}$ inches. What is its area in square inches?
   a. $\frac{11}{4}$ inch$^2$
   b. $\frac{11}{2}$ inch$^2$
   c. 22 inch$^2$
   d. 33 inch$^2$

4. You measure the width of your door to be 36 inches. The true width of the door is 35.75 inches. What is the relative error in your measurement?
   a. 0.7%
   b. 0.007%
   c. 0.99%
   d. 0.1%

5. A couple buys a house for $150,000. They sell it for $165,000. By what percentage did the house's value increase?
   a. 10%
   b. 13%
   c. 15%
   d. 17%

# Answer Explanations

**1. C:** An $x$-intercept is the point where the graph crosses the $x$-axis. At this point, the value of $y$ is 0. To determine if an equation has an $x$-intercept of -2, substitute -2 for $x$, and calculate the value of $y$. If the value of -2 for $x$ corresponds with a $y$-value of 0, then the equation has an $x$-intercept of -2. The only answer choice that produces this result is Choice $C$:

$$0 = (-2)^2 + 5(-2) + 6$$

**2. C:** There are 34 girls who are potty-trained out of a total of 52 girls:

$$34 \div 52 = 0.65 = 65\%$$

**3. D:** Recall the formula for area of a rectangle, area = length × width. The answer must be in square inches, so all values must be converted to inches. Half of a foot is equal to 6 inches. Therefore, the area of the rectangle is equal to:

$$6 \text{ in} \times \frac{11}{2} \text{ in} = \frac{66}{2} \text{ in}^2 = 33 \text{ in}^2$$

**4. A:** The relative error can be found by finding the absolute error and making it a percent of the true value. The absolute error is $36 - 35.75 = 0.25$. This error is then divided by 35.75—the true value—to find 0.7%.

**5. A:** The value went up by:

$$\$165,000 - \$150,000 = \$15,000$$

Out of $150,000, this is $\frac{15,000}{150,000} = \frac{1}{10}$. Convert this to having a denominator of 100, the result is $\frac{10}{100}$ or 10%.

# Reasoning Through Language Arts

## *Reading for Meaning*

### Events, Plots, Characters, Settings, and Ideas

#### Putting Events in Order

One of the most crucial skills for conquering the GED's Reasoning Through Language Arts questions is the ability to recognize the sequences of events for each passage and place them in the correct order. Every passage has a plot, whether it is from a short story, a manual, a newspaper article or editorial, or a history text. And each plot has a logical order, which is also known as a sequence. Some of the most straightforward sequences can be found in technology directions, science experiments, instructional materials, and recipes. These forms of writing list actions that must occur in a proper sequence in order to get sufficient results. Other forms of writing, however, use style and ideas in ways that completely change the sequence of events. Poetry, for instance, may introduce repetitions that make the events seem cyclical. Postmodern writers are famous for experimenting with different concepts of place and time, creating "cut scenes" that distort straightforward sequences and abruptly transport the audience to different contexts or times. Even everyday newspaper articles, editorials, and historical sources may experiment with different sequential forms for stylistic effect.

Most questions that call for test takers to apply their sequential knowledge use key words such as **sequence**, **sequence of events**, or **sequential order** to cue the test taker in to the task at hand. In social studies or history passages, the test questions might employ key words such as **chronology** or **chronological order** to cue the test taker. In some cases, sequence can be found through comprehension techniques. These literal passages number the sequences, or they use key words such as *firstly*, *secondly*, *finally*, *next*, or *then*. The sequences of these stories can be found by rereading the passage and charting these numbers or key words. In most cases, however, readers have to correctly order events through inferential and evaluative reading techniques; they have to place events in a logical order without explicit cues.

#### Making Inferences

##### *Predictions*

Some texts use suspense and foreshadowing to captivate readers. For example, an intriguing aspect of murder mysteries is that the reader is never sure of the culprit until the author reveals the individual's identity. Authors often build suspense and add depth and meaning to a work by leaving clues to provide hints or predict future events in the story; this is called foreshadowing. While some instances of foreshadowing are subtle, others are quite obvious.

##### *Inferences*

Another way to read actively is to identify examples of inference within text. Making an inference requires the reader to read between the lines and look for what is implied rather than what is explicitly stated. That is, using information that is known from the text, the reader is able to make a logical assumption about information that is not explicitly stated but is probably true.

Authors employ literary devices such as tone, characterization, and theme to engage the audience by showing details of the story instead of merely telling them. For example, if an author said *Bob is selfish*, there's little left to infer. If the author said, *Bob cheated on his test, ignored his mom's calls, and parked*

*illegally*, the reader can infer Bob is selfish. Authors also make implications through character dialogue, thoughts, effects on others, actions, and looks. Like in life, readers must assemble all the clues to form a complete picture.

Read the following passage:

"Hey, do you wanna meet my new puppy?" Jonathan asked.

"Oh, I'm sorry but please don't—" Jacinta began to protest, but before she could finish, Jonathan had already opened the passenger side door of his car and a perfect white ball of fur came bouncing towards Jacinta.

"Isn't he the cutest?" beamed Jonathan.

"Yes—achoo!—he's pretty—aaaachooo!!—adora—aaa—aaaachoo!" Jacinta managed to say in between sneezes. "But if you don't mind, I—I—achoo!—need to go inside."

Which of the following can be inferred from Jacinta's reaction to the puppy?
a. she hates animals
b. she is allergic to dogs
c. she prefers cats to dogs
d. she is angry at Jonathan

An inference requires the reader to consider the information presented and then form their own idea about what is probably true. Based on the details in the passage, what is the best answer to the question? Important details to pay attention to include the tone of Jacinta's dialogue, which is overall polite and apologetic, as well as her reaction itself, which is a long string of sneezes. Answer choices (a) and (d) both express strong emotions ("hates" and "angry") that are not evident in Jacinta's speech or actions. Answer choice (c) mentions cats, but there is nothing in the passage to indicate Jacinta's feelings about cats. Answer choice (b), "she is allergic to dogs," is the most logical choice—based on the fact that she began sneezing as soon as a fluffy dog approached her, it makes sense to guess that Jacinta might be allergic to dogs. So even though Jacinta never directly states, "Sorry, I'm allergic to dogs!" using the clues in the passage, it is still reasonable to guess that this is true.

Making inferences is crucial for readers of literature because literary texts often avoid presenting complete and direct information to readers about characters' thoughts or feelings, or they present this information in an unclear way, leaving it up to the reader to interpret clues given in the text. In order to make inferences while reading, readers should ask themselves:

- What details are being presented in the text?
- Is there any important information that seems to be missing?
- Based on the information that the author *does* include, what else is probably true?
- Is this inference reasonable based on what is already known?

## Conclusions

Active readers should also draw conclusions. When doing so, the reader should ask the following questions: What is this piece about? What does the author believe? Does this piece have merit? Do I believe the author? Would this piece support my argument? The reader should first determine the author's intent. Identify the author's viewpoint and connect relevant evidence to support it. Readers may then move to the most important step: deciding whether to agree and determining whether they

are correct. Always read cautiously and critically. Interact with text, and record reactions in the margins. These active reading skills help determine not only what the author thinks, but what you think as the reader.

## Analyzing Relationships within Passages

Inferences are useful in gaining a deeper understanding of how people, events, and ideas are connected in a passage. Readers can use the same strategies used with general inferences and analyzing texts—paying attention to details and using them to make reasonable guesses about the text—to read between the lines and get a more complete picture of how (and why) characters are thinking, feeling, and acting. Read the following passage from O. Henry's story "The Gift of the Magi":

> One dollar and eighty-seven cents. That was all. And sixty cents of it was in pennies. Pennies saved one and two at a time by bulldozing the grocer and the vegetable man and the butcher until one's cheeks burned with the silent imputation of parsimony that such close dealing implied. Three times Della counted it. One dollar and eighty-seven cents. And the next day would be Christmas.

> There was clearly nothing to do but flop down on the shabby little couch and howl. So Della did it.

These paragraphs introduce the reader to the character Della. Even though the author doesn't include a direct description of Della, the reader can already form a general impression of her personality and emotions. One detail that should stick out to the reader is repetition: "one dollar and eighty-seven cents." This amount is repeated twice in the first paragraph, along with other descriptions of money: "sixty cents of it was in pennies," "pennies saved one and two at a time." The story's preoccupation with money parallels how Della herself is constantly thinking about her finances—"three times Della counted" her meager savings. Already the reader can guess that Della is having money problems. Next, think about her emotions. The first paragraph describes haggling over groceries "until one's cheeks burned"—another way to describe blushing. People tend to blush when they are embarrassed or ashamed, so readers can infer that Della is ashamed by her financial situation. This inference is also supported by the second paragraph, when she flops down and howls on her "shabby little couch." Clearly, she's in distress. Without saying, "Della has no money and is embarrassed to be poor," O. Henry is able to communicate the same impression to readers through his careful inclusion of details.

A character's **motive** is their reason for acting a certain way. Usually, characters are motivated by something that they want. In the passage, above, why is Della upset about not having enough money? There's an important detail at the end of the first paragraph: "the next day would be Christmas." Why is money especially important around Christmas? Christmas is a holiday when people exchange gifts. If Della is struggling with money, she's probably also struggling to buy gifts. So a shrewd reader should be able to guess that Della's motivation is wanting to buy a gift for someone—but she's currently unable to afford it, leading to feelings of shame and frustration.

In order to understand characters in a text, readers should keep the following questions in mind:

- What words does the author use to describe the character? Are these words related to any specific emotions or personality traits (for example, characteristics like rude, friendly, unapproachable, or innocent)?

- What does the character say? Does their dialogue seem to be straightforward, or are they hiding some thoughts or emotions?

- What actions can be observed from this character? How do their actions reflect their feelings?

- What does the character want? What do they do to get it?

## Understanding Main Ideas and Details

### Determining the Relationship Between Ideas

It is very important to know the difference between the topic and the main idea of the text. Even though these two are similar because they both present the central point of a text, they have distinctive differences. A **topic** is the subject of the text; it can usually be described in a one- to two-word phrase and appears in the simplest form. On the other hand, the **main idea** is more detailed and provides the author's central point of the text. It can be expressed through a complete sentence and is often found in the beginning, middle, or end of a paragraph. In most nonfiction books, the first sentence of the passage usually (but not always) states the main idea.

Review the passage below to explore the topic versus the main idea:

> Cheetahs are one of the fastest mammals on the land, reaching up to 70 miles an hour over short distances. Even though cheetahs can run as fast as 70 miles an hour, they usually only have to run half that speed to catch up with their choice of prey. Cheetahs cannot maintain a fast pace over long periods of time because their bodies will overheat. After a chase, cheetahs need to rest for approximately 30 minutes prior to eating or returning to any other activity.

In the example above, the topic of the passage is "Cheetahs" simply because that is the subject of the text. The main idea of the text is "Cheetahs are one of the fastest mammals on the land but can only maintain a fast pace for shorter distances." While it covers the topic, it is more detailed and refers to the text in its entirety. The text continues to provide additional details called **supporting details**, which will be discussed in the next section.

### How Details Develop the Main Idea

Supporting details help readers better develop and understand the main idea. Supporting details answer questions like *who, what, where, when, why,* and *how*. Different types of supporting details include examples, facts and statistics, anecdotes, and sensory details.

Persuasive and informative texts often use supporting details. In persuasive texts, authors attempt to make readers agree with their points of view, and supporting details are often used as "selling points." If authors make a statement, they need to support the statement with evidence in order to adequately persuade readers. Informative texts use supporting details such as examples and facts to inform readers. Review the previous "Cheetahs" passage to find examples of supporting details.

> Cheetahs are one of the fastest mammals on the land, reaching up to 70 miles an hour over short distances. Even though cheetahs can run as fast as 70 miles an hour, they usually only have to run half that speed to catch up with their choice of prey. Cheetahs cannot maintain a fast pace over long periods of time because their bodies will overheat. After a chase, cheetahs need to rest for approximately 30 minutes prior to eating or returning to any other activity.

In the example, supporting details include:

- Cheetahs reach up to 70 miles per hour over short distances.
- They usually only have to run half that speed to catch up with their prey.
- Cheetahs will overheat if they exert a high speed over longer distances.
- Cheetahs need to rest for 30 minutes after a chase.

Look at the diagram below (applying the cheetah example) to help determine the hierarchy of topic, main idea, and supporting details.

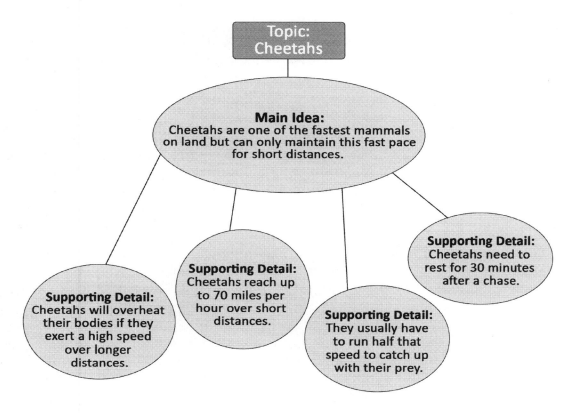

## Point of View and Purpose

### Author's Point of View and Purpose

When it comes to an author's writing, readers should always identify a **position** or **stance**. No matter how objective a text may seem, readers should assume the author has preconceived beliefs. One can reduce the likelihood of accepting an invalid argument by looking for multiple articles on the topic, including those with varying opinions. If several opinions point in the same direction and are backed by reputable peer-reviewed sources, it's more likely that the author has a valid argument. Positions that run contrary to widely held beliefs and existing data should invite scrutiny. There are exceptions to the rule, so readers should be careful consumers of information.

While themes, symbols, and motifs are buried deep within the text and can sometimes be difficult to infer, an author's **purpose** is usually obvious from the beginning. There are four purposes of writing: to inform, to persuade, to describe, and to entertain. **Informative** writing presents facts in an accessible way. **Persuasive** writing appeals to emotions and logic to inspire the reader to adopt a specific stance.

Readers should be wary of this type of writing, as it can mask a lack of objectivity with powerful emotion. **Descriptive** writing is designed to paint a picture in the reader's mind, while texts that **entertain** are often narratives designed to engage and delight the reader.

The various writing styles are usually blended, with one purpose dominating the rest. A persuasive text, for example, might begin with a humorous tale to make readers more receptive to the persuasive message, or a recipe in a cookbook designed to inform might be preceded by an entertaining anecdote that makes the recipes more appealing.

## Author's Position and Response to Different Viewpoints

If an author presents a differing opinion or a counterargument in order to refute it, the reader should consider how and why the information is being presented. It is meant to strengthen the original argument and shouldn't be confused with the author's intended conclusion, but it should also be considered in the reader's final evaluation.

Authors can also use bias if they ignore the opposing viewpoint or present their side in an unbalanced way. A strong argument considers the opposition and finds a way to refute it. Critical readers should look for an unfair or one-sided presentation of the argument and be skeptical, as a bias may be present. Even if this bias is unintentional, if it exists in the writing, the reader should be wary of the validity of the argument. Readers should also look for the use of stereotypes, which refer to specific groups. Stereotypes are often negative connotations about a person or place and should always be avoided. When a critical reader finds stereotypes in a piece of writing, they should be critical of the argument, and consider the validity of anything the author presents. Stereotypes reveal a flaw in the writer's thinking and may suggest a lack of knowledge or understanding about the subject.

## Inferring the Author's Purpose in the Passage

In nonfiction writing, authors employ argumentative techniques to present their opinion to readers in the most convincing way. Persuasive writing usually includes at least one type of appeal: an appeal to logic (**logos**), emotion (**pathos**), or credibility and trustworthiness (**ethos**). When a writer appeals to logic, they are asking readers to agree with them based on research, evidence, and an established line of reasoning. An author's argument might also appeal to readers' emotions, perhaps by including personal stories and anecdotes (a short narrative of a specific event). A final type of appeal—appeal to authority—asks the reader to agree with the author's argument on the basis of their expertise or credentials. Consider three different approaches to arguing the same opinion:

### Logic (Logos)

Below is an example of an appeal to logic. The author uses evidence to disprove the logic of the school's rule (the rule was supposed to reduce discipline problems, but the number of problems has not been reduced; therefore, the rule is not working) and he or she calls for its repeal.

> Our school should abolish its current ban on campus cell phone use. The ban was adopted last year as an attempt to reduce class disruptions and help students focus more on their lessons. However, since the rule was enacted, there has been no change in the number of disciplinary problems in class. Therefore, the rule is ineffective and should be done away with.

### Emotion (Pathos)

An author's argument might also appeal to readers' emotions, perhaps by including personal stories and anecdotes. The next example presents an appeal to emotion. By sharing the personal anecdote of one

student and speaking about emotional topics like family relationships, the author invokes the reader's empathy in asking them to reconsider the school rule.

> Our school should abolish its current ban on campus cell phone use. If students aren't able to use their phones during the school day, many of them feel isolated from their loved ones. For example, last semester, one student's grandmother had a heart attack in the morning. However, because he couldn't use his cell phone, the student didn't know about his grandmother's condition until the end of the day—when she had already passed away, and it was too late to say goodbye. By preventing students from contacting their friends and family, our school is placing undue stress and anxiety on students.

## Credibility (Ethos)

Finally, an appeal to authority includes a statement from a relevant expert. In this case, the author uses a doctor in the field of education to support the argument. All three examples begin from the same opinion—the school's phone ban needs to change—but rely on different argumentative styles to persuade the reader.

> Our school should abolish its current ban on campus cell phone use. According to Dr. Bartholomew Everett, a leading educational expert, "Research studies show that cell phone usage has no real impact on student attentiveness. Rather, phones provide a valuable technological resource for learning. Schools need to learn how to integrate this new technology into their curriculum." Rather than banning phones altogether, our school should follow the advice of experts and allow students to use phones as part of their learning.

## Rhetorical Questions

Another commonly used argumentative technique is asking **rhetorical questions**, questions that do not actually require an answer but that push the reader to consider the topic further.

> I wholly disagree with the proposal to ban restaurants from serving foods with high sugar and sodium contents. Do we really want to live in a world where the government can control what we eat? I prefer to make my own food choices.

Here, the author's rhetorical question prompts readers to put themselves in a hypothetical situation and imagine how they would feel about it.

## Tone and Figurative Language

### How Words Affect Tone

**Tone** refers to the writer's attitude toward the subject matter. For example, the tone conveys how the writer feels about the topic he or she is writing about. A lot of nonfiction writing has a neutral tone, which is an important tone for the writer to take. A neutral tone demonstrates that the writer is presenting a topic impartially and letting the information speak for itself. On the other hand, nonfiction

writing can be just as effective and appropriate if the tone isn't neutral. For instance, consider this example:

> Seat belts save more lives than any other automobile safety feature. Many studies show that airbags save lives as well; however, not all cars have airbags. For instance, some older cars don't. Furthermore, air bags aren't entirely reliable. For example, studies show that in 15% of accidents, airbags don't deploy as designed; but, on the other hand, seat belt malfunctions are extremely rare. The number of highway fatalities has plummeted since laws requiring seat belt usage were enacted.

In this passage, the writer mostly chooses to retain a neutral tone when presenting information. If the writer would instead include their own personal experience of losing a friend or family member in a car accident, the tone would change dramatically. The tone would no longer be neutral and would show that the writer has a personal stake in the content, allowing them to interpret the information in a different way. When analyzing tone, consider what the writer is trying to achieve in the text and how they *create* the tone using style.

An author's choice of words—also referred to as **diction**—helps to convey their meaning in a particular way. Through diction, an author can convey a particular tone—e.g., a humorous tone, a serious tone—in order to support the thesis in a meaningful way to the reader.

## Connotation and Denotation

**Connotation** is when an author chooses words or phrases that invoke ideas or feelings other than their literal meaning. An example of the use of connotation is the word *cheap*, which suggests something is poor in value or negatively describes a person as reluctant to spend money. When something or someone is described this way, the reader is more inclined to have a particular image or feeling about it or him/her. Thus, connotation can be a very effective language tool in creating emotion and swaying opinion. However, connotations are sometimes hard to pin down because varying emotions can be associated with a word. Generally, though, connotative meanings tend to be fairly consistent within a specific cultural group.

**Denotation** refers to words or phrases that mean exactly what they say. It is helpful when a writer wants to present hard facts or vocabulary terms with which readers may be unfamiliar. Some examples of denotation are the words *inexpensive* and *frugal*. *Inexpensive* refers to the cost of something, not its value, and *frugal* indicates that a person is conscientiously watching their spending. These terms do not elicit the same emotions that *cheap* does.

Authors sometimes choose to use both, but what they choose and when they use it is what critical readers need to differentiate. One method isn't inherently better than the other; however, one may create a better effect, depending upon an author's intent. If, for example, an author's purpose is to inform, to instruct, and to familiarize readers with a difficult subject, their use of connotation may be helpful. However, it may also undermine credibility and confuse readers. An author who wants to create a credible, scholarly effect in their text would most likely use denotation, which emphasizes literal, factual meaning and examples.

## How Figurative Language Affects the Meaning of Words

It's important to be able to recognize and interpret **figurative,** or non-literal, language. Literal statements rely directly on the denotations of words and express exactly what's happening in reality.

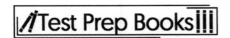 

Figurative language uses non-literal expressions to present information in a creative way. Consider the following sentences:

   a. His pillow was very soft, and he fell asleep quickly.

   b. His pillow was a fluffy cloud, and he floated away on it to the dream world.

Sentence *A* is literal, employing only the real meanings of each word. Sentence *B* is figurative. It employs a metaphor by stating that his pillow was a cloud. Of course, he isn't actually sleeping on a cloud, but the reader can draw on images of clouds as light, soft, fluffy, and relaxing to get a sense of how the character felt as he fell asleep. Also, in sentence *B*, the pillow becomes a vehicle that transports him to a magical dream world. The character isn't literally floating through the air—he's simply falling asleep! But by utilizing figurative language, the author creates a scene of peace, comfort, and relaxation that conveys stronger emotions and more creative imagery than the purely literal sentence. While there are countless types of figurative language, there are a few common ones that any reader should recognize.

**Simile** and **metaphor** are comparisons between two things, but their formats differ slightly. A simile says that two things are *similar* and makes a comparison using "like" or "as"—*A* is like *B*, or *A* is as [some characteristic] as *B*—whereas a metaphor states that two things are exactly the same—*A* is *B*. In both cases, simile and metaphor invite the reader to think more deeply about the characteristics of the two subjects and consider where they overlap. An example of metaphor can be found in the above sentence about the sleeper ("His pillow was a fluffy cloud"). For an example of simile, look at the first line of Robert Burns' famous poem:

   My love is like a red, red rose

This is comparison using "like," and the two things being compared are love and a rose. Some characteristics of a rose are that it's fragrant, beautiful, blossoming, colorful, vibrant—by comparing his love to a rose, Burns asks the reader to apply these qualities to his love. In this way, he implies that his love is also fresh, blossoming, and brilliant.

Similes can also compare things that appear dissimilar. Here's a song lyric from Florence and the Machine:

   Happiness hit her like a bullet in the back

"Happiness" has a very positive connotation, but getting "a bullet in the back" seems violent and aggressive, not at all related to happiness. By using an unexpected comparison, the writer forces readers to think more deeply about the comparison and ask themselves how could getting shot be similar to feeling happy. "A bullet in the back" is something that she doesn't see coming; it's sudden and forceful; and presumably, it has a strong impact on her life. So, in this way, the author seems to be saying that unexpected happiness made a sudden and powerful change in her life.

Another common form of figurative language is **personification,** when a non-human object is given human characteristics. William Blake uses personification here:

   . . . the stars threw down their spears,

   And watered heaven with their tears

He imagines the stars as combatants in a heavenly battle, giving them both action (throwing down their spears) and emotion (the sadness and disappointment of their tears). Personification helps to add emotion or develop relationships between characters and non-human objects. In fact, most people use personification in their everyday lives:

> My alarm clock betrayed me! It didn't go off this morning!

> The last piece of chocolate cake was staring at me from the refrigerator.

Next is **hyperbole,** a type of figurative language that uses extreme exaggeration. Sentences like, "I love you to the moon and back," or "I will love you for a million years," are examples of hyperbole. They aren't literally true—unfortunately, people cannot jump to outer space or live for a million years—but they're creative expressions that communicate the depth of feeling of the author.

Another way that writers add deeper meaning to their work is through **allusions.** An allusion is a reference to something from history, literature, or another cultural source. When the text is from a different culture or a time period, readers may not be familiar with every allusion. However, allusions tend to be well-known because the author wants the reader to make a connection between what's happening in the text and what's being referenced.

> I can't believe my best friend told our professor that I was skipping class to finish my final project! What a Judas!

This sentence contains a Biblical allusion to Judas, a friend and follower of Jesus who betrayed Jesus to the Romans. In this case, the allusion to Judas is used to give a deeper impression of betrayal and disloyalty from a trusted friend. Commonly used allusions in Western texts may come from the Bible, Greek or Roman mythology, or well-known literature such as Shakespeare. By familiarizing themselves with these touchstones of history and culture, readers can be more prepared to recognize allusions.

## How Figurative Language Influences the Author's Purpose

A **rhetorical strategy**—also referred to as a **rhetorical mode**—is the structural way an author chooses to present their argument. Though the terms noted below are similar to the organizational structures noted earlier, these strategies do not imply that the entire text follows the approach. For example, a cause and effect organizational structure is solely that, nothing more. A persuasive text may use cause and effect as a strategy to convey a singular point. Thus, an argument may include several of the strategies as the author strives to convince their audience to take action or accept a different point of view. It's important that readers are able to identify an author's thesis and position on the topic in order to be able to identify the careful construction through which the author speaks to the reader.

The following are some of the more common rhetorical strategies:

- **Cause and effect**—establishing a logical correlation or causation between two ideas
- **Classification/division**—the grouping of similar items together or division of something into parts
- **Comparison/contrast**—the distinguishing of similarities/differences to expand on an idea
- **Definition**—used to clarify abstract ideas, unfamiliar concepts, or to distinguish one idea from another
- **Description**—use of vivid imagery, active verbs, and clear adjectives to explain ideas
- **Exemplification**—the use of examples to explain an idea

- **Narration**—using anecdotes or personal experience to present or expand on a concept
- **Problem/Solution**—presentation of a problem or problems, followed by proposed solution(s)

## How Rhetorical Language Conveys Meaning, Emotion, or Persuades Readers

A **rhetorical device** is the phrasing and presentation of an idea that reinforces and emphasizes a point in an argument. A rhetorical device is often quite memorable. One of the more famous uses of a rhetorical device is in John F. Kennedy's 1961 inaugural address: "Ask not what your country can do for you, ask what you can do for your country." The contrast of ideas presented in the phrasing is an example of the rhetorical device of antimetabole. Some other common examples are provided below, but test takers should be aware that this is not a complete list.

| Device | Definition | Example |
|---|---|---|
| Allusion | A reference to a famous person, event, or significant literary text as a form of significant comparison | "We are apt to shut our eyes against a painful truth, and listen to the song of that siren till she transforms us into beasts." Patrick Henry |
| Anaphora | The repetition of the same words at the beginning of successive words, phrases, or clauses, designed to emphasize an idea | "We shall not flag or fail. We shall go on to the end. We shall fight in France, we shall fight on the seas and oceans, we shall fight with growing confidence … we shall fight in the fields and in the streets, we shall fight in the hills. We shall never surrender." Winston Churchill |
| Understatement | A statement meant to portray a situation as less important than it actually is to create an ironic effect | "The war in the Pacific has not necessarily developed in Japan's favor." Emperor Hirohito, surrendering Japan in World War II |
| Parallelism | A syntactical similarity in a structure or series of structures used for impact of an idea, making it memorable | "A penny saved is a penny earned." Ben Franklin |
| Rhetorical question | A question posed that is not answered by the writer though there is a desired response, most often designed to emphasize a point | "Can anyone look at our reduced standing in the world today and say, 'Let's have four more years of this?'" Ronald Reagan |

## Organizing Ideas

### How a Section Fits into a Passage and Helps Develop the Ideas

Being able to determine what is most important while reading is critical to synthesis. It is the difference between being able to tell what is necessary to full comprehension and that which is interesting but not necessary.

When determining the importance of an author's ideas, consider the following:

- Ask how critical an author's particular idea, assertion, or concept is to the overall message.

- Ask "is this an interesting fact or is this information essential to understanding the author's main idea?"

- Make a simple chart. On one side, list all of the important, essential points an author makes and on the other, list all of the interesting yet non-critical ideas.

- Highlight, circle, or underline any dates or data in non-fiction passages. Pay attention to headings, captions, and any graphs or diagrams.

- When reading a fictional passage, delineate important information such as theme, character, setting, conflict (what the problem is), and resolution (how the problem is fixed). Most often, these are the most important aspects contained in fictional text.

- If a non-fiction passage is instructional in nature, take physical note of any steps in the order of their importance as presented by the author. Look for words such as *first*, *next*, *then*, and *last*.

Determining the importance of an author's ideas is critical to synthesis in that it requires the test taker to parse out any unnecessary information and demonstrate they have the ability to make sound determination on what is important to the author, and what is merely a supporting or less critical detail.

### Analyzing How a Text is Organized

Depending on what the author is attempting to accomplish, certain formats or text structures work better than others. For example, a sequence structure might work for narration but not for identifying similarities and differences between concepts. Similarly, a comparison-contrast structure is not useful for narration. It's the author's job to put the right information in the correct format.

Readers should be familiar with the five main literary structures:

#### Sequence Structure

**Sequence structure** (sometimes referred to as the order structure) is when the order of events proceeds in a predictable order. In many cases, this means the text goes through the plot elements: exposition, rising action, climax, falling action, and resolution. Readers are introduced to characters, setting, and conflict in the **exposition**. In the **rising action**, there's an increase in tension and suspense. The **climax** is the height of tension and the point of no return. **Tension** decreases during the falling action. In the **resolution**, any conflicts presented in the exposition are resolved, and the story concludes. An informative text that is structured sequentially will often go in order from one step to the next.

## Problem-Solution

In the **problem-solution structure**, authors identify a potential problem and suggest a solution. This form of writing is usually divided into two paragraphs and can be found in informational texts. For example, cell phone, cable, and satellite providers use this structure in manuals to help customers troubleshoot or identify problems with services or products.

## Comparison-Contrast

When authors want to discuss similarities and differences between separate concepts, they arrange thoughts in a **comparison-contrast paragraph structure**. **Venn diagrams** are an effective graphic organizer for comparison-contrast structures because they feature two overlapping circles that can be used to organize similarities and differences. A comparison-contrast essay organizes one paragraph based on similarities and another based on differences. A comparison-contrast essay can also be arranged with the similarities and differences of individual traits addressed within individual paragraphs. Words such as *however, but,* and *nevertheless* help signal a contrast in ideas.

## Descriptive

**Descriptive writing** is designed to appeal to your senses. Much like an artist who constructs a painting, good descriptive writing builds an image in the reader's mind by appealing to the five senses: *sight, hearing, taste, touch,* and *smell.* However, overly descriptive writing can become tedious; likewise, sparse descriptions can make settings and characters seem flat. Good authors strike a balance by applying descriptions only to facts that are integral to the passage.

## Cause and Effect

Passages that use the **cause and effect structure** are simply asking *why* by demonstrating some type of connection between ideas. Words such as *if, since, because, then,* or *consequently* indicate a relationship. By switching the order of a complex sentence, the writer can rearrange the emphasis on different clauses. Saying, *If Sheryl is late, we'll miss the dance,* is different from saying *We'll miss the dance if Sheryl is late.* One emphasizes Sheryl's tardiness while the other emphasizes missing the dance. Paragraphs can also be arranged in a cause and effect format. Since the format—before and after—is sequential, it is useful when authors wish to discuss the impact of choices. Researchers often apply this paragraph structure to the scientific method.

## Understanding the Meaning and Purpose of Transition Words

The writer should act as a guide, showing the reader how all the sentences fit together. Consider this example:

> Seat belts save more lives than any other automobile safety feature. Many studies show that airbags save lives as well. Not all cars have airbags. Many older cars don't. Air bags aren't entirely reliable. Studies show that in 15% of accidents, airbags don't deploy as designed. Seat belt malfunctions are extremely rare.

There's nothing wrong with any of these sentences individually, but together they're disjointed and difficult to follow. The best way for the writer to communicate information is through the use of transition words. Here are examples of transition words and phrases that tie sentences together, enabling a more natural flow:

- To show causality: *as a result, therefore,* and *consequently*
- To compare and contrast: *however, but,* and *on the other hand*

- To introduce examples: *for instance, namely,* and *including*
- To show order of importance: *foremost, primarily, secondly,* and *lastly*

Note: This is not a complete list of transitions. There are many more that can be used; however, most fit into these or similar categories. The point is that the words should clearly show the relationship between sentences, supporting information, and the main idea.

Here is an update to the previous example using transition words. These changes make it easier to read and bring clarity to the writer's points:

> Seat belts save more lives than any other automobile safety feature. Many studies show that airbags save lives as well; however, not all cars have airbags. For instance, some older cars don't. Furthermore, air bags aren't entirely reliable. For example, studies show that in 15% of accidents, airbags don't deploy as designed; but, on the other hand, seat belt malfunctions are extremely rare.

Also, be prepared to analyze whether the writer is using the best transition word or phrase for the situation. Take this sentence for example: "As a result, seat belt malfunctions are extremely rare." This sentence doesn't make sense in the context above because the writer is trying to show the contrast between seat belts and airbags, not the causality.

## How the Passage Organization Supports the Author's Ideas

Even if the writer includes plenty of information to support their point, the writing is only coherent when the information is in a logical order. **Logical sequencing** is really just common sense, but it's also an important writing technique. First, the writer should introduce the main idea, whether for a paragraph, a section, or the entire piece. Second, they should present evidence to support the main idea by using transitional language. This shows the reader how the information relates to the main idea and the sentences around it. The writer should then take time to interpret the information, making sure necessary connections are obvious to the reader. Finally, the writer can summarize the information in a closing section.

Note: Though most writing follows this pattern, it isn't a set rule. Sometimes writers change the order for effect. For example, the writer can begin with a surprising piece of supporting information to grab the reader's attention, and then transition to the main idea. Thus, if a passage doesn't follow the logical order, don't immediately assume it's wrong. However, most writing usually settles into a logical sequence after a nontraditional beginning.

### Introductions and Conclusions

Examining the writer's strategies for introductions and conclusions puts the reader in the right mindset to interpret the rest of the text. Look for methods the writer might use for **introductions** such as:

- Stating the main point immediately, followed by outlining how the rest of the piece supports this claim.

- Establishing important, smaller pieces of the main idea first, and then grouping these points into a case for the main idea.

- Opening with a quotation, anecdote, question, seeming paradox, or other piece of interesting information, and then using it to lead to the main point.

- Whatever method the writer chooses, the introduction should make their intention clear, establish their voice as a credible one, and encourage a person to continue reading.

**Conclusions** tend to follow a similar pattern. In them, the writer restates their main idea a final time, often after summarizing the smaller pieces of that idea. If the introduction uses a quote or anecdote to grab the reader's attention, the conclusion often makes reference to it again. Whatever way the writer chooses to arrange the conclusion, the final restatement of the main idea should be clear and simple for the reader to interpret. Finally, conclusions shouldn't introduce any new information.

## Comparing Different Ways of Presenting Ideas

### Evaluating Two Different Texts

Every passage offered in the GED Reasoning Through Language Arts section has its own unique scope, purpose, and emphasis, or what it covers, why it is written, and what its specific focus is centered upon. Additionally, each passage is written with a particular audience in mind, and each passage affects its audience differently. The scope, purpose, and emphasis of each passage can be found by comparing the parts of the piece with the whole framework of the piece. Word choices, grammatical choices, and syntactical choices can help the reader figure out the scope, purpose, and emphasis. These choices are embedded in the words and sentences of the passage (the parts).

They help show the intentions and goals of the author (the "whole"). For example, if an author uses strong language like *enrage*, *ignite*, *infuriate*, and *antagonize*, then they may be cueing the reader in to their own rage, or they may be trying to incite anger in others. Likewise, if an author continually uses short, simple sentences, he or she might be trying to incite excitement or nervousness. These different choices and styles affect the overall message, or purpose. Sometimes the subject matter or audience is discussed explicitly, but often, on GED tests, test takers have to break a passage down, also known as decoding the passage. In this way, test takers can find the passage's target audience and intentions. Meanwhile, the impact of the article can be personal or historical, depending upon the passage—it can either speak to the test taker personally or capture a historical era.

When two passages are analyzed in juxtaposition—or side-by-side—it can help the audience have a clearer picture of the scope, purpose, emphasis, audience, and impact. Evaluating and comparing passages side-by-side helps shed light on similarities and differences that are helpful for test takers. The key is to figure out both the parts and the "wholes" of each passage. Compare the word choices, grammatical choices, and syntactical choices of each passage, and then compare the big picture of each passage. As a result, test takers will have a stronger basis for understanding the intricate details and broader frameworks of all passages they encounter.

### Evaluating Two Different Passages

Every passage offered in the GED Reasoning Through Language Arts section has its own view, tone, style, organization, purpose, or impact. It is extremely important to compare the parts to the "wholes" of each passage. Additionally, these parts and "wholes" are better understood through **intertextual analysis** (for example, comparing the texts as if they were side by side). The viewpoint of the text can be found through a close analysis of the author's biases, or personal opinions or perceptions. All biases are embedded in the word choices, grammatical choices, and syntactical choices of each passage. For example, if an author continually uses negative words like *dislike*, *hate*, *despise*, *detrimental*, or *loathe*,

they are trying to illustrate their own hatred of something or convey a character's hatred of something. These negative terms inevitably affect the view and tone of a passage. Comparing terminologies and biases can help a test taker better understand the similarities and differences of two or more passages. Similarly, the purposes of each can be better highlighted with a closer examination of word choices, grammatical choices, and syntactical choices.

Organization, on the other hand, is more easily understood by studying the passage on its own. Organizational differences on the page are likely to jump out at the test taker. A poetry passage, for instance, is traditionally organized differently than a prose passage. Test takers can see the differences in structures: one uses paragraphs, while the other uses stanzas. If organizational differences cannot be deduced through visual analysis, test takers should try to take a closer look at the sequence of events or the content of each paragraph. Organization, nevertheless, is not something that is separate from view, tone, purpose, style, and impact. It can skew or connect a viewpoint, shift or solidify tone, reinforce or undermine purpose, express or conceal a particular style, or establish or disestablish the impact of passage. Organization is the backbone of every form of written expression—it unifies all the parts and sets the parameters for the wholes. Thus, organization should be analyzed strategically when comparing passages.

# *Identifying and Creating Arguments*

## The Relationship Between Evidence and Main Ideas and Details

### Summarizing Information from a Passage
**Summarizing** is an effective way to draw a conclusion from a passage. A summary is a shortened version of the original text, written by the reader in their own words. Focusing on the main points of the original text and including only the relevant details can help readers reach a conclusion. It's important to retain the original meaning of the passage.

Like summarizing, **paraphrasing** can also help a reader fully understand different parts of a text. Paraphrasing calls for the reader to take a small part of the passage and list or describe its main points. Paraphrasing is more than rewording the original passage, though. It should be written in the reader's own words, while still retaining the meaning of the original source. This will indicate an understanding of the original source, yet still help the reader expand on their interpretation.

Readers should pay attention to the **sequence**, or the order in which details are laid out in the text, as this can be important to understanding its meaning as a whole. Writers will often use transitional words to help the reader understand the order of events and to stay on track. Words like *next, then, after*, and *finally* show that the order of events is important to the author. In some cases, the author omits these transitional words, and the sequence is implied. Authors may even purposely present the information out of order to make an impact or have an effect on the reader. An example might be when a narrative writer uses **flashback** to reveal information.

### Relationship Between the Main Idea and Details of a Passage
In order to understand any text, readers first must determine the **topic**, or what the text is about. In non-fiction writing, the topic can generally be expressed in a few words. For example, a passage might be about college education, moving to a new neighborhood, or dog breeds. Slightly more specific information is found in the **main idea**, or what the writer wants readers to know about the topic. An article might be about the history of popular dog breeds; another article might tell how certain dog

breeds are unfairly stereotyped. In both cases, the topic is the same—dog breeds—but the main ideas are quite different. Each writer has a distinct purpose for writing and a different set of details for what they want us to know about dog breeds. When a writer expresses their main idea in one sentence, this is known as a **thesis statement**. If a writer uses a thesis statement, it can generally be found at the beginning of the passage. Finally, the most specific information in a text is in the **supporting details**. An article about dog breed stereotyping might discuss a case study of pit bulls and provide statistics about how many dog attacks are caused by pit bulls versus other breeds.

## Main Idea of a Passage

Topics and main ideas are critical parts of writing. The **topic** is the subject matter of the piece. An example of a topic would be *the use of cell phones in a classroom*.

The **main idea** is what the writer wants to say about that topic. A writer may make the point that the use of cell phones in a classroom is a serious problem that must be addressed in order for students to learn better. Therefore, the topic is cell phone usage in a classroom, and the main idea is that it's *a serious problem needing to be addressed*. The topic can be expressed in a word or two, but the main idea should be a complete thought.

An author will likely identify the topic immediately within the title or the first sentence of the passage. The main idea is usually presented in the introduction. In a single passage, the main idea may be identified in the first or last sentence, but it will most likely be directly stated and easily recognized by the reader. Because it is not always stated immediately in a passage, it's important that readers carefully read the entire passage to identify the main idea.

The main idea should not be confused with the thesis statement. A **thesis statement** is a clear statement of the writer's specific stance and can often be found in the introduction of a nonfiction piece. The thesis is a specific sentence (or two) that offers the direction and focus of the discussion.

In order to illustrate the main idea, a writer will use **supporting details**, which provide evidence or examples to help make a point. Supporting details are typically found in nonfiction pieces that seek to inform or persuade the reader.

## Determining Which Details Support a Main Idea

An important skill is the ability to determine which details in a passage support the main idea. In the example of cell phone usage in the classroom, where the author's main idea is to show the seriousness of this problem and the need to "unplug", supporting details would be critical for effectively making that point. Supporting details used here might include statistics on a decline in student focus and studies showing the impact of digital technology usage on students' attention spans. The author could also include testimonies from teachers surveyed on the topic.

It's important that readers evaluate the author's supporting details to be sure that they are credible, provide evidence of the author's point, and directly support the main idea. Although shocking statistics grab readers' attention, their use may provide ineffective information in the piece. Details like this are crucial to understanding the passage and evaluating how well the author presents their argument and evidence.

## Drawing Conclusions, Making Inferences, and Evaluating Evidence

### Making Generalizations Based on Evidence

One way to make generalizations is to look for main topics. When doing so, pay particular attention to any titles, headlines, or opening statements made by the author. Topic sentences or repetitive ideas can be clues in gleaning inferred ideas. For example, if a passage contains the phrase *While some consider DNA testing to be infallible, it is an inherently flawed technique,* the test taker can infer the rest of the passage will contain information that points to problems with DNA testing.

The test taker may be asked to make a generalization based on prior knowledge but may also be asked to make predictions based on new ideas. For example, the test taker may have no prior knowledge of DNA other than its genetic property to replicate. However, if the reader is given passages on the flaws of DNA testing with enough factual evidence, the test taker may arrive at the inferred conclusion or generalization that the author does not support the infallibility of DNA testing in all identification cases.

When making generalizations, it is important to remember that the critical thinking process involved must be fluid and open to change. While a reader may infer an idea from a main topic, general statement, or other clues, they must be open to receiving new information within a particular passage. New ideas presented by an author may require the test taker to alter a generalization. Similarly, when asked questions that require making an inference, it's important to read the entire test passage and all of the answer options. Often, a test taker will need to refine a generalization based on new ideas that may be presented within the text itself.

### Using Main Ideas to Draw Conclusions

Determining conclusions requires being an active reader, as a reader must make a prediction and analyze facts to identify a conclusion. There are a few ways to determine a logical conclusion, but careful reading is the most important. It's helpful to read a passage a few times, noting details that seem important to the text. A reader should also identify key words in a passage to determine the logical conclusion or determination that flows from the information presented.

Textual evidence within the details helps readers draw a conclusion about a passage. **Textual evidence** refers to information—facts and examples that support the main point; it will likely come from outside sources and can be in the form of quoted or paraphrased material. In order to draw a conclusion from evidence, it's important to examine the credibility and validity of that evidence as well as how (and if) it relates to the main idea.

If an author presents a differing opinion or a **counterargument** in order to refute it, the reader should consider how and why the information is being presented. It is meant to strengthen the original argument and shouldn't be confused with the author's intended conclusion, but it should also be considered in the reader's final evaluation.

Sometimes, authors explicitly state the conclusion they want readers to understand. Alternatively, a conclusion may not be directly stated. In that case, readers must rely on the implications to form a logical conclusion:

> On the way to the bus stop, Michael realized his homework wasn't in his backpack. He ran back to the house to get it and made it back to the bus just in time.

In this example, though it's never explicitly stated, it can be inferred that Michael is a student on his way to school in the morning. When forming a conclusion from implied information, it's important to read the text carefully to find several pieces of evidence to support the conclusion.

## Describing the Steps of an Argument

Strong arguments tend to follow a fairly defined format. In the introduction, background information regarding the problem is shared, the implications of the issue are stated, and the author's thesis or claims are given. Supporting evidence is then presented in the body paragraphs, along with the counterargument, which then gets refuted with specific evidence. Lastly, in the conclusion, the author summarizes the points and claims again.

## Evidence Used to Support a Claim or Conclusion

**Premises** are the why, and **conclusions** are the what. Stated differently, premises are the evidence or facts supporting why the conclusion is logical and valid. GED Reasoning Through Language Arts questions do not require evaluation of the factual accuracy of the arguments; instead, the questions evaluate the test taker's ability to assess an argument's logical strength. For example, John eats all red food. Apples are red. Therefore, John eats apples. This argument is logically sound, despite having no factual basis in reality. Below is an example of a practice argument.

> Julie is an American track athlete. She's the star of the number one collegiate team in the country. Her times are consistently at the top of national rankings. Julie is extremely likely to represent the United States at the upcoming Olympics.

In this example, the conclusion, or the *what*, is that she will likely be on the American Olympic team. The author supports this conclusion with two premises. First, Julie is the star of an elite track team. Second, she runs some of the best times of the country. This is the *why* behind the conclusion. The following builds off this basic argument:

> Julie is an American track athlete. She's the star of the number one collegiate team in the country. Her times are consistently at the top of national rankings. Julie is extremely likely to represent the United States at the upcoming Olympics. Julie will continue to develop after the Olympic trials. She will be a frontrunner for the gold. Julie is likely to become a world-famous track star.

These additions to the argument make the conclusion different. Now, the conclusion is that Julie is likely to become a world-famous track star. The previous conclusion, Julie will likely be on the Olympic team, functions as a **sub-conclusion** in this argument. Like conclusions, premises must adequately support sub-conclusions. However, sub-conclusions function like premises, since sub-conclusions also support the overall conclusion.

## Determining Whether Evidence is Relevant and Sufficient

A **hasty generalization** involves an argument relying on insufficient statistical data or inaccurately generalizing. One common generalization occurs when a group of individuals under observation have some quality or attribute that is asserted to be universal or true for a much larger number of people than actually documented. Here's an example of a hasty generalization:

> A man smokes a lot of cigarettes, but so did his grandfather. The grandfather smoked nearly two packs per day since his World War II service until he died at ninety years of age. Continuing to smoke cigarettes will clearly not impact the grandson's long-term health.

This argument is a hasty generalization because it assumes that one person's addiction and lack of consequences will naturally be reflected in a different individual. There is no reasonable justification for such extrapolation. It is common knowledge that any smoking is detrimental to everyone's health. The fact that the man's grandfather smoked two packs per day and lived a long life has no logical connection with the grandson engaging in similar behavior. The hasty generalization doesn't take into account other reasons behind the grandfather's longevity. Nor does the author offer evidence that might support the idea that the man would share a similar lifetime if he smokes. It might be different if the author stated that the man's family shares some genetic trait rendering them immune to the effects of tar and chemicals on the lungs. If this were in the argument, we would assume it as truth and find the generalization to be valid rather than hasty. Of course, this is not the case in our example.

## Determining Whether a Statement Is or Is Not Supported

The basic tenet of reading comprehension is the ability to read and understand a text. One way to understand a text is to look for information that supports the author's main idea, topic, or position statement. This information may be factual, or it may be based on the author's opinion. This section will focus on the test taker's ability to identify factual information, as opposed to opinionated bias. The GED will ask test takers to read passages containing factual information, and then logically relate those passages by drawing conclusions based on evidence.

In order to identify factual information within one or more text passages, begin by looking for statements of fact. Factual statements can be either true or false. Identifying factual statements as opposed to opinion statements is important in demonstrating full command of evidence in reading. For example, the statement *The temperature outside was unbearably hot* may seem like a fact; however, it's not. While anyone can point to a temperature gauge as factual evidence, the statement itself reflects only an opinion. Some people may find the temperature unbearably hot. Others may find it comfortably warm. Thus, the sentence, *The temperature outside was unbearably hot,* reflects the opinion of the author who found it unbearable. If the text passage followed up the sentence with atmospheric conditions indicating heat indices above 140 degrees Fahrenheit, then the reader knows there is factual information that supports the author's assertion of *unbearably hot.*

In looking for information that can be proven or disproven, it's helpful to scan for dates, numbers, timelines, equations, statistics, and other similar data within any given text passage. These types of indicators will point to proven particulars. For example, the statement, *The temperature outside was unbearably hot on that summer day, July 10, 1913,* most likely indicates factual information, even if the reader is unaware that this is the hottest day on record in the United States. Be careful when reading biased words from an author. Biased words indicate opinion, as opposed to fact. The following list contains a sampling of common biased words:

- Good/bad
- Great/greatest
- Better/best/worst
- Amazing
- Terrible/bad/awful
- Beautiful/handsome/ugly
- More/most
- Exciting/dull/boring
- Favorite

- Very
- Probably/should/seem/possibly

Remember, most of what is written is actually opinion or carefully worded information that seems like fact when it isn't. To say, *duplicating DNA results is not cost-effective* sounds like it could be a scientific fact, but it isn't. Factual information can be verified through independent sources.

The simplest type of test question may provide a text passage, then ask the test taker to distinguish the correct factual supporting statement that best answers the corresponding question on the test. However, be aware that most questions may ask the test taker to read more than one text passage and identify which answer best supports an author's topic. While the ability to identify factual information is critical, these types of questions require the test taker to identify chunks of details, and then relate them to one another.

## Assessing Whether an Argument is Valid

Although different from conditions and If/Then Statements, **reasonableness** is another important foundational concept. Evaluating an argument for reasonableness and validity entails evaluating the evidence presented by the author to justify their conclusions. Everything contained in the argument should be considered, but remember to ignore outside biases, judgments, and knowledge. For the purposes of this test, the test taker is a one-person jury at a criminal trial using a standard of reasonableness under the circumstances presented by the argument.

These arguments are encountered on a daily basis through social media, entertainment, and cable news. An example is:

> Although many believe it to be a natural occurrence, some believe that the red tide that occurs in Florida each year may actually be a result of human sewage and agricultural runoff. However, it is arguable that both natural and human factors contribute to this annual phenomenon. On one hand, the red tide has been occurring every year since the time of explorers like Cabeza de Vaca in the 1500's. On the other hand, the red tide seems to be getting worse each year, and scientists from the Florida Fish & Wildlife Conservation say the bacteria found inside the tide feed off of nutrients found in fertilizer runoff.

The author's conclusion is that both natural phenomena and human activity contribute to the red tide that happens annually in Florida. The author backs this information up by historical data to prove the natural occurrence of the red tide, and then again with scientific data to back up the human contribution to the red tide. Both of these statements are examples of the premises in the argument. Evaluating the strength of the logical connection between the premises and conclusion is how reasonableness is determined. Another example is:

> The local railroad is a disaster. Tickets are exorbitantly priced, bathrooms leak, and the floor is sticky.

The author is clearly unhappy with the railroad service. They cite three examples of why they believe the railroad to be a disaster. An argument more familiar to everyday life is:

> Alexandra said the movie she just saw was amazing. We should go see it tonight.

Although not immediately apparent, this is an argument. The author is making the argument that they should go see the movie. This conclusion is based on the premise that Alexandra said the movie was

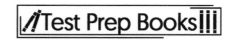

amazing. There's an inferred note that Alexandra is knowledgeable on the subject, and she's credible enough to prompt her friends to go see the movie. This seems like a reasonable argument. A less reasonable argument is:

> Alexandra is a film student, and she's written the perfect romantic comedy script. We should put our life savings toward its production as an investment in our future.

The author's conclusion is that they should invest their life savings into the production of a movie, and it is justified by referencing Alexandra's credibility and current work. However, the premises are entirely too weak to support the conclusion. Alexandra is only a film *student*, and the script is seemingly her first work. This is not enough evidence to justify investing one's life savings in the film's success.

## Assumptions in an Argument

Think of assumptions as unwritten premises. Although they never explicitly appear in the argument, the author is relying on it to defend the argument, just like a premise. Assumptions are the most important part of an argument that will never appear in an argument.

An argument in the abstract is: The author concludes Z based on W and X premises. But the W and X premises actually depend on the unmentioned assumption of Y. Therefore, what the author is really saying is that, X, W, and Y make Z correct, but Y is assumed.

People assume all of the time. Assumptions and inferences allow the human mind to process the constant flow of information. Many assumptions underlie even the most basic arguments. However, in the world of Legal Reasoning arguments, assumptions must be avoided. An argument must be fully presented to be valid; relying on an assumption is considered weak. The test requires that test takers identify these underlying assumptions. One example is:

> Peyton Manning is the most over-rated quarterback of all time. He lost more big games than anyone else. Plus, he allegedly assaulted his female trainer in college. Peyton clearly shouldn't make the Hall of Fame.

The author certainly relies on a lot of assumptions. A few assumptions are:

- Peyton Manning plays quarterback.

- He is considered to be a great quarterback by at least some people.

- He played in many big games.

- Allegations and past settlements without any admission of guilt from over a decade ago can be relied upon as evidence against Hall of Fame acceptance.

- The Hall of Fame voters factor in off-the-field incidents, even if true.

- The best players should make the Hall of Fame.

- Losing big games negates, at least in part, the achievement of making it to those big games

- Peyton Manning is retired, and people will vote on whether he makes the Hall of Fame at some point in the future.

The author is relying on all of these assumptions. Some are clearly more important to his argument than others. In fact, disproving a necessary assumption can destroy a premise and possibly an entire conclusion. For example, what if the Hall of Fame did not factor in any of the off-the-field incidents? Then the alleged assault no longer factors into the argument. Even worse, what if making the big games actually was more important than losing those games in the eyes of the Hall of Fame voters? Then the whole conclusion falls apart and is no longer justified if that premise is disproven.

Assumption questions test this exact point by asking the test taker to identify which assumption the argument relies upon. If the author is making numerous assumptions, then the most important assumption must be chosen.

If the author truly relies on an assumption, then the argument will completely fall apart if the assumption isn't true. **Negating** a necessary assumption will *always* make the argument fall apart. This is a universal rule of logic and should be the first thing done in testing answer choices.

Here are some ways that underlying assumptions will appear as questions:

- Which of the following is a hidden assumption that the author makes to advance his argument?
- Which assumption, if true, would support the argument's conclusion (make it more logical)?
- The strength of the argument depends on which of the following?
- Upon which of the following assumptions does the author rely?
- Which assumption does the argument presuppose?

An example is:

> Frank Underwood is a terrible president. The man is a typical spend, spend, spend liberal. His employment program would exponentially increase the annual deficit and pile on the national debt. Not to mention, Underwood is also on the verge of starting a war with Russia.

Upon which of the following assumptions does the author's argument most rely?
a. Frank Underwood is a terrible president.
b. The United States cannot afford Frank Underwood's policy plans without spending more than the country raises in revenue.
c. No spend, spend, spend liberal has ever succeeded as president.
d. Starting a war with Russia is beneficial to the United States.

Use the negation rule to find the correct answer in the choices below.

Choice *A* is not an assumption—it is the author's conclusion. This type of restatement will never be the correct answer, but test it anyway. After negating the choice, what remains is: *Frank Underwood is a fantastic president.* Does this make the argument fall apart? No, it just becomes the new conclusion. The argument is certainly worse since it does not seem reasonable for someone to praise a president for being a spend, spend, spend liberal or raising the national debt; however, the argument still makes *logical* sense. Eliminate this choice.

Choice *B* is certainly an assumption. It underlies the premises that the country cannot afford Underwood's economic plans. When reversed to: *The United States can afford Frank Underwood's policy plans without spending more than the country raises in revenue,* this destroys the argument. If the United States can afford his plans, then the annual deficit and national debt won't increase; therefore, Underwood being a terrible president would only be based on the final premise. The argument is much

weaker without the two sentences involving the financials. Keep it as a benchmark while working through the remaining choices.

Choice *C* is irrelevant. The author is not necessarily claiming that all loose-pocket liberals make for bad presidents. His argument specifically pertains to Underwood. Negate it— *Some spend, spend, spend liberals have succeeded as president.* This does not destroy the argument. Some other candidate could have succeeded as president. However, the author is pointing out that those policies would be disastrous considering the rising budget and debt. The author is not making an appeal to historical precedent. Although not a terrible choice, it is certainly weaker than Choice *B*. Eliminate this choice.

Choice *D* is definitely not an assumption made by the author. The author is assuming that a war with Russia is disastrous. Negate it anyway—*Starting a war with Russia is not beneficial for the United States.* This does not destroy the argument; it makes it stronger. Eliminate this choice.

## Analyzing Two Arguments and Evaluating the Types of Evidence Used to Support Each Claim

Arguments use evidence and reasoning to support a position or prove a point. Claims are typically controversial and may be faced with some degree of contention. Thus, authors support claims with evidence. Two arguments might present different types of evidence that readers will need to evaluate for merit, worthiness, accuracy, relevance, and impact. Evidence can take on many forms such as numbers (statistics, measurements, numerical data, etc.), expert opinions or quotes, testimonies, anecdotal evidence or stories from individuals, and textual evidence, such as that obtained from documents like diaries, newspapers, and laws.

### Data, Graphs, or Pictures as Evidence

Some writing in the test contains **infographics** such as charts, tables, or graphs. In these cases, interpret the information presented and determine how well it supports the claims made in the text. For example, if the writer makes a case that seat belts save more lives than other automobile safety measures, they might want to include a graph (like the one below) showing the number of lives saved by seat belts versus those saved by air bags.

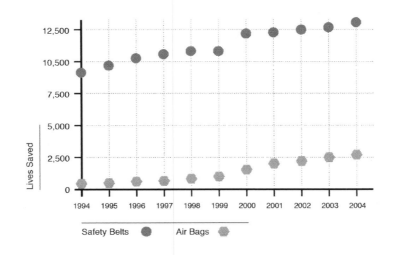

Based on data from the National Highway Traffic Safety Administration

If the graph clearly shows a higher number of lives are saved by seat belts, then it's effective. However, if the graph shows air bags save more lives than seat belts, then it doesn't support the writer's case.

Finally, graphs should be easy to understand. Their information should immediately be clear to the reader at a glance. Here are some basic things to keep in mind when interpreting infographics:

- In a **bar graph**, higher bars represent larger numbers. Lower bars represent smaller numbers.

- **Line graphs** often show trends over time. Points that are higher represent larger numbers than points that are lower. A line that consistently ascends from left to right shows a steady increase over time. A line that consistently descends from left to right shows a steady decrease over time. A line that bounces up and down represents instability or inconsistency in the trend. When interpreting a line graph, determine the point the writer is trying to make, and then see if the graph supports that point.

- **Pie charts** are used to show proportions or percentages of a whole but are less effective in showing change over time.

- **Tables** present information in numerical form, not as graphics. When interpreting a table, make sure to look for patterns in the numbers.

There can also be timelines, illustrations, or maps on the test. When interpreting these, keep in mind the writer's intentions and determine whether or not the graphic supports the case.

## Extending Your Understanding to New Situations

### Combining Information from Different Sources

Synthesizing, or combining, ideas and information from different sources is a skill that helps test takers pass the GED and also thrive in the workforce. The theories and concepts offered in different passages cannot just haphazardly be tossed together. Every test taker has to come up with their own recipe for success when it comes to synthesizing separate sources.

One way for test takers to think about synthesizing sources is to imagine their written responses as empty homes that need to be decorated. They can then imagine the words, concepts, and theories in the different sources as their desired décor. At times, two different sources combine to create perfectly matched décor—the words, concepts, and theories blend seamlessly upon the walls of the test taker's literary home, creating a balance. At other times, two different sources clash, forcing test takers to sort and separate the ideas into different rooms (for example, different paragraphs or sentences). At still other times, the two sources are incomplete, so test takers need to combine materials with their own interests and statements. If sources contradict one another, it is best to highlight these contradictions. A test taker should take note of the contradictions and use their best judgment in choosing which source is more aligned with their own theories. At times, the test taker may even disagree with information in both articles. It is perfectly acceptable to make the audience aware of all contradictions and disagreements.

Writers, like interior designers, must hone their craft through experience. The best way to begin synthesizing sources is to *practice*. There are four practical ways test takers can start practicing synthesis. Firstly, they need to learn how to properly identify and cite captivating quotations. Secondly, they need to learn how to summarize ideas succinctly in their own words. Thirdly, they need to create unique sentences that are part quotation and part summary. And, lastly, they need to ensure that all of the above

is backed by sound grammar, syntax, and organization. The best way to ensure quality is to read other high-quality works and enlist a group of friends or colleagues to edit.

## Transferring Information to New Situations

A natural extension of being able to make an inference from a given set of information is also being able to apply that information to a new context. This is especially useful in non-fiction or informative writing. Considering the facts and details presented in the text, readers should consider how the same information might be relevant in a different situation. The following is an example of applying an inferential conclusion to a different context:

> Often, individuals behave differently in large groups than they do as individuals. One example of this is the psychological phenomenon known as the bystander effect. According to the bystander effect, the more people who witness an accident or crime occur, the less likely each individual bystander is to respond or offer assistance to the victim. A classic example of this is the murder of Kitty Genovese in New York City in the 1960s. Although there were over thirty witnesses to her killing by a stabber, none of them intervened to help Kitty or contact the police.

Considering the phenomenon of the bystander effect, what would probably happen if somebody tripped on the stairs in a crowded subway station?
a. Everybody would stop to help the person who tripped
b. Bystanders would point and laugh at the person who tripped
c. Someone would call the police after walking away from the station
d. Few if any bystanders would offer assistance to the person who tripped

This question asks readers to apply the information they learned from the passage, which is an informative paragraph about the bystander effect. According to the passage, this is a concept in psychology that describes the way people in groups respond to an accident—the more people are present, the less likely any one person is to intervene. While the passage illustrates this effect with the example of a woman's murder, the question asks readers to apply it to a different context—in this case, someone falling down the stairs in front of many subway passengers. Although this specific situation is not discussed in the passage, readers should be able to apply the general concepts described in the paragraph. The definition of the bystander effect includes any instance of an accident or crime in front of a large group of people. The question asks about a situation that falls within the same definition, so the general concept should still hold true: in the midst of a large crowd, few individuals are likely to actually respond to an accident. In this case, Choice *D* is the best response.

# *Grammar and Language*

## Word Usage

### Correcting Errors with Frequently Confused Words

There are a handful of words in the English language that writers often confuse with other words because they sound similar or identical. Errors involving these words are hard to spot because they *sound* right even when they're wrong. Also, because these mistakes are so pervasive, many people think they're correct. Here are a few examples that may be encountered on the test:

### They're vs. Their vs. There

This set of words is probably the all-time winner of misuse. The word *they're* is a contraction of "they are." Remember that contractions combine two words, using an apostrophe to replace any eliminated letters. If a question asks whether the writer is using the word *they're* correctly, change the word to "they are" and reread the sentence. Look at the following example:

> Legislators can be proud of they're work on this issue.

This sentence *sounds* correct, but replace the contraction *they're* with "they are" to see what happens:

> Legislators can be proud of they are work on this issue.

The result doesn't make sense, which shows that it's an incorrect use of the word *they're*. Did the writer mean to use the word *their* instead? The word *their* indicates possession because it shows that something *belongs* to something else. Now put the word *their* into the sentence:

> Legislators can be proud of their work on this issue.

To check the answer, find the word that comes right after the word *their* (which in this case is *work*). Pose this question: whose *work* is it? If the question can be answered in the sentence, then the word signifies possession. In the sentence above, it's the legislators' work. Therefore, the writer is using the word *their* correctly.

If the words *they're* and *their* don't make sense in the sentence, then the correct word is almost always *there*. The word *there* can be used in many different ways, so it's easy to remember to use it when *they're* and *their* don't work. Now test these methods with the following sentences:

> Their going to have a hard time passing these laws.

> Enforcement officials will have there hands full.

> They're are many issues to consider when discussing car safety.

In the first sentence, asking the question "Whose going is it?" doesn't make sense. Thus the word *their* is incorrect. However, when replaced with the conjunction *they're* (or *they are*), the sentence works. Thus, the correct word for the first sentence should be *they're*.

In the second sentence, ask this question: "Whose hands are full?" The answer (*enforcement officials*) is correct in the sentence. Therefore, the word *their* should replace *there* in this sentence.

In the third sentence, changing the word *they're* to "they are" ("They are are many issues") doesn't make sense. Ask this question: "Whose are is it?" This makes even less sense, since neither of the words *they're* or *their* makes sense. Therefore, the correct word must be *there*.

### Who's vs. Whose

*Who's* is a contraction of "who is" while the word *whose* indicates possession. Look at the following sentence:

> Who's job is it to protect America's drivers?

The easiest way to check for correct usage is to replace the word *who's* with "who is" and see if the sentence makes sense:

> Who is job is it to protect America's drivers?

By changing the contraction to "Who is" the sentence no longer makes sense. Therefore, the correct word must be *whose*.

## Your vs. You're
The word *your* indicates possession, while *you're* is a contraction for "you are." Look at the following example:

> Your going to have to write your congressman if you want to see action.

Again, the easiest way to check correct usage is to replace the word *Your* with "You are" and see if the sentence still makes sense.

> You are going to have to write your congressman if you want to see action.

By replacing Your with "You are," the sentence still makes sense. Thus, in this case, the writer should have used "You're."

## Its vs. It's
*Its* is a word that indicates possession, while the word *it's* is a contraction of "it is." Once again, the easiest way to check for correct usage is to replace the word with "it is" and see if the sentence makes sense. Look at the following sentence:

> It's going to take a lot of work to pass this law.

Replacing *it's* with "it is" results in this: "It is going to take a lot of work to pass this law." This makes sense, so the contraction (*it's*) is correct. Now look at another example:

> The car company will have to redesign it's vehicles.

Replacing *it's* with "it is" results in this: "The car company will have to redesign it is vehicles." This sentence doesn't make sense, so the contraction (*it's*) is incorrect.

## Than vs. Then
*Than* is used in sentences that involve comparisons, while *then* is used to indicate an order of events. Consider the following sentence:

> Japan has more traffic fatalities than the U.S.

The use of the word *than* is correct because it compares Japan to the U.S. Now look at another example:

> Laws must be passed, and then we'll see a change in behavior.

Here the use of the word *then* is correct because one thing happens after the other.

## Affect vs. Effect

*Affect* is a verb that means to change something, while *effect* is a noun that indicates such a change. Look at the following sentence:

> There are thousands of people affected by the new law.

This sentence is correct because *affected* is a verb that tells what's happening. Now look at this sentence:

> The law will have a dramatic effect.

This sentence is also correct because *effect* is a noun and the thing that happens.

Note that a noun version of *affect* is occasionally used. It means "emotion" or "desire," usually in a psychological sense.

## Two vs. Too vs. To

*Two* is the number (2). *Too* refers to an amount of something, or it can mean *also*. *To* is used for everything else. Look at the following sentence:

> Two senators still haven't signed the bill.

This is correct because there are *two* (2) senators. Here's another example:

> There are too many questions about this issue.

In this sentence, the word *too* refers to an amount ("too many questions"). Now here's another example:

> Senator Wilson is supporting this legislation, too.

In this sentence, the word *also* can be substituted for the word *too*, so it's also correct. Finally, one last example:

> I look forward to signing this bill into law.

In this sentence, the tests for *two* and *too* don't work. Thus, the word *to* fits the bill!

## Other Common Writing Confusions

In addition to all of the above, there are other words that writers often misuse. This doesn't happen because the words sound alike, but because the writer is not aware of the proper way to use them.

## Correcting Subject-Verb Agreement Errors

In English, verbs must agree with the subject. The form of a verb may change depending on whether the subject is singular or plural, or whether it is first, second, or third person. For example, the verb *to be* has various forms:

> I <u>am</u> a student.

> You <u>are</u> a student.

> She <u>is</u> a student.

We <u>are</u> students.

They <u>are</u> students.

Errors occur when a verb does not agree with its subject. Sometimes, the error is readily apparent:

We is hungry.

*Is* is not the appropriate form of *to be* when used with the third person plural *we*.

We are hungry.

This sentence now has correct subject-verb agreement.

However, some cases are trickier, particularly when the subject consists of a lengthy noun phrase with many modifiers:

Students who are hoping to accompany the anthropology department on its annual summer trip to Ecuador needs to sign up by March 31st.

The verb in this sentence is *needs*. However, its subject is not the noun adjacent to it—Ecuador. The subject is the noun at the beginning of the sentence—students. Because *students* is plural, *needs* is the incorrect verb form.

*Students* who are hoping to accompany the anthropology department on its annual summer trip to Ecuador *need* to sign up by March 31st.

This sentence now uses correct agreement between *students* and *need*.

Another case to be aware of is a **collective noun**. A collective noun refers to a group of many things or people but can be singular in itself—e.g., *family, committee, army, pair team, council, jury*. Whether or not a collective noun uses a singular or plural verb depends on how the noun is being used. If the noun refers to the group performing a collective action as one unit, it should use a singular verb conjugation:

The family is moving to a new neighborhood.

The whole family is moving together in unison, so the singular verb form *is* is appropriate here.

The committee has made its decision.

The verb *has* and the possessive pronoun *its* both reflect the word *committee* as a singular noun in the sentence above; however, when a collective noun refers to the group as individuals, it can take a plural verb:

The newlywed pair spend every moment together.

This sentence emphasizes the love between two people in a pair, so it can use the plural verb *spend*.

The council are all newly elected members.

The sentence refers to the council in terms of its individual members and uses the plural verb *are*.

Overall, though, American English is more likely to pair a collective noun with a singular verb, while British English is more likely to pair a collective noun with a plural verb.

Which of the following sentences is correct?

A large crowd of protesters was on hand.

A large crowd of protesters were on hand.

Many people would say the second sentence is correct, but they'd be wrong. However, they probably wouldn't be alone. Most people just look at two words: *protesters were*. Together they make sense. They sound right. The problem is that the verb *were* doesn't refer to the word *protesters*. Here, the word *protesters* is part of a prepositional phrase that clarifies the actual subject of the sentence (*crowd*).

Take the phrase "of protesters" away and re-examine the sentences:

A large crowd was on hand.

A large crowd were on hand.

Without the prepositional phrase to separate the subject and verb, the answer is obvious. The first sentence is correct. On the test, look for confusing prepositional phrases when answering questions about subject-verb agreement. Take the phrase away, and then recheck the sentence.

## Correcting Pronoun Errors
### Pronoun Person
**Pronoun person** refers to the narrative voice the writer uses in a piece of writing. A great deal of nonfiction is written in third person, which uses pronouns like *he, she, it,* and *they* to convey meaning. Occasionally a writer uses first person (*I, me, we,* etc.) or second person (*you*). Any choice of pronoun person can be appropriate for a particular situation, but the writer must remain consistent and logical.

Test questions may cover examining samples that should stay in a single pronoun person, be it first, second, or third. Look out for shifts between words like *you* and *I* or *he* and *they*.

### Pronoun Clarity
Pronouns always refer back to a noun. However, as the writer composes longer, more complicated sentences, the reader may be unsure which noun the pronoun should replace. For example:

An amendment was made to the bill, but now it has been voted down.

Was the amendment voted down or the entire bill? It's impossible to tell from this sentence. To correct this error, the writer needs to restate the appropriate noun rather than using a pronoun:

An amendment was made to the bill, but now the bill has been voted down.

### Pronouns in Combination
Writers often make mistakes when choosing pronouns to use in combination with other nouns. The most common mistakes are found in sentences like this:

Please join Senator Wilson and I at the event tomorrow.

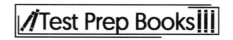

Notice anything wrong? Though many people think the sentence sounds perfectly fine, the use of the pronoun *I* is actually incorrect. To double-check this, take the other person out of the sentence:

Please join I at the event tomorrow.

Now the sentence is obviously incorrect, as it should read, "Please join *me* at the event tomorrow." Thus, the first sentence should replace *I* with *me*:

Please join Senator Wilson and me at the event tomorrow.

For many people, this sounds wrong because they're used to hearing and saying it incorrectly. Take extra care when answering this kind of question and follow the double-checking procedure.

## Eliminating Non-Standard English Words or Phrases

Non-standard English words and phrases, such as slang, should be eliminated, as it not only reduces the professionalism and formality of a text, but it also opens the door for confusion. Slang tends to evolve quickly, and it is less universally-understood than standard English. Therefore, unless working on a narrative fiction piece that purposely includes non-standard English as part of the dialogue, writers should make every effort to eliminate this type of language from their writing.

## Sentence Structure

## Eliminating Dangling or Misplaced Modifiers

**Modifiers** are words or phrases (often adjectives or nouns) that add detail to, explain, or limit the meaning of other parts of a sentence. Look at the following example:

A big pine tree is in the yard.

In the sentence, the words *big* (an adjective) and *pine* (a noun) modify *tree* (the head noun).

All related parts of a sentence must be placed together correctly. **Misplaced** and **dangling modifiers** are common writing mistakes. In fact, they're so common that many people are accustomed to seeing them and can decipher an incorrect sentence without much difficulty. On the test, expect to be asked to identify and correct this kind of error.

### *Misplaced Modifiers*

Since modifiers refer to something else in the sentence (*big* and *pine* refer to *tree* in the example above), they need to be placed close to what they modify. If a modifier is so far away that the reader isn't sure what it's describing, it becomes a **misplaced modifier**. For example:

Seat belts almost saved 5,000 lives in 2009.

It's likely that the writer means that the total number of lives saved by seat belts in 2009 is close to 5,000. However, due to the misplaced modifier (*almost*), the sentence actually says there are 5,000 instances when seat belts *almost saved lives*. In this case, the position of the modifier is actually the difference between life and death (at least in the meaning of the sentence). A clearer way to write the sentence is:

Seat belts saved almost 5,000 lives in 2009.

Now that the modifier is close to the 5,000 lives it references, the sentence's meaning is clearer.

Another common example of a misplaced modifier occurs when the writer uses the modifier to begin a sentence. For example:

Having saved 5,000 lives in 2009, Senator Wilson praised the seat belt legislation.

It seems unlikely that Senator Wilson saved 5,000 lives on her own, but that's what the writer is saying in this sentence. To correct this error, the writer should move the modifier closer to the intended object it modifies. Here are two possible solutions:

Having saved 5,000 lives in 2009, the seat belt legislation was praised by Senator Wilson.

Senator Wilson praised the seat belt legislation, which saved 5,000 lives in 2009.

When choosing a solution for a misplaced modifier, look for an option that places the modifier close to the object or idea it describes.

## Dangling Modifiers

A modifier must have a target word or phrase that it's modifying. Without this, it's a **dangling modifier**. Dangling modifiers are usually found at the beginning of sentences:

After passing the new law, there is sure to be an improvement in highway safety.

This sentence doesn't say anything about who is passing the law. Therefore, "After passing the new law" is a dangling modifier because it doesn't modify anything in the sentence. To correct this type of error, determine what the writer intended the modifier to point to:

After passing the new law, legislators are sure to see an improvement in highway safety.

"After passing the new law" now points to *legislators*, which makes the sentence clearer and eliminates the dangling modifier.

## Editing Sentences for Parallel Structure and Correct Use of Conjunctions

### Parallel Structure

**Parallel structure** occurs when phrases or clauses within a sentence contain the same structure. Parallelism increases readability and comprehensibility because it is easy to tell which sentence elements are paired with each other in meaning.

Jennifer enjoys cooking, knitting, and to spend time with her cat.

This sentence is not parallel because the items in the list appear in two different forms. Some are **gerunds**, which is the verb + ing: *cooking, knitting*. The other item uses the **infinitive** form, which is to + verb: *to spend*. To create parallelism, all items in the list may reflect the same form:

Jennifer enjoys cooking, knitting, and spending time with her cat.

All of the items in the list are now in gerund forms, so this sentence exhibits parallel structure. Here's another example:

The company is looking for employees who are responsible and with a lot of experience.

Again, the items that are listed in this sentence are not parallel. "Responsible" is an adjective, yet "with a lot of experience" is a prepositional phrase. The sentence elements do not utilize parallel parts of speech.

> The company is looking for employees who are responsible and experienced.

"Responsible" and "experienced" are both adjectives, so this sentence now has parallel structure.

## Conjunctions

**Conjunctions** join words, phrases, clauses, or sentences together, indicating the type of connection between these elements.

> I like pizza, *and* I enjoy spaghetti.

> I like to play baseball, *but* I'm allergic to mitts.

Some conjunctions are **coordinating**, meaning they give equal emphasis to two main clauses. Coordinating conjunctions are short, simple words that can be remembered using the mnemonic FANBOYS: for, and, nor, but, or, yet, so. Other conjunctions are subordinating. **Subordinating conjunctions** introduce dependent clauses and include words such as *because, since, before, after, if,* and *while*.

Conjunctions can also be classified as follows:

- **Cumulative conjunctions** add one statement to another.
  - Examples: *and, both, also, as well as, not only*
  - E.g. The juice is sweet *and* sour.
- **Adversative conjunctions** are used to contrast two clauses.
  - Examples: *but, while, still, yet, nevertheless*
  - E.g. She was tired, *but* she was happy.
- **Alternative conjunctions** express two alternatives.
  - Examples: *or, either, neither, nor, else, otherwise*
  - E.g. He must eat, *or* he will die.

## Editing for Subject-Verb and Pronoun-Antecedent Agreement

### Subject-Verb Agreement

The subject of a sentence and its verb must agree. The cornerstone rule of subject-verb agreement is that subject and verb must agree in number. Whether the subject is singular or plural, the verb must follow suit.

> Incorrect: The houses is new.

> Correct: The houses are new.

> Also Correct: The house is new.

In other words, a singular subject requires a singular verb; a plural subject requires a plural verb.

The words or phrases that come between the subject and verb do not alter this rule.

Incorrect: The houses built of brick is new.

Correct: The houses built of brick are new.

Incorrect: The houses with the sturdy porches is new.

Correct: The houses with the sturdy porches are new.

The subject will always follow the verb when a sentence begins with *here* or *there.* Identify these with care.

Incorrect: Here *is* the *houses* with sturdy porches.

Correct: Here *are* the *houses* with sturdy porches.

The subject in the sentences above is not *here*, it is *houses*. Remember, *here* and *there* are never subjects. Be careful that contractions such as *here's* or *there're* do not cause confusion!

Two subjects joined by *and* require a plural verb form, except when the two combine to make one thing:

Incorrect: Garrett and Jonathan is over there.

Correct: Garrett and Jonathan are over there.

Incorrect: Spaghetti and meatballs are a delicious meal!

Correct: Spaghetti and meatballs is a delicious meal!

In the example above, *spaghetti and meatballs* is a compound noun. However, *Garrett and Jonathan* is not a compound noun.

Two singular subjects joined by *or, either/or,* or *neither/nor* call for a singular verb form.

Incorrect: Butter or syrup are acceptable.

Correct: Butter or syrup is acceptable.

Plural subjects joined by *or, either/or*, or *neither/nor* are, indeed, plural.

The chairs or the boxes are being moved next.

If one subject is singular and the other is plural, the verb should agree with the closest noun.

Correct: The chair or the boxes are being moved next.

Correct: The chairs or the box is being moved next.

Some plurals of money, distance, and time call for a singular verb.

Incorrect: Three dollars *are* enough to buy that.

Correct: Three dollars *is* enough to buy that.

For words declaring degrees of quantity such as *many of, some of,* or *most of,* let the noun that follows *of* be the guide:

Incorrect: Many of the books is in the shelf.

Correct: Many of the books are in the shelf.

Incorrect: Most of the pie *are* on the table.

Correct: Most of the pie *is* on the table.

For indefinite pronouns like anybody or everybody, use singular verbs.

Everybody *is* going to the store.

However, the pronouns *few, many, several, all, some,* and *both* have their own rules and use plural forms.

Some *are* ready.

Some nouns like *crowd* and *congress* are called **collective nouns** and they require a singular verb form.

Congress *is* in session.

The news *is* over.

Books and movie titles, though, including plural nouns such as *Great Expectations*, also require a singular verb. Remember that only the subject affects the verb. While writing tricky subject-verb arrangements, say them aloud. Listen to them. Once the rules have been learned, one's ear will become sensitive to them, making it easier to pick out what's right and what's wrong.

## Pronoun-Antecedent Agreement

An **antecedent** is the noun to which a pronoun refers; it needs to be written or spoken before the pronoun is used. For many pronouns, antecedents are imperative for clarity. In particular, a lot of the personal, possessive, and demonstrative pronouns need antecedents. Otherwise, it would be unclear who or what someone is referring to when they use a pronoun like *he* or *this*.

**Pronoun reference** means that the pronoun should refer clearly to one, clear, unmistakable noun (the antecedent).

**Pronoun-antecedent agreement** refers to the need for the antecedent and the corresponding pronoun to agree in gender, person, and number. Here are some examples:

The *kidneys* (plural antecedent) are part of the urinary system. *They* (plural pronoun) serve several roles.

The kidneys are part of the *urinary system* (singular antecedent). *It* (singular pronoun) is also known as the renal system.

## Eliminating Wordiness or Awkward Sentence Structure

A great Facebook or Twitter post is witty, to the point, and even moving. Good writing is like a good social media post—it needs to be seamless, succinct, and sound in its organization. Alternatively, there

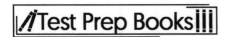 

are also social media rants so jumbled that they do not make sense or are so endless that readers lose interest. The most captivating social media entries are the ones that meet a high standard of organization. Likewise, the most captivating essays follow these same standards.

Wordiness and awkward sentence structure can happen as a result of many factors. Firstly, they can result from poor grammar or run-on sentences. In order to avoid this, test takers should try using punctuation with fidelity and breaking up independent and dependent clauses into simpler, bite-size nuggets of knowledge. Secondly, wordiness and awkward sentence structure can stem from the overuse of adjectives and adverbs. Test takers should try to limit adverbs and adjectives to ensure clarity. Lastly, wordiness and awkward sentence structure can be the product of flawed organization. Not only should sentences be succinct, but paragraphs and pages should also be succinct—they should use space efficiently and effectively. Test takers should try conveying a message using the fewest words possible.

Below are examples of ways to rectify wordiness and awkward sentences in writing.

**WORDINESS:**

| BEFORE: Science is an important subject of study, and it is important for all students to learn because it focuses on the way the world works and it has important subfields like biology, physics, and chemistry. | AFTER: Science—which is composed of important subfields like biology, physics, and chemistry—helps students understand the way the world works. |
| --- | --- |
| BEFORE: History is about important people, places, events, movements, and eras in the past it is a really, really interesting field with lots of different lenses of study such as economic history, political history, and cultural history to name a few types of history. | AFTER: History can be studied through many lenses: economics, politics, and culture. However, all types of history focus on interesting people, places, events, movements, and eras in the past. |

**AWKWARDNESS:**

| BEFORE: The administrative expertise of George Washington's presidential administration was known for its powerfully powerful administrators. | AFTER: George Washington's presidential administration was known for its powerful leadership and expertise. |
| --- | --- |
| BEFORE: I want to study history, working hard, and becoming a historian. | AFTER: I want to study history, work hard, and become a historian. |

## Eliminating Run-On Sentences and Sentence Fragments

A **sentence fragment** is a failed attempt to create a complete sentence because it's missing a required noun or verb. Fragments don't function properly because there isn't enough information to understand the writer's intended meaning. For example:

> Seat belt use corresponds to a lower rate of hospital visits, reducing strain on an already overburdened healthcare system. Insurance claims as well.

Look at the last sentence: *Insurance claims as well.* What does this mean? This is a fragment because it has a noun but no verb, and it leaves the reader guessing what the writer means about insurance claims. Many readers can probably infer what the writer means, but this distracts them from the flow of the writer's argument. Choosing a suitable replacement for a sentence fragment may be one of the questions on the test. The fragment is probably related to the surrounding content, so look at the overall point the writer is trying to make and choose the answer that best fits that idea.

Remember that sometimes a fragment can *look* like a complete sentence or have all the nouns and verbs it needs to make sense. Consider the following two examples:

> Seat belt use corresponds to a lower rate of hospital visits.

> Although seat belt use corresponds to a lower rate of hospital visits.

Both examples above have nouns and verbs, but only the first sentence is correct. The second sentence is a fragment, even though it's actually longer. The key is the writer's use of the word *although*. Starting a sentence with *although* turns that part into a *subordinate clause* (more on that next). Keep in mind that one doesn't have to remember that it's called a subordinate clause on the test. Just be able to recognize that the words form an incomplete thought and identify the problem as a sentence fragment.

A **run-on sentence** is, in some ways, the opposite of a fragment. It contains two or more sentences that have been improperly forced together into one. An example of a run-on sentence looks something like this:

> Seat belt use corresponds to a lower rate of hospital visits it also leads to fewer insurance claims.

Here, there are two separate ideas in one sentence. It's difficult for the reader to follow the writer's thinking because there is no transition from one idea to the next. On the test, choose the best way to correct the run-on sentence.

Here are two possibilities for the sentence above:

> Seat belt use corresponds to a lower rate of hospital visits. It also leads to fewer insurance claims.

> Seat belt use corresponds to a lower rate of hospital visits, but it also leads to fewer insurance claims.

Both solutions are grammatically correct, so which one is the best choice? That depends on the point that the writer is trying to make. Always read the surrounding text to determine what the writer wants to demonstrate, and choose the option that best supports that thought.

## Transition Words

**Transitions** are the glue that helps put ideas together seamlessly, within sentences and paragraphs, between them, and (in longer documents) even between sections. Transitions may be single words, sentences, or whole paragraphs (as in the prior example). Transitions help readers to digest and understand what to feel about what has gone on and clue readers in on what is going on, what will be, and how they might react to all these factors. Transitions are like good clues left at a crime scene.

Recall this list of some common transition words and phrases:

- To show causality: *as a result, therefore*, and *consequently*
- To compare and contrast: *however, but*, and *on the other hand*
- To introduce examples: *for instance, namely*, and *including*
- To show order of importance: *foremost, primarily, secondly*, and *lastly*

## Capitalization, Punctuation, and Apostrophes

### Correct Capitalization
Here's a non-exhaustive list of things that should be capitalized.

- The first word of every sentence
- The first word of every line of poetry
- The first letter of proper nouns (World War II)
- Holidays (Valentine's Day)
- The days of the week and months of the year (Tuesday, March)
- The first word, last word, and all major words in the titles of books, movies, songs, and other creative works (In the novel, *To Kill a Mockingbird*, note that *a* is lowercase since it's not a major word, but *to* is capitalized since it's the first word of the title.)
- Titles when preceding a proper noun (President Roberto Gonzales, Aunt Judy)

When simply using a word such as president or secretary, though, the word is not capitalized.

Officers of the new business must include a *president* and *treasurer*.

Seasons—spring, fall, etc.—are not capitalized.

*North*, *south*, *east*, and *west* are capitalized when referring to regions but are not when being used for directions. In general, if it's preceded by *the* it should be capitalized.

I'm from the South.

I drove south.

### Using Apostrophes with Possessive Nouns Correctly
*Possessives*
In grammar, **possessive nouns** show ownership, which was seen in previous examples like *mine, yours,* and *theirs*.

Singular nouns are generally made possessive with an apostrophe and an *s* (*'s*).

> My *uncle's* new car is silver.

> The *dog's* bowl is empty.

> *James's* ties are becoming outdated.

Plural nouns ending in *s* are generally made possessive by just adding an apostrophe (*'* ):

> The pistachio nuts' saltiness is added during roasting. (The saltiness of pistachio nuts is added during roasting.)

> The students' achievement tests are difficult. (The achievement tests of the students are difficult.)

If the plural noun does not end in an *s* such as *women,* then it is made possessive by adding an **apostrophe** *s* (*'s*)—*women's.*

Indefinite possessive pronouns such as *nobody* or *someone* become possessive by adding an *apostrophe s*— *nobody's* or *someone's.*

## Using Correct Punctuation
### *Ellipses*
An **ellipsis** (…) consists of three handy little dots that can speak volumes on behalf of irrelevant material. Writers use them in place of words, lines, phrases, list content, or paragraphs that might just as easily have been omitted from a passage of writing. This can be done to save space or to focus only on the specifically relevant material.

> Exercise is good for some unexpected reasons. Watkins writes, "Exercise has many benefits such as … reducing cancer risk."

In the example above, the ellipsis takes the place of the other benefits of exercise that are more expected.

The ellipsis may also be used to show a pause in sentence flow.

> "I'm wondering...how this could happen," Dylan said in a soft voice.

### *Commas*
A **comma** (,) is the punctuation mark that signifies a pause—breath—between parts of a sentence. It denotes a break of flow. As with so many aspects of writing structure, authors will benefit by reading their writing aloud or mouthing the words. This can be particularly helpful if one is uncertain about whether the comma is needed.

In a complex sentence—one that contains a **subordinate (dependent)** clause or clauses—the use of a comma is dictated by where the subordinate clause is located. If the subordinate clause is located before the main clause, a comma is needed between the two clauses.

> *Because I don't have that much money*, I will not pay for the steak.

Generally, if the subordinate clause is placed after the main clause, no punctuation is needed.

>I did well on my exam *because I studied two hours the night before*.

Notice how the last clause is dependent because it requires the earlier independent clauses to make sense.

Use a comma on both sides of an interrupting phrase.

>I will pay for the ice cream, *chocolate and vanilla*, and then will eat it all myself.

The words forming the phrase in italics are nonessential (extra) information. To determine if a phrase is nonessential, try reading the sentence without the phrase and see if it's still coherent.

A comma is not necessary in this next sentence because no interruption—nonessential or extra information—has occurred. Read sentences aloud when uncertain.

>I will pay for his chocolate and vanilla ice cream and then will eat it all myself.

If the nonessential phrase comes at the beginning of a sentence, a comma should only go at the end of the phrase. If the phrase comes at the end of a sentence, a comma should only go at the beginning of the phrase.

Other types of interruptions include the following:

- Interjections: Oh no, I am not going.
- Abbreviations: Barry Potter, M.D., specializes in heart disorders.
- Direct addresses: Yes, Claudia, I am tired and going to bed.
- Parenthetical phrases: His wife, lovely as she was, was not helpful.
- Transitional phrases: Also, it is not possible.

The second comma in the following sentence is called an Oxford comma.

>I will pay for ice cream, syrup, and pop.

It is a comma used after the second-to-last item in a series of three or more items. It comes before the word *or* or *and*. Not everyone uses the Oxford comma; it is optional, but many believe it is needed. The comma functions as a tool to reduce confusion in writing. So, if omitting the Oxford comma would cause confusion, then it's best to include it.

Commas are used in math to mark the place of thousands in numerals, breaking them up so they are easier to read. Other uses for commas are in dates (*March 19, 2016*), letter greetings (*Dear Sally,*), and in between cities and states (*Louisville, KY*).

## Semicolons
The **semicolon** (;) might be described as a heavy-handed comma. Take a look at these two examples:

>I will pay for the ice cream, but I will not pay for the steak.

>I will pay for the ice cream; I will not pay for the steak.

What's the difference? The first example has a comma and a conjunction separating the two independent clauses. The second example does not have a conjunction, but there are two independent clauses in the sentence, so something more than a comma is required. In this case, a semicolon is used.

Two independent clauses can only be joined in a sentence by either a comma and conjunction or a semicolon. If one of those tools is not used, the sentence will be a run-on. Remember that while the clauses are independent, they need to be closely related in order to be contained in one sentence.

Another use for the semicolon is to separate items in a list when the items themselves require commas.

> The family lived in Phoenix, Arizona; Oklahoma City, Oklahoma; and Raleigh, North Carolina.

## Colons

**Colons** (:) have many miscellaneous functions. Colons can be used to precede further information or a list. In these cases, a colon should only follow an independent clause.

> Humans take in sensory information through five basic senses: sight, hearing, smell, touch, and taste.

The meal includes the following components:

- Caesar salad
- Spaghetti
- Garlic bread
- Cake

The family got what they needed: a reliable vehicle.

While a comma is more common, a colon can also precede a formal quotation.

> He said to the crowd: "Let's begin!"

The colon is used after the greeting in a formal letter.

> Dear Sir:
> To Whom It May Concern:

In the writing of time, the colon separates the minutes from the hour (*4:45 p.m.*). The colon can also be used to indicate a ratio between two numbers (*50:1*).

## Hyphens

The **hyphen** (-) is a little hash mark that can be used to join words to show that they are linked.

Hyphenate two words that work together as a single adjective (a compound adjective).

> honey-covered biscuits

Some words always require hyphens, even if not serving as an adjective.

> merry-go-round

Hyphens always go after certain prefixes like *anti-* & *all-*.

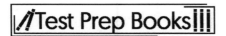 

Hyphens should also be used when the absence of the hyphen would cause a strange vowel combination (*semi-engineer*) or confusion. For example, *re-collect* should be used to describe something being gathered twice rather than being written as *recollect*, which means to remember.

## Parentheses and Dashes

**Parentheses** are half-round brackets that look like this: ( ). They set off a word, phrase, or sentence that is an afterthought, explanation, or side note relevant to the surrounding text but not essential. A pair of commas is often used to set off this sort of information, but parentheses are generally used for information that would not fit well within a sentence or that the writer deems not important enough to be structurally part of the sentence.

The picture of the heart (see above) shows the major parts you should memorize.

Mount Everest is one of three mountains in the world that are over 28,000 feet high (K2 and Kanchenjunga are the other two).

See how the sentences above are complete without the parenthetical statements? In the first example, *see above* would not have fit well within the flow of the sentence. The second parenthetical statement could have been a separate sentence, but the writer deemed the information not pertinent to the topic.

The **em-dash** (—) is a mark longer than a hyphen used as a punctuation mark in sentences and to set apart a relevant thought. Even after plucking out the line separated by the dash marks, the sentence will be intact and make sense.

Looking out the airplane window at the landmarks—Lake Clarke, Thompson Community College, and the bridge—she couldn't help but feel excited to be home.

The dashes use is similar to that of parentheses or a pair of commas. So, what's the difference? Many believe that using dashes makes the clause within them stand out while using parentheses is subtler. It's advised to not use dashes when commas could be used instead.

## Quotation Marks

Here are some instances where **quotation marks** should be used:

- Dialogue for characters in narratives. When characters speak, the first word should always be capitalized, and the punctuation goes inside the quotes. For example:

    Janie said, "The tree fell on my car during the hurricane."

- Around titles of songs, short stories, essays, and chapters in books
- To emphasize a certain word
- To refer to a word as the word itself

## Apostrophes

This punctuation mark, the apostrophe ('), is a versatile little mark. It has a few different functions:

- Quotes: Apostrophes are used when a second quote is needed within a quote.

    In my letter to my friend, I wrote, "The girl had to get a new purse, and guess what Mary did? She said, 'I'd like to go with you to the store.' I knew Mary would buy it for her."

162

- Contractions: Another use for an apostrophe in the quote above is a contraction. *I'd* is used for *I would.*

- Possession: An apostrophe followed by the letter *s* shows possession (*Mary's* purse). If the possessive word is plural, the apostrophe generally just follows the word.

    The trees' leaves are all over the ground.

# Practice Questions

*Questions 1-5 are based upon the following passage:*

### The Myth of Head Heat Loss

It has recently been brought to my attention that most people believe that 75% of your body heat is lost through your head. I had certainly heard this before, and am not going to attempt to say I didn't believe it when I first heard it. It is natural to be gullible to anything said with enough authority. But the "fact" that the majority of your body heat is lost through your head is a lie.

Let me explain. Heat loss is proportional to surface area exposed. An elephant loses a great deal more heat than an anteater because it has a much greater surface area than an anteater. Each cell has mitochondria that produce energy in the form of heat, and it takes a lot more energy to run an elephant than an anteater.

So, each part of your body loses its proportional amount of heat in accordance with its surface area. The human torso probably loses the most heat, though the legs lose a significant amount as well. Some people have asked, "Why does it feel so much warmer when you cover your head than when you don't?" Well, that's because your head, because it is not clothed, is losing a lot of heat while the clothing on the rest of your body provides insulation. If you went outside with a hat and pants but no shirt, not only would you look stupid but your heat loss would be significantly greater because so much more of you would be exposed. So, if given the choice to cover your chest or your head in the cold, choose the chest. It could save your life.

1. What is the primary purpose of this passage?
   a. To provide evidence that disproves a myth
   b. To compare elephants and anteaters
   c. To explain why it is appropriate to wear clothes in winter
   d. To show how people are gullible

2. Which of the following best describes the main idea of the passage?
   a. It is better to wear a shirt than a hat
   b. Heat loss is proportional to surface area exposed
   c. It is natural to be gullible
   d. The human chest loses the most heat

3. Why does the author compare elephants and anteaters?
   a. To express an opinion
   b. To give an example that helps clarify the main point
   c. To show the differences between them
   d. To persuade why one is better than the other

4. Which of the following best describes the tone of the passage?
   a. Harsh
   b. Angry
   c. Casual
   d. Indifferent

5. Which of the following sentences provides the best evidence to support the main idea?
   a. "It is natural to be gullible to anything said with enough authority."
   b. "Each part of your body loses its proportional amount of heat in accordance with its surface area."
   c. "If given the choice to cover your chest or your head in the cold, choose the chest."
   d. "But the 'fact' that the majority of your body heat is lost through your head is a lie."

# Answer Explanations

**1. A:** Not only does the article provide examples to disprove a myth, the title also suggests that the article is trying to disprove a myth. Further, the sentence, "But the 'fact' that the majority of your body heat is lost through your head is a lie," and then the subsequent "let me explain," demonstrates the author's intention in disproving a myth. *B* is incorrect because although the selection does compare elephants and anteaters, it does so in order to prove a point, and is not the primary reason that the selection was written. *C* is incorrect because even though the article mentions somebody wearing clothes in the winter, and that doing so could save your life, wearing clothes in the winter is not the primary reason this article was written. *D* is incorrect because the article only mentions that people are gullible once, and makes no further comment on the matter, so this cannot be the primary purpose.

**2. B:** If the myth is that most of one's body heat is lost through their head, then the fact that heat loss is proportional to surface area exposed is the best evidence that disproves it, since one's head has a great deal less surface area than the rest of the body, making *B* the correct choice. "It is better to wear a shirt than a hat" does not provide evidence that disproves the fact that the head loses more heat than the rest of the body. Thus, *A* is incorrect. *C* is incorrect because gullibility is mentioned only once in this passage and the rest of the article ignores this statement, so clearly it is not the main idea. Finally, *D* is incorrect because though the article mentions that the human chest probably loses the most heat, it is to provide an example of the evidence that heat loss is proportional to surface area exposed, so this is not the main idea of the passage.

**3. B:** Choice *B* is correct because the author is trying to demonstrate the main idea, which is that heat loss is proportional to surface area, and so they compare two animals with different surface areas to clarify the main point. Choice *A* is incorrect because the author uses elephants and anteaters to prove a point that heat loss is proportional to surface area, not to express an opinion. Choice *C* is incorrect because though the author does use them to show differences, they do so in order to give examples that prove the above points. Choice *D* is incorrect because there is no language to indicate favoritism between the two animals.

**4. C:** Because of the way the author addresses the reader and the colloquial language the author uses (i.e., "let me explain," "so," "well," didn't," "you would look stupid," etc.), Choice *C* is the best answer because it has a much more casual tone than the usual informative article. Choice *A* may be a tempting choice because the author says the "fact" that most of one's heat is lost through their head is a "lie" and that someone who does not wear a shirt in the cold looks stupid. However, this only happens twice within the passage, and the passage does not give an overall tone of harshness. Choice *B* is incorrect because again, while not necessarily nice, the language does not carry an angry charge. The author is clearly not indifferent to the subject because of the passionate language that they use, so Choice *D* is incorrect.

**5. B:** Choice *B* is correct. The primary purpose of the article is to provide evidence to disprove the myth that most of a person's heat is lost through their head. The fact that each part of the body loses heat in proportion to its surface area is the best evidence to disprove this myth. Choice *A* is incorrect because again, gullibility is not a main contributor to this article, but it may be common to see questions on the test that give the same wrong answer in order to try and trick the test taker. Choice *C* only suggests what you should do with this information; it is not the primary evidence itself. Choice *D*, while tempting, is actually not evidence. It does not give any reason for why it is a lie; it simply states that it is. Evidence is factual information that supports a claim.

# Science

## *Reading for Meaning in Science*

### Claims and Evidence in Science

#### Finding Evidence that Supports a Finding

Science is one of the most objective, straightforward fields of study. Thus, it is no surprise that scientists and science articles are focused on **evidence**. When reading science passages, test takers are sometimes asked to find supporting evidence that reinforces a particular finding. A **finding** in science is a result of the investigation; it is what scientists find out. The majority of science passages tend to avoid opinions; instead, they focus on facts. Although no results are infallible just because the texts are scientific, most results are quantified. Quantified results mean they are expressed in numbers or measurements. Thus, when in doubt, go straight to the data, or numbers, that are offered. Sometimes data is embedded in the text; other times it appears in charts, tables, or graphs. These tools use numbers to demonstrate the patterns discussed in scientific texts, and they help readers to visualize concrete patterns. In order to find evidence to support a finding in scientific passage, all test takers should try collecting and analyzing the relevant data offered. Regardless of whether the data is coming from the text or a graph, it is helpful when making conclusions.

The following steps are helpful for identifying evidence that supports a finding in a science passage:

- Apply critical analysis and critical thinking by asking the right questions.
- Determine the weight of the information by figuring out its relevance.
- Identify trends in the numbers.
- Make inferences.
- Determine the most appropriate methods for either quantifying or communicating inferences.

#### Making Sense of Information that Differs Between Various Science Sources

Science is often a process of checks and balances, and GED students are expected to carry out this process of checks and balances as they analyze and compare information that differs between various science sources. Science demands a high degree of communication, which, in turn, demands a high degree of scientific literacy and numeracy. GED students must be prepared to analyze the different data and written conclusions of various texts. Contrary to popular belief, science is not an authoritarian field—scientific worldviews and inquiries can be wrong. It is more fruitful to think of science as a living library that is shaped by the complex activities carried out by different groups in different places. This living library is filled with ideas that are shaped by various sources and methods of research. The explanations, inferences, and discussions carried out by scientists are filled with facts that may be flawed or biased. Science, like any other field, cannot completely escape bias. Even though science is meant to be objective, its findings can still lend themselves to biases.

Thus, it is important for GED students to get in the practice of not only making sense of information that differs between various science sources, but also to begin synthesizing this information into a unique worldview. The peer review process is also necessary to ensure checks and balances within the scientific field. The key to making this happen while taking the GED is to maintain an acute awareness of when and where information or data differs. Pay close attention to the ways in which each scientist uses specific words or data to back their overall conclusions.

Below are some key reasons why data and interpretations can differ:

- Historical bias
- Cultural bias
- Interpretation or personal bias
- Lack of implementation and data collection fidelity
- Different data collection approaches
- Different data collection and data analysis tools
- Weak hypotheses
- Compounding variables
- Failure to recognize certain variables
- User error
- Changes in the environment between two studies
- Computation or statistical errors
- Interpretive blind spots
- Lack of understanding of context or environment

## Science Vocabulary, Terms, and Phrases

Every field of study has its own specialized vocabulary, terms, and phrases. However, the field of science has one of the most unique living libraries when it comes to its specialized vocabulary, terms, and phrases. Many people mistakenly believe science is just about mathematical formulas. But scientific literacy is essential to becoming a marketable employee and an active global citizen. Thus, GED assessments try to test a student's scientific literacy by assessing their understanding of specialized vocabulary, terms, and phrases in passages, charts, graphs, and tables. Understanding the numbers is not enough to pass this portion of the exam. All students of science must have a basic understanding of science vocabulary, terms, and phrases in order to shape their scientific worldview, drive their scientific inquiry, and enhance their scientific enterprise.

Every person has the ability to formulate their own scientific worldview. Science is not only highly complex, but it is also tentative in nature—humans make educated guesses about the information and data they collect. This information and data change over time, and, as a result, new vocabulary, terms, and phrases are constantly shadowing new discoveries, data analysis, and findings. Scientific inquiry may begin with simple questions, or hypotheses, but it may end with new concepts and terminology. The more questions scientists ask, the more necessary it is to apply words to both the preconceived questions and logical answers. Scientific inquiry, in many ways, is a combination of logic and imagination, and scientific imagination is usually the force driving the creation of new specialized vocabulary, terms, and phrases. Scientific enterprise is a larger process of checks and balances, which allows scientific findings to be debated through intellectual dialogue. Words are an important component of the peer review process of scientific enterprise. Theories and findings always come into question, and GED students are expected to not only comprehend the words of passages, but also question their findings through intertextual analysis and data analysis.

Below are a few tables of commonly used scientific terms and their definitions:

**Earth Science Terms**

- **Carbon cycle**: The series of biochemical processes that transfer carbon, the main component of many biological compounds and minerals, into different reservoirs of the Earth's environment; these reservoirs include the Earth's interior, its geological sediments, its oceans and waterways, its terrestrial biosphere, and its atmosphere.

- **Climate**: The weather in a particular location averaged over a period of time.

- **Equator**: The line separating the Northern and Southern Hemispheres.

- **Hemisphere**: Literally "half a sphere"; the earth is divided into two pairs of hemispheres (Northern and Southern, Eastern and Western).

- **Orbit**: The path of a celestial body in its revolution about another.

- **Prime meridian**: A human-made geographic line that runs South-to-North and separates the globe into two: the Eastern and Western Hemispheres.

- **Revolve**: Turn on or around an axis.

- **Seismic**: Caused by an earthquake or geological vibration.

- **Solar system**: The Sun and the celestial bodies (for example, Earth and the other planets) that orbit it.

- **Tectonic**: Pertaining to the structure or movement of the Earth's crust.

- **Volcano**: A geological feature composed of a mountain or crevice that spews hot gases and magma into the atmosphere when agitated.

- **Water**: The liquid that sustains life; a colorless, odorless liquid that helps shape geography (for example, rivers, lakes, streams, oceans, glaciers) and biological functions (for example, hydration, blood flow).

- **Weather**: Atmospheric conditions such as temperature and precipitation.

- **Wind**: Air moving from high pressure to low pressure.

| Chemistry Terms |
| --- |

- **Acid**: a corrosive chemical substance that has the ability to neutralize alkali; opposite of a base on the pH scale.

- **Atom**: The microscopic building blocks of matter and the foundations of chemistry; every solid, liquid, and gas is composed of atoms.

- **Atomic mass**: Typically expressed in atomic mass units, atomic mass is the mass of an atom, which can be figured out by adding protons and neutrons to find the mass number.

- **Base**: Bases are substances that are the opposite of acids on the pH scale; when mixed with acids they create a chemical reaction that produces salts.

- **Boiling point**: A point at which a liquid reaches a temperature that allows it to transform into a vapor; the normal boiling point of water is 100 degrees Celsius.

- **Oxidation**: The process or result of oxidizing or being oxidized.

- **Chemical formula**: An arrangement of elemental symbols and subscripts that convey the structure of a compound.

- **Chemical reaction**: A process that transforms the molecular or ionic composition of a substance.

- **Condensation**: The conversion of a vapor or gas to a liquid.

- **Conductor**: Any material that can transmit sound, heat, or electricity; normally used to describe metals and other materials that serve as conduits for electricity.

- **Covalent bond**: The sharing of electrons between two atoms; sometimes called a molecular bond.

- **Decompose**: (With reference to a chemical compound) break down or cause to break down into component elements or simpler constituents.

- **Electron**: Subatomic particles that carry a negative charge; carries a charge that is opposite of a proton.

- **Ion**: Atoms or molecules that are not neutral in their charge; they are positively or negatively charged.

- **Ionic bond**: A type of ionic cohesion that occurs when two oppositely charged atoms or molecules attract one another.

- **Liquid**: A substance that is neither a solid nor a gas, but flows freely in a fluid-like state that is akin to oil or water.

- **Radioactivity**: A process by which atoms become unstable and emit radiation; an unstable, disintegrating atom losing energy.

- **Gas**: An air-like state of matter that has traits that are distinguishable from solids and liquids; gases are known for their ability to expand rapidly throughout free space because of their air-like qualities; in fact, air itself is a combination of gases.

- **Salt**: A substance created from a mixture of a base and an acid.

- **Solution**: A liquid combination of a solute (a chemical that dissolves in a solution) and a solvent (a chemical that other substances dissolve into)

---

**Physics Terms**

- **Acceleration**: Acceleration in physics can be found by dividing the change in velocity by the change in time; it is the rate of the overall change in velocity as analyzed in relationship to the overall change in time.

- **Activation energy**: The amount of energy that is required for a chemical reaction to be initiated; normally quantified by a measurement known as Joules (J).

- **Amplitude**: The peak strength of a vibration or wave, which is measured by its repetition over a single period.

- **Density**: The degree of compactness of a substance.

- **Electromagnetic spectrum**: The spectrum that includes all different types of electromagnetic radiation, including radio waves, infrared waves, visible light waves, ultraviolet waves, X-rays, and Gamma rays

- **Energy**: The scientific name describing the phenomenon that produces heat, light, or motion in an object; in biology, it is produced by cells and the body in order to fuel human functions.

- **Frequency**: The number of occurrences within a given period of time.

- **Friction**: The resistance when a body is moved in contact with another.

- **Gravity**: Discovered by Sir Isaac Newton, it is an invisible force that draws two objects or celestial bodies close together; this force is displayed in space when celestial objects orbit around one another.

- **Momentum**: Used by scientists to quantify the motion object.

- **Resistance**: The impeding, slowing, or stopping effect exerted by one material thing on another.

- **Voltage**: The electrical potential between two items, expressed in a measurement known as volts.

- **Volume**: The amount of space that a three-dimensional geometrical object (whether solid, liquid, or gas) occupies.

**General Science Terms**

- **Atmosphere**: In science, it is the combinations of gases that contribute to the mass and shape of a celestial body, particularly the planet Earth.

- **Cause**: The beginning of a chain reaction or the root an event; a phenomenological starting point that produces an effect.

- **Conclusion**: A definitive decision, assumption, or statement that is rooted in logic.

- **Context**: In science, it is the places, perspectives, and circumstances that helped influence a particular experiment or hypothesis.

- **Effect**: An event, process, or phenomenon that results from another event, process, or phenomenon (which is known as a cause).

- **Experiment**: A scientific procedure that helps test hypotheses by carrying out the scientific method.

- **Evaluate**: To assess the nature, content, necessity, or effectiveness of a particular fact, theory, or philosophy.

- **Evidence**: The details or facts needed to prove a hypothesis, theory, case, or argument.

- **Fact**: Information that can be substantiated as true, using science or accepted theory; information that can be cross-referenced with others' understanding of reality.

- **Hypothesis**: A postulation or prediction that is assessed via the scientific method.

- **Inference**: An implicit conclusion that can be reached by combining the details of a document or experience with logically sound background knowledge.

- **Implication**: Something that is inferred.

- **Generalization**: The process of abstracting common properties of instances.

- **Research**: The process of consolidating information, ideas, and theories in a systematized fashion (typically via writing books, articles, or reports).

- **Scientific method**: The consolidation of ideas, observations, experiments, and theories, using tested hypotheses as a guide for understanding the world.

- **Scientist**: A researcher or practitioner devoted to the study of science, which includes: physics, Earth sciences, chemistry, and biology.

- **Theory**: A worldview, or a system of philosophies, ideas, perceptions, and conjectures, that tries to make sense of reality.

## Understanding and Explaining Information from the Passages

Comprehension is a key component to passing the science portion of the GED. As previously mentioned, test takers must be able to make sense of the information presented in various scientific sources. This

demands a well-rounded scientific literacy, which is the ability to understand complex scientific vocabulary, terms, and phrases. Making sense of science passages also requires scientific numeracy, which is the ability to understand scientific formulas, scientific equations, and scientific data. Literacy and numeracy are the skills that help test takers understand and explain the information in scientific passages.

Additionally, basic reasoning and language arts skills are helpful, such as understanding the purpose, details, and main idea of the passage. It is also important for test takers to recognize the method of arriving at the findings. Method is what sets apart a scientific text from a literary one. Each experiment or data collection technique has its own unique method. When reading scientific passages, test takers should be aware of the different ways that scientists carry out their experiments or data collection.

## Understanding Symbols, Terms, and Phrases in Science

Much like in mathematics, scientific texts rely on symbols to convey certain messages. These symbols may be in a text, or they may be in graphs, charts, tables, or pictures. These symbols are key components of evaluating data and communicating results.

In physics-based passages, students may encounter symbols and variables that are particular to that field of science. For instance, in studies focusing on electricity and magnetism, students are likely to encounter a symbol that looks like this: $\lambda$. This symbol is the Greek letter "lambda." Scientists uses the $\lambda$ symbol in order to communicate or compute a wavelength, measured in meters, of the electromagnetic spectrum. Scientists might also use a symbol like this: $f$. This is a symbol that represents the frequency, measured in hertz, of the electromagnetic spectrum.

In chemistry, symbols are also used on a regular basis. For instance, when discussing temperature, whether in Celsius or Fahrenheit, scientists often use the following symbol: °. Instead of saying 35 degrees, a scientist might just present the finding as 35°. Chemistry also uses symbols for the periodic table. For example, mercury is represented on the periodic table by using the following symbol: Hg. All elements have their own unique symbols.

In most cases, test takers have access to a table that offers definitions for each symbol. At times, the symbols have units or need units attached to them in order to explain the measure of a particular property. The International System of Units (SI) is usually used for science. Some of the most frequently used standard measures include: the meter (m) for length, the kilogram (kg) for mass, the ampere (A) for electric current, the kelvin (K) for temperature, and the mole (mol) for the amount of a substance. It never hurts to familiarize oneself with these commonly repeated symbols in scientific texts.

## Using Scientific Words to Express Science Information

Numbers and symbols alone, however, do not fully convey scientific knowledge. Scientists rely heavily on specialized words to express scientific information. Presenting graphs, tables, and charts without any words would create a lot of confusion. Scientists use words to enhance the numbers and symbols they record and evaluate. Scientific literacy, therefore, requires a specialized synthesis of numbers, symbols, and scientific words. Many of these words are not used much outside the field of science.

Take the Linnaean system of classification as an example. It was created by Carl Linnaeus, a Swedish scientist working in the 18th century. This classification system helps scientists organize all living organisms into different phyla, classes, orders, families, genera, and species. The Linnaean scheme for organizing living organisms is still in use today. However, the entire scheme is founded upon a highly specialized naming system that draws on an archaic Latin language. The American coyote for example

{}

carries a common name—most people refer to it simply as the "coyote," whether they are using French, Spanish, or English. However, its taxonomic name in the Linnaean system is *Canis latrans*. A difficult name like *Canis latrans* illustrates just how specialized scientific words can be. For someone taking the GED, it is not necessary to memorize the specialized names of all species and all chemical compounds. However, it is certainly important to understand that this highly specialized language may emerge within a passage to express scientific information. Together, along with symbols and numbers, these specialized words help create an entire scientific language. Scientific literacy at the GED level entails comprehending that such complex terms exist, and using context clues, dictionary definition keys, and other literacy-based tools to understand their meaning within the broader scope of the passage and its related assessment items.

# *Designing and Interpreting Science Experiments*

## Science Investigations

### Designing a Science Investigation
Human beings are, by nature, very curious. Long before the scientific method was established, people have been making observations and predicting outcomes, manipulating the physical world to create extraordinary things—from the first man-made fire in 6000 B.C.E. to the satellite that orbited Pluto in 2016. Although the history of the scientific method is sporadic and attributed to many different people, it remains the most reliable way to obtain and utilize knowledge about the observable universe. Designing a science investigation is based on the scientific method, which consists of the following steps:

- Make an observation
- Create a question
- Form a hypothesis
- Conduct an experiment
- Collect and analyze data
- Form a conclusion

The first step is to identify a problem based on an observation—the who, what, when, where, why, and how. An **observation** is the analysis of information using basic human senses: sight, sound, touch, taste, and smell. Observations can be two different types—qualitative or quantitative. A **qualitative observation** describes what is being observed, such as the color of a house or the smell of a flower. **Quantitative observations** measure what is being observed, such as the number of windows on a house or the intensity of a flower's smell on a scale of 1–5.

Observations lead to the identification of a problem, also called an **inference**. For example, if a fire truck is barreling down a busy street, the inferences could be:

- There's a fire.
- Someone is hurt.
- Some kid pulled the fire alarm at a local school.

Inferences are logical predictions based on experience or education that lead to the formation of a hypothesis.

## Forming and Testing a Hypothesis

A hypothesis is a testable explanation of an observed scenario and is presented in the form of a statement. It's an attempt to answer a question based on an observation, and it allows a scientist to predict an outcome. A hypothesis makes assumptions on the relationship between two different variables, and answers the question: "If I do this, what happens to that?"

In order to form a hypothesis, there must be an independent variable and a dependent variable that can be measured. The **independent variable** is the variable that is manipulated, and the **dependent variable** is the result of the change.

For example, suppose a student wants to know how light affects plant growth. Based upon what he or she already knows, the student proposes (hypothesizes) that the more light to which a plant is exposed, the faster it will grow.

- Observation: Plants exposed to lots of light seem to grow taller.
- Question: Will plants grow faster if there's more light available?
- Hypothesis: The more light the plant has, the faster it will grow.
- Independent variable: The amount of time exposed to light (able to be manipulated)
- Dependent variable: Plant growth (the result of the manipulation)

Once a hypothesis has been formed, it must be tested to determine whether it's true or false. (How to test a hypothesis is described in a subsequent section.) After it has been tested and validated as true over and over, then a hypothesis can develop into a theory, model, or law.

## Experimental Design

To test a hypothesis, one must conduct a carefully designed experiment. There are four basic requirements that must be present for an experiment to be valid:

- A control
- Variables
- A constant
- Repeated and collected data

The control is a standard to which the resultant findings are compared. It's the baseline measurement that allows for scientists to determine whether the results are positive or negative. For the example of light affecting plant growth, the control may be a plant that receives no light at all.

The independent variable is manipulated (a good way to remember this is I manipulate the Independent variable), and the dependent variable is the result of changes to the independent variable. In the plant example, the independent variable is the amount of time exposed to light, and the dependent variable is the resulting growth (or lack thereof) of the plant. For this experiment, there may be three plants—one that receives a minimal amount of light, the control, and one that receives a lot of light.

Finally, there must be constants in an experiment. A constant is an element of the experiment that remains unchanged. Constants are extremely important in minimizing inconsistencies within the experiment that may lead to results outside the parameters of the hypothesis. For example, some constants in the above case are that all plants receive the same amount of water, all plants are potted in the same kind of soil, the species of the plant used in each condition is the same, and the plants are

stored at the same temperature. If, for instance, the plants received different amounts of water as well as light, it would be impossible to tell whether the plants responded to changes in water or light.

Once the experiment begins, a disciplined scientist must always record the observations in meticulous detail, usually in a journal. A good journal includes dates, times, and exact values of both variables and constants. Upon reading this journal, a different scientist should be able to clearly understand the experiment and recreate it exactly. The journal includes all collected data, or any observed changes. In this case, the data is rates of plant growth, as well as any other phenomena that occurred as a result of the experiment. A well-designed experiment also includes repetition in order to get the most accurate possible readings and to account for any errors, so several trials may be conducted.

Even in the presence of diligent constants, there are an infinite number of reasons that an experiment can (and will) go wrong, known as sources of error. All experimental results are inherently accepted as imperfect, if ever so slightly, because experiments are conducted by human beings, and no instrument can measure anything perfectly. The goal of scientists is to minimize those errors to the best of their ability.

## Identifying and Explaining Independent and Dependent Variables

In an experiment, variables are the key to analyzing data, especially when data is in a graph or table. Variables can represent anything, including objects, conditions, events, and amounts of time.

**Covariance** is a general term referring to how two variables move in relation to each other. Take for example an employee that gets paid by the hour. For them, hours worked and total pay have a positive covariance. As hours worked increases, so does pay.

**Constant variables** remain unchanged by the scientist across all trials. Because they are held constant for all groups in an experiment, they aren't being measured in the experiment, and they are usually ignored. Constants can either be controlled by the scientist directly like the nutrition, water, and sunlight given to plants, or they can be selected by the scientist specifically for an experiment like using a certain animal species or choosing to investigate only people of a certain age group.

**Independent variables** are also controlled by the scientist, but they are the same only for each group or trial in the experiment. Each group might be composed of students that all have the same color of car or each trial may be run on different soda brands. The independent variable of an experiment is what is being indirectly tested because it causes change in the dependent variables.

**Dependent variables** experience change caused by the independent variable and are what is being measured or observed. For example, college acceptance rates could be a dependent variable of an experiment that sorted a large sample of high school students by an independent variable such as test scores. In this experiment, the scientist groups the high school students by the independent variable (test scores) to see how it affects the dependent variable (their college acceptance rates).

Note that most variables can be held constant in one experiment, but also serve as the independent variable or a dependent variable in another. For example, when testing how well a fertilizer aids plant growth, its amount of sunlight should be held constant for each group of plants, but if the experiment is being done to determine the proper amount of sunlight a plant should have, the amount of sunlight is an independent variable because it is necessarily changed for each group of plants.

## Identifying and Improving Hypotheses for Science Investigations

When presented with fundamental, scientific concepts, it is important to read for understanding. The most basic skill in achieving this literacy is to understand the concept of hypothesis and moreover, to be able to identify it in a particular passage. A **hypothesis** is a proposed idea that needs further investigation in order to be proven true or false. While it can be considered an educated guess, a hypothesis goes more in depth in its attempt to explain something that is not currently accepted within scientific theory. It requires further experimentation and data gathering to test its validity and is subject to change, based on scientifically conducted test results. Being able to read a science passage and understand its main purpose, including any hypotheses, helps the test taker understand data-driven evidence. It helps the test taker to be able to correctly answer questions about the science excerpt they are asked to read.

When reading to identify a hypothesis, a test taker should ask, "What is the passage trying to establish? What is the passage's main idea? What evidence does the passage contain that either supports or refutes this idea?" Asking oneself these questions will help identify a hypothesis. Additionally, hypotheses are logical statements that are testable and use very precise language.

Review the following hypothesis example:

Consuming excess sugar in the form of beverages has a greater impact on childhood obesity and subsequent weight gain than excessive sugar from food.

While this is likely a true statement, it is still only a conceptual idea in a text passage regarding how sugar consumption affects childhood obesity, unless the passage also contains tested data that either proves or disproves the statement. A test taker could expect the rest of the passage to cite data proving that children who drink empty calories and don't exercise will, in fact, be obese.

A hypothesis goes further in that, given its ability to be proven or disproven, it may result in further hypotheses that require extended research. For example, the hypothesis regarding sugar consumption in drinks, after undergoing rigorous testing, may lead scientists to state another hypothesis such as the following:

Consuming excess sugar in the form of beverages as opposed to food items is a habit found in mostly sedentary children.

This new, working hypothesis further focuses not just on the source of an excess of calories, but tries an "educated guess" that empty caloric intake has a direct, subsequent impact on physical behavior.

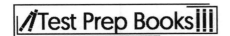 
The data-driven chart below is similar to an illustration a test taker might see in relation to the hypothesis on sugar consumption in children:

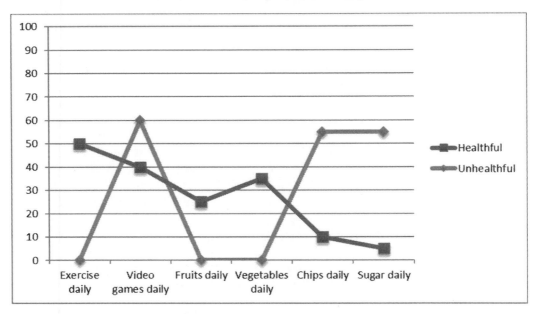

**Behaviors of Healthy and Unhealthy Kids**

While this guide will address other data-driven passages a test taker could expect to see within a given science excerpt, note that the hypothesis regarding childhood sugar intake and rate of exercise has undergone scientific examination and yielded results that support its truth.

When reading a science passage to determine its hypothesis, a test taker should look for a concept that attempts to explain a phenomenon, is testable, logical, precisely worded, and yields data-driven results. The test taker should scan the presented passage for any word or data-driven clues that will help identify the hypothesis, and then be able to correctly answer test questions regarding the hypothesis based on their critical thinking skills.

## Identifying Possible Errors in a Science Investigation and Changing the Design to Correct Them

For a hypothesis to be proven true or false, all experiments are subject to multiple trials in order to verify accuracy and precision. A measurement is **accurate** if the observed value is close to the "true value." For example, if someone measured the pH of water at 6.9, this measurement would be considered accurate (the pH of water is 7). On the other hand, a measurement is **precise** if the measurements are consistent—that is, if they are reproducible. If someone had a series of values for a pH of water that were 6.9, 7.0, 7.2, and 7.3, their measurements would not be precise. However, if all measured values were 6.9, or the average of these values was 6.9 with a small range, then their measurements would be precise. Measurements can fall into the following categories:

- Both accurate and precise
- Accurate but not precise
- Precise but not accurate
- Neither accurate nor precise

The accuracy and precision of observed values most frequently correspond to the amount of error present in the experiment. Aside from general carelessness, there are two primary types of error: random and systematic. **Random errors** are unpredictable variations in the experiment that occur by chance. They can be difficult to detect, but they can often be nullified using a statistical analysis and minimized by taking repeated measurements and taking an average. **Systematic errors** occur when there are imperfections in the design of the experiment itself—usually errors that affect the accuracy of the measurements. These errors can be minimized by using the most accurate equipment available and by taking proper care of instruments and measuring techniques. Common examples of errors are listed below.

| Random | Systematic |
|---|---|
| Environmental factors (random changes in vibration, temperature, humidity, etc.) | Poorly maintained instruments |
| | Old or out-of-date instruments |
| Differences in instrument use among scientists | Faulty calibration of instruments |
| Errors in judgment—can be affected by state of mind | Reading the instruments at an angle (parallax error) or other faulty reading errors |
| Incorrectly recorded observations | Not accounting for lag time |

The most basic method to account for the possibility of errors is to take an average (also called a **mean**) of all observed values. To do so, one must divide the number of measurements taken from the sum of all measurements.

$$\frac{Sum\ of\ Measurements}{Total\ \#\ of\ Measurements}$$

For the above example of the pH values, the average is calculated by finding the sum of the pH values ascertained and dividing by the number of values recorded.

$$\frac{6.9 + 7.0 + 7.2 + 7.3}{4} = 7.1$$

The more observations recorded, the greater the precision. It's important to first assess the accuracy of measurements before proceeding to collect multiple trials of data. If a particular trial results in measurements that are vastly different from the average, it may indicate that a random or systematic error occurred during the trial. When this happens, a scientist might decide to "throw out" the trial and run the experiment again.

## Identifying the Strengths and Weaknesses of Different Types of Science Investigations

In order to address the strengths and weaknesses of different types of scientific investigations, GED test takers must first strengthen their capacity for scientific literacy and numeracy. It is important to familiarize oneself with methods for decoding highly specialized scientific terms, formulas, and symbols. Additionally, test takers can take the following suggestions to help identify unique weaknesses and strengths in different types of scientific investigations:

- Using critical analysis, test takers begin asking questions about the accuracy of the methods used to collect, analyze, and display data. They should carefully look at text and graphics that show scientific findings.

- Test takers should determine whether or not the words, data, and symbols provided by the author actually offer information that is relevant for testing a hypothesis or making an inference.

- When two or more passages on the same topic are offered, test takers should cross-analyze the findings to determine what data is accurate or relevant and which findings are most objective.

- Although scientific research strives for objectivity, test takers should highlight any subjective biases that may be embedded in a text. In particular, they should be aware of certain historical or ethical biases that might appear.

- Test takers should double check for any computational inaccuracies.

- Test takers should make suggestions for better ways to present the findings in both texts and visual images.

## Using Evidence to Draw Conclusions or Make Predictions

### Deciding Whether Conclusions are Supported by Data
Drawing conclusions is the process of analyzing patterns in data and determining whether the relationship is **causal**, meaning that one variable is the cause of the change in the other. There are many correlations that aren't casual, such as a city where alcohol sales increase as crime increases. Although there's a positive correlation between the two, crime may not be the factor that causes an increase in alcohol sales. There could be other factors, such as an increase in unemployment, which increases both alcohol sales and crime rates. Although crime and alcohol sales are positively correlated, they aren't causally correlated.

For this reason, it's important for scientists to carefully design their experiments with all the appropriate constants to ensure that the relationships are causal. If a relationship is determined to be causal by isolating the variables from all other factors, only then can conclusions be drawn based on data. In the plant growth experiment, the conclusion is that light affects plant growth because the data shows they are causally correlated since the two variables were entirely isolated.

### Making Conclusions Based on Data
The Science section of the GED will contain one data-driven science passage that require the test taker to examine evidence within a particular type of graphic. The test taker will then be required to interpret the data and answer questions demonstrating their ability to draw logical conclusions.

In general, there are two types of data: qualitative and quantitative. Science passages may contain both, but simply put, **quantitative** data is reflected numerically and qualitative is not. **Qualitative** data is based on its qualities. In other words, qualitative data tends to present information more in subjective generalities (for example, relating to size or appearance). Quantitative data is based on numerical findings such as percentages. Quantitative data will be described in numerical terms. While both types of data are valid, the test taker will more likely be faced with having to interpret quantitative data through one or more graphic(s), and then be required to answer questions regarding the numerical data. A test taker should take the time to learn the skills it takes to interpret quantitative data so that they can make sound conclusions.

An example of a line graph is as follows:

**Cell Phone Use in Kiteville, 2000-2006**

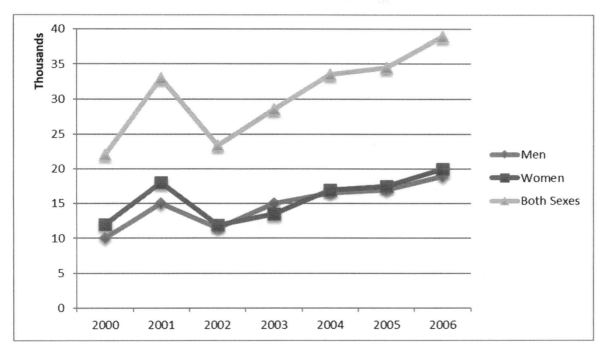

A **line graph** presents quantitative data on both horizontal (side to side) and vertical (up and down) axes. It requires the test taker to examine information across varying data points. When reading a line graph, a test taker should pay attention to any headings, as these indicate a title for the data it contains. In the above example, the test taker can anticipate the line graph contains numerical data regarding the use of cellphones during a certain time period. From there, a test taker should carefully read any outlying words or phrases that will help determine the meaning of data within the horizontal and vertical axes. In this example, the vertical axis displays the total number of people in increments of 5,000. Horizontally, the graph displays yearly markers, and the reader can assume the data presented accounts for a full calendar year. In addition, the line graph also uses different shapes to mark its data points. Some data points represent the number of men. Some data points represent the number of women, and a third type of data point represents the number of both sexes combined.

A test taker may be asked to read and interpret the graph's data, then answer questions about it. For example, the test may ask, *In which year did men seem to decrease cellphone use?* then require the test taker to select the correct answer. Similarly, the test taker may encounter a question such as *Which year yielded the highest number of cellphone users overall?* The test taker should be able to identify the correct answer as 2006.

A **bar graph** presents quantitative data through the use of lines or rectangles. The height and length of these lines or rectangles corresponds to the magnitude of the numerical data for that particular category or attribute. The data presented may represent information over time, showing shaded data

over time or over other defined parameters. A bar graph will also utilize horizontal and vertical axes. An example of a bar graph is as follows:

**Population Growth in Major U.S. Cities**

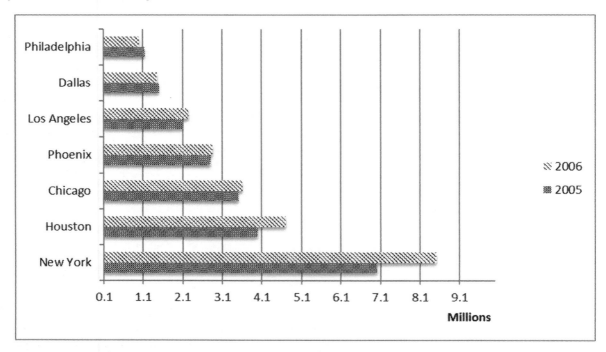

Reading the data in a bar graph is similar to the skills needed to read a line graph. The test taker should read and comprehend all heading information, as well as information provided along the horizontal and vertical axes. Note that the graph pertains to the population of some major U.S. cities. The "values" of these cities can be found along the left side of the graph, along the vertical axis. The population values can be found along the horizontal axes. Notice how the graph uses shaded bars to depict the change in population over time, as the heading indicates. Therefore, when the test taker is asked a question such as, *Which major U.S. city experienced the greatest amount of population growth during the depicted two year cycle,* the reader should be able to determine a correct answer of New York. It is important to pay particular attention to color, length, data points, and both axes, as well as any outlying header information in order to be able to answer graph-like test questions.

A **circle graph** (also sometimes referred to as a **pie chart**) presents quantitative data in the form of a circle. The same principles apply: the test taker should look for numerical data within the confines of the circle itself but also note any outlying information that may be included in a header, footer, or to the side of the circle. A circle graph will not depict horizontal or vertical axis information but will instead rely

on the reader's ability to visually take note of segmented circle pieces and apply information accordingly. An example of a circle graph is as follows:

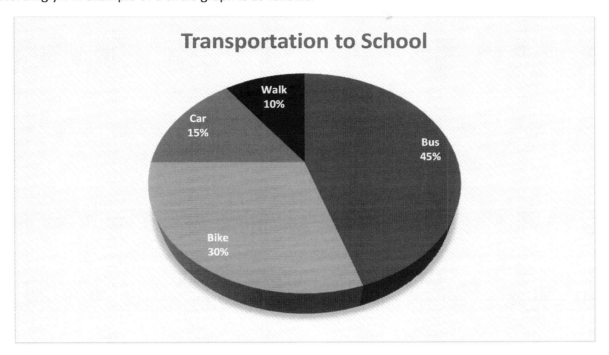

Notice the heading "Transportation to School." This should indicate to the test taker that the topic of the circle graph is how people traditionally get to school. To the right of the graph, the reader should comprehend that the data percentages contained within it directly correspond to the method of transportation. In this graph, the data is represented through the use shades and pattern. Each transportation method has its own shade. For example, if the test taker was then asked, *Which method of school transportation is most widely utilized,* the reader should be able to identify school bus as the correct answer.

Be wary of test questions that ask test takers to draw conclusions based on information that is not present. For example, it is not possible to determine, given the parameters of this circle graph, whether the population presented is of a particular gender or ethnic group. This graph does not represent data from a particular city or school district. It does not distinguish between student grade levels and, although the reader could infer that the typical student must be of driving age if cars are included, this is not necessarily the case. Elementary school students may rely on parents or others to drive them by personal methods. Therefore, do not read too much into data that is not presented. Only rely on the quantitative data that is presented in order to answer questions.

A **scatter plot** or **scatter diagram** is a graph that depicts quantitative data across plotted points. It will involve at least two sets of data. It will also involve horizontal and vertical axes.

An example of a scatter plot is as follows:

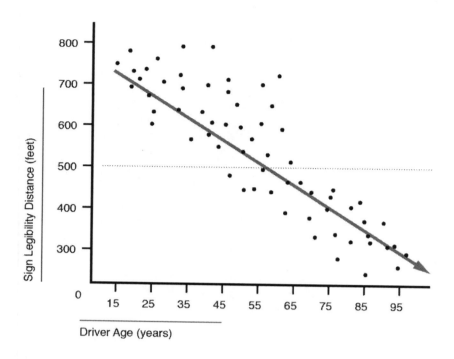

The skills needed to address a scatter plot are essentially the same as in other graph examples. Note any topic headings, as well as horizontal or vertical axis information. In the sample above, the reader can determine the data addresses a driver's ability to correctly and legibly read road signs as related to their age. Again, note the information that is absent. The test taker is not given the data to assess a time period, location, or driver gender. It simply requires the reader to note an approximate age to the ability to correctly identify road signs from a distance measured in feet. Notice that the overall graph also displays a trend. In this case, the data indicates a negative one and possibly supports the hypothesis that as a driver ages, their ability to correctly read a road sign at over 500 feet tends to decline over time. If the test taker were to be asked, *At what approximation in feet does a sixteen-year-old driver correctly see and read a street sign,* the answer would be the option closest to 500 feet.

Reading and examining scientific data in excerpts involves all of a reader's contextual reading, data interpretation, drawing logical conclusions based only on the information presented, and their application of critical thinking skills across a set of interpretive questions. Thorough comprehension and attention to detail is necessary to achieve test success.

## Making Predictions Based on Data

Science is amazing in that it actually allows people to predict the future and see into the past with a certain degree of accuracy. Using numerical correlations created from quantitative data, one can see in a general way what will happen to *y* when something happens to *x*.

The best way to get a useful overview of quantitative data to facilitate predictions is to use a scatter plot, which plots each data point individually. As shown above, there may be slight fluctuations from the correlation line, so one may not be able to predict what happens with *every* change, but he or she will be able to have a general idea of what is going to happen to y with a change in x. To demonstrate, the graph with a line of best fit created from the plant growth experiment is below.

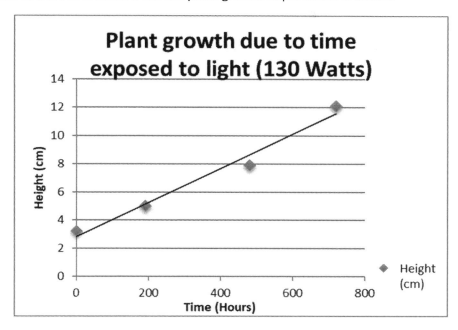

Using the trend line within the data, one can estimate what will happen to plant growth at a given length of time exposed to light. For example, it can be estimated that with 700 hours of time, the plant is expected to grow to a height of about 11 cm. The plant may not grow to exactly 11 cm, but it will likely grow to about that height based on previous data. This process allows scientists to draw conclusions based on data.

## Science Theories and Processes

Theories, models, and laws have one thing in common: *they develop on the basis of scientific evidence that has been tested and verified by multiple researchers on many different occasions*. Listed below are their exact definitions:

- **Theory:** An explanation of natural patterns or occurrences—i.e., the theory of relativity, the kinetic theory of gases, etc.

- **Model:** A representation of a natural pattern or occurrence that's difficult or impossible to experience directly, usually in the form of a picture or 3-D representation—i.e., Bohr's atomic model, the double-helix model of DNA, etc.

- **Law:** A mathematical or concise description of a pattern or occurrence in the observable universe—i.e., Newton's law of gravity, the laws of thermodynamics, etc.

The terms *theory, model,* and *law* are often used interchangeably in the sciences, although there's an essential difference: theories and models are used to explain *how* and *why* something happens, while

laws describe exactly *what* happens. A common misconception is that theories develop into laws. But theories and models never become laws because they inherently describe different things.

| Type | Function | Examples |
|------|----------|----------|
| Theory | To explain how and why something happens | Einstein's Theory of Special Relativity<br>The Big Bang Theory |
| Model | To represent how and why something happens | A graphical model or drawing of an atom |
| Laws | To describe exactly what happens | $E = mc^2$<br>$F = ma$<br>$PV = nRT$ |

In order to ensure that scientific theories are consistent, scientists continually gather information and evidence on existing theories to improve their accuracy.

# *Using Numbers and Graphics in Science*

## Science Formulas and Statistics

### Applying Science Formulas

Scientific inquiry includes the fields of chemistry and physics. It incorporates mathematical problems, which are described with science formulas. Science formulas cannot be used haphazardly. In fact, these science formulas have very specific standards for use. These formulas stand at the intersection of mathematics and science. And, like math, science extracts all of its meaning through its specificity. On any standardized science test, the biggest challenge is knowing when to employ a particular science formula. All formulas are provided on the examination. Thus, the test taker does not need to memorize these formulas; they just need to use the formulas correctly.

Take the dynamics of motion as an example. In science, dynamics is the study of the relationship between motion and the forces affecting motion. In science, there is a formula that is universally used for force: F = m/a. This equation is shorthand for force (F) equals mass (m) divided by (/) acceleration (a). This equation is used to describe the relationship with three components of science: force, mass, and acceleration. For instance, an object remains at rest unless the force (F) is strong enough to move the mass (m) and cause the object to accelerate (a).

However, the equation F = m/a would NOT be helpful for figuring out the weight of an object. The weight of an object demands another formula: $W = m \times g$. This formula is shorthand for weight (W) equals mass (m) times (×) gravity (g). Force and weight have their own scientific formulas. The formulas do not need to be memorized, but every test taker needs to know *when* and *how* to use a particular formula. Otherwise, their results will be incorrect.

## Using Statistics to Describe Science Data

The most common relationship examined in an experiment is between two variables (independent and dependent), most often referred to as *x* and *y*. The independent variable (*x*) is displayed on the horizontal axis of a coordinate plane, and the dependent variable (*y*) is displayed on the vertical axis.

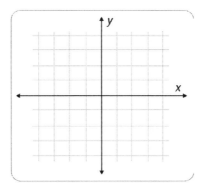

The placement of the variables in this way provides a visual representation of what happens to *y* when *x* is manipulated. In analyzing trends, *x* is used to predict *y*, and since *y* is the result of *x*, then *x* comes before *y* in time. For example, in the experiment on plant growth, the hours the plant was exposed to light had to happen before growth could occur.

When analyzing the relationship between the variables, scientists will consider the following questions:

- Does *y* increase or decrease with *x*, or does it do both?

- If it increases or decreases, how fast does it change?

- Does *y* stay steady through certain values of *x*, or does it jump dramatically from one value to the other?

- Is there a strong relationship? If given a value of *x*, can one predict what will happen to *y*?

If, in general, *y* increases as *x* increases, or *y* decreases and *x* decreases, it is known as a **positive correlation**. The data from the plant experiment show a positive correlation—as time exposed to light (*x*) increases, plant growth (*y*) increases. If the variables trend in the opposite direction of each other—that is, if *y* increases as *x* decreases, or vice versa—it is called a **negative correlation**. If there doesn't seem to be any visible pattern to the relationship, it is referred to as **no** or **zero correlation**.

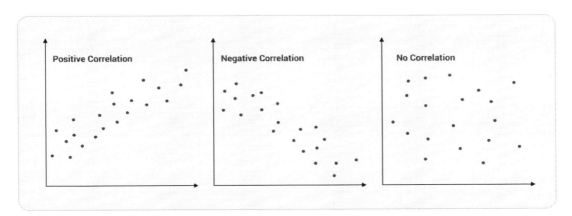

Science

Experiments that show positive or negative correlation within their data indicate that the variables are related. This allows scientists to make predictions based on the data.

## Probability and Sampling in Science

### Determining the Probability or Likelihood of Something Happening

A **simple event** consists of only one outcome. The most popular simple event is flipping a coin, which results in either heads or tails. A **compound event** results in more than one outcome and consists of more than one simple event. An example of a compound event is flipping a coin while tossing a die. The result is either heads or tails on the coin and a number from one to six on the die. The probability of a simple event is calculated by dividing the number of possible outcomes by the total number of outcomes. Therefore, the probability of obtaining heads on a coin is $\frac{1}{2}$, and the probability of rolling a 6 on a die is $\frac{1}{6}$. The probability of compound events is calculated using the basic idea of the probability of simple events. If the two events are independent, the probability of one outcome is equal to the product of the probabilities of each simple event. For example, the probability of obtaining heads on a coin and rolling a 6 is equal to:

$$\frac{1}{2} \times \frac{1}{6} = \frac{1}{12}$$

The probability of either A or B occurring is equal to the sum of the probabilities minus the probability that both A and B will occur. Therefore, the probability of obtaining either heads on a coin or rolling a 6 on a die is:

$$\frac{1}{2} + \frac{1}{6} - \frac{1}{12} = \frac{7}{12}$$

The two events aren't mutually exclusive because they can happen at the same time. If two events are mutually exclusive, and the probability of both events occurring at the same time is zero, the probability of event A or B occurring equals the sum of both probabilities. An example of calculating the probability of two mutually exclusive events is determining the probability of pulling a king or a queen from a deck of cards. The two events cannot occur at the same time.

### Using a Sample to Answer Science Questions

When conducting a scientific experiment, once a hypothesis is conceived, it is important for scientists and students to adequately test their hypothesis. In order to test a hypothesis, scientists and students must analyze a particular **sample** of the larger population. Every sample must be composed of two comparable groups: a treatment (or experimental) group and a control group. Control groups can be used to acquire baseline measurements for analysis. When conducting the experiment, the treatment groups are the ones affected by experimental manipulation. From this sample, scientists and students can compare relevant data from each group to test their hypothesis.

If the experimental manipulation is effective, then scientists and students notice evident differences in the data collected from each sub-sample. In some cases, when scientists are merely carrying out observations, they may not split the sample into any subgroups but instead try to create new sub-samples through observation and data collection. Regardless of the approach, these kinds of samples, whether physical or observatory, are necessary for conducting scientific research. For the GED, test takers should be aware of how scientists use these samples, how they display their results, and how they compare samples through qualitative and quantitative data. Additionally, they should be prepared

to extrapolate findings from the sample, comparing it to the larger population or other subpopulations. This extrapolation helps test takers better understand whether the sample is a good representation of the larger population or comparative to other subpopulations.

## Using Counting to Solve Science Problems

In some instances, test takers have to use counting in order to solve science problems. Because the subject is science, a lot of quantitative data is offered in the form of charts, graphs, and tables. Additionally, numbers are referred to in science passages. At times, problems can be solved by counting the quantitative data offered in the text, charts, graphs, or tables. For example, if the scientific experiment compares two sub-samples of a larger sample of animals exposed to nuclear radiation, then the test taker may have to compute or count the number of animals from each sub-sample that are impacted by the radiation. Alternatively, test takers may have to compute or count the total number of animals from the larger population impacted by radiation. The author may choose to illustrate their findings with just text, just graphics, or a combination of text and graphics. Basic mathematics come in handy whenever quantitative data is offered. Basic mathematics consists of addition, subtraction, multiplication, and division. Complex formulas are not needed in these cases, but often test takers have to convey their ability to do basic arithmetic computations.

## Presenting Science Information Using Numbers, Symbols, and Graphics

## Using Graphics to Display Science Information

Observations made during a scientific experiment are organized and presented as data. Data can be collected in a variety of ways, depending on the purpose of the experiment. In testing how light exposure affects plant growth, for example, the data collected would be changes in the height of the plant relative to the amount of light it received. The easiest way to organize collected data is to use a **data table**.

A data table always contains a title that relates the two variables in the experiment. Each column or row must contain the units of measurement in the heading only. See the below example (note: this is not actual data).

| Plant Growth During Time Exposed to Light (130 Watts) | |
|---|---|
| Time (Hours) | Height (cm) |
| 0 | 3.2 |
| 192 | 5.0 |
| 480 | 7.9 |
| 720 | 12.1 |

Data must be presented in a concise, coherent way. Most data are presented in graph form. The fundamental rule for creating a graph based on data is that the independent variable (i.e., amount of time exposed to light) is on the x-axis, and the dependent variable (i.e., height of plant) is on the y-axis.

There are many types of graphs that a person may choose to use depending on which best represents the data.

The **illustrative diagram** provides a graphic representation or picture of some process. Questions may address specific details of the process depicted in the graphic. For example, "At which stage of the sliding filament theory of muscle contraction does the physical length of the fibers shorten (and contract)?"

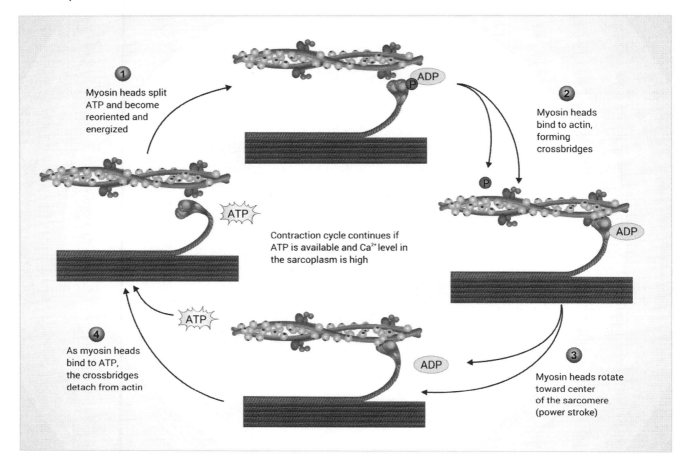

Bar graphs depict the passage data as parallel lines of varying heights. GED bar graphs will be printed in black and white. Data may be oriented vertically or horizontally. Questions may ask, "During the fall season, in what habitat do bears spend the most time?"

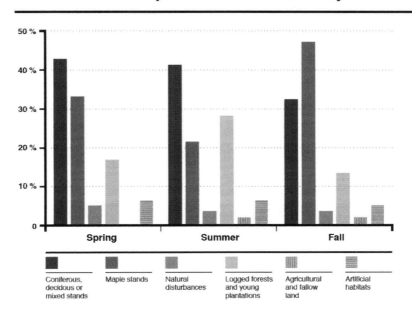

Bar graphs can also be horizontal, like the graph below.

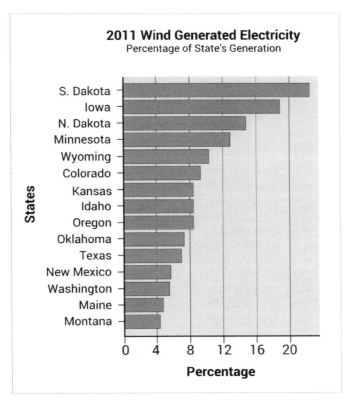

Recall that scatter plots provide a visual representation of the passage data along the x- and y-axes. This representation indicates the nature of the relationship between the two variables. It is important to note that correlation doesn't equal causation. The relationship may be linear, curvilinear, positive, negative, inverse, or there may be no relationship. Questions may ask "What is the relationship between x and y?"

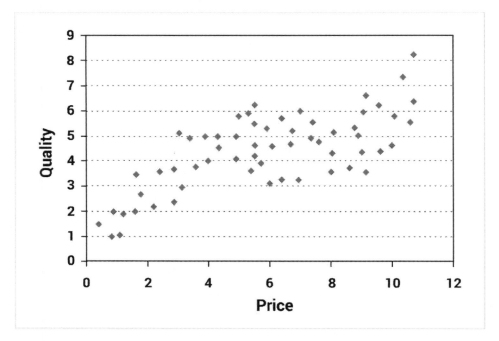

Line graphs are scatter plots that compare and contrast the relationships between two or more data sets. The horizontal axis represents the passage data sets that are compared over time. The vertical axis is the scale for measurement of that data. The scale points are equidistant from one another. There will always be a title for the line graph. Questions related to line graphs might ask," Which of the following conclusions is supported by the provided graph of tropical storms?"

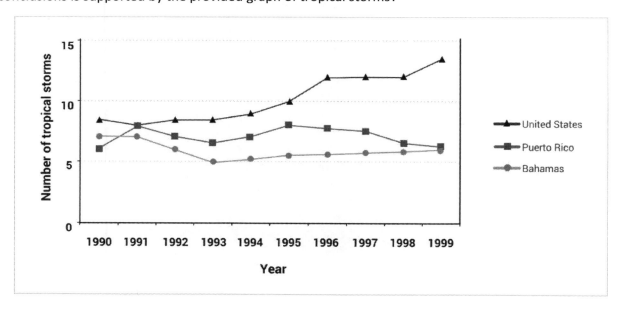

A **region graph** is a visual representation of the passage data set used to display the properties of a given substance under different conditions or at different points in time. Questions relating to this graph may ask, "According to the figure, what is the temperature range associated with liquid nitrogen?"

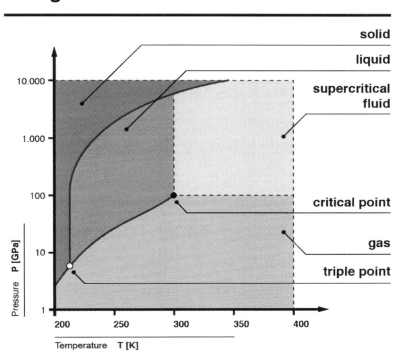

A pie or circle graph is used when the data sum to 100%, such as the percentage of students in each high school class interested in a trip to a local museum.

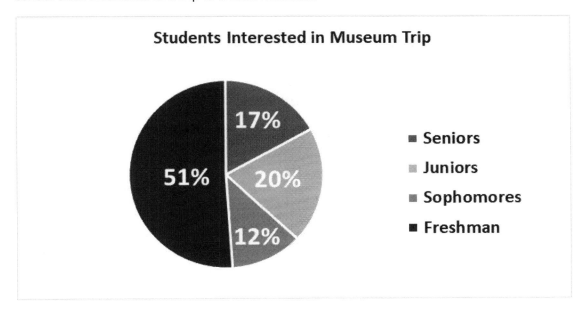

## Using Numbers or Symbols to Display Science Information

### Scientific Notation

Scientific notation is the conversion of extremely small or large numbers into a format that is easier to comprehend and manipulate. It changes the number into a product of two separate numbers: a digit term and an exponential term.

$$Scientific\ notation = digit\ term \times exponential\ term$$

To put a number into scientific notation, one should use the following steps:

- Move the decimal point to after the first non-zero number to find the digit number.
- Count how many places the decimal point was moved in step 1.
- Determine if the exponent is positive or negative.
- Create an exponential term using the information from steps 2 and 3.
- Combine the digit term and exponential term to get scientific notation.

For example, to put 0.0000098 into scientific notation, the decimal should be moved so that it lies between the last two numbers: 000009.8. This creates the digit number:

$$9.8$$

Next, the number of places that the decimal point moved is determined; to get between the 9 and the 8, the decimal was moved six places to the right. It may be helpful to remember that a decimal moved to the right creates a negative exponent, and a decimal moved to the left creates a positive exponent. Because the decimal was moved six places to the right, the exponent is negative.

Now, the exponential term can be created by using the base 10 (this is *always* the base in scientific notation) and the number of places moved as the exponent, in this case:

$$10^{-6}$$

Finally, the digit term and the exponential term can be combined as a product. Therefore, the scientific notation for the number 0.0000098 is:

$$9.8 \times 10^{-6}$$

### Significant Figures

Significant figures are numbers that contribute meaning to a measurement. Reporting values in significant figures reduces unnecessary numbers while increasing accuracy and minimizing confusion. For example, if a scale measures a sample to four significant figures, say, 12.56 grams, it would be inaccurate to write the number as 12.5600, because it very well may be more or less than 12.5600, but the scale cannot provide the measurement to that degree of precision. Therefore, all data must be presented with the number of figures that accurately reflect the precision of the measuring instrument.

There are rules for identifying the number of significant figures in a number:

- All non-zero digits are significant. For example, the number 23 has two significant figures, and the number 165.74 has five significant figures.

- Any zeros between two non-zero numbers are significant.

- For example, the number 203 has three significant figures: 2, 0, and 3.

- Leading zeros are never significant.

- For example, the value 0.000034 has two significant figures: 3 and 4.

- Trailing zeros (those following a non-zero number) are only significant after a decimal point.

- For example, the value 0.034500 has five significant figures: 3, 4, 5, 0, and 0.

- In numbers without decimals, trailing zeros may or may not be significant.

- For example, a number like 1,600 may have two or four significant figures, depending on if the number is precise to the nearest unit (four) or if it's just an estimate (two).

Scientific notation is often used to reduce numbers to significant figures. In scientific notation, the exponent doesn't count as a significant figure. For example, to reduce the number 0.0000098 (which has two significant figures) into a number that only has significant figures, it can be written in scientific notation;

$$9.8 \times 10^{-6}$$

where the 9 and the 8 are the only significant numbers. It's important to notice here that the number of significant figures remains the same, but one has an unnecessary number of zeros, and the other has none.

## Different Ways in Which Scientific Information is Presented

The purpose of scientific experimentation is to gain knowledge and share it with others, particularly in the scientific field. In scientific practice, there are structures in place that allow scientists to share new ideas and groundbreaking discoveries with other scientists and potentially the public.

The following lists some outlets that scientists use to present information:

- **Scientific journals**: Scientific journals are magazines that publish scholarly articles relating to important discoveries or new research conducted by scientists. The articles in scientific journals are peer-reviewed, which means that other experts in the scientific community review the information for fallacies or bias before the information is published. Therefore, scholarly journals publish credible information written and reviewed by experts in the field.

- **Academic conferences**: In order to formally present new developments and meet up with others in the field, scientists frequently hold and attend scientific conferences. Presenting information is usually given by a panel or keynote speakers. Networking is an especially important part of academic conferences, as up-and-coming scientists have the opportunity to meet noteworthy experts in their field.

- **Popular media**: Communicating new research to the public is also an important way for scientists to gain acknowledgement and funding for their work. Scientists are able to reach a large audience by using newspapers, magazines, or TV stations. A few examples of popular media outlets are *National Geographic*, *The New York Times*, and *CNN*, among others.

# GED Science Questions

More so than simply presenting fact-based science questions that assess the test taker's knowledge of scientific concepts, the Science section of the GED primarily includes passage- and graphic-based questions. These questions test one's ability to interpret scientific data and concepts represented in a graphical format instead of written text. The following provides descriptions about what to expect:

## Data Representation

Scientific data will be presented in tables, graphs, diagrams, or models designed to test one's ability to interpret scientific data represented in a graphical format instead of written text. These questions do *not* necessarily examine scientific content knowledge (e.g., the equation for photosynthesis); rather, they test students' ability to interpret raw data represented in a table or graph. Therefore, it's possible to do well on this portion of the exam without a detailed understanding of the scientific topic at hand. Questions may ask for factual information, identification of data trends, or graph calculations. For example:

- Based on the attached graph, how did Study 1 differ from Study 2?
- What is the nature of the relationship between Experiment 1 and Experiment 2?
- What is *x* at the given *y*-value?

## Research Summaries

Passages present the design, implementation, and conclusion of various scientific experiments. These passages typically contain 5 or 6 questions designed to test one's ability to identify the following:

- What question is the experiment trying to answer?
- What is the researcher's predicted answer to the question?
- How did the researchers test the hypotheses?
- Based on data obtained from the experiments, was the prediction correct?
- What would happen if . . .?
- 2 × 2 Matrix questions: "Yes, because . . ." or "No, because . . ."

## Conflicting Viewpoints

This section will present a disagreement between two scientists about a specific scientific hypothesis or concept. The opinions of each researcher are presented in two separate passages. There are two formats for these questions. The test taker must demonstrate an understanding of the content or compare and contrast the main differences between the two opinions. For example:

- Based on the data presented by Scientist 1, which of the following is correct?
- What is the main difference between the conclusions of Expert A and Expert B?

## Elements of Science Passages

### Short Answer Questions

Short answer questions are usually one to five words long and require the reader to recall basic facts presented in the passage.

*An example answer choice*: "Research group #1 finished last."

### Long Answer Questions

Long answer questions are composed of one to three sentences that require the reader to make comparisons, summaries, generalizations, or conclusions about the passage.

*An example answer choice*: "Scientist 2 disagreed with Scientist 1 on the effects of Bisphenol A pollution and its presumed correlation to birth defects in mice and humans. Scientist 2 proposes that current environmental Bisphenol A levels are not sufficient to cause adverse effects on human health."

### Fact Questions

Fact questions are the most basic type of question on the test. They ask the reader to recall a specific term, definition, number, or meaning.

*An example question/answer*: "Which of the following organisms was present in fresh water samples from Pond #1?"
    a. Water flea
    b. Dragonfly nymph
    c. Snail
    d. Tadpole

## Graphs

As mentioned, there are different graph types used in the GED Science Test to represent the passage data. Tables will also present passage data sets in tabular form. The **independent variable** is positioned on the left side, while the **dependent variable** is on the right side of the table. The content of the tables is always discussed in the corresponding passage. Knowledge of all table content isn't required.

# Sample Table for Analysis

| Data type | Seismic sources | | | | | | Area/volume sources | |
|---|---|---|---|---|---|---|---|---|
| | Individual faults | | | | | | | |
| | Location | Activity | Length | Dip | Depth | Style | Area | Depth |
| **Geological/Remote Sensing** | | | | | | | | |
| Detailed mapping | X | X | X | X | | X | | |
| Geomorphic data | X | X | X | | | X | X | |
| Quatenary surface rupture | X | X | X | | | X | | |
| Fault trenching data | X | X | | X | | X | | |
| Paleoliquefaction data | X | X | | | | | X | |
| Borehole data | X | X | | X | | X | | |
| Aerial photography | X | X | X | | | | | |
| Low sun-angle photography | X | X | X | | | | | |
| Satellite imagery | X | | X | | | | X | |
| Regional structure | X | | | X | | X | X | |
| Balanced Cross Section | X | | | X | X | | X | |
| **Geophysical/Geodetic** | | | | | | | | |
| Regional potential field data | X | | X | | | | X | X |
| Local potential field data | X | | X | X | X | X | | |
| High resolution reflection data | X | X | | X | | X | | |
| Standard reflexing data | X | | | X | | X | | |
| Deep crustal reflection data | X | | | X | X | | X | X |
| Tectonic geodetic/strain data | X | X | | X | X | X | X | X |
| Regional stress data | | | | | | X | X | |
| **Seismological** | | | | | | | | |
| Reflected crustal phase data | | | | | | | X | X |
| Pre-instrumental earthquake data | X | X | | | | X | X | |
| Teleseismic earthquake data | | | | | | | X | |
| Regional network seismicity data | X | X | X | X | X | | X | X |
| Local network seismicity data | X | X | X | X | X | | | X |
| Focal mechanism data | | | | X | | X | | |

# Practice Questions

*Questions 1–5 pertain to the following information:*

Worldwide, fungal infections of the lung account for significant mortality in individuals with compromised immune function. Three of the most common infecting agents are *Aspergillus, Histoplasma*, and *Candida*. Successful treatment of infections caused by these agents depends on an early and accurate diagnosis. Three tests used to identify specific markers for these mold species include ELISA (enzyme-linked immunosorbent assay), GM Assay (Galactomannan Assay), and PCR (polymerase chain reaction).

Two important characteristics of these tests include sensitivity and specificity. Sensitivity relates to the probability that the test will identify the presence of the infecting agent, resulting in a true positive result. Higher sensitivity equals fewer false-positive results. Specificity relates to the probability that if the test doesn't detect the infecting agent, the test is truly negative for that agent. Higher specificity equals fewer false-negatives.

Figure 1 shows the timeline for the process of infection from exposure to the pathogen to recovery or death.

Figure 1:
## Natural History of the Process of Infection

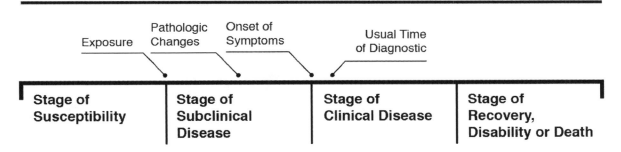

Figure 2 (below) shows the sensitivity and specificity for ELISA, GM assay and PCR related to the diagnosis of infection by *Aspergillus*, *Histoplasma* and *Candida*.

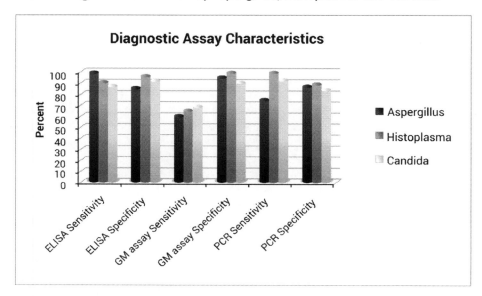

The table below identifies the process of infection in days from exposure for each of the species.

| Process of Infection – Days Since Pathogen Exposure | | | |
|---|---|---|---|
| | Aspergillus | Histoplasma | Candida |
| Sub-clinical Disease | Day 90 | Day 28 | Day 7 |
| Detection Possible | Day 118 | Day 90 | Day 45 |
| Symptoms Appear | Day 145 | Day 100 | Day 120 |

Figure 3 (below) identifies the point at which each test can detect the organism. Time is measured in days from the time an individual is exposed to the pathogen.

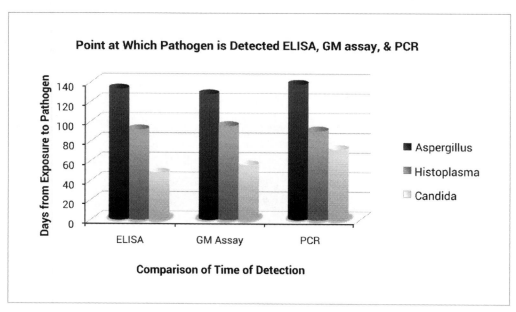

1. Which of the following statements is supported by Figure 2?
   a. For *Candida*, the GM assay will provide the most reliable results.
   b. ELISA testing for *Aspergillus* is the most specific of the three tests.
   c. PCR is the most sensitive method for testing *Histoplasma*.
   d. True positive rates were greater than 75% for all three testing methods.

2. In reference to the table and Figure 3, which pathogen can be detected earlier in the disease process, and by which method?
   a. *Candida* by PCR testing
   b. *Aspergillus* by ELISA testing
   c. *Candida* by GM assay
   d. *Histoplasma* by PCR testing

3. In reference to Figure 2, which statement is correct?
   a. There is a 20% probability that ELISA testing will NOT correctly identify the presence of *Histoplasma*.
   b. When GM assay testing for *Candida* is conducted, there is a 31% probability that it will NOT be identified if the organism is present.
   c. The probability that GM assay testing for *Aspergillus* will correctly identify the presence of the organism is 99%.
   d. The false-negative probabilities for each of the three testing methods identified in Figure 2 indicate that the organism will be detected when present less than 70% of the time.

4. Physicians caring for individuals with suspected *Histoplasma* infections order diagnostic testing prior to instituting treatment. PCR testing results will not be available for 10 days. GM assay results can be obtained more quickly. The physicians opt to wait for the PCR testing. Choose the best possible rationale for that decision.
   a. The treatment will be the same regardless of the test results.
   b. The individual was not exhibiting any disease symptoms.
   c. The probability of PCR testing identifying the presence of the organism is greater than the GM assay.
   d. The subclinical disease phase for *Histoplasma* is more than 100 days.

5. Referencing the data in Figures 2 and 3, if ELISA testing costs twice as much as PCR testing, why might it still be the best choice to test for *Candida*?
   a. ELISA testing detects the presence of *Candida* sooner than PCR testing.
   b. ELISA testing has fewer false-positives than PCR testing.
   c. There is only a 69% probability that PCR testing will correctly identify the presence of *Candida*.
   d. PCR testing is less sensitive than ELISA testing for *Candida*.

# Answer Explanations

**1. C:** There is a 99% probability of PCR testing identifying *Histoplasma*. GM assay was more specific for identifying *Aspergillus,* 95% to 85%. True positive is defined by sensitivity. The sensitivity of GM assay testing is less than 70%.

**2. D:** *Histoplasma* is detectable 90 days from exposure. PCR testing is able to detect *Histoplasma* 91 days from exposure—one day after sufficient organisms exist for detection. *Candida* is detectable 45 days from exposure. PCR testing is able to detect *Candida* 72 days from exposure—27 days after a sufficient number of organisms exist for detection. *Aspergillus* is detectable 118 days from exposure. ELISA testing is able to detect *Aspergillus* 134 days from exposure—16 days after a sufficient number of organisms exist for detection. *Candida* is detectable 45 days from exposure. GM assay testing is able to detect *Candida* 56 days from exposure—11 days after a sufficient number of organisms exist for detection.

**3. B:** The probability that the GM assay will identify *Candida* is 69%. Therefore, there's a 31% probability that it won't be identified. ELISA sensitivity and specificity for *Histoplasma* are both greater than 80%. False-negative probabilities are represented by the specificity of a given testing method. The sensitivity and specificity for GM assay testing for Aspergillus is 59% and 96% respectively. All testing methods had greater than 90% specificity for the organisms.

**4. C:** The sensitivity of PCR testing for *Histoplasma* is 99%, and the test can identify the organism one day after it reaches a detectable colony size. The sensitivity for GM assay testing for *Histoplasma* is 65%. If physicians rely on GM assay testing, they may determine that the individual doesn't have the *Histoplasma* infection. Treatment will depend on the presence or absence of the infection as indicated by testing. Waiting for PCR testing is based on the sensitivity of the test, not the individual's current symptoms. The subclinical phase of *Histoplasma* is 28 days.

**5. A:** ELISA testing detects *Candida* three days after the organism is present in sufficient numbers to be recognized. PCR detects the organism more than three weeks after it is first detectable. ELISA testing sensitivity for *Candida* is 87% and PCR testing is 92%. However, the ability to identify the presence of the organism earlier in the process of infection (allowing early intervention) outweighs the differences in the probability of identifying the presence of the organism. There's a 92% probability that PCR testing will identify the presence of *Candida*. PCR testing is more sensitive than ELISA: 92% versus 87%.

# Social Studies

## *Reading for Meaning in Social Studies*

### Main Ideas and Details in Social Studies Readings

#### Determining the Main Ideas

As mentioned, the **main idea** is more detailed than the topic of a piece of writing and it provides the author's central point of the text. It can be expressed through a complete sentence and is often found in the beginning, middle, or end of a paragraph. In most nonfiction books, the first sentence of the passage usually (but not always) states the main idea.

#### Using Details to Make Inferences or Claims

Once a reader has determined an author's thesis or main idea, he or she will need to understand how textual evidence supports interpretation of that thesis or main idea. Test takers will be asked direct questions regarding an author's main idea and may be asked to identify evidence that would support those ideas. This will require test takers to comprehend literal and figurative meanings within the text passage, be able to draw inferences from provided information, and be able to separate important evidence from minor supporting detail. It's often helpful to skim test questions and answer options prior to critically reading informational text; however, test takers should avoid the temptation to solely look for the correct answers. Just trying to find the "right answer" may cause test takers to miss important supporting textual evidence. Making mental note of test questions is only helpful as a guide when reading.

After identifying an author's thesis or main idea, a test taker should look at the supporting details that the author provides to back up their assertions, identifying those additional pieces of information that help expand the thesis. From there, test takers should examine the additional information and related details for credibility, the author's use of outside sources, and be able to point to direct evidence that supports the author's claims. It's also imperative that test takers be able to identify what is strong support and what is merely additional information that is nice to know but not necessary. Being able to make this differentiation will help test takers effectively answer questions regarding an author's use of supporting evidence within informational text.

### Social Studies Vocabulary

Although general literacy is usually enough to understand social studies texts, some authors use specialized vocabulary for the field of social studies. Traditionally, these specialized vocabulary terms can be separated into eight major categories: people, places, events, groups, movements, eras, documents, and analytical trends. The field of social studies centers on those who have shaped history on both the microcosmic and macrocosmic levels. Much of the social studies vocabulary terms test takers encounter is focused on famous leaders or historical agents. An **agent** is someone who does something; historical agents do something historically significant.

Social studies concepts also include geography and are linked with geography in general, so it is important that test takers have a good understanding of place and its influences on history. Additionally, it is important for test takers to understand historical events: wars, assassinations, political victories, resignations, marches, parades, and celebrations. Groups are also important to understanding social

studies. In particular, some groups form social movements, factions of people devoted to some larger changes. At times, these movements succeed in changing history; at other times, they fail. Historians tend to also categorize history in segments of time known as eras. Eras can be as strict as decades (for example, the Roaring Twenties) or as fluid as ideas (for example, the Progressive Era).

Sometimes social studies texts also refer to the titles of primary and secondary texts, which have their own unique vocabulary terms. An example of an important primary text is the Declaration of Independence, while a secondary text might be a textbook discussing the Declaration of Independence. All these concepts—from people to documents—influence historical analyses, which are usually secondary texts. Historians and scholars may create their own analytical paradigms, which carry their own specialized vocabulary. For instance, some historians refer to themselves as quantitative historians because their analytical lenses are influenced heavily by quantitative data. Quantitative historians have their own specialized vocabulary for analytical trends.

Below are examples of the eight major categories of social studies vocabulary: people, places, events, groups, movements, eras, documents, and analytical trends.

| People |
|---|

**King James I of England:** The King of England who granted the charter that would help found the Jamestown Colony; the Jamestown colony is named after him.

**John Smith:** A famous English explorer who played an important role in the survival of the Jamestown colony.

**Powhatan:** A well-known Native American leader who led a tribe known as the Powhatans; he was the father of a famous Native American woman known as Pocahontas.

**Pocahontas:** A well-known Native American woman who served as a mediator between the Powhatans and the Jamestown colony; she was the daughter of a respected Native American chief known as Powhatan.

**William Bradford**: A famous Puritan settler who signed the Mayflower Compact, served as governor for nearly 30 years, and wrote *Of Plymouth Plantation*.

**Bartolome de las Casas:** Known as the "Protector of the Indians," he was a priest who wrote a treatise that shed light on the mistreatment of Native Americans in the New World.

**Charles Townshend:** British chancellor of the exchequer and responsible for the passage of the highly controversial Townshend Acts in 1767.

**Crispus Attucks:** Murdered by British soldiers in reaction to colonial protests, Crispus Attucks, a black colonist, became the first casualty of the so-called Boston Massacre. Some people even memorialize him as a martyr of the American Revolution, claiming that his bloodshed marked the beginning of the struggle for independence.

**Thomas Paine:** Thomas Paine was an English-born American political activist, philosopher, political theorist and revolutionary. He was the author of *Common Sense*, a foundational document that helped stir the American Revolution.

**James Madison:** Known as both a Founding Father and the Father of the Constitution, he served as the fourth president of the United States, preceded by Thomas Jefferson and succeeded by James Monroe.

**Thomas Jefferson:** A Founding Father who became the third president of the United States, Jefferson was famous for his involvement in the Declaration of Independence, the Louisiana Purchase, and the creation of the Jeffersonian Republican platform.

**General Andrew Jackson:** A famous general during the War of 1812, who led the United States to an impressive victory at the Battle of New Orleans. He later became a controversial US president known for expanding democracy while simultaneously perpetuating white supremacy.

**James K. Polk:** Known for his expansionist policies in an era that witnessed rapid westward annexation, occupation, and settlement, he is forever known as the president who led the United States in a (successful) border war with Mexico, the Mexican-American War.

**Dred Scott:** An escaped slave who catapulted the United States in a US Supreme Court case known as *Dred Scott v. Sanford* (1857). The Dred Scott decision, which reinforced the rights of slave owners and slave states, helped pave the way to the ideological battles over slavery that culminated in the Civil War.

**Abraham Lincoln:** Known for entering office when the nation was divided over slavery between the North and South, he is one of the most recognized presidents because of his involvement in the Civil War, his approval of the Emancipation Proclamation, and his untimely assassination by John Wilkes Booth.

**Ulysses S. Grant:** A famous Civil War general whose presidency was marred by corruptions such as the Whiskey Ring during the Gilded Age.

**General Robert E. Lee:** The most skilled Confederate military leader during the Civil War, Lee ended up surrendering at the Appomattox Courthouse in Virginia, which marked the end of the conflict between North and South.

| Places | |
| --- | --- |

**Mesoamerica:** A historical region that includes modern-day Mexico and Central America.

**Mississippi River:** The longest river on the North American continent, the Mississippi is known for its vast estuaries and its cultural contributions to American history.

**Great Lakes Region:** A geographic region in North America that surrounds the large lakes that separate the modern-day United States and Canada

**Reservations:** Federal land, often of poor quality, set aside for Native Americans to live on in the United States.

**Jamestown:** Located on the coast of modern-day Virginia and founded in 1607, it became the first successful English colony in North America. Previous colonization attempts by the English (for example, Roanoke Island) were failures.

**Plymouth:** A religiously based English colony founded by Puritan Separatists in 1620.

**Roanoke Island:** A colony off the coast of Virginia that the English tried to settle in the 16th century.

**James River:** A river near coastal Virginia that served as a source of water for the Jamestown colony.

**Chesapeake Bay:** A large coastal estuary that served as a harbor for the early Jamestown colony.

**Plymouth Harbor:** The anchorage site of the *Mayflower*; it is located in modern-day Massachusetts.

**Massachusetts Bay Colony:** An English colony composed of modern-day Maine, New Hampshire, Vermont, Massachusetts, and Connecticut; it was created through a joint-stock charter and eventually subsumed the old Plymouth Colony.

**New England Colonies:** The English colonies of the Northeast; this region included the Massachusetts Bay Colony (which acquired the Plymouth Colony), Rhode Island, Connecticut, and New Hampshire.

**Middle Colonies:** The English colonies located between the New England colonies and the Southern Colonies; this region included New York, New Jersey, Pennsylvania, and Delaware.

**Southern Colonies:** The English colonies located between Florida and the Middle Colonies; this region included Maryland, Virginia, North Carolina, South Carolina, and Georgia.

**Mystic River Valley:** A region in southeastern Connecticut that witnessed the massacre of the Pequot Native Americans by the English colonists.

**Atlantic World:** A word historians use to describe interactions that took place on either side of and on the Atlantic Ocean, particularly during the Age of Exploration and Colonization.

**Appalachian Mountains:** A well-known North American mountain range that extends from Georgia to Maine.

**Louisiana Territory:** A large tract of land west of the Mississippi River in North America. This land exchanged hands from one empire to the next throughout the 16th, 17th, and 18th centuries; the United States eventually purchased the land from the French in 1803.

**Rio Grande River:** The body of water that serves as a natural boundary between the United States and Mexico, flowing around the border of Texas and into the Gulf of Mexico.

**Republic of Texas:** Prior to American annexation, the name given to the independent state that emerged out of the Texas Revolution against Mexico; this republic lasted roughly ten years before statehood.

**Trans-Appalachia:** The region west of the Appalachian Mountains.

**Confederate States of America:** The name given to states that seceded from the United States Union during the Civil War. The Confederate States, also known as the Confederacy, formed a short-lived independent nation that lost to the Union during the Civil War.

**Events**

**French and Indian War:** English colonists in the New World fought against the French and their Native American allies. This conflict was an extension of a larger conflict between England and France called the Seven Years' War. The French and Indian War caused the Thirteen Colonies to accumulate a lot of debt, paving the way to the American Revolution.

**American Revolution:** A colonial revolt and war for independence that pitted American colonists against the British Crown.

**Starving Time**: Refers to a harsh period of struggle and starvation in the Jamestown colony in the winter of 1609–1610.

**Pequot War:** An armed conflict that pitted the English colonists and their Native American allies against the Pequot Indians of New England; this conflict lasted from 1636 to 1638.

**King Philip's War:** A bloody war pitting the English colonists and their allies against the Wampanoag indigenous tribe of New England and their chief, Metacom. The war resulted in over 5,000 deaths.

**Boston Massacre:** A conflict that stemmed from American protests over British quartering and taxation policies in the Thirteen Colonies. It led to the death of several American colonists and was sensationalized by Patriots as a strategic massacre.

**Boston Tea Party:** A famous protest that witnessed English colonists dumping dozens of tea crates into Boston harbor. It is known as one of the events that helped ignite the American Revolution.

**Lexington and Concord:** Often categorized as the locations of the first shots fired in the American War for Independence. These battles were fought in 1775, before the Declaration of Independence was even signed or even created.

**Stamp Act Controversy:** The controversy and protests in the American colonies surrounding the passage of the Stamp Act of 1765.

**Constitutional Convention:** A historical event, hosted in Philadelphia, Pennsylvania, that witnessed the end of the Articles of Confederation (and its coinciding Critical Period) and the adoption of a new national Constitution with a Bill of Rights.

**Shays' Rebellion:** Typically seen as a symbol of the weakness of the United States under the Articles of Confederation, it was a lengthy uprising by disaffected farmers in western Massachusetts under the leadership of Daniel Shays.

**Great Compromise:** A famous agreement during the Constitutional Convention that helped establish Congress into a two-part (or "bicameral") legislature with a House and Senate.

**Three-Fifths Compromise:** A controversial constitutional compromise that designated a slave as three fifths of a person when it came to census data, for electoral and legislative reasons.

**Louisiana Purchase:** This transaction, carried out by Thomas Jefferson, saw the United States expand by one third and the French lose most of its territory in the New World.

**War of 1812:** A three-year war between the United States and Great Britain that witnessed the burning of the original White House and an eventual American victory in 1815.

**Battle at Baltimore:** The famous battle in the War of 1812 that inspired Francis Scott Key to write the "Star-Spangled Banner," a poem that later became the United States' national anthem.

**Battle of New Orleans:** A battle made famous by the leadership and victory of Andrew Jackson; it is considered part of the War of 1812, but it actually occurred after the war ended via official treaty between the United States and Great Britain.

**Mexican-American War:** An armed conflict that lasted between 1846 to 1848 that began as a skirmish over borders and territories, but ended with the official cession of one third of the Mexican nation to the United States.

**American Civil War:** A deadly civil conflict between the North and South—the Union and Confederacy—that helped end slavery and eventually reunified a nation that had long been divided over the institution of slavery.

**Battle of Gettysburg:** A Civil War victory by the Union at Gettysburg, Pennsylvania in 1863 that helped turn the tide against the Confederates.

## Groups

**Olmec:** The earliest Native American civilization in Mexico.

**Maya:** An early Mesoamerican civilization that began building its great pyramids around 250 CE and then disappeared around 900 CE.

**Aztec:** A Mesoamerican civilization that flourished in Mexico from about 1300 CE to 1521 CE but was eventually conquered by Spanish conquistadors under leadership of Hernán Cortés.

**Inca:** The largest civilization in the pre-Columbian Americas, it emerged in the highlands of Peru in the 13th century and was eventually conquered by Spanish conquistadors in 1572.

**Iroquois:** A political confederation of five northeastern Native American tribes that rose to prominence during colonial times.

**Five Civilized Tribes:** A group of prominent tribes in the Southeast region of North American continent that collaborated and traded with the colonists; the tribes included the Cherokee, Chickasaw, Choctaw, Creek, and Seminole tribes.

**Separatists:** Radical English Protestants who wanted to separate from the Church of England, this group founded Plymouth Colony.

**Church of England:** The official Protestant church of England; it separated from the Catholic Church in the 16th century under the leadership of King Henry VIII.

**Pequot Indians:** A group of Native Americans who originally resided in a territory that is now the modern-day state of Connecticut; this group fought against the English settlers in the Pequot War (1636–1638).

**Mohegan:** A Native American tribe that unified with the Pequot in present-day Connecticut during the era of European colonization.

**Narragansett:** An Algonquin Native American tribe that allied with the New England colonists during the Pequot War (1636–1638).

**Parliament:** The name given to the British legislature, which created taxes and acts that displeased the colonists in the years leading up to the American Revolution.

**Patriots:** The name given to the network of leaders, organizers, and militiamen who led a revolution against the British government in the Thirteen Colonies.

**First Continental Congress:** One of the first examples of colonial unity, it witnessed several colonies, represented by delegates, coming together to petition the alleged wrongdoings and overstepped boundaries of King George III and the British Crown in America.

**Second Continental Congress:** The second famous convening of the colonists during the revolutionary era in American history, which helped birth the Declaration of Independence on July 4, 1776.

**Minutemen:** A fast-acting group of civilian militiamen who were ready to form a standing army within a minute's time during the years of the American Revolution.

**Tories:** A group of American colonists who chose not to side with the revolutionists during the American War for Independence; they chose instead to stay loyal to the British.

**Liberty Boys:** A secret network of discontented colonists who strategically participated in both acts of protest and espionage against the British Crown in the Revolutionary Era.

**Federalists:** A group that emerged in the years leading up to the Constitutional Convention; they preferred federal rights over states' rights.

**Anti-Federalists:** A group that emerged in the years leading up to the Constitutional Convention; they preferred states' rights over federal rights.

**Democratic-Republican Party:** Also known as the Democratic Republicans and formed by Thomas Jefferson and James Madison around 1792, this American political party opposed the new Federalist Party's centralizing policies.

**Jeffersonian Republicans:** Named after Thomas Jefferson, the third president of the United States, this group trusted agrarian (farming) values.

**Republican Party:** Still in existence today as one of the main two political parties in the U.S., it was organized in the years prior to the Civil War. The first Republican President was Abraham Lincoln.

**Democratic Party:** Still in existence today as one of the main two political parties in the U.S., this political party emerged during the 1820s and 1830s with the democratic fervor surrounding the rise of President Andrew Jackson.

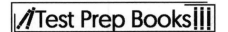 

## Movements

**Women's Suffrage:** The name given to the movement that secured women's right to vote in the United States in the early 20th century; women were the last group to gain this right in America.

**Jacksonian Democracy:** A phrase used to describe the rapid expansion of suffrage to include working class white men during Andrew Jackson's ascendancy to the presidency.

## Eras

**Industrial Revolution:** The term used to refer to an era in global history that witnessed a paradigm shift in culture and economics; an 18th, 19th, and early 20th century global transformation that emphasized mechanized manufacturing processes over agrarian production.

**Market Revolution:** America's transition from an agrarian economy to a full-blown market economy, which eventually paved the way to the Industrial Revolution.

**Critical Period**: A phrase sometimes used to refer to the instability of the nation under the Articles of Confederation.

**Age of Expansion:** Refers to an era in US history following the Louisiana Purchase and extending all the way to the early 20th century, characterized by expansion of territories and borders.

**Sectional Crisis:** An era of political crisis in the United States in the antebellum period that created a division between North and South, free states and slave states.

**Antebellum:** Literally means "before the war"; it refers to the time period leading up to the American Civil War.

**Populism:** Support for the concerns of ordinary people.

**Reconstruction:** Deemed a failure by some historians because it perpetuated the oppression of African-Americans and resolved little tension between North and South, the era of Reconstruction directly followed the Civil War and tried to rebuild a devastated nation.

## Documents

**Mayflower Compact:** The first governing document of the Plymouth Colony, which was signed by William Bradford and his fellow Puritan Separatists.

**Declaration of Independence:** A document adopted by the American colonies in 1776 to declare the colonies free from British rule.

**Treaty of Paris:** A treaty between the Spanish, British, and French Empires following the Seven Years' War; as a result of the treaty, the French relinquished a significant amount of land in North America.

**Townshend Acts:** These acts, created and implemented by Charles Townshend, a British Parliamentary leader, offended the American colonists because they enforced more taxes (on things such as tea) and greater British control over the colonies.

**Tea Act of 1773:** This law led to the Boston Tea Party because American colonists were enraged that the British would tax one of their favorite commodities, tea.

**Proclamation of 1763:** This royal directive angered American colonists because it stated that they were not allowed to transverse or settle territory west of the Appalachian Mountains.

**Stamp Act of 1765:** This act allowed the British to tax all stamps, which were needed on official documents in the colonies such as marriage licenses.

**The Quartering Act:** The colonists were angered by this act because it mandated that all colonists must house, or quarter, British soldiers without any royal compensation.

**Treaty of Paris (1783):** The documents, signed by the United States and Great Britain, that officially ended the American War for Independence in 1783.

**Common Sense:** A pamphlet written by Thomas Paine in 1775–76 advocating independence from Great Britain to people in the Thirteen Colonies.

**Coercive Acts:** Also known as the Intolerable Acts, a series of aggressive British statutes that were passed in 1774. They were designed to punish the Massachusetts colonists for their participation in the protests of Boston Tea Party; the colonists claimed the acts were "coercive" or "intolerable" in their revolutionary propaganda.

**Quebec Act:** A controversial act that instigated the Protestant sensitivities of the American colonists by making it legal for Roman Catholics to practice in Quebec.

**Articles of Confederation:** Created in 1777, this document established the first central government for the United States; it was replaced by the US Constitution in 1789.

**US Constitution:** The governing document of the United States that replaced the Articles of Confederation in 1789 and strengthened the federal government.

**Bill of Rights:** The first ten proposed and ratified amendments to the US Constitution, which spelled out specific personal rights such as the right to free speech.

**Star-Spangled Banner:** Written by Francis Scott Key at the Battle of Baltimore during the War of 1812, this poem became the national anthem of the United States 100 years after its creation.

**Treaty of Ghent:** The official end of the War of 1812 came about as a result of the signing of this treaty. However, some skirmishes between the United States and Great Britain continued for months after its signing, due to delays in communication.

**Indian Removal Act:** A controversial act signed by President Andrew Jackson in 1830 that removed Native Americans to federal territory in the West, which resulted in the Trail of Tears.

**Treaty of Guadalupe Hidalgo:** Bringing about the end of the Mexican-American War, this 1848 treaty transitioned about one third of Mexican territory into the hands of the United States.

**Gadsden Purchase:** Following the Mexican Cession after the Mexican-American War, this 1853 purchase from Mexico transferred a small sliver of northern Mexico (modern-day Arizona and New Mexico) into the possession of the United States.

**Fugitive Slave Act:** A divisive law created during the antebellum period in American history that made it illegal to house or assist runaway slaves in any capacity.

**Emancipation Proclamation:** The document that freed slaves in the United States; it was created by President Lincoln during the Civil War in 1863.

**Gettysburg Address:** A famous Abraham Lincoln speech, delivered in 1863 on the site of the Battle of Gettysburg, that is iconic for its passion and brevity

**Jim Crow laws:** Laws that reinforced the institutionalized segregation of the South from Reconstruction until the Civil Rights Movement of the 1960s.

### Analytical Trends

**Consensus History:** A style of American historiography that downplays conflict and complexity, focusing on unity and nationalism.

**Modernism:** A philosophy that took hold in the late 19th and early 20th century that gave rise to histories and literature that emphasized the beauties and the pangs of modernity.

**New Left:** A 1960s political movement that championed such causes as anti-war activism, women's rights, and other issues.

**Postmodernism:** A departure from modernism, this literary, artistic, and architectural movement also affected history and philosophy. It focuses on the tenuousness of authority and truth and interpretation of texts.

**Progressivism:** A view of history and philosophy categorized by a larger search for order and a belief in human progress.

### General Social Studies Terms

**American Exceptionalism:** A worldview that claims the United States is historically unique and more powerful than other nations.

**Reductive:** Oversimplifying a subject, debate, or narrative.

**Nuanced:** A subtly different view or varying argument that promotes a unique perspective.

**Historically Accurate:** Authentic or true, in terms of historical validity or honesty.

**Indigenous People:** A way of referring to any group who originated in a particular place, in contrast to people who arrived later, as conquerors, immigrants, or slaves.

**Historical Narrative:** A spoken or written account of history, as told from a specific viewpoint or perspective.

**Eurocentrism:** A worldview that favors a European narrative of progress.

**Colonial Economy:** A phrase used to describe the system of production, consumption, and trade that emerged during the period of European colonization.

**Joint-Stock Company:** A business entity in which shareholders own a share of the company's profit; many joint-stock companies are responsible for founding colonies in the New World.

**Mayflower:** The English ship that famously transported the Separatist Puritans to their new settlement at Plymouth.

**Archive:** To place or organize documents or materials in storage for future use.

**Savage:** A pejorative term the English used to describe the Native Americans as barbarous or uncivilized.

**Bolster:** A verb that means to support or reinforce.

**Proselytizing:** Trying to convert someone to a particular faith or religion.

**Exploitation:** Taking advantage of someone or something for selfish reasons, such as profit.

**Genocidal:** An adjective used to describe the systematic attempt to kill off an entire group of people, whether defined by religion, ethnicity, or race.

**Paradigm Shifting:** A phrase coined by Thomas Kuhn to describe large waves of historical and scientific change that fundamentally change the ways people understand the world around them.

**Capitalism:** The dominant political and economic philosophy of the United States, which focuses on creating a free market in which there is competition between businesses.

**Slavery:** An institution built upon the bondage and forced labor of human beings. Slavery preceded the foundation of the United States and continued until the Civil War era and the Emancipation Proclamation.

**Protesting:** When a person or group makes a public statement of disagreement; it can take the form of marches, gatherings, silences, and even boycotts.

**Boycotting:** A specific type of protest that focuses on finances and economics; it is the refusal to purchase or use a particular service or product, in an effort to force political or social change.

**Electoral College:** In the United States, it is a voting system that allows selected representatives to vote on behalf of the people. It is an example of limited democracy.

**Industrialization:** The widespread development of manufacturing industries in a region, country, or culture.

**Agrarian:** A term used to describe a society or culture that relies heavily on farming for trade and subsistence.

**Republic:** A classical form of government adopted by the United States (and the Republic of Texas) because it placed the power of the people in the hands of elected officials who are supposed to stand for public opinion.

**Self-Sufficiency:** Needing no outside help to sustain one's own life, especially when it comes to food production.

**Virtue:** Behavior showing high moral standards.

**Yeoman:** A term for a farmer who works a small, individually owned plot of land. Thomas Jefferson believed democracy could be sustained through the independence of yeoman farmers.

**Discontent:** A feeling of dissatisfaction, typically with the prevailing social or political situation.

**Revisionism:** The re-interpretation of the historical record, usually in a way that distorts or alters the prevailing understanding.

**Sanitize:** Literally, to clean; in social sciences it means to alter something regarded as less acceptable so as to make it more palatable.

**Subjugation:** The action of bringing someone or something under domination or control.

**Terminological:** Connected with the meanings of words, especially the technical words and expressions used in a particular subject.

**Egalitarian:** A term that is synonymous with ultimate equality or when people or society share material or immaterial power equally.

**Anti-Egalitarian:** Contrary to principles of social equality and fairness.

**Cultural Milieu:** The cultural and social environment that surrounds a person. It comes from a French term meaning "middle place."

**Working Class:** A term used as label for a laboring class that gained momentum during the Industrial Revolution.

**White Supremacy:** A system of beliefs that upholds white people as the supreme race while discriminating against other races.

**Duel:** An archaic way of resolving disputes that involved a highly structured form of violence; it was often performed with guns and involved a series of sport-like rules and procedures.

**Immigration:** The action of coming to live permanently in a foreign country.

**Urbanization:** The process of making an area more urban or populated.

**Industrialization:** The widespread development of manufacturing industries in a region, country, or culture.

**Artisan:** A worker who is highly skilled in a trade, especially one involving handicrafts.

**Cash-Crop Agriculture:** The growing of agricultural crops for money, in contrast to crops grown for subsistence. Before to the Civil War, cotton was an American cash crop.

**Manufacturing:** Using mechanized instruments or technology to make a particular good or product (for example, automobile manufacturing).

**Suffrage:** A term used to describe the right to vote; historically, it originally belonged to men or land-owners. It was extended gradually to other groups, with women being the last to earn the right.

**Aristocratic:** Having to do with a form of government that places strength in the hands of a small, privileged ruling class.

**Insurgency:** An act of rebellion or revolt against a government or ruler.

**Elitism:** A tendency to promote the wealthier portions of the population.

**Hierarchical:** Organized in order of rank.

**Deference:** Humble submission and respect.

**Angst:** Intense feelings of distress or anxiety that can be felt either personally or collectively.

**Tyranny:** Cruel and oppressive government or rule.

**Spurious:** Not what it purports to be; false or fake.

**Rhetoric:** The name given to any form of communication, written or oral, that carries power as an art and discourse; a personalized and recognizable style of personal or collective communication.

**Plebeian:** A commoner; a common person.

**Racist:** An individual who takes seriously the strict parameters of racial constructs and discriminates against other races as a result.

**Racial Exclusivity:** Excluding a person or group of persons because of their race.

**Cotton Gin:** A cotton-separating invention created by Eli Whitney in 1793 that was supposed to ease the burden of slavery through mechanized means but actually increased the demand for slave labor on cotton plantations.

**Plantations:** A large estate farmed by slaves or tenant farmers who live there but do not own the land. During the antebellum period in American history, plantations served as the epicenter of slave labor; these plantations capitalized on the institution of slavery to produce large cash crops such as tobacco and cotton.

## How Authors Use Language in Social Studies

Often history is interpreted or taught as a mere timeline or a series of bland facts about the past, but history should also be understood as a "lived experience." All humans are *a part of* history—they are the historical actors and personas who make positive (or negative) changes in the world. Human beings are constantly interacting with the super-structural forces of history. History occurs in interlocking webs of mutual reciprocity.

History happens in a context of local and global events. The people recording that history (in whatever format) are part of that context and therefore shaped by it. No one merely records statistics, facts, and figures. Each thing recorded is done so because it is important for some reason to the one recording it.

Those who study history must do their best to understand the people and places they study as well as understand themselves in their own historical context.

Good historians ask questions prior to reading or studying what has been left for them by prior generations. What was important to the person who left this record? Were they rich or poor? Were they weak or powerful? What was their particular view of the world? What was their view of themselves and the group(s) they belonged to and their perceived place in history? These and other questions are critical to better understanding what was recorded and why it was considered important. It also helps provide a context for understanding the record left for posterity.

The historian must also understand their own biases, worldview, preconceptions, and context so that they can be aware of who they are and what they believe, because it influences the way they read, interpret, and understand the historical record.

Social studies deal with many different documents and recordings, all using written or spoken language. Language can be found in diaries, journals, political cartoons, old maps, treatises, constitutions, treaties, laws, advertisements, deeds, archives, inventory reports, and financial receipts. These are all examples of **primary sources**. Social studies also uses language in textbooks, monographs, academic journals, encyclopedias, online blogs, contemporary maps, charts, tables, and graphs. These are all examples of **secondary sources**. Language can even be found on old artifacts, archeological discoveries, monuments, and museum exhibits. These are all examples of historical objects that can fall into the categories of either primary or secondary sources. Language is the primary method of capturing history and documenting its meaning. Although social studies can examine artifacts without language (for example, the artifacts used in anthropology and archeology), most social studies documents use language. The languages may change from culture to culture, but language use is itself a unifying component of all major cultural histories.

Thus, it is important for test takers to become detectives of social studies language. Every student must be prepared to understand the purpose and biases embedded in language. For instance, if a document repeatedly uses words such as *liberty*, *freedom*, and *inalienable rights*, it is likely that the authors of these documents believe in these concepts so much that they wanted to disseminate these words to a broader audience. Additionally, if advertisements consistently use the word "cool," then the creators of these advertisements are likely using this word for a specific purpose, such as to appeal to teenagers concerned with their image. Every language-based source carries its own perspective and biases. Thus, students must be prepared to link language to not only the historical context (for example, the era of the Early Republic), but also to the beliefs of the author(s).

## Fact Versus Opinion

A fact is information that can be proven true. If information can be disproved, it is not a fact. For example, water freezes at or below thirty-two degrees Fahrenheit. An argument stating that water freezes at seventy degrees Fahrenheit cannot be supported by data and is therefore not a fact. Facts tend to be associated with science, mathematics, and statistics.

Opinions are information open to debate. Opinions are often tied to subjective concepts like equality, morals, and rights. They can also be controversial. An affirmative argument for a position—such as gun control—can be just as effective as an opposing argument against it.

Biases and stereotypes are viewpoints based in opinion and held despite evidence that they are incorrect. A bias is an individual prejudice. Biased people ignore evidence that contradicts their position

while offering as proof any evidence that supports it. A stereotype is a widely held belief projected onto a group. Those who stereotype tend to make assumptions based on what others have told them and usually have little firsthand experience with the group or item in question.

Readers must read critically to discern between fact and opinion and to notice bias and stereotypes.

## Claims and Evidence in Social Studies

### Determining Whether a Claim Is or Is Not Supported by Evidence

Valid claims must have sufficient evidence that fully support the claims and conclusions. Critical readers examine the facts and evidence used to support an author's claim. They check the facts against other sources to be sure those facts are correct. They also check the validity of the sources used to be sure those sources are credible, academic, and/or peer-reviewed. Consider that when an author uses another person's opinion to support their argument, even if it is an expert's opinion, it is still only an opinion and should not be taken as fact. A strong argument uses valid, measurable facts to support ideas. Even then, the reader may disagree with the argument as it may be rooted in their personal beliefs.

An authoritative argument may use the facts to sway the reader. For example, in a paper on global warming, many experts differ in their opinions of what alternative fuels can be used to aid in offsetting it. Because of this, a writer may choose to only use the information and expert opinion that supports their viewpoint.

Students must be able to distinguish between reliable and unreliable sources in order to develop a well-written research report. When choosing print sources, typically published works that have been edited and clearly identify the author or authors are considered credible sources. Peer-reviewed journals and research conducted by scholars are likewise considered to be credible sources of information.

When deciding on what Internet sources to use, it is also a sound practice for researchers to look closely at each website's universal resource locator, the *URL*. Generally speaking, websites with .edu, .gov, or .org as the Top Level Domain are considered reliable, but the researcher must still question any possible political or social bias. Personal blogs, tweets, personal websites, online forums, and any site that clearly demonstrates bias, strong opinions, or persuasive language are considered unreliable sources.

### Comparing Information that Differs Between Sources

If one were to analyze current events, they will get a clearer view of how this works. The same event can be recorded by two different people and sound like two different events because of the way the information is reported. For example, two people might report on an event during a time of war. The first might be a pacifist and therefore would be opposed to the war and that bias would be seen in how they reported on the conflict. Someone else might speak of the same events and make them seem heroic because they are very much in favor of their country's involvement in the conflict. The same historical event is being recorded but with two very different intents, understandings, and interpretations.

The historian who comes to this information (or the modern reader in the current events case) needs to also be aware of their personal views and how that affects their understanding of what they are reading. They may read sympathetically if they share the bias of the original author. They may also react in great opposition to what was recorded if their own view varies sharply from that of the original recorder.

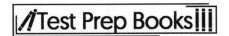 

Awareness of the times, backgrounds, purposes, and influences on both the original recorder and the one examining the record must be taken into account when analyzing historical sources.

# *Analyzing Historical Events and Arguments*

## Making Inferences

**Inference** refers to the reader's ability to understand the unwritten text, i.e., "read between the lines" in terms of an author's intent or message. The strategy asks that a reader not take everything he or she reads at face value but instead, add their own interpretation of what the author seems to be trying to convey. A reader's ability to make inferences relies on their ability to think clearly and logically about the text. It does not ask that the reader make wild speculation or guess about the material but demands that he or she be able to come to a sound conclusion about the material.

An author's use of less literal words and phrases requires readers to make more inference when they read. Since inference involves **deduction**—deriving conclusions from ideas assumed to be true—there's more room for interpretation. Still, critical readers who employ inference, if careful in their thinking, can still arrive at the logical, sound conclusions the author intends.

## Connections Between Different Social Studies Elements (People, Events, Places, Processes)

### Analyzing Cause-and-Effect Relationships

Every time someone studies history, it is very much a collision of past, present, and future. Historians are concerned for the past, rooted in the present, and thinking about the future. Historical analysis is, therefore, a process infusing the present in the past in hopes of predicting (or deterring) certain social interactions in the future.

When examining the historical narratives of events, it is important to understand the relationship between causes and effects. A cause can be defined as something, whether an event, social change, or other factor, that contributes to the occurrence of certain events; the results of causes are called effects. Those terms may seem simple enough, but they have drastic implications on how one explores history. Events such as the American Revolution or the Civil Rights Movement may appear to occur spontaneously, but a closer examination will reveal that these events depended on earlier phenomena and patterns that influenced the course of history.

There can be multiple causes and effects for any situation. The existence of multiple causes can be seen through the settling of the American West. Many historians have emphasized the role of manifest destiny—the national vision of expanding across the continent—as a driving force behind the growth of the United States. Yet there were many different influences behind the expansion westward. Northern abolitionists and southern planters saw the frontier as a way to either extend or limit slavery. Economic opportunities in the West also encouraged travel westward, as did the gradual pacification, relocation, or eradication of Native American tribes. In fact, manifest destiny as well as economic and political reasons played significant roles in justifying the pacification, relocation, or eradication of the Native American tribal nations.

Even an individual cause can be subdivided into smaller factors or stretched out in a gradual process. Although there were numerous issues that led to the Civil War, slavery was the primary cause. However, that topic stretched back to the very founding of the nation, and the existence of slavery was a

controversial topic during the creation of the Declaration of Independence and the Constitution. The abolition movement as a whole did not start until the 1830s, but nevertheless, slavery is a cause that gradually grew more important over the following decades. In addition, opponents of slavery were divided by different motivations—some believed that it stifled the economy, while others focused on moral issues.

On the other end of the spectrum, a single event can have numerous results. The rise of the telegraph, for example, had several effects on American history. The telegraph allowed news to travel much quicker and turned events into immediate national news, such as the sinking of the USS Maine, which sparked the Spanish-American War. In addition, the telegraph helped make railroads run more efficiently by improving the links between stations. The faster speed of both travel and communications led to a shift in time itself, and localized times were replaced by standardized time zones across the nation.

By looking at different examples of cause and effect closely, it becomes clear that no event occurs without one—if not multiple—causes behind it, and that each historical event can have a variety of direct and indirect consequences.

One of the most critical elements of cause-and-effect relationships is how they are relevant not only in studying history but also in contemporary events. People must realize that events and developments today will likely have a number of consequences later on. Therefore, the study of cause and effect remains vital in understanding the past, the present, and the future.

## Describing the Connections Between People, Places, Environments, Processes, and Events

The primary role of social studies is to illuminate connections between people, places, environments, processes, and events. Therefore, test takers must be prepared to examine correlations and causations in social studies. Correlations are connections that do not necessarily show any signs of causation. Two things are correlated when they happen to the same people, or in the same circumstances, or at the same time. For example, the increased popularity of apocalyptic literature in 2008 and 2009 can be **correlated** with the Great Recession that occurred around that time. However, these two events might not be **causally related**. A relationship is causal when one thing causes another to happen. In other words, the rise in apocalyptic literature may be caused by other cultural changes, such as an increasing disenchantment with humanity, a disenchantment caused by an increase in global wars and genocide.

Other connections can be discovered by analyzing causation. For instance, the mass immigration of Irish workers to the United States in the 19th century can likely be understood as a cause and effect scenario spawned by the great potato famine of that era—immigrants had to flee Ireland because their families were going to starve to death. In this instance, one thing caused another. Students of social studies must constantly be on the search for these connections. They must study the ways in which geography (for example, the Rio Grande River) affects immigration patterns (for example, undocumented immigration from Mexico to America in the 20th and 21st centuries). They must even be aware of the ways in which people (for example, Adolf Hitler) influence events (the rise of Nazi Germany in the 1930s and 1940s).

Connections are discussed in passages, political cartoons, and test questions. Test takers must be able to contextualize, historicize, and analyze connections. Too often the field of social studies is taught as a linear timeline. But, in reality, the field of social studies is more like a complex web of ideas, characters, events, eras, movements, counter-movements, and belief systems. Additionally, views of historical events change throughout history. Today we may analyze slavery differently than the era in which

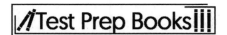 
slavery was legal in the United States. Therefore, students of social studies must also be aware of their own connections to history and all the variables that form its foundations. Below is one example of a cognitive map showing the connections between people, places, environments, processes, and events in social studies.

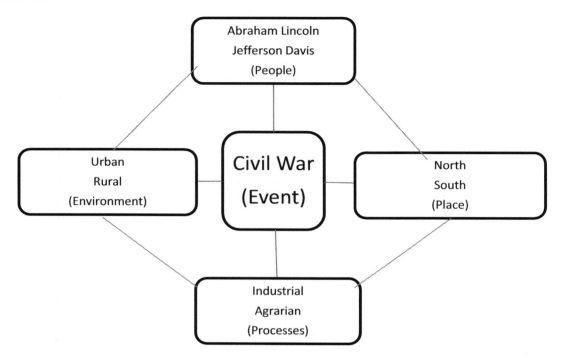

## Putting Events in Order and Understanding the Steps in a Process

Social studies students must understand how to determine the timeline/chronology of events through a process called sequencing. Sequencing allows students to gain a better understanding of change over time in history. Social studies classrooms often employ test questions that force students to recall the correct chronology, or time order, of important historical events.

Along with sequencing, social studies students should be able to carry out a process known as categorizing. Categorizing is the process by which historical themes, events, agents, persons, movements, or ideas are placed in designated categories that help students understand their historical significance. Categorization is usually most effective when certain words or phrases are organized by themes or concepts. For instance, the categorical concept of "economic depression" could help students better understand such historical events as the Panic of 1819, the Great Depression, and the Great Recession. Categorization allows students to link unrelated events in history.

Identifying associations and cause-and-effect relationships strengthens a student's ability to sequence events in history. All U.S. history is a series of associated events leading to still other events. A cause is what made something happen. An effect is what happens because of something. Understanding cause-and-effect helps students to understand the proverbial *why* of history; it helps them breathe more meaning into history.

Comparing and contrasting is another strategy that will make students more historically informed. In history, we often compare two or more things to understand their similarities and differences better. Part of the historical process is understanding what historical characteristics are unique or utterly common. Students might, for instance, compare and contrast the American Revolution to the Texas

Revolution to gain a better understanding of the ways in which such variables as time, geographic location, and contributing persons affect history.

Summarizing is a strategy that is also used often throughout the historical process in a social studies classroom. Students will not only have to summarize the meaning of historical events or eras, but they will also need to know how to summarize the important points of primary and secondary sources. Summaries allow students to convey their knowledge in a short, concise, digestible fashion. Part of summarizing requires that students find the main idea of a particular article, source, or paragraph. Main ideas help students make their summaries even more concise and effective. Summarizing sometimes requires students to make generalizations or draw inferences/conclusions. Often there are "gaps of information" in the sources provided to students. Students will have to use background knowledge and critical-thinking skills to fill in these gaps with generalizations (broad, sweeping statements) or inferences/conclusions (educated guesses, predictions, or assumptions).

## Analyzing the Relationship of Events, Processes, and/or Ideas

Events, processes, and ideas can be related in different ways. Earlier events don't necessarily *cause* later ones; in many cases, they simply occurred prior to the later event. For example, although the battles at Concord and Lexington may seem to be instantaneous eruptions of violence during the American Revolution, they stemmed from a variety of factors. The most obvious influences behind those two battles were the assortment of taxes and policies imposed on the Thirteen Colonies following the French and Indian War from 1754 to 1763. Taxation without direct representation, combined with the deployment of British soldiers to enforce these policies, greatly increased American resistance. Earlier events, such as the Boston Massacre and the Boston Tea Party, similarly stemmed from conflicts between British soldiers and local colonists over perceived tyranny and rebelliousness. Therefore, the start of the American Revolution progressed from earlier developments.

## The Effect of Different Social Studies Concepts on an Argument or Point Of View

## Analyzing How Events and Situations Shape the Author's Point of View

Many people want to rise above their historical contexts, but it is an impossibility. Whether one likes it or not, the ideas of humanity are always influenced by the forces of history. The individual and collective consciousness of humanity is often dictated by historical events and situations. A Jew writing in Germany during World War II would inevitably be affected in some capacity by the anti-Semitic tendencies of Nazism. A Texas-based Mexican national writing during the Mexican-American War of the 1840s would inevitably be influenced by American expansionism. A college student writing and liking posts on Facebook during the Great Recession of 2008 would inevitably be exposed to the effects of the stock market's decline. Even if the author does not comment on these events, they still shape the author's point of view. When analyzing a history text or a historical cartoon, test takers should first ask key questions: "When, where, and why was this documented created?" Often the answers to these questions provide test takers with the evidence they need to properly analyze the documents and answer multiple choice questions.

In some cases, the author of a document explicitly comments on history. The author may refer to historical persons, events, or dates. Test takers should take note of these persons, events, and dates because they offer evidence for answering questions or prompts. For instance, a primary source such as Anne Frank's diary directly refers to the events of World War II and the aggressions of Germans. In other cases, it is up to the test taker to decode the implicit messages embedded in a text in order to gain a better understanding of historical influences. A good place to start with this decoding process is the date

the document was created. If test takers know the date of a document, they can begin to illuminate historical correlations. For instance, a historian writing in the 1960s might not explicitly discuss the historical opinions of the New Left (a political movement of the 1960s), but a test taker may be able to decode the implicit messages embedded in the text and infer that the historian may have been influenced by that era of political thought.

## Evaluating Whether the Author's Evidence is Factual, Relevant, and Sufficient

It's important to read any piece of writing critically. The goal is to discover the point and purpose of what the author is writing about through analysis. It's also crucial to establish the point or stance the author has taken on the topic of the piece. After determining the author's perspective, readers can then more effectively develop their own viewpoints on the subject.

If the argument is that wind energy is the best solution, the author will use facts that support this idea. That same author may leave out relevant facts on solar energy. The way the author uses facts can influence the reader, so it's important to consider the facts being used, how those facts are being presented, and what information might be left out.

## Making Judgments About How Different Ideas Impact the Author's Argument

To reach supportable judgments and conclusions in social studies, teachers and students must be prepared to categorize and synthesize a variety of primary and secondary sources, paying close attention to which sources are legitimate sources of fact or opinion. Students must also be able to justifiably quote information from these sources to establish historical generalizations, or "general statements that identify themes that unite or separate source materials." Often, a generalization identifies key features, relationships, or differences found throughout multiple sources.

## Identifying Bias

Bias exists in all forms of written and visual documentation. In social studies, it is especially important to look out for bias, in both primary and secondary sources. Bias can stem from various sources, including: historical context, cultural background, personal beliefs, political affiliation, and religious values. All these things shape the way an individual sees and writes about history and society. For example, a conservative author writing in the late 1980s may have been likely to support the political initiative known as the War on Drugs.

This likelihood is due to political affiliation and historical context. The 1980s was a conservative era in American politics, thanks to the rise of President Ronald Reagan. It was also a historical era that responded accordingly to the crack epidemic and gained conservative support for expanded police enforcement. Additionally, a communist political cartoonist in the Soviet Union during the Cold War may be likely to paint a picture of the United States as an aggressor. That era of history pitted the Soviet Union against the United States on a global level. Biases even emerge in secondary sources; people analyzing history are influenced by their own cultural-historical contexts.

## Propaganda in Social Studies Readings

There are times in which biases are so extreme that they take the form of propaganda. Propaganda means written, spoken, or visual texts that try to influence or control the opinions of audiences. Two examples of propaganda are the texts and political cartoons published by Nazi Germany during Adolf Hitler's era of leadership. These materials tried to influence or control the beliefs of Germany by exposing them to extreme biases. GED test takers often have to decode texts and political cartoons by exposing biases or propagandistic tendencies.

# *Using Numbers and Graphics in Social Studies*

## Using Data Presented in Visual Form, Including Maps, Charts, Graphs, and Tables

### Making Sense of Information that is Presented in Different Ways

Primary sources contain firsthand documentation of a historical event or era. Primary sources are provided by people who have experienced an historical era or event. Primary sources capture a specific moment, context, or era in history. They are valued as eyewitness accounts and personal perspectives. Examples include diaries, memoirs, journals, letters, interviews, photographs, context-specific artwork, government documents, constitutions, newspapers, personal items, libraries, and archives. Another example of a primary source is the Declaration of Independence. This historical document captures the revolutionary sentiment of an era in American history.

Authors of secondary sources write about events, contexts, and eras in history with a relative amount of experiential, geographic, or temporal distance. Normally, secondary source authors aren't firsthand witnesses. In some cases, they may have experienced an event, but they are offering secondhand, retrospective accounts of their experience. All scholars and historians produce secondary sources—they gather primary source information and synthesize it for a new generation of students. Monographs, biographies, magazine articles, scholarly journals, theses, dissertations, textbooks, and encyclopedias are all secondary sources. In some rare instances, secondary sources become so enmeshed in their era of inquiry that they later become primary sources for future scholars and analysts.

Both primary and secondary sources of information are useful. They both offer invaluable insight that helps the writer learn more about the subject matter. However, researchers are cautioned to examine the information closely and to consider the time period as well as the cultural, political, and social climate in which accounts were given. Learning to distinguish between reliable sources of information and questionable accounts is paramount to a quality research report.

### Analyzing Information from Maps, Tables, Charts, Photographs, and Political Cartoons

Geographers utilize a variety of maps in their study of the spatial world. Projections are maps that represent the spherical globe on a flat surface. Conformal projections attempt to preserve shape but distort size and area. For example, the most well-known projection, the Mercator projection, drastically distorts the size of land areas at the poles. In this particular map, Antarctica, one of the smallest continents, appears massive, while the areas closer to the equator are depicted more accurately.

Other projections attempt to lessen the amount of distortion; the equal-area projection, for example, attempts to accurately represent the size of landforms. However, equal-area projections alter the shapes and angles of landforms regardless of their positioning on the map. Other projections are hybrids of the two primary models. For example, the Robinson projection tries to balance form and area in order to create a more visually accurate representation of the spatial world. Despite the efforts to maintain consistency with shapes, projections cannot provide accurate representations of the Earth's surface due to their flat, two-dimensional nature. In this sense, projections are useful symbols of space, but they do not always provide the most accurate portrayal of reality.

Unlike projections, topographic maps display contour lines, which represent the relative elevation of a particular place and are very useful for surveyors, engineers, and/or travelers. For example, hikers may refer to topographic maps to calculate their daily climbs.

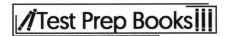

Similar to topographic maps, **isoline maps** are also useful for calculating data and differentiating between the characteristics of two places. These maps use symbols to represent values and lines to connect points with the same value. For example, an isoline map could display average temperatures of a given area. The sections which share the same average temperature would be grouped together by lines. Additionally, isoline maps can help geographers study the world by generating questions. For example, is elevation the only reason for differences in temperature? If not, what other factors could cause the disparity between the values?

Thematic maps are also quite useful because they display the geographical distribution of complex political, physical, social, cultural, economic, or historical themes. For example, a thematic map could indicate an area's election results using a different color for each candidate. There are several different kinds of thematic maps, including dot-density maps and flow-line maps. A *dot-density map* uses dots to illustrate volume and density; these dots could represent a certain population, or the number of specific events that have taken place in an area. Flow-line maps utilize lines of varying thicknesses to illustrate the movement of goods, people, or even animals between two places. Thicker lines represent a greater number of moving elements, and thinner lines represent a smaller number.

## Representing Textual Data into Visual Form

Students should not only be able to analyze maps and other infographics, but they should also be able to create graphs, charts, tables, documents, maps, timelines, and other visual materials to represent geographic, political, historical, economic, and cultural features. Students should be made aware of the different options they have to present data. They should understand that maps visually display geographic features, and they can be used to illustrate key relationships in human geography and natural geography. Maps can indicate themes in history, politics, economics, culture, social relationships, and demographic distributions.

Students can also choose to display data or information in a variety of graphs: Bar graphs compare two or more things with parallel bars; line graphs show change over time with strategic points placed carefully between vertical and horizontal axes; and pie graphs divide wholes into percentages or parts. Likewise, students can choose to use timelines or tables to present data/information. Timelines arrange events or ideas into chronological order, and tables arrange words or numbers into columns or rows. These are just some of the visual tools teachers and students can use to help visually convey their historical questions or ideas.

## Using Graphs with Appropriate Labeling, and Using the Data to Predict Trends

Being "literate" in social studies means that teachers and students must be ready to interpret a variety of forms of data. In social studies, data is usually numerical or statistical information offered in the form of a graph, chart, table, document, map, or timeline.

Sometimes valuable data can also be embedded in documents, maps, or timelines. Thus, it is important that every student is also exposed to these data-based tools in a social studies classroom. Much like all sources, students should be challenged to determine the validity of the data presented in graphs, charts, tables, documents, maps, and timelines.

## Dependent and Independent Variables

As mentioned, the independent variable in an experiment or process is the one that is manipulated, while the dependent one experiences change because of the manipulations to the independent variable.

## Correlation Versus Causation

In social studies, much like in basic statistics, correlation does not always imply causation. Correlation means events occur together, in a relation of more than just random chance. Causation means one thing causes other another. In social studies, one event can be shown to lead to another. For example, the bombing of Pearl Harbor by the Japanese led to the entrance of the United States in the Second World War. The bombing of Pearl Harbor encouraged President Franklin Delano Roosevelt and the United States Congress to declare war on Japan. This example shows a clear line of cause and effect, one that is indisputable in terms of historical evidence.

However, when discussing the Great Depression in America, historians are far less likely to come to a consensus about the cause. Since there are a multitude of variables contributing to the Great Depression, delineating a clear line of causation is more difficult. Instead, historians can discuss the correlation of factors that led to the Depression, which include: increased inflation, increased debt, various taxes and policies, fear, isolationism, corruption, and the excesses of the Roaring Twenties. It is hard to come up with a clear formula of "this equaled that" when it comes to the Great Depression. Thus, it is more applicable to discuss the historical correlations between people, trends, and events.

## Using Statistics in Social Studies

### Mean, Median, Mode, and Range of a Data Set

Recall that the center of a set of data (statistical values) can be represented by its mean, median, or mode. These are sometimes referred to as measures of central tendency. Measures of central tendency can also be used to analyze and understand data related to history and social studies.

The mean is the average of the data set. The mean can be calculated by adding the data values and dividing by the sample size (the number of data points). Suppose a student has test scores of 93, 84, 88, 72, 91, and 77. To find the mean, or average, the scores are added and the sum is divided by 6 because there are 6 test scores:

$$\frac{93 + 84 + 88 + 72 + 91 + 77}{6} = \frac{505}{6} = 84.17$$

Given the mean of a data set and the sum of the data points, the sample size can be determined by dividing the sum by the mean. Suppose you are told that Kate averaged 12 points per game and scored a total of 156 points for the season. The number of games that she played (the sample size or the number of data points) can be determined by dividing the total points (sum of data points) by her average (mean of data points): $\frac{156}{12} = 13$. Therefore, Kate played in 13 games this season.

If given the mean of a data set and the sample size, the sum of the data points can be determined by multiplying the mean and sample size. Suppose you are told that Tom worked 6 days last week for an average of 5.5 hours per day. The total number of hours worked for the week (sum of data points) can be determined by multiplying his daily average (mean of data points) by the number of days worked (sample size):

$$5.5 \times 6 = 33$$

Therefore, Tom worked a total of 33 hours last week.

The median of a data set is the value of the data point in the middle when the sample is arranged in numerical order. To find the median of a data set, the values are written in order from least to greatest. The lowest and highest values are simultaneously eliminated, repeating until the value in the middle remains. Suppose the salaries of math teachers are: $35,000; $38,500; $41,000; $42,000; $42,000; $44,500; $49,000. The values are listed from least to greatest to find the median. The lowest and highest values are eliminated until only the middle value remains. Repeating this step three times reveals a median salary of $42,000. If the sample set has an even number of data points, two values will remain after all others are eliminated. In this case, the mean of the two middle values is the median. Consider the following data set: 7, 9, 10, 13, 14, 14. Eliminating the lowest and highest values twice leaves two values, 10 and 13, in the middle. The mean of these values $\left(\frac{10+13}{2}\right)$ is the median. Therefore, the set has a median of 11.5.

The mode of a data set is the value that appears most often. A data set may have a single mode, multiple modes, or no mode. If different values repeat equally as often, multiple modes exist. If no value repeats, no mode exists. Consider the following data sets:

- A: 7, 9, 10, 13, 14, 14
- B: 37, 44, 33, 37, 49, 44, 51, 34, 37, 33, 44
- C: 173, 154, 151, 168, 155

Set A has a mode of 14. Set B has modes of 37 and 44. Set C has no mode.

The range of a data set is the difference between the highest and the lowest values in the set. The range can be considered the span of the data set. To determine the range, the smallest value in the set is subtracted from the largest value. The ranges for the data sets A, B, and C above are calculated as follows:

A: $14 - 7 = 7$

B: $51 - 33 = 18$

C: $173 - 151 = 22$

# Practice Questions

*Questions 1–3 refer to the passage below*:

> It hath been shewn to have been the constant Opinion of there being a North-west Passage, from the Time soon after which the South Sea was discovered near the Western Part of America, and that this Opinion was adopted by the greatest Men not only in the Time they lived, but whose Eminence and great Abilities are revered by the present Age. That there is a Sea to Westward of Hudson's Bay, there hath been given the concurrent Testimony of Indians; and of Navigators and Indians that there is a Streight which unites such Sea with the Western Ocean. The Voyage which lead us into these Considerations, hath so many Circumstances relating to it, which, now they have been considered, shew the greatest Probability of its being authentick; which carry with them as much the Evidence of a Fact, afford as great a Degree of Credibility as we have for any Transaction done a long Time since, which hath not been of a publick Nature and transacted in the Face of the World, so as to fall under the Notice of every one, though under the Disadvantage that the Intent on one Part must have been to have it concealed and buried in Oblivion.

Excerpt from *The Great Probability of a Northwest Passage* by Thomas Jefferys, 1768

1. Which of the following events most directly triggered increased interest in the maritime route described in the passage?
    a. Vasco da Gama sailing around the Cape of Good Hope in 1488.
    b. Christopher Columbus reaching the Caribbean in 1492.
    c. Ferdinand Magellan's expedition circumnavigating the world in 1522.
    d. Henry Hudson exploring the Hudson Bay in 1611.

2. Which of the following was a long-term consequence of explorers looking for a "North-west passage"?
    a. European powers gained a faster route to the Pacific Ocean.
    b. European powers abandoned international trade networks.
    c. European powers forged alliances with Amerindian empires.
    d. European powers colonized the Americas.

3. Which of the following people most likely funded the expeditions alluded to in the passage?
    a. Monarch
    b. Feudal lord
    c. Leader of a merchant trade guild
    d. Military general

*Questions 4–5 refer to the passage below*:

> What is dangerous for Japan is, not the imitation of the outer features of the West, but the acceptance of the motive force of the Western nationalism as her own. Her social ideals are already showing signs of defeat at the hands of politics. I can see her motto, taken from science, "Survival of the Fittest," writ large at the entrance of her present-day history—the motto whose meaning is, "Help yourself, and never heed what it costs to others"; the motto of the blind man who only believes in what he can touch, because he cannot see. But those who can see know that men are so closely knit that when you strike others the blow comes back to yourself. The moral law, which is the greatest discovery of man, is the discovery of this wonderful truth, that man becomes all the truer the more he realizes himself in others. This truth has not only a subjective value but is manifested in every department of our life. And nations who sedulously cultivate moral blindness as the cult of patriotism will end their existence in a sudden and violent death.

Excerpt from the essay "Nationalism in Japan" by Rabindranath Tagore, 1917

4. Which of the following BEST summarizes the "outer features of the West" that Japan adopted in the nineteenth century?
    a. Japan enacted a written constitution and modernized its military in the nineteenth century.
    b. Japan outlawed Shintoism and orchestrated mass conversions to Christianity.
    c. Japan encouraged nationalism to strengthen the Shogun.
    d. Japan adopted European moral laws and other positive social ideals.

5. Nationalism had the LEAST influence on which one of the following world events?
    a. German unification
    b. Latin American wars of independence
    c. Russo-Turkish War
    d. War of the Spanish Succession

# Answer Explanations

**1. B:** Jefferys is referencing the Northwest Passage. There were rumors about a Northwest Passage to Asia prior to Columbus reaching the Caribbean, and his voyage ignited a firestorm of interest. From 1492 to 1800, European powers sponsored many hundreds of expeditions to locate the route. Thus, Choice *B* is the correct answer. Vasco da Gama sailing around the Cape of Good Hope led to increased European trade with East Africa, India, and China, but his journey around Africa was unrelated to the Northwest Passage. So, Choice *A* is incorrect. Ferdinand Magellan's circumnavigation of the world didn't increase interest in a Northwest Passage because his expedition traveled to Asia across the southern portion of the Atlantic Ocean. So, Choice *C* is incorrect. Choice *D* is the second best answer. European explorers believed the Northwest Passage was located to the west of Hudson Bay, and the passage mentions Hudson Bay. However, the voyage of Christopher Columbus was the inciting incident for the entire Age of Discovery, so Choice *D* is incorrect.

**2. D:** European explorers never found the Northwest Passage, but the search uncovered the Americas' economic potential. European colonization started almost immediately after Columbus reached the Caribbean, and it spread across both continents as explorers continued to search for the elusive route to Asia. Thus, Choice *D* is the correct answer. Although Ferdinand Magellan found a passage to Asia through the southern Atlantic, it was much slower than sailing around the Cape of Good Hope. So, Choice *A* is incorrect. The search for a Northwest Passage exponentially increased international trade, so Choice *B* is incorrect. European powers occasionally made strategic short-term alliances with individual Amerindian tribes, but alliances weren't a long-term consequence of European exploration in the Americas. As such, Choice *C* is incorrect.

**3. A:** European monarchies were the primary sponsors of maritime expeditions that searched for an alternative route to Asia via a Northwest Passage in the Atlantic Ocean. Thus, Choice *A* is the correct answer. Feudal political systems collapsed in the fifteenth century, and the passage was published in 1768. So, Choice *B* is incorrect. Choice *C* is the second best answer. Some wealthy merchants invested in joint-stock companies that sponsored expeditions, but maritime expeditions typically required a royal charter. As such, the monarchy was still always involved in maritime expeditions during the eighteenth century. In addition, joint-stock companies were independent legal entities, so they were rarely connected to trade guilds. Therefore, Choice *C* is incorrect. Although maritime expeditions usually included a militarized component, military generals were not a primary source of funding. So, Choice *D* is incorrect.

**4. A:** The passage mentions that Japan has already imitated the "outer features of the West" before issuing a warning against nationalism. During the late nineteenth century, Japan followed the example of great European powers by modernizing its navy and adopting the Meiji Constitution in writing. Both of these reforms fall under the category of "outer features of the West" as the phrase is used in the passage. Nationalism is defined in spiritual terms throughout the passage, so it would be an "inner feature of the West." Thus, Choice *A* is the correct answer. Shintoism is a traditional Japanese religion, and it's not mentioned in the passage. Japan also didn't orchestrate mass conversions to Christianity, so Choice *B* is incorrect. The Shogun was a Japanese military dictatorship that held power between 1185 and 1868. Japanese modernization efforts dissolved the Shogun, and nationalism was adopted under the new imperial Japanese regime. So, Choice *C* is incorrect. Choice *D* is incorrect because Japan didn't adopt European moral laws or social ideals; rather, Japan embraced nationalism in the late-eighteenth and early-nineteenth centuries.

**5. D:** The Prussian political leader Otto von Bismarck leveraged nationalism to rally support for German unification, which occurred in 1871. So, Choice *A* is incorrect. Mexican nationalists defeated Spanish colonizers in the Mexican Revolution, and Simon Bolivar led nationalist revolts across South America during the early nineteenth century. So, Choice *B* is incorrect. The Russo-Turkish War was largely caused by nationalist revolts in Bulgaria, Montenegro, and Romania against the Ottoman Empire, so Choice *C* is incorrect. The War of the Spanish Succession was fought in the early eighteenth century, which predates the rise of nationalism in continental Europe. Thus, Choice *D* is the correct answer.

# GED Practice Test #1

## *Mathematical Reasoning*

### No Calculator Questions

1. $\frac{3}{25} =$

    a. 0.15
    b. 0.1
    c. 0.9
    d. 0.12

2. What is the value of the following expression?

$$\sqrt{8^2 + 6^2}$$

    a. 14
    b. 10
    c. 9
    d. 100

3. $864 \div 36 =$
    a. 24
    b. 25
    c. 34
    d. 18

4. Ms. Temple's fifth grade class has received some grades for the geometry math unit. Each student who achieves at least an 80% overall average on the three graded criteria will receive a star. Each score is weighted equally so they all contribute equally toward the overall average. Using the scores for the quiz, homework, and participation for each student, determine which students have met the 80% minimum and place a star in the appropriate box.

| Name | Quiz Score | Homework Score | Participation | Star |
|------|-----------|----------------|---------------|------|
| Brian | 8/10 | 2/5 | 9/10 | |
| Kelsey | 6/10 | 4/5 | 8/10 | |
| Brad | 7/10 | 4/5 | 9/10 | |
| Xavier | 9/10 | 3/5 | 9/10 | |
| Julie | 10/10 | 3/5 | 9/10 | |
| Taylor | 5/10 | 4/5 | 10/10 | |
| Paulina | 6/10 | 5/5 | 8/10 | |
| Mario | 8/10 | 1/5 | 7/10 | |

5. A pizzeria owner regularly creates jumbo pizzas, each with a radius of 9 inches. She is mathematically inclined and wants to know the area of the pizza to purchase the correct boxes and know how much she is feeding her customers. What is the area of the circle, in terms of $\pi$, with a radius of 9 inches?

## Calculator Questions

1. $5.88 \times 3.2 =$
   a. 18.816
   b. 16.44
   c. 20.352
   d. 17

2. How will the following number be written in standard form: $(1 \times 10^4) + (3 \times 10^3) + (7 \times 10^1) + (8 \times 10^0)$
   a. 137
   b. 13,078
   c. 1,378
   d. 8,731

3. What is the value of the expression: $7^2 - 3 \times (4 + 2) + 15 \div 5$?
   a. 12.2
   b. 40.2
   c. 34
   d. 58.2

4. Four people split a bill. The first person pays for $\frac{1}{5}$, the second person pays for $\frac{1}{4}$, and the third person pays for $\frac{1}{3}$. What fraction of the bill does the fourth person pay?

   a. $\frac{13}{60}$

   b. $\frac{47}{60}$

   c. $\frac{1}{4}$

   d. $\frac{4}{15}$

5. A student gets an 85% on a test with 20 questions. How many answers did the student solve correctly?
   a. 15
   b. 16
   c. 17
   d. 18

6. What is $\frac{420}{98}$ rounded to the nearest integer?

    a. 4
    b. 3
    c. 5
    d. 6

7. If Danny takes 48 minutes to walk 3 miles, how long should it take him to walk 5 miles maintaining the same speed?
    a. 32 min
    b. 64 min
    c. 80 min
    d. 96 min

8. Is the following function even, odd, neither, or both?

$$y = \frac{1}{2}x^4 + 2x^2 - 6$$

    a. Even
    b. Odd
    c. Neither
    d. Both

9. An investment of $2,000 is made into an account with an annual interest rate of 5%, compounded continuously. What is the total value for the investment after eight years?
    a. $2,954.91
    b. $3,000
    c. $2,983.65
    d. $2,800

10. What is the volume of a rectangular prism with a height of 2 inches, a width of 4 inches, and a depth of 6 inches?
    a. 12 in³
    b. 24 in³
    c. 48 in³
    d. 96 in³

11. What is the volume of a cylinder, in terms of $\pi$, with a radius of 5 inches and a height of 10 inches?
    a. 250 $\pi$ in³
    b. 50 $\pi$ in³
    c. 100 $\pi$ in³
    d. 200 $\pi$ in³

12. Ten students take a test. Five students get a 50. Four students get a 70. If the average score is 55, what was the last student's score?
    a. 20
    b. 40
    c. 50
    d. 60

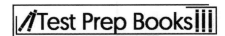 

13. Given the value of a given stock at monthly intervals, which graph should be used to best represent the trend of the stock?
    a. Box plot
    b. Line plot
    c. Line graph
    d. Circle graph

14. A six-sided die is rolled. What is the probability that the roll is 1 or 2?
    a. $\frac{1}{6}$

    b. $\frac{1}{4}$

    c. $\frac{1}{3}$

    d. $\frac{1}{2}$

15. An equilateral triangle has a perimeter of 18 feet. If a square whose sides have the same length as one side of the triangle is built, what will be the area of the square?
    a. 6 square feet
    b. 36 square feet
    c. 256 square feet
    d. 1000 square feet

16. What is the value of $x^2 - 2xy + 2y^2$ when $x = 2, y = 3$?
    a. 8
    b. 10
    c. 12
    d. 14

17. The square and circle have the same center. The circle has a radius of $r$. What is the area of the shaded region?

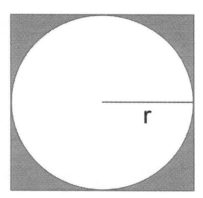

    a. $r^2 - \pi r^2$
    b. $4r^2 - 2\pi r$
    c. $(4 - \pi)r^2$
    d. $(\pi - 1)r^2$

18. What is the expression that represents three times the sum of twice a number and one minus 6?
    a. $2x + 1 - 6$
    b. $3x + 1 - 6$
    c. $3(x + 1) - 6$
    d. $3(2x + 1) - 6$

19. What is the area of a circle, in terms of $\pi$, with a radius of 10 centimeters?
    a. $10\,\pi$ cm $^2$
    b. $20\,\pi$ cm $^2$
    c. $100\,\pi$ cm $^2$
    d. $200\,\pi$ cm $^2$

20. A landscaper is making a circular garden in his back yard, with a radius of 13 feet. He needs to compute the area to know how much soil to purchase. What is the area of the circle in terms of $\pi$?
    a. $26\,\pi$ ft $^2$
    b. $169\,\pi$ ft $^2$
    c. $130\,\pi$ ft $^2$
    d. $260\,\pi$ ft $^2$

21. A cube has sides that are 7 inches long. What is the cube's volume?
    a. $49in^3$
    b. $343in^3$
    c. $294in^3$
    d. $28in^3$

22. Which of the following is largest?
    a. 0.45
    b. 0.096
    c. 0.3
    d. 0.313

23. Which of the following is NOT a way to write 40 percent of $N$?
    a. $(0.4)N$
    b. $\frac{2}{5}N$
    c. $40N$
    d. $\frac{4N}{10}$

24. An equation for the line passing through the origin and the point (2, 1) is
    a. $y = 2x$
    b. $y = \frac{1}{2}x$
    c. $y = x - 2$
    d. $2y = x + 1$

25. A farmer owns two (non-adjacent) square plots of land, which he wishes to fence. The area of one is 1000 square feet, while the area of the other is 10 square feet. How much fencing does he need, in feet?

    a. 44

    b. $40\sqrt{10}$

    c. $440\sqrt{10}$

    d. $44\sqrt{10}$

26. If $\log_{10} x = 2$, then $x$ is

    a. 4

    b. 20

    c. 100

    d. 1000

27. Five of six numbers have a sum of 25. The average of all six numbers is 6. What is the sixth number?

    a. 8

    b. 10

    c. 11

    d. 12

28. $52.3 \times 10^{-3} =$

    a. 0.00523

    b. 0.0523

    c. 0.523

    d. 523

29. If $\frac{5}{2} \div \frac{1}{3} = n$, then $n$ is between:

    a. 5 and 7

    b. 7 and 9

    c. 9 and 11

    d. 3 and 5

30. A closet is filled with red, blue, and green shirts. If $\frac{1}{3}$ of the shirts are green and $\frac{2}{5}$ are red, what fraction of the shirts are blue?

    a. $\frac{4}{15}$

    b. $\frac{1}{5}$

    c. $\frac{7}{15}$

    d. $\frac{1}{2}$

31. Express as an improper fraction $11\frac{5}{8}$.

a. $\frac{55}{8}$

b. $\frac{93}{8}$

c. $\frac{16}{11}$

d. $\frac{19}{5}$

32. Round to the nearest tenth: 8.067

a. 8.70

b. 8.1

c. 8.0

d. 8.07

33. Which of the following is the result of simplifying the expression:

$$\frac{4a^{-1}b^3}{a^4b^{-2}} \times \frac{3a}{b}$$

a. $12a^3b^5$

b. $12\frac{b^4}{a^4}$

c. $\frac{12}{a^4}$

d. $7\frac{b^4}{a}$

34. The graph shows the position of a car over a 10-second time interval. Which of the following is the correct interpretation of the graph for the interval 1 to 3 seconds?

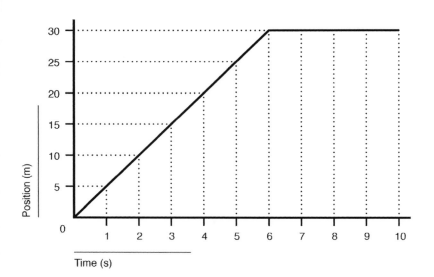

a. The car remains in the same position.
b. The car is traveling at a speed of 5 m/s.
c. The car is traveling up a hill.
d. The car is traveling at 20mph.

35. What is the product of the following expression?

$$(4x - 8)(5x^2 + x + 6)$$

a. $20x^3 - 36x^2 + 16x - 48$
b. $6x^3 - 41x^2 + 12x + 15$
c. $204 + 11x^2 - 37x - 12$
d. $2x^3 - 11x^2 - 32x + 20$

36. What is the solution for the following equation?

$$\frac{x^2 + x - 30}{x - 5} = 11$$

a. $x = -6$
b. There is no solution.
c. $x = 16$
d. $x = 5$

37. If $\sqrt{1 + x} = 4$, what is $x$?
a. 10
b. 15
c. 20
d. 25

38. This chart indicates how many sales of CDs, vinyl records, and MP3 downloads occurred over the last year. Approximately what percentage of the total sales was from CDs?

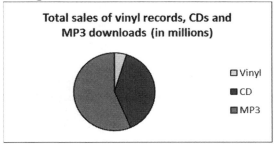

**Total sales of vinyl records, CDs and MP3 downloads (in millions)**

☐ Vinyl
■ CD
■ MP3

a. 55%
b. 25%
c. 40%
d. 5%

39. What is the y-intercept for $y = x^2 + 3x - 4$?
   a. $y = 1$
   b. $y = -4$
   c. $y = 3$
   d. $y = 4$

40. Which equation is not a function?
   a. $y = |x|$
   b. $y = \sqrt{x}$
   c. $x = 3$
   d. $y = 4$

41. What is the answer to $(2 + 2i)(2 - 2i)$?
   a. 8
   b. $8i$
   c. 4
   d. $4i$

# If you want to test your knowledge further on the math section of the GED test, take our online practice quiz. **testprepbooks.com/ged-quiz**

SCAN HERE

# Reasoning Through Language Arts

*Questions 1–6 are based on the following passage:*

As long ago as 1860 it was the proper thing to be born at home. At present, so I am told, the high gods of medicine have decreed that the first cries of the young shall be uttered upon the anesthetic air of a hospital, preferably a fashionable one. So young Mr. and Mrs. Roger Button were fifty years ahead of style when they decided, one day in the summer of 1860, that their first baby should be born in a hospital. Whether this anachronism had any bearing upon the astonishing history I am about to set down will never be known.

I shall tell you what occurred, and let you judge for yourself.

The Roger Buttons held an enviable position, both social and financial, in ante-bellum Baltimore. They were related to the This Family and the That Family, which, as every Southerner knew, entitled them to membership in that enormous peerage which largely populated the Confederacy. This was their first experience with the charming old custom of having babies—Mr. Button was naturally nervous. He hoped it would be a boy so that he could be sent to Yale College in Connecticut, at which institution Mr. Button himself had been known for four years by the somewhat obvious nickname of "Cuff."

On the September morning <u>consecrated</u> to the enormous event he arose nervously at six o'clock, dressed himself, adjusted an impeccable stock, and hurried forth through the streets of Baltimore to the hospital, to determine whether the darkness of the night had borne in new life upon its bosom.

When he was approximately a hundred yards from the Maryland Private Hospital for Ladies and Gentlemen he saw Doctor Keene, the family physician, descending the front steps, rubbing his hands together with a washing movement—as all doctors are required to do by the unwritten ethics of their profession.

Mr. Roger Button, the president of Roger Button & Co., Wholesale Hardware, began to run toward Doctor Keene with much less dignity than was expected from a Southern gentleman of that picturesque period. "Doctor Keene!" he called. "Oh, Doctor Keene!"

The doctor heard him, faced around, and stood waiting, a curious expression settling on his harsh, medicinal face as Mr. Button drew near.

"What happened?" demanded Mr. Button, as he came up in a gasping rush. "What was it? How is she? A boy? Who is it? What—"

"Talk sense!" said Doctor Keene sharply. He appeared somewhat irritated.

"Is the child born?" begged Mr. Button.

Doctor Keene frowned. "Why, yes, I suppose so—after a fashion." Again he threw a curious glance at Mr. Button.

The Curious Case of Benjamin Button, F.S. Fitzgerald, 1922

1. What major event is about to happen in this story?
   a. Mr. Button is about to go to a funeral.
   b. Mr. Button's wife is about to have a baby.
   c. Mr. Button is getting ready to go to the doctor's office.
   d. Mr. Button is about to go shopping for new clothes.

2. What kind of tone does the above passage have?
   a. Nervous and Excited
   b. Sad and Angry
   c. Shameful and Confused
   d. Grateful and Joyous

3. What is the meaning of the word "consecrated" in paragraph 4?
   a. Numbed
   b. Chained
   c. Dedicated
   d. Moved

4. What does the author mean to do by adding the following statement?

   "rubbing his hands together with a washing movement—as all doctors are required to do by the unwritten ethics of their profession."

   a. Suggesting that Mr. Button is tired of the doctor.
   b. Trying to explain the detail of the doctor's profession.
   c. Hinting to readers that the doctor is an unethical man.
   d. Giving readers a visual picture of what the doctor is doing.

5. Which of the following best describes the development of this passage?
   a. It starts in the middle of a narrative in order to transition smoothly to a conclusion.
   b. It is a chronological narrative from beginning to end.
   c. The sequence of events is backwards—we go from future events to past events.
   d. To introduce the setting of the story and its characters.

6. Which of the following is an example of an imperative sentence?
   a. "Oh, Doctor Keene!"
   b. "Talk sense!"
   c. "Is the child born?"
   d. "Why, yes, I suppose so—"

*Questions 7–12 are based on the following passage:*

> Knowing that Mrs. Mallard was afflicted with heart trouble, great care was taken to break to her as gently as possible the news of her husband's death.
>
> It was her sister Josephine who told her, in broken sentences; veiled hints that revealed in half concealing. Her husband's friend Richards was there, too, near her. It was he who had been in the newspaper office when intelligence of the railroad disaster was received, with Brently Mallard's name leading the list of "killed." He had only taken the time to assure himself of its

truth by a second telegram, and had hastened to forestall any less careful, less tender friend in bearing the sad message.

She did not hear the story as many women have heard the same, with a paralyzed inability to accept its significance. She wept at once, with sudden, wild abandonment, in her sister's arms. When the storm of grief had spent itself she went away to her room alone. She would have no one follow her.

There stood, facing the open window, a comfortable, roomy armchair. Into this she sank, pressed down by a physical exhaustion that haunted her body and seemed to reach into her soul.

She could see in the open square before her house the tops of trees that were all aquiver with the new spring life. The delicious breath of rain was in the air. In the street below a peddler was crying his wares. The notes of a distant song which some one was singing reached her faintly, and countless sparrows were twittering in the eaves.

There were patches of blue sky showing here and there through the clouds that had met and piled one above the other in the west facing her window.

She sat with her head thrown back upon the cushion of the chair, quite motionless, except when a sob came up into her throat and shook her, as a child who has cried itself to sleep continues to sob in its dreams.

She was young, with a fair, calm face, whose lines bespoke repression and even a certain strength. But now here was a dull stare in her eyes, whose gaze was fixed away off yonder on one of those patches of blue sky. It was not a glance of reflection, but rather indicated a suspension of intelligent thought.

There was something coming to her and she was waiting for it, fearfully. What was it? She did not know; it was too subtle and elusive to name. But she felt it, creeping out of the sky, reaching toward her through the sounds, the scents, and color that filled the air.

Now her bosom rose and fell tumultuously. She was beginning to recognize this thing that was approaching to possess her, and she was striving to beat it back with her will—as powerless as her two white slender hands would have been. When she abandoned herself a little whispered word escaped her slightly parted lips. She said it over and over under her breath: "free, free, free!" The vacant stare and the look of terror that had followed it went from her eyes. They stayed keen and bright. Her pulses beat fast, and the coursing blood warmed and relaxed every inch of her body.

She did not stop to ask if it were or were not a monstrous joy that held her. A clear and exalted perception enabled her to dismiss the suggestion as trivial. She knew that she would weep again when she saw the kind, tender hands folded in death; the face that had never looked save with love upon her, fixed and gray and dead. But she saw beyond that bitter moment a long procession of years to come that would belong to her absolutely. And she opened and spread her arms out to them in welcome.

Excerpt from "The Story of An Hour," Kate Chopin, 1894

7. What point of view is the above passage told in?
    a. First person
    b. Second person
    c. Third person omniscient
    d. Third person limited

8. What kind of irony are we presented with in this story?
    a. The way Mrs. Mallard reacted to her husband's death.
    b. The way in which Mr. Mallard died.
    c. The way in which the news of her husband's death was presented to Mrs. Mallard.
    d. The way in which nature is compared with death in the story.

9. What is the meaning of the word "elusive" in paragraph 9?
    a. Horrible
    b. Indefinable
    c. Quiet
    d. Joyful

10. What is the best summary of the passage above?
    a. Mr. Mallard, a soldier during World War I, is killed by the enemy and leaves his wife widowed.
    b. Mrs. Mallard understands the value of friendship when her friends show up for her after her husband's death.
    c. Mrs. Mallard combats mental illness daily and will perhaps be sent to a mental institution soon.
    d. Mrs. Mallard, a newly widowed woman, finds unexpected relief in her husband's death.

11. What is the tone of this story?
    a. Confused
    b. Joyful
    c. Depressive
    d. All of the above

12. What is the meaning of the word "tumultuously" in paragraph 10?
    a. Orderly
    b. Unashamedly
    c. Violently
    d. Calmly

*Question 13 is based on the following passage:*

In 2015, 28 countries, including Estonia, Portugal, Slovenia, and Latvia, scored significantly higher than the United States on standardized high school math tests. In the 1960s, the United States consistently ranked first in the world. Today, the United States spends more than $800 billion dollars on education, which exceeds the next highest country by more than $600 billion dollars. The United States also leads the world in spending per school-aged child by an enormous margin.

13. If these statements above are factual, which of the following statements must be correct?
    a. Outspending other countries on education has benefits beyond standardized math tests.
    b. The United States' education system is corrupt and broken.
    c. The standardized math tests are not representative of American academic prowess.
    d. Spending more money does not guarantee success on standardized math tests.

*Questions 14–17 are based on the following passage:*

I have thought that an example of the intelligence (instinct?) of a class of fish which has come under my observation during my excursions into the Adirondack region of New York State might possibly be of interest to your readers, especially as I am not aware that any one except myself has noticed it, or, at least, has given it publicity.

The female sun-fish (called, I believe, in England, the roach or bream) makes a "hatchery" for her eggs in this wise. Selecting a spot near the banks of the numerous lakes in which this region abounds, and where the water is about 4 inches deep, and still, she builds, with her tail and snout, a circular embankment 3 inches in height and 2 thick. The circle, which is as perfect a one as could be formed with mathematical instruments, is usually a foot and a half in diameter; and at one side of this circular wall an opening is left by the fish of just sufficient width to admit her body.

The mother sun-fish, having now built or provided her "hatchery," deposits her spawn within the circular inclosure, and mounts guard at the entrance until the fry are hatched out and are sufficiently large to take charge of themselves. As the embankment, moreover, is built up to the surface of the water, no enemy can very easily obtain an entrance within the inclosure from the top; while there being only one entrance, the fish is able, with comparative ease, to keep out all intruders.

I have, as I say, noticed this beautiful instinct of the sun-fish for the perpetuity of her species more particularly in the lakes of this region; but doubtless the same habit is common to these fish in other waters.

This excerpt is adapted from "The 'Hatchery' of the Sun-Fish"--- *Scientific American*, #711

14. What is the purpose of this passage?
    a. To show the effects of fish hatcheries on the Adirondack region
    b. To persuade the audience to study Ichthyology (fish science)
    c. To depict the sequence of mating among sun-fish
    d. To enlighten the audience on the habits of sun-fish and their hatcheries

15. What does the word *wise* in this passage most closely mean?
    a. Knowledge
    b. Manner
    c. Shrewd
    d. Ignorance

16. What is the definition of the word *fry* as it appears in the following passage?

> The mother sun-fish, having now built or provided her "hatchery," deposits her spawn within the circular inclosure, and mounts guard at the entrance until the fry are hatched out and are sufficiently large to take charge of themselves.

    a. Fish at the stage of development where they are capable of feeding themselves.
    b. Fish eggs that have been fertilized.
    c. A place where larvae is kept out of danger from other predators.
    d. A dish where fish is placed in oil and fried until golden brown.

17. How is the circle that keeps the larvae of the sun-fish made?
    a. It is formed with mathematical instruments.
    b. The sun-fish builds it with her tail and snout.
    c. It is provided to her as a "hatchery" by Mother Nature.
    d. The sun-fish builds it with her larvae.

*Questions 18–23 are based on the following passage:*

> When researchers and engineers undertake a large-scale scientific project, they may end up making discoveries and developing technologies that have far wider uses than originally intended. This is especially true in NASA, one of the most influential and innovative scientific organizations in America. NASA spinoff technology refers to innovations originally developed for NASA space projects that are now used in a wide range of different commercial fields. Many consumers are unaware that products they are buying are based on NASA research! Spinoff technology proves that it is worthwhile to invest in science research because it could enrich people's lives in unexpected ways.
>
> The first spinoff technology worth mentioning is baby food. In space, where astronauts have limited access to fresh food and fewer options with their daily meals, malnutrition is a serious concern. Consequently, NASA researchers were looking for ways to enhance the nutritional value of astronauts' food. Scientists found that a certain type of algae could be added to food, improving the food's neurological benefits. When experts in the commercial food industry learned of this algae's potential to boost brain health, they were quick to begin their own research. The nutritional substance from algae then developed into a product called life's DHA, which can be found in over 90 percent of infant food sold in America.
>
> Another intriguing example of a spinoff technology can be found in fashion. People who are always dropping their sunglasses may have invested in a pair of sunglasses with scratch resistant lenses—that is, it's impossible to scratch the glass, even if the glasses are dropped on an abrasive surface. This innovation is incredibly advantageous for people who are clumsy, but most shoppers don't know that this technology was originally developed by NASA. Scientists first created scratch resistant glass to help protect costly and crucial equipment from getting scratched in space, especially the helmet visors in space suits. However, sunglass companies

245

later realized that this technology could be profitable for their products, and they licensed the technology from NASA.

18. What is the main purpose of this article?
    a. To advise consumers to do more research before making a purchase
    b. To persuade readers to support NASA research
    c. To tell a narrative about the history of space technology
    d. To define and describe instances of spinoff technology

19. What is the organizational structure of this article?
    a. A general definition followed by more specific examples
    b. A general opinion followed by supporting arguments
    c. An important moment in history followed by chronological details
    d. A popular misconception followed by counterevidence

20. Why did NASA scientists research algae?
    a. They already knew algae was healthy for babies.
    b. They were interested in how to grow food in space.
    c. They were looking for ways to add health benefits to food.
    d. They hoped to use it to protect expensive research equipment.

21. What does the word "neurological" mean in the second paragraph?
    a. Related to the body
    b. Related to the brain
    c. Related to vitamins
    d. Related to technology

22. Why does the author mention space suit helmets?
    a. To give an example of astronaut fashion
    b. To explain where sunglasses got their shape
    c. To explain how astronauts protect their eyes
    d. To give an example of valuable space equipment

23. Which statement would the author probably NOT agree with?
    a. Consumers don't always know the history of the products they are buying.
    b. Sometimes new innovations have unexpected applications.
    c. It is difficult to make money from scientific research.
    d. Space equipment is often very expensive.

*Questions 24–28 are based on the following passage:*

In the quest to understand existence, modern philosophers must question if humans can fully comprehend the world. Classical western approaches to philosophy tend to hold that one can understand something, be it an event or object, by standing outside of the phenomena and observing it. It is then by unbiased observation that one can grasp the details of the world. This seems to hold true for many things. Scientists conduct experiments and record their findings, and thus many natural phenomena become comprehendible. However, several of these observations were possible because humans used tools in order to make these discoveries.

This may seem like an extraneous matter. After all, people invented things like microscopes and telescopes in order to enhance their capacity to view cells or the movement of stars. While humans are still capable of seeing things, the question remains if human beings have the capacity to fully observe and see the world in order to understand it. It would not be an impossible stretch to argue that what humans see through a microscope is not the exact thing itself, but a human interpretation of it.

This would seem to be the case in the "Business of the Holes" experiment conducted by Richard Feynman. To study the way electrons behave, Feynman set up a barrier with two holes and a plate. The plate was there to indicate how many times the electrons would pass through the hole(s). Rather than casually observe the electrons acting under normal circumstances, Feynman discovered that electrons behave in two totally different ways depending on whether or not they are observed. The electrons that were observed had passed through either one of the holes or were caught on the plate as particles. However, electrons that weren't observed acted as waves instead of particles and passed through both holes. This indicated that electrons have a dual nature. Electrons seen by the human eye act like particles, while unseen electrons act like waves of energy.

This dual nature of the electrons presents a conundrum. While humans now have a better understanding of electrons, the fact remains that people cannot entirely perceive how electrons behave without the use of instruments. We can only observe one of the mentioned behaviors, which only provides a partial understanding of the entire function of electrons. Therefore, we're forced to ask ourselves whether the world we observe is objective or if it is subjectively perceived by humans. Or, an alternative question: can man understand the world only through machines that will allow them to observe natural phenomena?

Both questions humble man's capacity to grasp the world. However, those ideas don't consider that many phenomena have been proven by human beings without the use of machines, such as the discovery of gravity. Like all philosophical questions, whether man's reason and observation alone can understand the universe can be approached from many angles.

24. The word *extraneous* in paragraph two can be best interpreted as referring to which one of the following?
    a. Indispensable
    b. Bewildering
    c. Superfluous
    d. Exuberant

25. What is the author's motivation for writing the passage?
    a. To bring to light an alternative view on human perception by examining the role of technology in human understanding.
    b. To educate the reader on the latest astroparticle physics discovery and offer terms that may be unfamiliar to the reader.
    c. To argue that humans are totally blind to the realities of the world by presenting an experiment that proves that electrons are not what they seem on the surface.
    d. To reflect on opposing views of human understanding.

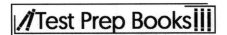 

26. Which of the following most closely resembles the way in which paragraph four is structured?
    a. It offers one solution, questions the solution, and then ends with an alternative solution.
    b. It presents an inquiry, explains the details of that inquiry, and then offers a solution.
    c. It presents a problem, explains the details of that problem, and then ends with more inquiry.
    d. It gives a definition, offers an explanation, and then ends with an inquiry.

27. For the classical approach to understanding to hold true, which of the following must be required?
    a. A telescope
    b. A recording device
    c. Multiple witnesses present
    d. The person observing must be unbiased

28. Which best describes how the electrons in the experiment behaved like waves?
    a. The electrons moved up and down like actual waves.
    b. The electrons passed through both holes and then onto the plate.
    c. The electrons converted to photons upon touching the plate.
    d. Electrons were seen passing through one hole or the other.

*Read the passage below and answer questions 29 & 30:*

To Whom It May Concern:

I'm writing in regards to the Writer/Producer position at Shadow Heat. I graduated with my MA degree in English at the University of Texas in May 2016 where I taught technical writing and writing arguments for my fellowship. My years taking and teaching English courses have enabled me to develop strong writing skills, which I believe will contribute greatly to the position in question.

Although a work in progress, my website, attached below, features technical writing, graphic design, blog writing, and creative writing samples. My passion for writing in order to connect with a specific audience is demonstrated by my various publications as well as my degrees that focus heavily on academic and creative writing. I would love to write for your company and hope you'll consider me for this position.

I'm highly motivated, carrying energy and creativity to my work. My nine years' experience in higher education enables me to adapt to changing ideals and trends while also maintaining personal values. I hope that you'll consider me for this position. I look forward to hearing from you!

Thanks!

29. What type of writing does this passage sound like?
    a. A how-to document on teaching
    b. A consumer email to a corporation
    c. A letter of interest for a resume
    d. A memo concerning employees in the workplace

30. Which of the following is correct information?
    a. The writer of the letter is a writer/producer at Shadow Heat.
    b. The writer of the letter has a Master's degree in English.
    c. The writer of the letter has ten years' experience in higher education.
    d. The writer of the letter is applying to be a website designer.

*Questions 31–36 are based on the following passage:*

> My gentleness and good behaviour had gained so far on the emperor and his court, and indeed upon the army and people in general, that I began to conceive hopes of getting my liberty in a short time. I took all possible methods to cultivate this favourable disposition. The natives came, by degrees, to be less apprehensive of any danger from me. I would sometimes lie down, and let five or six of them dance on my hand; and at last the boys and girls would venture to come and play at hide-and-seek in my hair. I had now made a good progress in understanding and speaking the language. The emperor had a mind one day to entertain me with several of the country shows, wherein they exceed all nations I have known, both for dexterity and magnificence. I was diverted with none so much as that of the rope-dancers, performed upon a slender white thread, extended about two feet, and twelve inches from the ground. Upon which I shall desire liberty, with the reader's patience, to enlarge a little.
>
> This diversion is only practised by those persons who are candidates for great employments, and high favour at court. They are trained in this art from their youth, and are not always of noble birth, or liberal education. When a great office is vacant, either by death or disgrace (which often happens,) five or six of those candidates petition the emperor to entertain his majesty and the court with a dance on the rope; and whoever jumps the highest, without falling, succeeds in the office. Very often the chief ministers themselves are commanded to show their skill, and to convince the emperor that they have not lost their faculty. Flimnap, the treasurer, is allowed to cut a caper on the straight rope, at least an inch higher than any other lord in the whole empire. I have seen him do the summerset several times together, upon a trencher fixed on a rope which is no thicker than a common packthread in England. My friend Reldresal, principal secretary for private affairs, is, in my opinion, if I am not partial, the second after the treasurer; the rest of the great officers are much upon a par.

from Jonathan Swift's *Gulliver's Travels into Several Remote Nations of the World*

31. Which of the following statements best summarizes the central purpose of this text?
    a. Gulliver details his fondness for the archaic yet interesting practices of his captors.
    b. Gulliver conjectures about the intentions of the aristocratic sector of society.
    c. Gulliver becomes acquainted with the people and practices of his new surroundings.
    d. Gulliver's differences cause him to become penitent around new acquaintances.

32. What is the word *principal* referring to in the following text?

> My friend Reldresal, principal secretary for private affairs, is, in my opinion, if I am not partial, the second after the treasurer; the rest of the great officers are much upon a par.

a. Primary or chief
b. An acolyte
c. An individual who provides nurturing
d. One in a subordinate position

33. What can the reader infer from this passage?

> I would sometimes lie down, and let five or six of them dance on my hand; and at last the boys and girls would venture to come and play at hide-and-seek in my hair.

a. The children tortured Gulliver.
b. Gulliver traveled because he wanted to meet new people.
c. Gulliver is considerably larger than the children who are playing around him.
d. Gulliver has a genuine love and enthusiasm for people of all sizes.

34. What is the significance of the word *mind* in the following passage?

> The emperor had a mind one day to entertain me with several of the country shows, wherein they exceed all nations I have known, both for dexterity and magnificence.

a. The ability to think
b. A collective vote
c. A definitive decision
d. A mythological question

35. Which of the following assertions does NOT support the fact that games are a commonplace event in this culture?

a. My gentleness and good behavior . . . short time.
b. They are trained in this art from their youth . . . liberal education.
c. Very often the chief ministers themselves are commanded to show their skill . . . not lost their faculty.
d. Flimnap, the treasurer, is allowed to cut a caper on the straight rope . . . higher than any other lord in the whole empire.

36. How do Flimnap and Reldresal demonstrate the community's emphasis on physical strength and leadership abilities?

a. Only children used Gulliver's hands as a playground.
b. The two men who exhibited superior abilities held prominent positions in the community.
c. Only common townspeople, not leaders, walk the straight rope.
d. No one could jump higher than Gulliver.

*Questions 37 & 38 are based on the following passage:*

Insects as a whole are preeminently creatures of the land and the air. This is shown not only by the possession of wings by a vast majority of the class, but by the mode of breathing to which reference has already been made, a system of branching air-tubes carrying atmospheric air with its combustion-supporting oxygen to all the insect's tissues. The air gains access to these tubes through a number of paired air-holes or spiracles, arranged segmentally in series.

It is of great interest to find that, nevertheless, a number of insects spend much of their time under water. This is true of not a few in the perfect winged state, as for example aquatic beetles and water-bugs ('boatmen' and 'scorpions') which have some way of protecting their spiracles when submerged, and, possessing usually the power of flight, can pass on occasion from pond or stream to upper air. But it is advisable in connection with our present subject to dwell especially on some insects that remain continually under water till they are ready to undergo their final moult and attain the winged state, which they pass entirely in the air. The preparatory instars of such insects are aquatic; the adult instar is aerial. All may-flies, dragon-flies, and caddis-flies, many beetles and two-winged flies, and a few moths thus divide their life-story between the water and the air. For the present we confine attention to the Stone-flies, the May-flies, and the Dragon-flies, three well-known orders of insects respectively called by systematists the Plecoptera, the Ephemeroptera and the Odonata.

In the case of many insects that have aquatic larvae, the latter are provided with some arrangement for enabling them to reach atmospheric air through the surface-film of the water. But the larva of a stone-fly, a dragon-fly, or a may-fly is adapted more completely than these for aquatic life; it can, by means of gills of some kind, breathe the air dissolved in water.

*from The Life-Story of Insects, by Geo H. Carpenter*

37. Which statement best details the central idea in this passage?
    a. It introduces certain insects that transition from water to air.
    b. It delves into entomology, especially where gills are concerned.
    c. It defines what constitutes as insects' breathing.
    d. It invites readers to have a hand in the preservation of insects.

38. Which definition most closely relates to the usage of the word *moult* in the passage?
    a. An adventure of sorts, especially underwater
    b. Mating act between two insects
    c. The act of shedding part or all of the outer shell
    d. Death of an organism that ends in a revival of life

*Questions 39 & 40 are based on the following passage:*

Smoking tobacco products is terribly destructive. A single cigarette contains over 4,000 chemicals, including 43 known carcinogens and 400 deadly toxins. Some of the most dangerous ingredients include tar, carbon monoxide, formaldehyde, ammonia, arsenic, and DDT. Smoking can cause numerous types of cancer including throat, mouth, nasal cavity, esophageal, gastric, pancreatic, renal, bladder, and cervical cancer.

Cigarettes contain a drug called nicotine, one of the most addictive substances known to man. Addiction is defined as a compulsion to seek the substance despite negative consequences. According to the National Institute of Drug Abuse, nearly 35 million smokers expressed a desire to quit smoking in 2015; however, more than 85 percent of those who struggle with addiction will not achieve their goal. Almost all smokers regret picking up that first cigarette. You would be wise to learn from their mistake if you have not yet started smoking.

According to the U.S. Department of Health and Human Services, 16 million people in the United States presently suffer from a smoking-related condition and nearly nine million suffer from a serious smoking-related illness. According to the Centers for Disease Control and Prevention (CDC), tobacco products cause nearly six million deaths per year. This number is projected to rise to over eight million deaths by 2030. Smokers, on average, die ten years earlier than their nonsmoking peers.

In the United States, local, state, and federal governments typically tax tobacco products, which leads to high prices. Nicotine users who struggle with addiction sometimes pay more for a pack of cigarettes than for a few gallons of gas. Additionally, smokers tend to stink. The smell of smoke is all-consuming and creates a pervasive nastiness. Smokers also risk staining their teeth and fingers with yellow residue from the tar.

Smoking is deadly, expensive, and socially unappealing. Clearly, smoking is not worth the risks.

39. Which of the following best describes the passage?
    a. Narrative
    b. Persuasive
    c. Expository
    d. Technical

40. Which of the following statements most accurately summarizes the passage?
    a. Tobacco is less healthy than many alternatives.
    b. Tobacco is deadly, expensive, and socially unappealing, and smokers would be much better off kicking the addiction.
    c. In the United States, local, state, and federal governments typically tax tobacco products, which leads to high prices.
    d. Tobacco products shorten smokers' lives by ten years and kill more than six million people per year.

41. Read the following poem. Which option best expresses the symbolic meaning of the "road" and the overall theme?

> Two roads diverged in a yellow wood,
> And sorry I could not travel both
> And be one traveler, long I stood
> And looked down one as far as I could
> To where it bent in the undergrowth;
> Then took the other, as just as fair,
> And having perhaps the better claim,
> Because it was grassy and wanted wear;
> Though as for that the passing there
> Had worn them really about the same,
> And both that morning equally lay
> In leaves no step had trodden black.
> Oh, I kept the first for another day!
> Yet knowing how way leads on to way,
> I doubted if I should ever come back.
> I shall be telling this with a sigh
> Somewhere ages and ages hence:
> Two roads diverged in a wood, and I—
> I took the one less traveled by,
> And that has made all the difference.

Robert Frost, "The Road Not Taken"

a. A divergent spot where the traveler had to choose the correct path to his destination
b. A choice between good and evil that the traveler needs to make
c. The traveler's struggle between his lost love and his future prospects
d. Life's journey and the choices with which humans are faced

42. Kimmy is a world-famous actress. Millions of people downloaded her leaked movie co-starring her previous boyfriend. Kimmy earns millions through her television show and marketing appearances. There's little wonder that paparazzi track her every move.

What is the argument's primary purpose?
a. Kimmy does not deserve her fame.
b. Kimmy starred in an extremely popular movie.
c. Kimmy earns millions of dollars through her television show and marketing appearances.
d. Kimmy is a highly compensated and extremely popular television and movie actress.

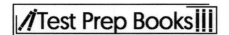
43. Dwight works at a mid-sized regional tech company. He approaches all tasks with unmatched enthusiasm and leads the company in annual sales. The top salesman is always the best employee. Therefore, Dwight is the best employee.

Which of the following most accurately describes how the argument proceeds?

a. The argument proceeds by first stating a conclusion and then offering several premises to justify that conclusion.

b. The argument proceeds by stating a universal rule and then proceeds to show how this situation is the exception.

c. The argument proceeds by stating several facts that serve as the basis for the conclusion at the end of the argument.

d. The argument proceeds by stating several facts, offering a universal rule, and then drawing a conclusion by applying the facts to the rule.

44. Read the following passage:

Last week, we adopted a dog from the local animal shelter, after looking for our perfect pet for several months. We wanted a dog that was not too old, but also past the puppy stage, so that training would be less time-intensive and to give an older animal a home. Robin, as she's called, was a perfect match and we filled out our application and upon approval, were permitted to bring her home. Her physical exam and lab work all confirmed she was healthy. We went to the pet store and bought all sorts of bedding, food, toys, and treats to outfit our house as a dog-friendly and fun place. The shelter told us she liked dry food only, which is a relief because wet food is expensive and pretty off-putting. We even got fencing and installed a dog run in the backyard for Robin to roam unattended. Then we took her to the vet to make sure she was healthy. Next week, she starts the dog obedience class that we enrolled her in with a discount coupon from the shelter. It will be a good opportunity to bond with her and establish commands and dominance. When we took her to the park the afternoon after we adopted her, it was clear that she is a sociable and friendly dog, easily playing cohesively with dogs of all sizes and dispositions.

Which of the following is out of sequence in the story?

a. Last week, we adopted a dog from the local animal shelter, after looking for our perfect pet for several months.

b. Robin, as she's called, was a perfect match and we filled out our application and upon approval, were permitted to bring her home.

c. Her physical exam and lab work all confirmed she was healthy.

d. Next week, she starts the dog obedience class that we enrolled her in with a discount coupon from the shelter.

# *Extended Response*

There are two passages below. Read both of the passages carefully all the way through. Then, choose which passage you think is better supported by evidence. In your response, be sure to use your own evidence from the passages. You will have forty-five minutes to plan, write, and edit your response. Your essay should be around 500 words.

**Passage I**

Shakespeare and His Plays

People who argue that William Shakespeare is not responsible for the plays attributed to his name are known as anti-Stratfordians (from the name of Shakespeare's birthplace, Stratford-upon-Avon). The most common anti-Stratfordian claim is that William Shakespeare simply was not educated enough or from a high enough social class to have written plays overflowing with references to such a wide range of subjects like history, the classics, religion, and international culture. William Shakespeare was the son of a glove-maker, he only had a basic grade school education, and he never set foot outside of England—so how could he have produced plays of such sophistication and imagination? How could he have written in such detail about historical figures and events, or about different cultures and locations around Europe? According to anti-Stratfordians, the depth of knowledge contained in Shakespeare's plays suggests a well-traveled writer from a wealthy background with a university education, not a countryside writer like Shakespeare. But in fact, there is not much substance to such speculation, and most anti-Stratfordian arguments can be refuted with a little background about Shakespeare's time and upbringing.

First of all, those who doubt Shakespeare's authorship often point to his common birth and brief education as stumbling blocks to his writerly genius. Although it is true that Shakespeare did not come from a noble class, his father was a very *successful* glove-maker and his mother was from a very wealthy land-owning family—so while Shakespeare may have had a country upbringing, he was certainly from a well-off family and would have been educated accordingly. Also, even though he did not attend university, grade school education in Shakespeare's time was actually quite rigorous and exposed students to classic drama through writers like Seneca and Ovid. It is not unreasonable to believe that Shakespeare received a very solid foundation in poetry and literature from his early schooling.

Next, anti-Stratfordians tend to question how Shakespeare could write so extensively about countries and cultures he had never visited before (for instance, several of his most famous works like *Romeo and Juliet* and *The Merchant of Venice* were set in Italy, on the opposite side of Europe!). But again, this criticism does not hold up under scrutiny. For one thing, Shakespeare was living in London, a bustling metropolis of international trade, the most populous city in England, and a political and cultural hub of Europe. In the daily crowds of people, Shakespeare would certainly have been able to meet travelers from other countries and hear firsthand accounts of life in their home country. And, in addition to the influx of information from world travelers, this was also the age of the printing press, a jump in technology that made it possible to print and circulate books much more easily than in the past. This also allowed for a freer flow of information across different countries, allowing people to read about life and ideas from throughout Europe. One needn't travel the continent in order to learn and write about its culture.

**Passage II**

*The following passage is from* The Shakespeare Problem Restated *by G.G. Greenwood:*

Now there is very good authority for saying, and I think the truth is so, that at least two of the plays published among the works of Shakespeare are not his at all; that at least three others contain very little, if any, of his writing; and that of the remainder, many contain long passages that are non-Shakespearean. But when we have submitted them all the crucible of criticism we have a magnificent residuum of the purest gold. Here is the true Shakespeare; here is the great magician who, by a wave of his wand, could transmute brass into gold, or make dry bones live and move and have immortal being. Who was this great magician—this mighty dramatist who was "not of an age, but for all time"? Who was the writer of *Venus* and *Lucrece* and the *Sonnets* and *Lear* and *Hamlet*? Was it William Shakespeare of Stratford, the Player? So it is generally believed, and that hypothesis I had accepted in unquestioning faith till my love of the works naturally led me to an examination of the life of the supposed author of them. Then I found that as I read my faith melted away "into thin air." It was not, certainly, that I had (nor have I now) any wish to disbelieve. I was, and I am, altogether willing to accept the Player as the immortal poet if only my reason would allow me to do so. Why not? . . . But the question of authorship is, nevertheless, a most fascinating one. If it be true, as the Rev. Leonard Bacon wrote that "The great world does not care sixpence who wrote *Hamlet*," the great world must, at the same time, be a very small world, and many of us must be content to be outside it. Having given, then, the best attention I was able to give to the question, and more time, I fear, than I ought to have devoted to it, I was brought to the conclusion, as many others have been, that the man who is, truly enough, designated by Messrs. Garnett and Gosse as a "Stratford rustic" is not the true Shakespeare. . .

That Shakespeare the "Stratford rustic and London actor" should have acquired this learning, this culture, and this polish; that *he* should have travelled into foreign lands, studied the life and topography of foreign cities, and the manners and customs of all sorts and conditions of men; that *he* should have written some half-dozen dramas . . . besides qualifying himself as a professional actor; that *he* should have done all this and a good deal more between 1587 and 1592 is a supposition so wild that it can only be entertained by those who are prepared to accept it as a miracle. "And miracles do not happen!"

# If you want to test your knowledge further on the reading comprehension section of the GED test, take our online practice quiz. testprepbooks.com/ged-quiz

# *Science*

## Passage 1

*Questions 1–5 pertain to Passage 1:*

Predators are animals that eat other animals. Prey are animals that are eaten by a predator. Predators and prey have a distinct relationship. Predators rely on the prey population for food and nutrition. They evolve physically to catch their prey. For example, they develop a keen sense of sight, smell, or hearing. They may also be able to run very fast or camouflage to their environment in order to sneak up on their prey. Likewise, the prey population may develop these features to escape and hide from their predators. As predators catch more prey, the prey population dwindles. With fewer prey to catch, the predator population also dwindles. This happens in a cyclical manner over time.

Figure 1 below shows the cyclical population growth in a predator-prey relationship.

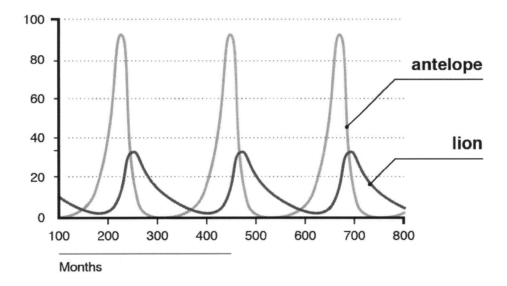

Figure 2 below shows a predator-prey cycle in a circular picture diagram

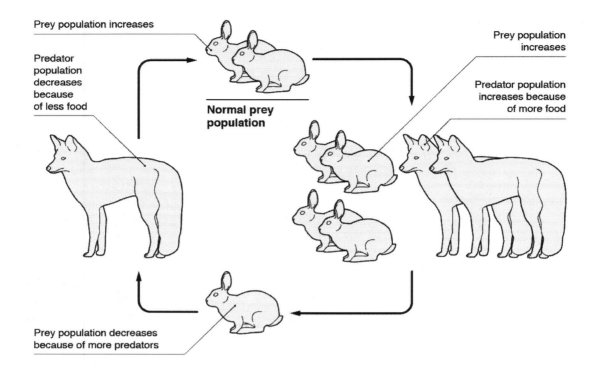

1. Looking at Figure 1, approximately how long is one cycle of the prey population, which includes the population being low, reaching a peak, and then becoming low again?
   a. 300 months
   b. 200 months
   c. 800 months
   d. 400 months

2. In Figure 2, which animal is the predator?
   a. Both the fox and rabbit
   b. Fox only
   c. Rabbit only
   d. Neither the fox nor the rabbit

3. What causes the predator population to decrease?
   a. When there's an increase in the prey population
   b. When winter arrives
   c. When the prey start attacking the predators
   d. When there are fewer prey to find

4. What causes the prey population to increase?
   a. When the predator population decreases, so more prey survive and reproduce.
   b. When there's an increase in the predator population
   c. When there's more sunlight
   d. The prey population always remains the same size.

5. Which is NOT a feature that a prey population can develop to hide from their predator?
   a. Keen sense of smell
   b. Camouflage ability
   c. A loud voice
   d. Keen sense of hearing

## Passage 2

*Questions 6–10 pertain to Passage 2:*

Greenhouses are glass structures that people grow plants in. They allow plants to survive and grow even in the cold winter months by providing light and trapping warm air inside. Light is allowed in through the clear glass walls and roof. Warm air comes in as sunlight through the glass roof. The sunlight is converted into heat, or infrared energy, by the surfaces inside the greenhouse. This heat energy then takes longer to pass back through the glass surfaces and causes the interior of the greenhouse to feel warmer than the outside climate.

Plants may grow better inside a greenhouse versus outside for several reasons. There is more control of the temperature and humidity of the environment inside the greenhouse. The carbon dioxide produced by plants is trapped inside the greenhouse and can increase the rate of photosynthesis of the plants. There are also fewer pests and diseases inside the greenhouse.

Figure 1 below shows how a greenhouse works.

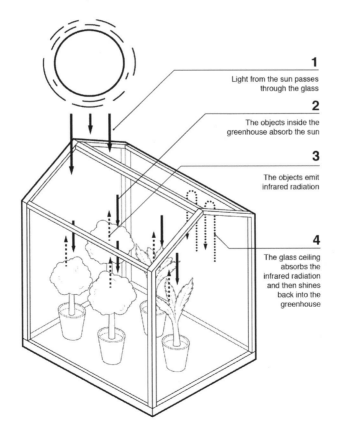

1 Light from the sun passes through the glass

2 The objects inside the greenhouse absorb the sun

3 The objects emit infrared radiation

4 The glass ceiling absorbs the infrared radiation and then shines back into the greenhouse

Scientist A wants to compare how a tomato plant grows inside a greenhouse versus outside a greenhouse.

Figure 2 below shows a graph of her results over 3 months.

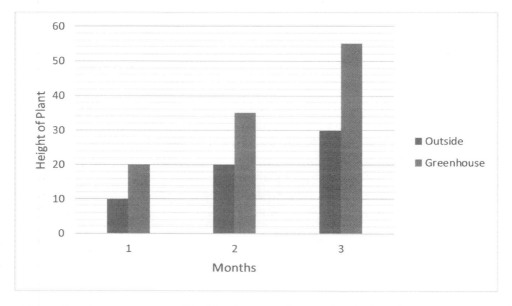

6. Looking at Figure 1, what gets trapped inside the greenhouse that helps plants grow?
   a. Short-wavelength IR
   b. Long-wavelength IR
   c. Cold air
   d. Water

7. Which plant grew taller from Scientist A's experiment?
   a. Outside
   b. Both grew to the same height.
   c. They both remained the same height for 3 months.
   d. Greenhouse

8. What gets converted to heat inside a greenhouse?
   a. Water
   b. Sunlight
   c. Plants
   d. Oxygen

9. What type of wavelength moves through the greenhouse glass easily according to Figure 1?
   a. Short-wavelength IR
   b. Oxygen
   c. Carbon dioxide
   d. Long-wavelength IR

10. What is one reason that plants may grow better inside a greenhouse?
   a. Colder air
   b. Less photosynthesis occurs in the greenhouse
   c. Fewer pests
   d. Less sunlight comes into the greenhouse

## Passage 3

*Questions 11–15 pertain to Passage 3:*

In chemistry, a titration is a method that is used to determine the concentration of an unknown solution. Generally, a known volume of a solution of known concentration is mixed with the unknown solution. Once the reaction of the two solutions has been completed, the concentration of the unknown solution can be calculated. When acids and bases are titrated, the progress of the reaction is monitored by changes in the pH of the known solution. The equivalence point is when just enough of the unknown solution has been added to neutralize the known solution. A color reaction may also occur so that with the drop of solution that causes complete neutralization, the solution turns bright pink, for example. For acids that only have one proton, usually a hydrogen atom, the halfway point between the beginning of the curve and the equivalence point is where the amount of acid and base are equal in the solution. At this point, the pH is equal to the $pK_a$, or the acid dissociation constant.

Figure 1 below shows a general titration curve of a strong acid with a strong base.

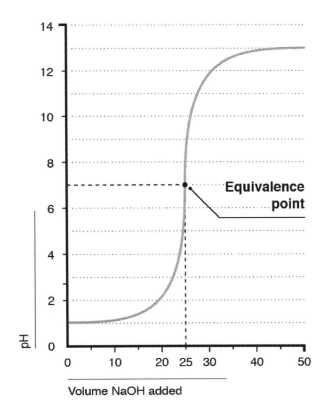

Figure 2 below shows the chemical reaction of a strong acid with a strong base.

Figure 3 shows the titration curve for acetic acid.

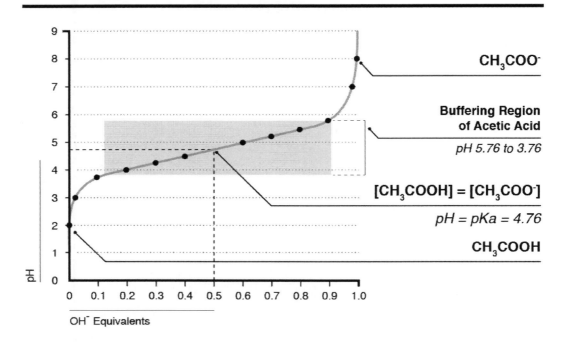

11. How much NaOH is added to the HCl solution to reach the equivalence point in Figure 1?
    a. 10
    b. 40
    c. 50
    d. 25

12. What is the acid dissociation constant of the titration curve in the Figure 3?
    a. 4.21
    b. 3.50
    c. 4.76
    d. 6.52

13. What is the pH of the acetic acid before the titration has started in Figure 3?
   a. 1
   b. 2
   c. 4.76
   d. 6

14. What is one of the products of the chemical equation in Figure 2?
   a. HCl
   b. NaCl
   c. NaOH
   d. Cl⁻

15. How would you describe the solution at the equivalence point in Figure 1?
   a. Neutral
   b. Acidic
   c. Basic
   d. Unknown

## Passage 4

*Questions 16–20 pertain to Passage 4:*

The heart is a muscle that is responsible for pumping blood through the body. It is divided into four chambers: the right atrium, right ventricle, left atrium, and left ventricle. Blood enters the atria and is then pumped into the ventricles below them. There is a valve between the atria and ventricles that prevents the blood from flowing back into the atria. The valve between the right atrium and ventricle has three folds whereas the valve between the left atrium and ventricle has two folds. Arteries carry oxygen-rich blood away from the heart to the body. Veins carry oxygen-poor blood from the body back to the heart. From there, the blood gets pumped to the lungs to get re-oxygenated and then back to the heart before circulating to the body. The heart beats every second of the day. For an adult, the normal heartrate is between 60 and 100 beats per minute. For a child, a normal heartrate is between 90 and 120 beats per minute.

Figure 1 below shows how blood gets pumped through the body.

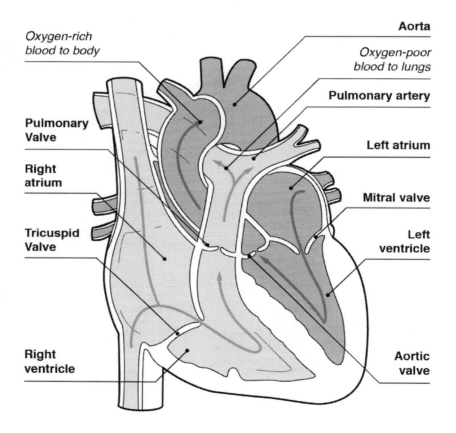

16. Where is the oxygen-poor blood pumped to before returning to the heart to get circulated to the rest of the body?
    a. Lungs
    b. Brain
    c. Stomach
    d. Kidney

17. Which heart valve has two folds?
    a. Pulmonary artery
    b. Tricuspid valve
    c. Mitral valve
    d. Aorta

18. If the aorta contains oxygen-rich blood, what type of vessel is it?
    a. Vein
    b. Pulmonary
    c. Airway
    d. Artery

19. Which heartrate (beats per minute) would be considered normal for a child during resting conditions?
    a. 85
    b. 125
    c. 100
    d. 60

20. The aorta is the artery that breaks into smaller vessels to transport blood to the rest of the body. Looking at the figure, which is the final chamber that the blood flows through before entering the aorta?
    a. Right ventricle
    b. Left ventricle
    c. Right atrium
    d. Left atrium

GED Practice Test #1

## Passage 5

*Questions 21–25 pertain to Passage 5:*

There are three types of rocks: sedimentary, metamorphic, and igneous. Sedimentary rock is formed from sediment, such as sand, shells, and pebbles. The sediment gathers together and hardens over time. It is generally soft and breaks apart easily. This is the only type of rock that contains fossils, which are the remains of animals and plants that lived a long time ago. Metamorphic rock forms under the surface of the earth due to changes in heat and pressure. These rocks usually have ribbon-like layers and may contain shiny crystals. Igneous rock forms when molten rock, or magma, cools and hardens. An example of molten rock is lava, which escapes from an erupting volcano. This type of rock looks shiny and glasslike.

Figure 1 below is a chart of different types of rocks.

| Igneous | | Sedimentary | | Metamorphic | |
|---|---|---|---|---|---|
| Obsidian | Pumice | Shale | Gypsum | Slate | Marble |
| Scoria | Rhyolite | Sandstone | Dolomite | Schist | Quartzite |
| Granite | Gabbro | Conglomerate | Limestone | Gneiss | Anthracite |

21. A volcano erupts and lava comes out and hardens once it is cooled. What type of rock is formed?
    A. Sedimentary
    B. Metamorphic
    C. Igneous
    D. Lava does not cool

22. Scientist A found a piece of granite rock, as seen in Figure 1. What type of rock is it?
    a. Igneous
    b. Metamorphic
    c. Sedimentary
    d. Fossil

266

23. Which type of rock could a fossil be found in?
    a. Igneous
    b. Bone
    c. Metamorphic
    d. Sedimentary

24. Which is an example of a metamorphic rock in the figure?
    a. Sandstone
    b. Slate
    c. Granite
    d. Limestone

25. What type of rock would most likely be formed at and found on the beach?
    a. Sedimentary
    b. Shells
    c. Igneous
    d. Metamorphic

## Passage 6

*Questions 26–30 pertain to Passage 6:*

The greenhouse effect is a natural process that warms the Earth's surface, similar to what occurs in a greenhouse meant to grow plants. Solar energy reaches the Earth's atmosphere and warms the air and land. Some of the energy is absorbed by the greenhouse gases found in the Earth's atmosphere and by the land, and the rest is reflected back into space. Greenhouse gases include water vapor, carbon dioxide, methane, nitrous oxide, and chlorofluorocarbons. In recent decades, human activity has increased the amount of greenhouse gases present in the Earth's atmosphere, which has created a warmer atmosphere than normal and increased the Earth's temperature.

Figure 1 below shows the process of the greenhouse effect.

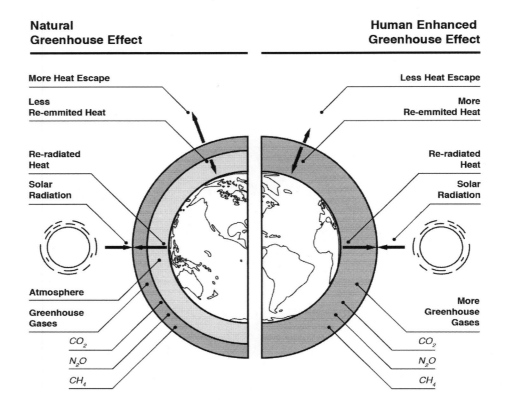

Figure 2 below describes the greenhouse gases that are produced from human activity.

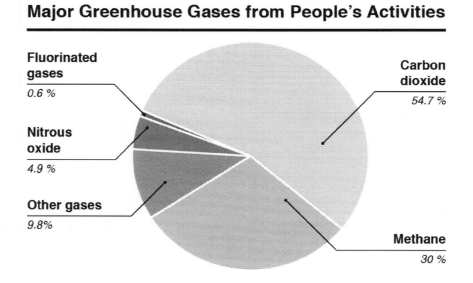

Figure 3 below describes the human activities that produce carbon dioxide.

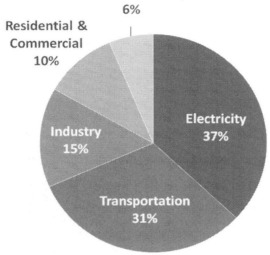

## U.S. Carbon Dioxide Emissions, By Source

U.S. Environmental Protection Agency (2014).
*U.S. Greenhouse Gas Inventory Report: 1990-2014.*

26. Which is not an example of a greenhouse gas?
    a. Methane
    b. Carbon dioxide
    c. Nitrous oxide
    d. Helium gas

27. Looking at Figure 3, what could a person do to decrease how much carbon dioxide they produce?
    a. Leave lights on all the time
    b. Walk instead of drive a car
    c. Always drive in their own car everywhere
    d. Leave the television on all the time

28. Looking at Figure 2, which is the second highest greenhouse gas produced by human activity?
    a. Methane
    b. Fluorinated gases
    c. Nitrous oxide
    d. Carbon dioxide

29. Looking at Figure 1, what gets increasingly trapped in the Earth's atmosphere with increased human activity?
    a. Space
    b. The Sun
    c. Heat
    d. Water vapor

30. What type of charts are found in Figures 2 and 3?
    a. Scatter plots
    b. Line graphs
    c. Bar graphs
    d. Pie charts

## Passage 7

*Questions 31–35 pertain to Passage 7:*

A meteorologist uses many different tools to predict the weather. They study the atmosphere and changes that are occurring to predict what the weather will be like in the future. Listed below are some of the tools that a meteorologist uses:

- Thermometer: measures air temperature
- Barometer: measures air pressure
- Rain gauge: measures rainfall over a specific time
- Anemometer: measures air speed
- Wind vane: shows which direction the wind is blowing

Figure 1 below shows data that is collected by a meteorologist.

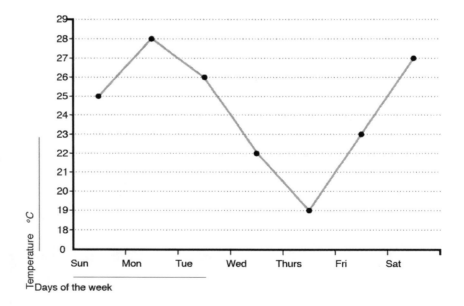

Figure 2 below shows data collected from a rain gauge.

**Rainfall**

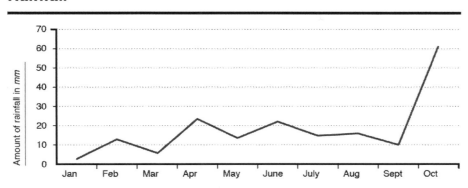

31. What tool would a meteorologist use to find out how fast the wind is blowing?
    a. Anemometer
    b. Barometer
    c. Thermometer
    d. Wind vane

32. What tool was used to collect the data shown in Figure 1?
    a. Rain gauge
    b. Thermometer
    c. Barometer
    d. Anemometer

33. The wind vane is pointing north. What does this tell us?
    a. Wind is blowing in an eastern direction.
    b. A storm is coming.
    c. The wind is blowing in a northern direction.
    d. The wind is blowing in a southern direction.

34. Looking at Figure 2, which month had the lowest rainfall?
    a. January
    b. April
    c. September
    d. October

35. Looking at Figure 2, what was the approximate amount of rain that fell in June?
    a. 0 mm
    b. 10 mm
    c. 50 mm
    d. 20 mm

## Passage 8

*Questions 36–40 pertain to Passage 8:*

Cells are the smallest functional unit of living organisms. Organisms can be single-celled or multicellular. Each cell contains organelles that are responsible for distinct functions and are essential for the organism's life. Plants and animals have different necessities for generating energy and nutrients. Their cells are similar but also have unique features.

Figure 1 below is a depiction of the organelles in an animal cell.

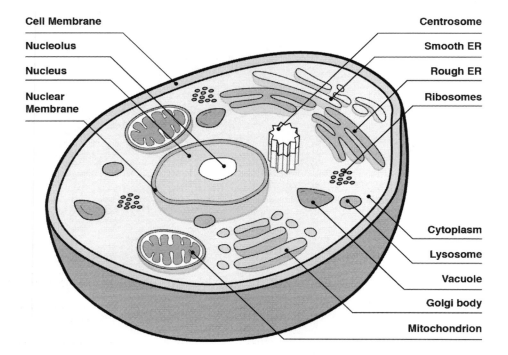

Figure 2 below depicts the organelles of a plant cell.

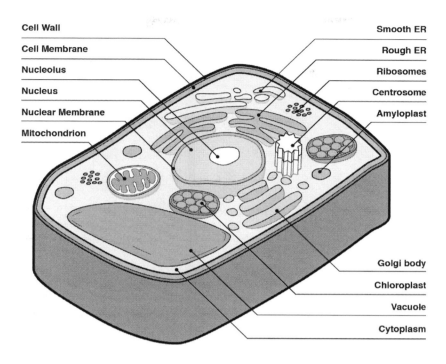

Figure 3 below describes the function of many important organelles.

| Cell Organelle | Function |
|---|---|
| Cell wall | *(Plants only)* Maintains the shape of the cell and is a protective barrier for the internal contents of the cell. |
| Chloroplasts | *(Plants only)* Site of photosynthesis, which converts sunlight energy to glucose storage energy. |
| Nucleus | *(Plants and Animals)* Contains the cell's DNA. |
| Ribosomes | *(Plants and Animals)* Puts together long chains of amino acids to build proteins. Smallest organelle in the cell. |
| Mitochondria | *(Plants and Animals)* The powerhouse of the cell. Converts the stored glucose energy to ATP energy, which drives forward almost all of the cell's reactions. |
| Cell membrane | *(Plants and Animals)* Regulates what molecules can move in and out of the cell. Made of a phospholipid bilayer. |
| Cytoplasm | *(Plants and Animals)* The liquid that fills the inside of the cell. |
| Vacuole | *(Plants and Animals)* A membranous sac that encloses anything in the cell that needs to be kept separate, such as food and water. |
| Golgi Body | *(Plants and Animals)* Receives products produced by the endoplasmic reticulum (ER) and adds final changes to them. |
| Lysosomes | *(Plants and Animals)* A membranous sac that is full of digestive juices. Breaks down larger molecules into smaller parts so that they can be used to build new parts of the cell. |

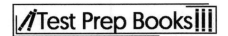

| Cell Organelle | Function |
|---|---|
| Rough endoplasmic reticulum (ER) | *(Plants and Animals)* A large folded membrane that is covered with ribosomes. Helps fold and modify the proteins built by the ribosomes before sending them to the Golgi body. |
| Smooth endoplasmic reticulum (ER) | *(Plants and Animals)* A large folded membrane that puts together lipids. |
| Microtubules and microfilaments | *(Plants and Animals)* Long tubes that allow the cell to move and provide an internal structure of support for the cell. |

36. Which is an organelle found in a plant cell but not an animal cell?
    a. Mitochondria
    b. Chloroplast
    c. Golgi body
    d. Nucleus

37. Where is the nucleolus located in both plant and animal cells?
    a. Near the chloroplast
    b. Inside the mitochondria
    c. Inside the nucleus
    d. Attached to the cell membrane

38. Which organelle is responsible for generating energy for the cell and is referred to as the powerhouse of the cell?
    a. Mitochondria
    b. Nucleus
    c. Ribosomes
    d. Cell wall

39. What does the cell membrane do?
    a. Builds proteins
    b. Breaks down large molecules
    c. Contains the cell's DNA
    d. Controls which molecules are allowed in and out of the cell

40. What are chloroplasts responsible for in plant cells?
    a. Maintaining the cell's shape
    b. Containing the cell's DNA
    c. Converting energy from sunlight to glucose
    d. Building proteins

If you want to test your knowledge further on the science section of the GED test, take our online practice quiz. **testprepbooks.com/ged-quiz**

## *Social Studies*

*Questions 1–5 are based on the following passage:*

Christopher Columbus is often credited for discovering America. This is incorrect. First, it is impossible to "discover" somewhere where people already live; however, Christopher Columbus did explore places in the New World that were previously untouched by Europe, so the term "explorer" would be more accurate. Another correction must be made, as well: Christopher Columbus was not the first European explorer to reach the present-day Americas! Rather, it was Leif Erikson who first came to the New World and contacted the natives, nearly five hundred years before Christopher Columbus.

Leif Erikson, the son of Erik the Red (a famous Viking outlaw and explorer in his own right), was born in either 970 or 980, depending on which historian you seek. His own family, though, did not raise Leif, which was a Viking tradition. Instead, one of Erik's prisoners taught Leif reading and writing, languages, sailing, and weaponry. At age 12, Leif was considered a man and returned to his family. He killed a man during a dispute shortly after his return, and the council banished the Erikson clan to Greenland.

In 999, Leif left Greenland and traveled to Norway where he would serve as a guard to King Olaf Tryggvason. It was there that he became a convert to Christianity. Leif later tried to return home with the intention of taking supplies and spreading Christianity to Greenland, however his ship was blown off course and he arrived in a strange new land: present day Newfoundland, Canada.

When he finally returned to his adopted homeland Greenland, Leif consulted with a merchant who had also seen the shores of this previously unknown land we now know as Canada. The son of the legendary Viking explorer then gathered a crew of 35 men and set sail. Leif became the first European to touch foot in the New World as he explored present-day Baffin Island and Labrador, Canada. His crew called the land "Vinland," since it was plentiful with grapes.

During their time in present-day Newfoundland, Leif's expedition made contact with the natives whom they referred to as Skraelings (which translates to "wretched ones" in Norse). There are several secondhand accounts of their meetings. Some contemporaries described trade between the peoples. Other accounts describe clashes where the Skraelings defeated the Viking explorers with long spears, while still others claim the Vikings dominated the natives. Regardless of the circumstances, it seems that the

Vikings made contact of some kind. This happened around 1000, nearly five hundred years before Columbus famously sailed the ocean blue.

Eventually, in 1003, Leif set sail for home and arrived at Greenland with a ship full of timber. In 1020, seventeen years later, the legendary Viking died. Many believe that Leif Erikson should receive more credit for his contributions in exploring the New World.

1. Which of the following best describes how the author generally presents the information?
   a. Chronological order
   b. Comparison-contrast
   c. Cause-effect
   d. Conclusion-premises

2. Which of the following is an opinion, rather than historical fact, expressed by the author?
   a. Leif Erikson was definitely the son of Erik the Red; however, historians debate the year of his birth.
   b. Leif Erikson's crew called the land "Vinland," since it was plentiful with grapes.
   c. Leif Erikson deserves more credit for his contributions in exploring the New World.
   d. Leif Erikson explored the Americas nearly five hundred years before Christopher Columbus.

3. Which of the following most accurately describes the author's main conclusion?
   a. Leif Erikson is a legendary Viking explorer.
   b. Leif Erikson deserves more credit for exploring America hundreds of years before Columbus.
   c. Spreading Christianity motivated Leif Erikson's expeditions more than any other factor.
   d. Leif Erikson contacted the natives nearly five hundred years before Columbus.

4. Which of the following best describes the author's intent in the passage?
   a. To entertain
   b. To inform
   c. To alert
   d. To suggest

5. Which of the following can be logically inferred from the passage?
   a. The Vikings disliked exploring the New World.
   b. Leif Erikson's banishment from Iceland led to his exploration of present-day Canada.
   c. Leif Erikson never shared his stories of exploration with the King of Norway.
   d. Historians have difficulty definitively pinpointing events in the Vikings' history.

6. Regime types fall along a continuum between which two extremes?
   a. Constitutional and non-constitutional
   b. Military and judicial
   c. Federal and communist
   d. Authoritarian and democratic

7. Which political concept describes a ruling body's ability to influence the actions, behaviors, or attitudes of a person or community?
   a. Authority
   b. Sovereignty
   c. Power
   d. Legitimacy

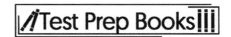

8. The period of business and industrial growth from 1876 through the turn of the twentieth century was deemed by author Mark Twain as what?
   a. Manifest Destiny
   b. The Columbian Exchange
   c. The New Deal
   d. The Gilded Age

9. Which of the following statements would make the best conclusion to an essay about civil rights activist Rosa Parks?
   a. On December 1, 1955, Rosa Parks refused to give up her bus seat to a white passenger, setting in motion the Montgomery bus boycott.
   b. Rosa Parks was a hero to many and came to symbolize the way that ordinary people could bring about real change in the Civil Rights Movement.
   c. Rosa Parks died in 2005 in Detroit, having moved from Montgomery shortly after the bus boycott.
   d. Rosa Parks' arrest was an early part of the Civil Rights Movement and helped lead to the passage of the Civil Rights Act of 1964.

*Questions 10 and 11 are based on the graphic that follows a brief introduction to the topic:*

The United States Constitution directs Congress to conduct a census of the population to determine the country's population and demographic information. The United States Census Bureau carries out the survey. In 1790, then Secretary of State Thomas Jefferson conducted the first census, and the most recent U.S. census was in 2010. The next U.S. census will be the first to be issued primarily through the Internet.

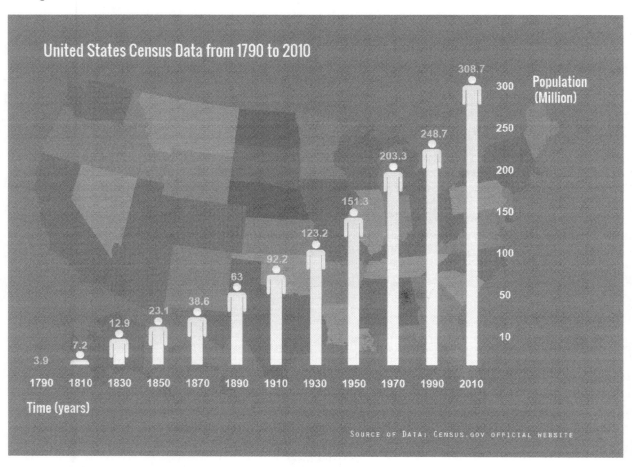

10. In which of the following years was the United States population less than it was in 1930?
    a. 1950
    b. 1970
    c. 1910
    d. 1990

11. In what year did the population increase the most during a twenty-year interval?
    a. From 1930 to 1950
    b. From 1950 to 1970
    c. From 1970 to 1990
    d. From 1990 to 2010

12. Latitudinal lines are used to measure distance
    a. from East to west
    b. from North to south
    c. Between two sets of coordinates
    d. In an inexact manner

13. Which best describes ethnic groups?
    a. Subgroups within a population who share a common history, language, or religion
    b. Divisive groups within a nation's boundaries seeking independence
    c. People who choose to leave a location
    d. Any minority group within a nation's boundaries

14. Which kind of market does not involve government interventions or monopolies while trades are made between suppliers and buyers?
    a. Free
    b. Command
    c. Gross
    d. Exchange

*Questions 15–20 are based upon the following passage:*

*This excerpt is an adaptation from Abraham Lincoln's Address Delivered at the Dedication of the Cemetery at Gettysburg, November 19, 1863.*

> Four score and seven years ago our fathers brought forth on this continent, a new nation, conceived in liberty, and dedicated to the proposition that all men are created equal.
>
> Now we are engaged in a great civil war, testing whether that nation, or any nation so conceived and so dedicated, can long endure. We are met on a great battlefield of that war. We have come to dedicate a portion of that field, as a final resting place for those who here gave their lives that this nation might live. It is altogether fitting and proper that we should do this.
>
> But, in a larger sense, we cannot dedicate, we cannot consecrate, we cannot hallow this ground.. The brave men, living and dead, who struggled here, have consecrated it, far above our poor power to add or detract. The world will little note, nor long remember what we say here, but it can never forget what they did here. It is for us the living, rather, to be dedicated here to the unfinished work which they who fought here have thus far so nobly advanced. It is rather for us to be here and dedicated to the great task remaining before us—that from these honored dead we take increased devotion to that cause for which they gave the last full measure of devotion—that we here highly resolve that these dead shall not have died in vain—that this nation, under God, shall have a new birth of freedom—and that government of people, by the people, for the people, shall not perish from the earth.

15. The best description for the phrase *four score and seven years ago* is which of the following?
    a. A unit of measurement
    b. A period of time
    c. A literary movement
    d. A statement of political reform

16. What is the setting of this text?
    a. A battleship off of the coast of France
    b. A desert plain on the Sahara Desert
    c. A battlefield in North America
    d. The residence of Abraham Lincoln

17. Which war is Abraham Lincoln referring to in the following passage?

    Now we are engaged in a great civil war, testing whether that nation, or any nation so conceived and so dedicated, can long endure.

    a. World War I
    b. The War of the Spanish Succession
    c. World War II
    d. The American Civil War

18. What message is the author trying to convey through this address?
    a. The audience should perpetuate the ideals of freedom that the soldiers died fighting for.
    b. The audience should honor the dead by establishing an annual memorial service.
    c. The audience should form a militia that would overturn the current political structure.
    d. The audience should forget the lives that were lost and discredit the soldiers.

19. In the following selection, what does the word *resolve* mean?

    . . . we here highly resolve that these dead shall not have died in vain—that this nation, under God, shall have a new birth of freedom—and that government of people, by the people, for the people, shall not perish from the earth.

    a. Foresee
    b. Request
    c. Prescribe
    d. Decide

20. What is the effect of Lincoln's statement in the following passage?

> But, in a larger sense, we cannot dedicate, we cannot consecrate, we cannot hallow this
> ground.. The brave men, living and dead, who struggled here, have consecrated it, far above our
> poor power to add or detract.

a. His comparison emphasizes the great sacrifice of the soldiers who fought in the war.
b. His comparison serves as a reminder of the inadequacies of his audience.
c. His comparison serves as a catalyst for guilt and shame among audience members.
d. His comparison attempts to illuminate the great differences between soldiers and civilians.

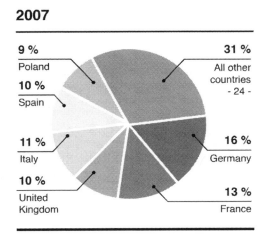

**Populations of Countries of the European Union in 1998 and 2007 by percentage**

**1998**

8 % Poland
9 % Spain
11 % Italy
12 % United Kingdom
30 % All other countries - 24 -
17 % Germany
13 % France

**2007**

9 % Poland
10 % Spain
11 % Italy
10 % United Kingdom
31 % All other countries - 24 -
16 % Germany
13 % France

21. According to the pie charts above, how did the population of Germany change from 1998 to 2007?
    a. It decreased one percent
    b. It increased one percent
    c. It decreased three percent
    d. It increased three percent

22. First-hand accounts of an event, subject matter, time period, or an individual are referred to as what type of source?
    a. Primary sources
    b. Secondary sources
    c. Direct sources
    d. Indirect sources

23. Once the Constitution had been drafted, nine of the thirteen states had to ratify it. Vigorous debate erupted over whether or not the Constitution should be approved. Two different political factions emerged. The Federalists supported the Constitution because they felt a stronger central government was necessary in order to promote economic growth and improve national security. Several leading federalists published a series of articles urging voters to support the Constitution. However, the Anti-Federalists felt that the Constitution took too much power away from the states and gave it to the national government. They also thought there weren't enough protections for individual rights and lobbied for the addition of a Bill of Rights that guaranteed basic liberties. Ultimately, the Constitution was ratified in 1788 and the Bill of Rights was approved a year later.

Based on the passage above and your knowledge of social studies, which of the following people would most likely have agreed with the following statement:

The Constitution should not be approved as is because it gives too much power to the national government.

    a. Alexander Hamilton
    b. James Madison
    c. Thomas Jefferson
    d. John Jay

*Questions 24–25 are based on the following passage:*

In general, the orientations on the left emphasize social and economic equality and advocate for government intervention to achieve it. Orientations on the right of the spectrum generally value the existing and historical political institutions and oppose government intervention, especially in regard to the economy.

**Communism** is a radical political ideology that seeks to establish common ownership over production and abolish social status and money. Communists believe that the world is split between two social classes—capitalists and the working class (often referred to as the proletariat). Communist politics assert that conflict arises from the inequality between the ruling class and the working class; thus, Communism favors a classless society.

**Conservatism** is a political ideology that prioritizes traditional institutions within a culture and civilization. Conservatives, in general, oppose modern developments and value stability. Since Conservatism depends on the traditional institution, this ideology differs greatly from country to

country. Conservatives often emphasize the traditional family structure and the importance of individual self-reliance. Fiscal Conservatism is one of the most common variants, and in general, the proponents of fiscal Conservatism oppose government spending and public debt.

**Progressivism** maintains that progress in the form of scientific and technological advancement, social change, and economic development improve the quality of human life. Progressive ideals include the view that the political and economic interests of the ruling class suppress progress, which results in perpetual social and economic inequality.

**Libertarianism** opposes state intervention on society and the economy. Libertarians advocate for a weak central government, favoring more local rule, and seek to maximize personal autonomy and protect personal freedom. Libertarians often follow a conservative approach to government, especially in the context of power and intervention, but favor a progressive approach to rights and freedom, especially those tied to personal liberty, like freedom of speech.

**Liberalism** developed during the Age of Enlightenment in opposition to absolute monarchy, royal privilege, and state religion. In general, Liberalism emphasizes liberty and equality, and liberals support freedom of speech, freedom of religion, free markets, civil rights, gender equality, and secular governance. Liberals support government intervention into private matters to further social justice and fight inequality; thus, liberals often favor social welfare organizations and economic safety nets to combat income inequality.

**Fascism** is a form of totalitarianism that became popular in Europe after World War I. Fascists advocate for a centralized government led by an all-powerful dictator, tasked with preparing for total war and mobilizing all resources to benefit the state. This orientation's distinguishing features include a consolidated and centralized government.

**Socialism** is closely tied to an economic system. Socialists prioritize the health of the community over the rights of individuals, seeking collective and equitable ownership over the means of production. Socialists tend to be willing to work to elect Socialist policies, like social security, universal health care, unemployment benefits, and other programs related to building a societal safety net.

24. Using the information from the passages above and the introduction about left-axis and right-axis political orientations, which of the following correctly categorizes the orientations mentioned in the passage?

    a. Left-axis ideologies: Socialism, Progressivism, Liberalism; Right-axis ideologies: Fascism, Libertarianism, Communism, Conservatism

    b. Left-axis ideologies: Socialism, Progressivism, Liberalism, Communism; Right-axis ideologies: Fascism, Libertarianism, Conservatism

    c. Left-axis ideologies: Socialism, Progressivism, Libertarianism, Liberalism; Right-axis ideologies: Fascism, Communism, Conservatism

    d. Left-axis ideologies: Socialism, Progressivism, Libertarianism, Communism; Right-axis ideologies: Fascism, Liberalism, Conservatism

25. Which of the following correctly states one of the biggest differences between Fascism and Libertarianism?
   a. Fascists favor a powerful, centralized government, whereas Libertarians favor powerful local rule.
   b. Fascists prioritize governmental spending on strengthening the military, whereas Libertarians believe governmental involvement in terms of power and intervention should be minimal.
   c. Fascists favor a powerful localized government, whereas Libertarians favor a powerful, centralized government.
   d. Fascists believe governmental involvement in terms of power and intervention should be minimal, whereas Libertarians prioritize governmental spending on strengthening the military.

*Questions 26–29 are based on the following passage:*

> Immigrants and emigrants move for physical, cultural, economic, and political reasons. An immigrant is a person who comes from another country to the one currently being discussed, while an emigrant is a person who leaves their home country to settle elsewhere. Geographers traditionally separate reasons for migration into push and pull factors. Political push factors include war, government-induced violence and intimidation, genocide, or oppression. Economic push factors include economic depressions or panics, among other factors. Political pull factors include things like the lure of democracy, safety, and liberty. Economic pull factors include job creation, higher wages, and low unemployment rates. Environmental push factors include flooding, natural disasters, droughts, nuclear contamination, and water contamination. Environmental pull factors include more hospitable climates, low chances of natural disasters, and outdoor aesthetics.

26. Using the information from the passage, as well as your knowledge of social studies concepts, which of the following statements is correct?
   a. Refugees may immigrate from their country because of political push factors.
   b. Refugees may emigrate from their country because of political push factors.
   c. Refugees may immigrate from their country because of political pull factors.
   d. Refugees may emigrate from their country because of political pull factors.

27. During the 1960s–1980s, deindustrialization in cities in the Industrial North (now called the "Rust Belt"), including hubs like Buffalo, Cleveland, Chicago, and Milwaukee, would be considered an example of which of the following?
   a. Political push factor
   b. Political pull factor
   c. Economic push factor
   d. Economic pull factor

28. In the late 19th and early 20th centuries, millions of people immigrated to the United States from Europe because they were enamored by the purported freedoms in the United States. This would be an example of which of the following?
   a. Political push factor
   b. Political pull factor
   c. Economic push factor
   d. Economic pull factor

29. The relocation of many people from the Sahel region of North Africa to other areas because of intense droughts is an example of which of the following?
    a. Political push factor
    b. Political pull factor
    c. Environmental push factor
    d. Environmental pull factor

30. Which of the following is an example of how one main cause of a given effect can actually be subdivided into smaller factors or stretched out in a gradual process?
    a. The way the invention of the telegraph caused changes to the way news traveled
    b. The way the Japanese attack on Pearl Harbor in 1941 caused the United States to enter into World War II
    c. The way Franz Ferdinand's death caused the start of World War I
    d. The way slavery caused the Civil War

*Please use the graphic below to answer Questions 31 and 32:*

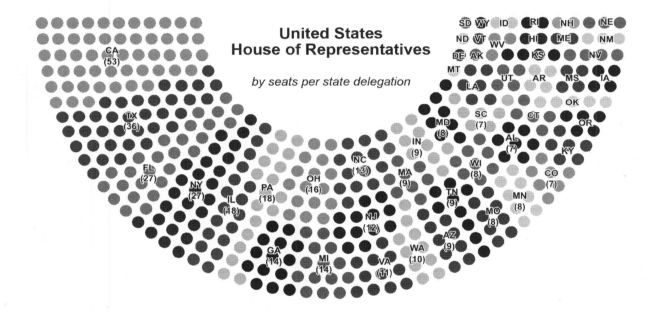

31. Which of the following statements is reflected in the graphic?
    a. The ten least-populated states possess a greater collective representation than the two most-populated states.
    b. The two most-populated states possess a greater collective representation than the ten least-populated states.
    c. The two most-populated states and ten least-populated states possess an equal number of representation.
    d. The ten most-populated states and two least-populated states possess an equal number of representatives.

32. Which of the following states would have the most votes within the Electoral College?
    a. Ohio
    b. Iowa
    c. Michigan
    d. South Dakota

*Questions 33 and 34 are based on the following table:*

| Branch | Role | Checks & Balances on Other Branches | |
|---|---|---|---|
| Executive | Carries out the laws | Legislative Branch<br>• Proposes laws<br>• Vetoes laws<br>• Calls special sessions of Congress<br>• Makes appointments<br>• Negotiates foreign treaties | Judicial Branch<br>• Appoints federal judges<br>• Grants pardons to federal offenders |
| Legislative | Makes the laws | Executive Branch<br>• Has the ability to override a President's veto<br>• Confirms executive appointments<br>• Ratifies treaties<br>• Has the ability to declare war<br>• Appropriates money<br>• Has the ability to impeach and remove President | Judicial Branch<br>• Creates lower federal courts<br>• Has the ability to impeach and remove judges<br>• Has the ability to propose amendments to overrule judicial decisions<br>• Approves appointments of federal judges |
| Judicial | Interprets the laws | Executive Branch<br>• Has the ability to declare executive actions unconstitutional | Legislative Branch<br>• Has the ability to declare acts of Congress unconstitutional |

33. Using the table provided and your understanding of checks and balances, which of the following is true regarding legislation?

a. Members of Congress debate and vote on legislation, although the president may request that legislators consider a certain proposal. The legislation will pass through Congress if it receives a three-quarters majority in both chambers, but the president can veto legislation that he or she disagrees with. The Supreme Court may review legislation and declare it unconstitutional.

b. Members of Congress debate and vote on legislation, although the president may request that legislators consider a certain proposal. The legislation will pass through Congress if it receives a two-thirds majority in both chambers, but the president can veto legislation that he or she disagrees with. The Supreme Court may review legislation and declare it unconstitutional.

c. Members of Congress debate and vote on legislation, although the president may request that legislators consider a certain proposal. The president may veto legislation that he or she disagrees with, but Congress can override the veto with a three-quarters majority in both chambers. The Supreme Court may review legislation and declare it unconstitutional.

d. Members of Congress debate and vote on legislation, although the president may request that legislators consider a certain proposal. The president may veto legislation that he or she disagrees with, but Congress can override the veto with a two-thirds majority in both chambers. The Supreme Court may review legislation and declare it unconstitutional.

34. Using the table provided and your understanding of checks and balances, which of the following is true regarding federal judges?

a. The Legislative branch appoints federal judges, but the Executive branch can impeach and remove judges.
b. The Executive branch appoints federal judges, but the Legislative branch can impeach and remove judges.
c. The Judicial branch appoints federal judges, but the Executive branch can impeach and remove judges.
d. The Judicial branch appoints federal judges, but the Legislative branch can impeach and remove judges.

35. In 1850, the ten most populous cities in the United States, in order from most populous to least were: New York, NY; Baltimore, MD; Boston, MA; Philadelphia, PA; New Orleans, LA; Cincinnati, OH; Brooklyn, NY; St. Louis, MO, Spring Garden, PA; Albany, NY. How many of these cities are located in a state that was one of the original thirteen colonies?

a. 6
b. 7
c. 8
d. 9

If you want to test your knowledge further on the social studies section of the GED test, take our online practice quiz. **testprepbooks.com/ged-quiz**

# Answer Explanations for Practice Test #1

## *Mathematical Reasoning*

### No Calculator Questions

**1. D:** The fraction is converted so that the denominator is 100 by multiplying the numerator and denominator by 4, to get $\frac{3}{25} = \frac{12}{100}$. Dividing a number by 100 just moves the decimal point two places to the left, with a result of 0.12.

**2. B:** 8 squared is 64, and 6 squared is 36. These should be added together to get $64 + 36 = 100$. Then, the last step is to find the square root of 100 which is 10.

**3. A:** The long division would be completed as follows:

$$
\begin{array}{r}
24 \\
36\overline{)864} \\
-72\downarrow \\
\hline
144
\end{array}
$$

**4.** The table below shows the students who achieved at least an 80% average and earned a star.

| Name | Quiz Score | Homework Score | Participation | Star |
|------|-----------|----------------|---------------|------|
| Brian | 8/10 | 2/5 | 9/10 | |
| Kelsey | 6/10 | 4/5 | 8/10 | |
| Brad | 7/10 | 4/5 | 9/10 | ☆ |
| Xavier | 9/10 | 3/5 | 9/10 | ☆ |
| Julie | 10/10 | 3/5 | 9/10 | ☆ |
| Taylor | 5/10 | 4/5 | 10/10 | |
| Paulina | 6/10 | 5/5 | 8/10 | ☆ |
| Mario | 8/10 | 1/5 | 7/10 | |

This problem involved summing the three fractional scores for each student and then converting that total to a percentage. The quiz and participation scores were conveniently presented as fractions out of ten, but in order to add the homework score, which is out of five, a common denominator (of 10) needed to be used. This simply involved multiplying both the numerator and denominator of the homework score by 2. Because a cutoff of 80% was all that was needed to earn a star, it is actually not necessary to convert every student's score to a percentage. The minimum summed fraction that equals 80% can be found and then scores could be compared to that value. After converting the homework

scores to fractions out of ten, each student's score will be some number out of 30. The fraction out of 30 that is equivalent to 80 percent is 24:

$$\frac{x}{30} = \frac{80}{100}$$

Cross-multiplying finds that $100x = 2400, x = 24$.

Therefore, each student must achieve at least 24 points out of the possible 30 to get the star. The completed table showing the calculated scores is below:

| Name | Quiz Score | Homework Score | Participation | Total |
|---|---|---|---|---|
| Brian | 8/10 | 2/5 = 4/10 | 9/10 | 21/30 |
| Kelsey | 6/10 | 4/5 = 8/10 | 8/10 | 22/30 |
| Brad | 7/10 | 4/5 = 8/10 | 9/10 | **24/30** |
| Xavier | 9/10 | 3/5 = 6/10 | 9/10 | **24/30** |
| Julie | 10/10 | 3/5 = 6/10 | 9/10 | **25/30** |
| Taylor | 5/10 | 4/5 = 8/10 | 10/10 | 22/30 |
| Paulina | 6/10 | 5/5 = 10/10 | 8/10 | **24/30** |
| Mario | 8/10 | 1/5 = 2/10 | 7/10 | 17/30 |

**5. 81$\pi$:** The formula for the area of the circle is $\pi r^2$ and 9 squared is 81.

## Calculator Questions

**1. A:** This problem can be multiplied as $588 \times 32$, except at the end, the decimal point needs to be moved three places to the left. Performing the multiplication will give 18,816 and moving the decimal place over three places results in 18.816.

**2. B:** 13,078. The power of 10 by which a digit is multiplied corresponds with the number of zeros following the digit when expressing its value in standard form. Therefore:

$$(1 \times 10^4) + (3 \times 10^3) + (7 \times 10^1) + (8 \times 10^0)$$

$$10,000 + 3,000 + 70 + 8$$

$$13,078$$

**3. C:** 34. When performing calculations consisting of more than one operation, the order of operations should be followed: *Parenthesis, Exponents, Multiplication/Division, Addition/Subtraction.* Parenthesis:

$$7^2 - 3 \times (4 + 2) + 15 \div 5$$

$$7^2 - 3 \times (6) + 15 \div 5$$

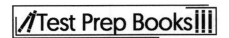

Exponents:

$$7^2 - 3 \times 6 + 15 \div 5 = 49 - 3 \times 6 + 15 \div 5$$

Multiplication/Division (from left to right):

$$49 - 3 \times 6 + 15 \div 5 = 49 - 18 + 3$$

Addition/Subtraction (from left to right):

$$49 - 18 + 3 = 34$$

**4. A:** To find the fraction of the bill that the first three people pay, the fractions need to be added, which means finding the common denominator. The common denominator will be 60.

$$\frac{1}{5} + \frac{1}{4} + \frac{1}{3}$$

$$\frac{12}{60} + \frac{15}{60} + \frac{20}{60} = \frac{47}{60}$$

The remainder of the bill is:

$$1 - \frac{47}{60} = \frac{60}{60} - \frac{47}{60} = \frac{13}{60}$$

**5. C:** 85% of a number means multiplying that number by 0.85.

$$0.85 \times 20 = \frac{85}{100} \times \frac{20}{1}$$

This can be simplified to:

$$\frac{17}{20} \times \frac{20}{1} = 17$$

**6. A:** Dividing by 98 can be approximated by dividing by 100, which would mean shifting the decimal point of the numerator to the left by 2. The result is 4.2 and rounds to 4.

**7. C:** 80 min. To solve the problem, a proportion is written consisting of ratios comparing distance and time. One way to set up the proportion is:

$$\frac{3}{48} = \frac{5}{x} \left( \frac{distance}{time} = \frac{distance}{time} \right)$$

To solve a proportion, the ratios are cross-multiplied:

$$(3)(x) = (5)(48) \rightarrow 3x = 240$$

The equation is solved by isolating the variable, or dividing by 3 on both sides, to produce $x = 80$.

**8. A:** The equation is *even* because:

$$f(-x) = f(x)$$

Plugging in a negative value will result in the same answer as when plugging in the positive of that same value. The function:

$$f(-2) = \frac{1}{2}(-2)^4 + 2(-2)^2 - 6$$

$$8 + 8 - 6 = 10$$

yields the same value as:

$$f(2) = \frac{1}{2}(2)^4 + 2(2)^2 - 6$$

$$8 + 8 - 6$$

$$10$$

**9. C:** The formula for continually compounded interest is:

$$A = Pe^{rt}$$

Plugging in the given values to find the total amount in the account yields the equation:

$$A = 2000e^{0.05 \times 8} = 2983.65$$

Choice A is incorrect because it uses annually compounded interest instead of continuous,

$$A = 2000 \times 1.05^8 = 2954.91$$

Choice B is incorrect because it fails to apply the formula for continuously compounded interest. Choice D is incorrect because it simply adds 40% (or eight times 5%) to the original investment rather than compounding annually.

**10. C:** The volume of a rectangular prism is:

$$length \times width \times height, \text{ and } 2 \ inches \times 4 \ inches \times 6 \ inches \text{ is } 48 \ in^3$$

Choice A is not the correct answer because that is $2 \ inches \times 6 \ inches$. Choice B is not the correct answer because that is $4 \ inches \times 6 \ inches$. Choice D is not the correct answer because that is double of all the sides multiplied together.

**11. A:** The volume of a cylinder is $\pi r^2 h$, and $\pi \times 5^2 \times 10$ is $250 \ \pi \ in^3$. Choice B is not the correct answer because that is $5^2 \times 2\pi$. Choice C is not the correct answer since that is $5cm \times 10\pi \times 2$. Choice D is not the correct answer because that is $10^2 \times 2cm$.

**12. A:** Let the unknown score be $x$. The average will be:

$$\frac{5 \times 50 + 4 \times 70 + x}{10} = \frac{530 + x}{10} = 55$$

Multiply both sides by 10 to get $530 + x = 550$, or $x = 20$.

**13. C:** Line graph. The scenario involves data consisting of two variables, month and stock value. Box plots display data consisting of values for one variable. Therefore, a box plot is not an appropriate choice. Both line plots and circle graphs are used to display frequencies within categorical data. Neither can be used for the given scenario. Line graphs display two numerical variables on a coordinate grid and show trends among the variables.

**14. C:** A die has an equal chance for each outcome. Since it has six sides, each outcome has a probability of $\frac{1}{6}$. The chance of a 1 or a 2 is therefore:

$$\frac{1}{6} + \frac{1}{6} = \frac{1}{3}$$

**15. B:** An equilateral triangle has three sides of equal length, so if the total perimeter is 18 feet, each side must be 6 feet long. A square with sides of 6 feet will have an area of $6^2 = 36$ square feet.

**16. B:** Start with the original equation: $x^2 - 2xy + 2y^2$, then replace each instance of $x$ with a 2, and each instance of $y$ with a 3 to get:

$$2^2 - 2 \times 2 \times 3 + 2 \times 3^2$$

$$4 - 12 + 18$$

$$10$$

**17. C:** The area of the shaded region is the area of the square minus the area of the circle. The area of the circle is $\pi r^2$. The side of the square will be $2r$, so the area of the square will be $4r^2$. Therefore, the difference is:

$$4r^2 - \pi r^2 = (4 - \pi)r^2$$

**18. D:** The expression is three times the sum of twice a number and 1, which is $3(2x + 1)$. Then, 6 is subtracted from this expression.

**19. C:** The formula for the area of the circle is $\pi r^2$ and $10^2$ is 100. Choice *A* is not the correct answer because 10 is not squared. Choice *B* is not the correct answer because that is $2 \times 10$. Choice *D* is not the correct answer because that is $r^2 \times 2$.

**20. B:** The formula for the area of the circle is $\pi r^2$ and 13 squared is 169. Choice *A* is not the correct answer because that is $13 \times 2$. Choice *C* is not the correct answer because that is $13 \times 10$. Choice *D* is not the correct answer because that is $2 \times 13 \times 10$.

**21. B:** The formula for the volume of a cube is $V = s^3$. Substitute the side length of $7in$ to get:

$$V = 7^3 = 343in^3$$

**22. A:** Figure out which is largest by looking at the first non-zero digits. Choice *B*'s first non-zero digit is in the hundredths place. The other three all have non-zero digits in the tenths place, so it must be *A*, *C*, or *D*. Of these, *A* has the largest first non-zero digit.

**23. C:** $40N$ would be 4,000% of $N$. All of the other coefficients are equivalent to $\frac{40}{100}$ or 40%.

**24. B:** The slope will be given by:

$$\frac{1-0}{2-0} = \frac{1}{2}$$

The *y*-intercept will be 0, since it passes through the origin. Using slope-intercept form, the equation for this line is $y = \frac{1}{2}x$.

**25. D:** The first field has an area of 1000 feet, so the length of one side is $\sqrt{1000} = 10\sqrt{10}$. Since there are four sides to a square, the total perimeter is $40\sqrt{10}$. The second square has an area of 10 square feet, so the length of one side is $\sqrt{10}$, and the total perimeter is $4\sqrt{10}$. Adding these together gives:

$$40\sqrt{10} + 4\sqrt{10}$$

$$(40+4)\sqrt{10}$$

$$44\sqrt{10}$$

**26. C:** If $\log_{10} x = 2$, then $10^2 = x$, which equals 100.

**27. C:** The average is calculated by adding all six numbers, then dividing by 6. The first five numbers have a sum of 25. If the total divided by 6 is equal to 6, then the total itself must be 36. The sixth number must be $36 - 25 = 11$.

**28. B:** Multiplying by $10^{-3}$ means moving the decimal point three places to the left, putting in zeroes as necessary.

**29. B:** $\frac{5}{2} \div \frac{1}{3} = \frac{5}{2} \times \frac{3}{1} = \frac{15}{2} = 7.5$.

**30. A:** The total fraction taken up by green and red shirts will be:

$$\frac{1}{3} + \frac{2}{5} = \frac{5}{15} + \frac{6}{15} = \frac{11}{15}$$

The remaining fraction is:

$$1 - \frac{11}{15} = \frac{15}{15} - \frac{11}{15} = \frac{4}{15}$$

**31. B:** $\frac{93}{8}$

The original number was $11\frac{5}{8}$. Multiply the denominator by the whole number portion. Add the numerator and put the total over the original denominator.

$$\frac{(8 \times 11) + 5}{8} = \frac{93}{8}$$

**32. B:** 8.1

To round 8.067 to the nearest tenths, use the digit in the hundredths.

6 in the hundredths is greater than 5, so round up in the tenths.

8.0̲67

0 becomes a 1.

8.1

**33. B:** To simplify the given equation, the first step is to make all exponents positive by moving them to the opposite place in the fraction. This expression becomes:

$$\frac{4b^3b^2}{a^1a^4} \times \frac{3a}{b}$$

Then the rules for exponents can be used to simplify. Multiplying the same bases means the exponents can be added. Dividing the same bases means the exponents are subtracted. Thus, after multiplying the exponents in the first fraction, the equation becomes:

$$\frac{4b^5}{a^5} \times \frac{3a}{b}$$

Therefore, we can first multiply to get $\frac{12ab^5}{a^5b}$. Then, dividing yields $12\frac{b^4}{a^4}$.

**34. B:** The car is traveling at a speed of five meters per second. On the interval from one to three seconds, the position changes by ten meters. By making this change in position over time into a rate, the speed becomes ten meters in two seconds or five meters in one second.

**35. A:** Finding the product means distributing one polynomial over the other so that each term in the first is multiplied by each term in the second. Then, like terms can be collected. Multiplying the factors yields the expression:

$$20x^3 + 4x^2 + 24x - 40x^2 - 8x - 48$$

Collecting like terms means adding the $x^2$ terms and adding the $x$ terms. The final answer after simplifying the expression is:

$$20x^3 - 36x^2 + 16x - 48$$

**36. B:** The equation can be solved by factoring the numerator into:

$$(x + 6)(x - 5)$$

Since that same factor $(x - 5)$ exists on top and bottom, that factor cancels. This leaves the equation $x + 6 = 11$. Solving the equation gives the answer $x = 5$. When this value is plugged into the equation, it yields a zero in the denominator of the fraction. Since this is undefined, there is no solution.

**37. B:** Start by squaring both sides to get $1 + x = 16$. Then subtract 1 from both sides to get $x = 15$.

**38. C:** The sum total percentage of a pie chart must equal 100%. Since the CD sales take up less than half of the chart and more than a quarter (25%), it can be determined to be 40% overall. This can also be

measured with a protractor. The angle of a circle is 360°. Since 25% of 360° would be 90° and 50% would be 180°, the angle percentage of CD sales falls in between; therefore, it would be Choice *C*.

**39. B:** The y-intercept of an equation is found where the $x$-value is zero. Plugging zero into the equation for $x$, the first two terms cancel out, leaving -4.

**40. C:** The equation $x = 3$ is not a function because it does not pass the vertical line test. This test is made from the definition of a function, where each $x$-value must be mapped to one and only one y-value. This equation is a vertical line, so the $x$-value of 3 is mapped with an infinite number of y-values.

**41. A:** This answer is correct because $(2 + 2i)(2 - 2i)$, using the FOIL method and rules for imaginary numbers, is:

$$4 - 4i + 4i - 4i^2 = 8$$

Choice *B* is not the answer because there is no *i* in the final answer, since the *i*'s cancel out in the FOIL. Choice *C*, 4, is not the final answer because we add $4 + 4$ in the end to equal 8. Choice *D*, 4*i*, is not the final answer because there is neither a 4 nor an *i* in the final answer.

## *Reasoning Through Language Arts*

**1. B:** Mr. Button's wife is about to have a baby. The passage begins by giving the reader information about traditional birthing situations. Then, we are told that Mr. and Mrs. Button decide to go against tradition to have their baby in a hospital. The next few passages are dedicated to letting the reader know how Mr. Button dresses and goes to the hospital to welcome his new baby. There is a doctor in this excerpt, as Choice *C* indicates, and Mr. Button does put on clothes, as Choice *D* indicates. However, Mr. Button is not going to the doctor's office nor is he about to go shopping for new clothes.

**2. A:** The tone of the above passage is nervous and excited. We are told in the fourth paragraph that Mr. Button "arose nervously." We also see him running without caution to the doctor to find out about his wife and baby—this indicates his excitement. We also see him stuttering in a nervous yet excited fashion as he asks the doctor if it's a boy or girl. Though the doctor may seem a bit abrupt at the end, indicating a bit of anger or shame, neither of these choices is the overwhelming tone of the entire passage. Despite the circumstances, joy and gratitude are not the main tone in the passage.

**3. C:** Dedicated. Mr. Button is dedicated to the task before him. Choice *A*, numbed, Choice *B*, chained, and Choice *D*, moved, all could grammatically fit in the sentence. However, they are not synonyms with *consecrated* like Choice *C* is.

**4. D:** Giving readers a visual picture of what the doctor is doing. The author describes a visual image—the doctor rubbing his hands together—first and foremost. The author may be trying to make a comment about the profession; however, the author does not "explain the detail of the doctor's profession" as Choice *B* suggests.

**5. D:** To introduce the setting of the story and its characters. We know we are being introduced to the setting because we are given the year in the very first paragraph along with the season: "one day in the summer of 1860." This is a classic structure of an introduction of the setting. We are also getting a long explanation of Mr. Button, what his work is, who is related to him, and what his life is like in the third paragraph.

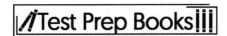

**6. B:** "Talk sense!" is an example of an imperative sentence. An imperative sentence gives a command. The doctor is commanding Mr. Button to talk sense. Choice *A* is an example of an exclamatory sentence, which expresses excitement. Choice *C* is an example of an interrogative sentence—these types of sentences ask questions. Choice *D* is an example of a declarative sentence. This means that the character is simply making a statement.

**7. C:** The point of view is told in third-person omniscient. We know this because the story starts out with us knowing something that the character does not know: that her husband has died. Mrs. Mallard eventually comes to know this, but we as readers know this information before it is broken to her. In third person limited, Choice *D*, we would only see and know what Mrs. Mallard herself knew, and we would find out the news of her husband's death when she found out the news, not before.

**8. A:** The way Mrs. Mallard reacted to her husband's death. The irony in this story is called situational irony, which means the situation that takes place is different than what the audience anticipated. At the beginning of the story, we see Mrs. Mallard react with a burst of grief to her husband's death. However, once she's alone, she begins to contemplate her future and says the word "free" over and over. This is quite a different reaction from Mrs. Mallard than what readers expected from the first of the story.

**9. B:** The word "elusive" most closely means "indefinable." Horrible, Choice *A*, doesn't quite fit with the tone of the word "subtle" that comes before it. Choice *C*, "quiet," is more closely related to the word "subtle." Choice *D*, "joyful," also doesn't quite fit the context here. "Indefinable" is the best option.

**10. D:** Mrs. Mallard, a newly widowed woman, finds unexpected relief in her husband's death. A summary is a brief explanation of the main point of a story. The story mostly focuses on Mrs. Mallard and her reaction to her husband's death, especially in the room when she's alone and contemplating the present and future. All of the other answer choices except Choice *C* are briefly mentioned in the story; however, they are not the main focus of the story.

**11. D:** The interesting thing about this story is that feelings that are confused, joyful, and depressive all play a unique and almost equal part of this story. There is no one right answer here, because the author seems to display all of these emotions through the character of Mrs. Mallard. She displays feelings of depressiveness by her grief at the beginning; then, when she receives feelings of joy, she feels moments of confusion. We as readers cannot help but go through these feelings with the character. Thus, the author creates a tone of depression, joy, and confusion, all in one story.

**12. C:** The word "tumultuously" most nearly means "violently." Even if you don't know the word "tumultuously," look at the surrounding context to figure it out. The next few sentences we see Mrs. Mallard striving to "beat back" the "thing that was approaching to possess her." We see a fearful and almost violent reaction to the emotion that she's having. Thus, her chest would rise and fall tumultuously, or violently.

**13. D:** Outspending other countries on education could have other benefits, but there is no reference to this in the passage, so Choice *A* is incorrect. Choice *B* is incorrect because the author does not mention corruption. Choice *C* is incorrect because there is nothing in the passage stating that the tests are not genuinely representative. Choice *D* is accurate because spending more money has not brought success. The United States already spends the most money, and the country is not excelling on these tests. Choice *D* is the correct answer.

**14. D:** To enlighten the audience on the habits of sun-fish and their hatcheries. Choice *A* is incorrect because although the Adirondack region is mentioned in the text, there is no cause or effect

relationships between the region and fish hatcheries depicted here. Choice *B* is incorrect because the text does not have an agenda, but rather is meant to inform the audience. Finally, Choice *C* is incorrect because the text says nothing of how sun-fish mate.

**15. B:** The word *wise* in this passage most closely means *manner*. Choices *A* and *C* are synonyms of *wise*; however, they are not relevant in the context of the text. Choice *D*, *ignorance*, is opposite of the word wise and is therefore incorrect.

**16. A:** Fish at the stage of development where they are capable of feeding themselves. Even if the word *fry* isn't immediately known to the reader, the context gives a hint when it says "until the fry are hatched out and are sufficiently large to take charge of themselves."

**17. B:** The sun-fish builds it with her tail and snout. The text explains this in the second paragraph: "she builds, with her tail and snout, a circular embankment 3 inches in height and 2 thick." Choice *A* is used in the text as a simile.

**18. D:** To define and describe instances of spinoff technology. This is an example of a purpose question—*why* did the author write this? The article contains facts, definitions, and other objective information without telling a story or arguing an opinion. In this case, the purpose of the article is to inform the reader. The only answer choice that is related to giving information is Choice *D*: to define and describe.

**19. A:** A general definition followed by more specific examples. This organization question asks readers to analyze the structure of the essay. The topic of the essay is about spinoff technology; the first paragraph gives a general definition of the concept, while the following two paragraphs offer more detailed examples to help illustrate this idea.

**20. C:** They were looking for ways to add health benefits to food. This reading comprehension question can be answered based on the second paragraph—scientists were concerned about astronauts' nutrition and began researching useful nutritional supplements. Choice *A* in particular is not true because it reverses the order of discovery (first NASA identified algae for astronaut use, and then it was further developed for use in baby food).

**21. B:** Related to the brain. This vocabulary question could be answered based on the reader's prior knowledge; but even for readers who have never encountered the word "neurological" before, the passage does provide context clues. The very next sentence talks about "this algae's potential to boost brain health," which is a paraphrase of "neurological benefits." From this context, readers should be able to infer that "neurological" is related to the brain.

**22. D:** To give an example of valuable space equipment. This purpose question requires readers to understand the relevance of the given detail. In this case, the author mentions "costly and crucial equipment" before mentioning space suit visors, which are given as an example of something that is very valuable. Choice *A* is not correct because fashion is only related to sunglasses, not to NASA equipment. Choice *B* can be eliminated because it is simply not mentioned in the passage. While Choice *C* seems like it could be a true statement, it is also not relevant to what is being explained by the author.

**23. C:** It is difficult to make money from scientific research. The article gives several examples of how businesses have been able to capitalize on NASA research, so it is unlikely that the author would agree with this statement. Evidence for the other answer choices can be found in the article: for Choice *A*, the author mentions that "many consumers are unaware that products they are buying are based on NASA

research"; Choice *B* is a general definition of spinoff technology; and Choice *D* is mentioned in the final paragraph.

**24. C:** *Extraneous* most nearly means *superfluous*, or *trivial*. Choice *A*, *indispensable*, is incorrect because it means the opposite of *extraneous*. Choice *B, bewildering*, means *confusing* and is not relevant to the context of the sentence. Finally, Choice *D* is incorrect because although the prefix of the word is the same, *ex-*, the word *exuberant* means *elated* or *enthusiastic*, and is irrelevant to the context of the sentence.

**25. A:** The author's purpose is to bring to light an alternative view on human perception by examining the role of technology in human understanding. This is a challenging question because the author's purpose is somewhat open-ended. The author concludes by stating that the questions regarding human perception and observation can be approached from many angles. Thus, the author does not seem to be attempting to prove one thing or another. Choice B is incorrect because we cannot know for certain whether the electron experiment is the latest discovery in astroparticle physics because no date is given. Choice *C* is a broad generalization that does not reflect accurately on the writer's views. While the author does appear to reflect on opposing views of human understanding (Choice *D*), the best answer is Choice *A*.

**26. C:** It presents a problem, explains the details of that problem, and then ends with more inquiry. The beginning of this paragraph literally "presents a conundrum," explains the problem of partial understanding, and then ends with more questions, or inquiry. There is no solution offered in this paragraph, making Choices *A and B* incorrect. Choice *D* is incorrect because the paragraph does not begin with a definition.

**27. D:** Looking back in the text, the author describes that classical philosophy holds that understanding can be reached by careful observation. This will not work if they are overly invested or biased in their pursuit. Choices *A*, *B*, and *C* are in no way related and are completely unnecessary. A specific theory is not necessary to understanding, according to classical philosophy mentioned by the author.

**28. B:** The electrons passed through both holes and then onto the plate. Choices *A* and *C* are incorrect because such movement is not mentioned at all in the text. In the passage, the author says that electrons that were physically observed appeared to pass through one hole or another. Remember, the electrons that were observed doing this were described as acting like particles. Therefore, Choice *D* is incorrect. Recall that the plate actually recorded electrons passing through both holes simultaneously and hitting the plate. This behavior, the electron activity that wasn't seen by humans, was characteristic of waves. Thus, Choice *B* is the right answer.

**29. C:** A letter of interest for a resume. The passage mentions teaching, Choice *A*, but it does not fit the format of a how-to document. A how-to document is a set of instructions for the reader to follow. Choice *B* is incorrect; the writer of the letter is not a consumer of products but trying to apply for a certain position within the company. Choice *D* is also incorrect, as the writer of the letter is not yet an employee, and therefore is incapable of writing the company's memo.

**30. B:** The writer of the letter has a Master's degree in English. Choice *A* is incorrect because the writer of the letter is applying to be a writer/producer at Shadow Heat—they aren't currently a writer/producer there. Choice *C* is also incorrect because the passage states that the writer has nine years' experience in higher education, not ten. Choice *D* is incorrect because the position is listed in the very first sentence: writer/producer, not website designer.

**31. C:** Gulliver becomes acquainted with the people and practices of his new surroundings. Choice *C* is the correct answer because it most extensively summarizes the entire passage. While Choices *A* and *B* are reasonable possibilities, they reference portions of Gulliver's experiences, not the whole. Choice *D* is incorrect because Gulliver doesn't express repentance or sorrow in this particular passage.

**32. A:** Principal refers to *chief* or *primary* within the context of this text. Choice *A* is the answer that most closely aligns with this definition. Choices *B* and *D* make reference to a helper or followers while Choice *C* doesn't meet the description of Reldresal from the passage.

**33. C:** One can reasonably infer that Gulliver is considerably larger than the children who were playing around him because multiple children could fit into his hand. Choice *B* is incorrect because there is no indication of stress in Gulliver's tone. Choices *A* and *D* aren't the best answer because though Gulliver seems fond of his new acquaintances, he didn't travel there with the intentions of meeting new people or to express a definite love for them in this particular portion of the text.

**34. C:** The emperor made a *definitive decision* to expose Gulliver to their native customs. In this instance, the word *mind* was not related to a vote, question, or cognitive ability.

**35. A:** Choice *A* is correct. This assertion does *not* support the fact that games are a commonplace event in this culture because it mentions conduct, not games. Choices *B*, *C*, and *D* are incorrect because these do support the fact that games were a commonplace event.

**36. B:** Choice *B* is the only option that mentions the correlation between physical ability and leadership positions. Choices *A* and *D* are unrelated to physical strength and leadership abilities. Choice *C* does not make a deduction that would lead to the correct answer—it only comments upon the abilities of common townspeople.

**37. A:** It introduces certain insects that transition from water to air. Choice *B* is incorrect because although the passage talks about gills, it is not the central idea of the passage. Choices *C* and *D* are incorrect because the passage does not "define" or "invite," but only serves as an introduction to stoneflies, dragonflies, and mayflies and their transition from water to air.

**38. C:** The act of shedding part or all of the outer shell. Choices *A*, *B*, and *D* are incorrect.

**39. B:** Narrative, Choice *A*, means a written account of connected events. Think of narrative writing as a story. Choice *C*, expository writing, generally seeks to explain or describe some phenomena, whereas Choice *D*, technical writing, includes directions, instructions, and/or explanations. This passage is persuasive writing, which hopes to change someone's beliefs based on an appeal to reason or emotion. The author is aiming to convince the reader that smoking is terrible. They use health, price, and beauty in their argument against smoking, so Choice *B*, persuasive, is the correct answer.

**40. B:** The author is opposed to tobacco. They cite disease and deaths associated with smoking. They point to the monetary expense and aesthetic costs. Choice *A* is incorrect because alternatives to smoking are not addressed in the passage. Choice *C* is incorrect because it does not summarize the passage but is just a premise. Choice *D* is incorrect because, while these statistics are a premise in the argument, they do not represent a summary of the piece. Choice *B* is the correct answer because it states the three critiques offered against tobacco and expresses the author's conclusion.

**41. D:** Choice *D* correctly summarizes Frost's theme of life's journey and the choices one makes. While Choice *A* can be seen as an interpretation, it is a literal one and is incorrect. Literal is not symbolic.

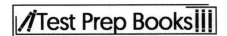 

Choice *B* presents the idea of good and evil as a theme, and the poem does not specify this struggle for the traveler. Choice *C* is a similarly incorrect answer. Love is not the theme.

**42. D:** Choice *A* is irrelevant. The argument does not address whether Kimmy deserves her fame. Eliminate this choice. Choice *B* restates a premise. Kimmy starring in an extremely popular movie is only one piece of the argument. It is not the main purpose. Eliminate this choice. Choice *C* also restates a premise, and it is incorrect for the same reasons as Choice *B*. Eliminate this choice. Choice *D* accurately expresses the argument's conclusion, and it best describes the argument's primary purpose. The argument concludes that Kimmy is a world-famous actress. Choice *D* is the best expression of the argument's purpose. Therefore, Choice *D* is the correct answer.

**43. D:** Choice *A* is incorrect. The argument does not start with a conclusion. Eliminate this choice. Choice *B* is incorrect. Although the argument states a universal rule—the top salesman is always a company's best employee—it does not argue that Dwight is the exception. Eliminate this choice. Choice *C* is fairly strong. The argument does state several facts and offers a conclusion based on those facts. Leave this choice for now. Choice *D* looks extremely promising. The argument first states several facts—Dwight works at a mid-sized regional tech company and leads the company in sales—then states a rule. Lastly, the argument applies the facts to the rule and concludes that Dwight is the best employee. This is a better fit than Choice *C* since it includes the rule and its application. Therefore, Choice *D* is the correct answer.

**44. C:** The passage is told in chronological order, detailing the steps the family took to adopt their dog. The narrator mentions that Robin's physical exam and lab work confirmed she was healthy before discussing that they brought her to the vet to evaluate her health.

# *Science*

**1. A:** One cycle takes 300 months. It starts with the population being low, rising and reaching a peak, and then falling again. It takes 200 months to reach the peak, Choice *B*. Three cycles could be completed in 800 months, Choice *C*, and the second cycle would have started by 400 months, Choice *D*.

**2. B:** Looking at Figure 2, the fox is the predator. When the diagram notes that the predator population decreases on the left side, there is only one fox left. As it increases, as noted on the right side, there are two foxes drawn. Foxes are also much larger than rabbits and would be able to catch them much easier than the other way around.

**3. D:** When the prey population decreases, the predators have less food, i.e. prey, to feed on. This causes the predator population to dwindle. An increase in the prey population, Choice *A*, would actually increase the predator population because they would have more food, which would lengthen survival and increase reproduction. Seasons do not affect the predator population in this situation, Choice *B*. Generally, prey do not have the ability to attack their predators, Choice *C*, due to physical constraints, such as differences in size.

**4. A:** When the predator population decreases, the rate of survival of the prey population increases, and they can then also reproduce more. An increase in the predator population, Choice *B*, would cause the prey population to decrease. Weather and amount of sunlight, Choice *C*, does not affect the growth of the prey population. The prey population is cyclical and does not remain the same size, Choice *D*.

**5. C:** Prey populations can develop different features to try and hide from and escape the predator population. The features help them blend into their environment, such as Choice *B*, or help them

identify predators early and quickly, Choices *A* and *D*. Choice *C* would just allow the predators to hear the prey easily.

**6. B:** Sunlight comes into the greenhouse as short-wavelength IR. As it is absorbed by surfaces in the greenhouse, it is converted to long-wavelength IR. The long-wavelength IR gets trapped inside the greenhouse and bounces off the surfaces and glass and remains inside the greenhouse. Since short-wavelength IR can enter the greenhouse, it also has the ability to leave the greenhouse, making Choice *A* incorrect. The greenhouse feels warmer, not cooler, than outside, so Choice *C* is incorrect. Water is not involved in the reaction noted in Figure 1, so Choice *D* is also incorrect.

**7. D:** Looking at the graph in Figure 2, the greenhouse plant grew taller than the outside plant. The bars representing the greenhouse plant are taller at 3 time points that Scientist A measured. Greenhouses trap sunlight, warm air, and gases, such as $CO_2$ inside the greenhouse, so plants have an increased rate of photosynthesis, allowing them to grow faster. The plants are also protected from pests inside the greenhouse.

**8. B:** Sunlight enters the greenhouse as short-wavelength IR and gets converted to long-wavelength IR. This process also gives off heat and makes the greenhouse feel warmer than the outside climate. Water and oxygen, Choices *A* and *D*, are not involved in this reaction. The plants remain the same and do not get converted into anything else, Choice *C*.

**9. A:** Short-wavelength IR enters the greenhouse in the form of sunlight. It can pass easily through the glass and can therefore pass easily back out to the outside environment. The long-wavelength IR, Choice *D*, gets trapped inside the greenhouse.

**10. C:** The plants inside a greenhouse are protected from many pests that can be found in the outside environment. The air is warmer in the greenhouse, so Choice *A* is incorrect. More photosynthesis occurs because of the increased sunlight energy that stays in the greenhouse, making Choices *B* and *D* incorrect.

**11. D:** The equivalence point occurs when just enough of the unknown solution is added to completely neutralize the known solution. In Figure 1, at the halfway point of the curve, the equivalence point is when 25 volumes of NaOH have been added to the solution. The pH is 7 at this point also, which is a neutralization of the HCl, strong acid.

**12. C:** The acid dissociation constant is the $pK_a$ of the solution. It is found at the halfway point between the beginning of the curve and the equivalence point, where the solution would have a pH of 7 and be completely neutralized. In Figure 3, it is marked as 4.76.

**13. B:** Looking at Figure 3, the vertical axis on the left side has information about the pH of the solution. The horizontal axis at the bottom has information about how much basic solution containing $OH^-$ is being added to the acetic acid. When the $OH^-$ is at 0, and none has been added yet, the pH of the acetic acid is marked as 2.

**14. B:** Looking at the chemical equation in Figure 2, the reactants are on the left side and the products are on the right side. HCl and NaOH, Choices *A* and *C*, are the reactants of the equation. NaCl is the salt that is formed as one of the products of the reaction. The chloride ion, Choice *D*, is not formed in this reaction.

**15. A:** The equivalence point occurs in all titration reactions when the solution is neutralized. If an acid and base are being titrated, the solution is no longer acidic or basic, Choices *B* and *C*. It reaches a pH of 7 and is considered neutral.

**16. A:** Oxygen-poor blood is pumped to the lungs before returning to the heart. Oxygen is transferred from the airways of the lungs into the blood. The blood becomes rich with oxygen and then returns to the heart so that it can bring oxygen and nutrients to other organs of the body, such as the brain, stomach, and kidney, Choices *B*, *C*, and *D*.

**17. C:** The mitral valve has two folds. The tricuspid valve, Choice *B*, has three folds. The valve between the left atrium and ventricle has two valves, as was noted in the descriptive passage. Correlating this information to Figure 1, the name of the valve between these two chambers is the mitral valve. Choices *A* and *D* are vessels that carry blood through them and are not names of valves.

**18. D:** Arteries carry oxygen-rich blood away from the heart to the rest of the body. The aorta is the largest artery in the body. Veins, Choice *A*, carry oxygen-poor blood to the heart and lungs. Airway, Choice *C*, is found in the respiratory system and carries air in and out of the body.

**19. C:** A normal heartrate for a child is between 90 and 120 beats per minute. Choice *C*, 100 beats per minute, falls within this range. Choices *A* and *D* are within the normal range for an adult but not for a child. Children's hearts pump blood faster than adults' hearts through the body. Choice *B*, 125, is higher than the normal range for children.

**20. B:** Looking at Figure 1 and following the arrow in the aorta backwards, the left ventricle is where the blood is coming from directly before it enters the aorta. Blood flows from the atria to the ventricles, so it enters the left atrium before the left ventricle and then the aorta, Choice *D*. Oxygen-poor blood is on the right side of the heart and flows from the right atrium to the right ventricle before flowing to the lungs to get re-oxygenated, Choices *A* and *C*.

**21. C:** Lava is a type of molten rock. When molten rock cools down and hardens, it forms igneous rock. Sedimentary and metamorphic rocks, Choices *A* and *B*, are not formed from molten rock. Choice *D* is incorrect because lava does cool down eventually and becomes hard.

**22: A:** Looking at Figure 1, the granite is found in column A. The description of the rocks in these columns says that these rocks were formed from molten rock. When molten rock cools, it forms igneous rock. Column C describes how metamorphic rocks are formed, Choice *B*. Column B describes how sedimentary rocks are formed, Choice *C*. Fossils, Choice *D*, are not rocks but are formed into sedimentary rock.

**23: D:** Sedimentary rocks are formed from soft materials, such as sand, shells, and pebbles. This allows for fossils to form because the remains of animals or plants can be pressed into the softer rock material and leave their imprint. Fossils cannot form in igneous, Choice *A*, or metamorphic, Choice *C*, rocks. Bones are something that can actually make a fossil imprint, Choice *B*.

**24. B:** Rocks that are formed by changes in heat and pressure are called metamorphic rocks, which is how the rocks in Column C are described. Slate is found in Column C of Figure 1. Sandstone and limestone, Choices *A* and *D*, are both found in Column B, which describes sedimentary rock. Granite, Choice *B*, is found in Column A, which describes sedimentary rock.

**25. A:** Sedimentary rock is formed from sand, shells, and pebbles, all of which are found in abundance at the beach. Shells, Choice *B*, are something that contribute to the formation of sedimentary rock. Igneous rock, Choice *C*, is formed from molten rock, which would likely be much too hot to be found on most beaches. The surface environment of a beach likely does not undergo changes in heat and pressure enough to form metamorphic rock, Choice *D*.

**26. D:** Helium gas is not one of the major direct or indirect greenhouse gases. Looking at Figure 2, Choices *A*, *B*, and *C* are part of the pie chart as greenhouse gases found in the atmosphere.

**27. B:** The two major wedges of the pie chart in Figure 3 are Transportation and Electricity. Using a car, Choice *C*, produces a lot of carbon dioxide. Walking instead of driving a car would not produce any carbon dioxide. Choices *A* and *D* use electricity and leaving either the lights or the television on would need a constant source of electricity, producing lots of carbon dioxide.

**28. A:** Looking at Figure 2, carbon dioxide, Choice *D*, takes up the largest wedge of the pie chart at 54.7%. The next largest wedge is methane at 30%. Nitrous oxide, Choice *C*, takes up only 4.9% and fluorinated gases, Choice *B*, takes up 0.6%.

**29. C:** Looking at Figure 1, in the right picture where there are more greenhouse gases, the re-emitted heat arrow is larger as more heat gets trapped in the Earth's atmosphere. Space and the Sun, Choices *A* and *B*, remain outside the Earth's atmosphere. Water vapor, Choice *D*, is not a part of the diagrams for the greenhouse effect.

**30. D:** Figures 2 and 3 are pie charts. Circular charts that are broken up into wedges, or pie pieces, are called pie charts. Scatter plots, Choice *A*, have specific point markers to mark each data point. In line graphs, Choice *B*, data are represented by connecting lines. In bar graphs, Choice *C*, data are represented by vertical or horizontal bars.

**31. A:** An anemometer measures air speed. Wind is the movement of air, so an anemometer would be able to measure wind speed. A barometer, Choice *B*, measures air pressure. A thermometer, Choice *C*, measures temperature. A wind vane, Choice *D*, shows which direction the wind is blowing.

**32. B:** Figure 1 is a graph showing the temperature on different days. Temperature is measured using a thermometer. A rain gauge, Choice *A*, would allow a meteorologist to record amounts of rainfall. A barometer, Choice *C*, measures air pressure. An anemometer, Choice *D*, measures air speed.

**33. C:** A wind vane shows which direction the wind is blowing. If it is pointing north, the wind is blowing in a northern direction. It would not be blowing in an eastern direction, Choice *A*, or a southern direction, Choice *D*, since that is the opposite direction of north. A wind vane simply tells wind direction and does not determine whether a storm is coming, Choice *B*.

**34. A:** Looking at the line graph in Figure 2, the lowest point is marked for January, with approximately 2 mm of rainfall. April, Choice *B*, has approximately 23 mm rainfall, September, Choice *C*, has 10 mm of rainfall, and October, Choice *D*, has the highest rainfall at 60 mm.

**35. D:** Reading the graph in Figure 2, at June, the rainfall is approximately 20 mm. The trend line marks all of the data collected for each month. For June, the trend line is just about at the 20 mm mark from the vertical axis on the left side of the graph.

**36. B:** Plants use chloroplasts to turn light energy into glucose. Animal cells do not have this ability. Comparing Figures 1 and 2, chloroplasts can be found in the plant cell but not the animal cell.

**37. C:** The nucleolus is always located inside the nucleus. It contains important hereditary information about the cell that is critical for the reproductive process. Chloroplasts, Choice *A*, are only located in plant cells. It is not found in the mitochondria, Choice *B*, or attached to the cell membrane, Choice *D*.

**38. A:** Looking at the table in Figure 3, each organelle is described, and mitochondria is described as the powerhouse of the cell. The nucleus, Choice *B*, contains the cell's DNA. The ribosomes, Choice *C*, build proteins. The cell wall, Choice *D*, maintains the shape of plant cells and protects its contents.

**39. D:** Figure 3 describes the functions of the organelles. The cell membrane surrounds the cell and regulates which molecules can move in and out of the cell. Ribosomes build proteins, Choice *A*. Lysosomes, Choice *B*, break down large molecules. The nucleus, Choice *C*, contains the cell's DNA.

**40. C:** Figure 3 describes the functions of the organelles. Chloroplasts are responsible for photosynthesis in plant cells, which is the process of converting sunlight energy to glucose energy. The cell wall helps maintain the cell's shape, Choice *A*. The nucleus contains the cell's DNA, Choice *B*. Ribosomes build proteins, Choice *D*.

# *Social Studies*

**1. D:** The passage does not proceed in chronological order since it begins by pointing out Christopher Columbus's explorations in America, so Choice *A* does not work. Although the author compares and contrasts Erikson with Christopher Columbus, this is not the main way in which the information is presented; therefore, Choice *B* does not work. Neither does Choice *C* because there is no mention of or reference to cause and effect in the passage. However, the passage does offer a conclusion (Leif Erikson deserves more credit) and premises (first European to set foot in the New World and first to contact the natives) to substantiate Erikson's historical importance. Thus, Choice *D* is correct.

**2. C:** Choice *C* is the correct answer because it is the author's opinion that Erikson deserves more credit. That, in fact, is the conclusion in the piece, but another person could argue that Columbus or another explorer deserves more credit for opening up the New World to exploration. Rather than being an indisputable fact, it is a subjective value claim. Choice *A* is incorrect because it describes facts: Leif Erikson was the son of Erik the Red and historians debate Leif's date of birth. These are not opinions. Choice *B* is incorrect; that Erikson called the land "Vinland" is a verifiable fact, as is Choice *D* because he did contact the natives almost 500 years before Columbus.

**3. B:** Choice *B* is correct because, as stated in the previous answer, it accurately identifies the author's statement that Erikson deserves more credit than he has received for being the first European to explore the New World. Choice *A* is incorrect because the author aims to go beyond describing Erikson as a mere legendary Viking. Choice *C* is incorrect because the author does not focus on Erikson's motivations, let alone name the spreading of Christianity as his primary objective. Choice *D* is incorrect because it is a premise that Erikson contacted the natives 500 years before Columbus, which is simply a part of supporting the author's conclusion.

**4. B:** Choice *A* is incorrect because the author is not in any way trying to entertain the reader. Choice *D* is incorrect because he goes beyond a mere suggestion; "suggest" is too vague. Although the author is certainly trying to alert the readers of Leif Erikson's unheralded accomplishments, the nature of the writing does not indicate the author would be satisfied with the reader merely knowing of Erikson's exploration (Choice *C*). Rather, the author would want the reader to be informed about it, which is more substantial (Choice *B*).

**5. D:** Choice *D* is correct because there are two examples of historians having trouble pinning down important dates in Viking history: Leif Erikson's date of birth and what happened during the encounter with the natives. Choice *A* is incorrect because the author never addresses the Vikings' state of mind or emotions. Choice *B* is incorrect because the author does not elaborate on Erikson's exile and whether he would have become an explorer if not for his banishment. Choice *C* is incorrect because there is not enough information to support this premise. It is unclear whether Erikson informed the King of Norway of his finding. Although it is true that the King did not send a follow-up expedition, he could have simply chosen not to expend the resources after receiving Erikson's news. It is not possible to logically infer whether Erikson told him.

**6. D:** Governmental regimes fall along a continuum between total authoritarianism and complete direct democracy. Most countries are neither totally authoritarian, nor a complete direct democracy, but they do all fall along this continuum. China and Iran would be towards the authoritarian end of the spectrum and the United States, United Kingdom, and Mexico would be towards the democratic end.

**7. C:** Power is the ability of a ruling body or political entity to influence the actions, behavior, and attitude of a person or group of people. Authority, Choice *A*, is the right and justification of the government to exercise power as recognized by the citizens or influential elites. Similarly, legitimacy, Choice *D*, is another way of expressing the concept of authority. Sovereignty, Choice *B*, refers to the ability of a state to determine and control their territory without foreign interference.

**8. D:** This period was called the Gilded Age since it appeared shiny and golden on the surface but was fueled by undercurrents of corruption led by big businessmen known as robber barons. Choice *A*, Manifest Destiny, is the concept referring to the pursuit and acquisition of new lands by the U.S., which led to the purchase of Alaska from Russia in 1867 and the annexation of Hawaii in 1898. The Columbian Exchange, Choice *B*, was an era of discovery, conquest, and colonization of the Americas by the Europeans. The New Deal, Choice *C*, was a plan launched by President Franklin Delano Roosevelt to help rebuild America's economy after the Great Depression.

**9. B:** Choice *A*, Choice *C*, and Choice *D* all relate facts but do not present the kind of general statement needed for a conclusion.

**10. C:** The correct answer choice is C, *1910*. There are two ways to arrive at the correct answer. You could find the four answer choices on the graph, or you could have identified that the population never dips at any point. Thus, the correct answer needs to be the only answer choice that is earlier in time than the others, Choice *C*.

**11. D:** The population increased the most between 1990 and 2010. The question is asking you to identify the rate of change for each interval. Between 1930 and 1950, the population increased by approximately 28 million. Between 1950 and 1970, the population increased by approximately 52 million. Between 1970 and 1990, the population increased by approximately 45 million. Between 1990 and 2010, the population increased by approximately 60 million. Thus, Choice *D* is the correct answer. The slope is also the steepest in this interval, which represents its higher increase.

**12. B:** Lines of latitude measure distance North and South. The Equator is zero degrees, and the Tropic of Cancer is 23 ½ degrees north of the equator. The distance between those two lines measures degrees North to South, as with any other two lines of latitude. Longitudinal lines, or meridians, measure distance East and West, even though they run north and south down the Globe. Latitude is not inexact, in that there are set distances between the lines. Furthermore, coordinates can only exist with the use of longitude and latitude.

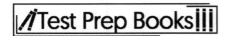

**13. A:** Ethnic groups are simply a group of people with a religious, cultural, economic, or linguistic commonality. Additionally, ethnic groups don't always choose to leave places. Many have called certain locations home for centuries. Also, some ethnic groups actually make up the majority in some countries and are not always minority groups.

**14. A:** Free. A free market does not involve government interventions or monopolies while trading between buyers and suppliers. However, in a command market, the government determines the price of goods and services. Gross and exchange markets refer to situations where brokers and traders make exchanges in the financial realm.

**15. B:** A period of time. It is apparent that Lincoln is referring to a period of time within the context of the passage because of how the sentence is structured with the word *ago*.

**16. C:** Lincoln's reference to *the brave men, living and dead, who struggled here,* proves that he is referring to a battlefield. Choices *A* and *B* are incorrect, as a *civil war* is mentioned and not a war with France or a war in the Sahara Desert. Choice *D* is incorrect because it does not make sense to consecrate a President's ground instead of a battlefield ground for soldiers who died during the American Civil War.

**17. D:** Abraham Lincoln, the president of the United States when he gave that address, was referencing the Civil War.

**18. A:** The audience should perpetuate the ideals of freedom that the soldiers died fighting for. Lincoln doesn't address any of the topics outlined in Choices *B*, *C*, or *D*. Therefore, Choice *A* is the correct answer.

**19. D:** The word *resolve* means to make up one's mind or decide upon something.

**20. A:** Choice *A* is correct because Lincoln's intention was to memorialize the soldiers who had fallen as a result of war as well as celebrate those who had put their lives in danger for the sake of their country. Choices *B* and *D* are incorrect because Lincoln's speech was supposed to foster a sense of pride among the members of the audience while connecting them to the soldiers' experiences.

**21. A:** It decreased one percent. In the first pie chart, the percentage of the European Union population that lived in Germany was 17%. In the second pie chart, we can see that this percentage drops to 16%. Therefore, there was a one percent decrease.

**22. A:** Firsthand accounts are given by primary sources—individuals who provide personal or expert accounts of an event, subject matter, time period, or of an individual. They are viewed more as objective accounts than subjective. Secondary sources are accounts given by an individual or group of individuals who were not physically present at the event or who did not have firsthand knowledge of an individual or time period. Secondary sources are sources that have used research in order to create a written work. Direct and indirect sources are not terms used in literary circles.

**23. C:** The passage makes clear that the Anti-Federalists wanted the Constitution to be altered prior to its approval in a way that would give states and individuals more power rather than the national government. Of the listed men, Thomas Jefferson was the only Anti-Federalist. The other people listed were notable Federalists.

**24. B:** As stated in the passage, left-axis political orientations typically favor social and economic equality and advocate for government intervention to achieve these goals. Communism, Socialism, Liberalism, and Progressivism are examples of political orientations on the left side of the spectrum that are

discussed in the passage. Right-axis political orientations generally value the existing and historical political institutions and oppose government intervention, especially in regard to the economy. Libertarianism, Conservatism, and Fascism are the three orientations from the passage that are considered right-axis orientations. It is true that Libertarians have some progressive ideals; however, Libertarianism is still usually considered a right-axis orientation because the political ideals are conservative.

**25. A:** Fascists advocate for a strong, consolidated, centralized government led by an all-powerful dictator. They believe a key role of this centralized government is to prepare for war. While Libertarians still tend to maintain a conservative approach to government, especially in the context of power and military intervention, they favor a weaker central government, with powerful local rule instead.

**26. B:** Emigration occurs when a person or entire group of people move *from* a location. Immigration occurs when a person or entire group of people move *to* a location. Push factors encourage (or force) people to move from their homes. Pull factors attract people to a location. As the passage mentioned, political push factors include war, government-induced violence and intimidation, genocide, or oppression. Refugees are those pushed from their home country because of such political factors. Refugees are often forcefully expunged from their home states when new countries are formed or when national boundaries are redrawn. For example, the unification of North Vietnam and South Vietnam after the Vietnam War brought hundreds of thousands of Vietnamese refugees to the United States during the 1970s. Choices A and C are incorrect because refugees *leave* their country, so they emigrate from their country; they immigrate *to* another country. Choice D is incorrect because refugees leave their country because of push factors, not pull factors.

**27. C:** Deindustrialization in cities in the Industrial North during the 1960s–1980s pushed away many residents from industrial hubs like Buffalo, Cleveland, Chicago, and Milwaukee because the number of jobs dropped significantly. Thus, people needed to move elsewhere to find employment. This is an example of an economic push factor—pushing people out of the area because of an economic downturn.

**28. B:** This scenario describes a political pull factor because it involves people moving to capitalize on the hopes of a better political situation; this enticement "pulls" them to the new location.

**29. C:** Environmental push factors include flooding, natural disasters, droughts, nuclear contamination, and water contamination, among others. In the Sahel region of North Africa, many people have found new lands due to the intense droughts. As another example, after Hurricane Katrina, many New Orleans residents had to relocate to Houston, Baton Rouge, or other cities to find refuge from the environmental and economic devastation.

**30. D:** An individual cause can be subdivided into smaller factors or stretched out in a gradual process. Although there were numerous issues that led to the Civil War, slavery was the primary cause. However, that issue stretched back to the very founding of the nation, and the existence of slavery was a controversial topic during the creation of the Declaration of Independence and the Constitution. The abolition movement as a whole did not start until the 1830s, but nevertheless, slavery is a cause that gradually grew more important over the following decades. In addition, opponents of slavery were divided by different motivations—some believed that it stifled the economy, while others focused on moral issues. On the other end of the spectrum, a single event can have numerous results. The rise of the telegraph, for example, had several effects on American history. The telegraph allowed news to travel much quicker and turned events into immediate national news, such as the sinking of the USS

Maine, which sparked the Spanish-American War. In addition, the telegraph helped make railroads run more efficiently by improving the links between stations. The faster speed of both travel and communications led to a shift in time itself, and localized times were replaced by standardized time zones across the nation. Therefore, Choice *A* is incorrect. Choices *B* and *C* are incorrect because those are examples of single causes for the given effects.

**31. B:** The two most-populous states (California and Texas) possess a greater collective representation (eighty-nine representatives) than the ten least-populous states. All other answer choices do not reflect accurate comparisons of representation.

**32. A:** Ohio would have the most votes (seventeen) compared to Iowa (four), Michigan (fifteen), and South Dakota (one).

**33. D:** According to the system of checks and balances outlined in the Constitution, members of Congress debate and vote on legislation, although the president may request that legislators consider a certain proposal. The president may veto legislation that he or she disagrees with, but Congress can override the veto with a two-thirds majority in both chambers. The Supreme Court may review legislation and declare it unconstitutional.

**34. B:** According to the system of checks and balances, the Executive branch appoints federal judges, but the Legislative branch can impeach and remove judges. The Legislative branch must approve the appointment of federal judges.

**35. B:** The original thirteen colonies were Virginia, New York, Massachusetts, Maryland, Rhode Island, Connecticut, New Hampshire, Delaware, North Carolina, South Carolina, New Jersey, Pennsylvania, and Georgia. Thus, all but three cities on the list (New Orleans, Cincinnati, St. Louis) are in states that were one of the original thirteen colonies, so the correct answer is Choice *B*, 7.

# GED Practice Test #2

## *Mathematical Reasoning*

### No Calculator Questions

1. Jessica buys 10 cans of paint. Red paint costs $1 per can and blue paint costs $2 per can. In total, she spends $16. How many red cans did she buy?
  a. 2
  b. 3
  c. 4
  d. 5

2. If $\log_{10} x = 2$, then $x$ is
  a. 4
  b. 20
  c. 100
  d. 1000

3. Mo needs to buy enough material to cover the walls around the stage for a theater performance. If he needs 79 feet of wall covering, what is the minimum number of yards of material he should purchase if the material is sold only by whole yards?
  a. 23 yards
  b. 25 yards
  c. 26 yards
  d. 27 yards

4. Taylor is buying things at the bake sale at his sister's basketball game. Here is the price list:
  - Brownies: $0.50
  - Cookies: $0.20
  - Cupcakes: $0.75
  - Lemon Squares: $0.60
  - Milk: $0.35

He buys 1 brownie, 2 cookies, 1 cupcake, 2 lemon squares, and 1 container of milk. He gives the cashier the following money:

How much change should he receive?
    a. $0.20
    b. $0.25
    c. $0.40
    d. $0.75

5. It costs Shea $12 to produce 3 necklaces. If he can sell each necklace for $20, how much profit would he make if he sold 60 necklaces?
    a. $240
    b. $360
    c. $960
    d. $1200

## Calculator Questions

1. A farmer owns two (non-adjacent) square plots of land, which he wishes to fence. The area of one is 1000 square feet, while the area of the other is 10 square feet. How much fencing does he need, in feet?
    a. 44
    b. $40\sqrt{10}$
    c. $440\sqrt{10}$
    d. $44\sqrt{10}$

2. A construction company is building a new housing development with the property of each house measuring 30 feet wide. If the length of the street is zoned off at 345 feet, how many houses can be built on the street?
    a. 11
    b. 115
    c. 11.5
    d. 12

3. Karen gets paid a weekly salary and a commission for every sale that she makes. The table below shows the number of sales and her pay for different weeks.

| Sales | 2 | 7 | 4 | 8 |
|-------|------|------|------|------|
| Pay | $380 | $580 | $460 | $620 |

Which of the following equations represents Karen's weekly pay?
    a. $y = 90x + 200$
    b. $y = 90x - 200$
    c. $y = 40x + 300$
    d. $y = 40x - 300$

4. Which of the following equations best represents the problem below?

The width of a rectangle is 2 centimeters less than the length. If the perimeter of the rectangle is 44 centimeters, then what are the dimensions of the rectangle?

    a. $2l + 2(l - 2) = 44$
    b. $(l + 2) + (l + 2) + l = 48$
    c. $l \times (l - 2) = 44$
    d. $(l + 2) + (l + 2) + l = 44$

5. For which real numbers $x$ is $-3x^2 + x - 8 > 0$?
    a. All real numbers $x$

    b. $-2\sqrt{\frac{2}{3}} < x < 2\sqrt{\frac{2}{3}}$

    c. $1 - 2\sqrt{\frac{2}{3}} < x < 1 + 2\sqrt{\frac{2}{3}}$

    d. For no real numbers $x$

6. A rectangle has a length that is 5 feet longer than three times its width. If the perimeter is 90 feet, what is the length in feet?
    a. 20
    b. 25
    c. 30
    d. 35

7. A line goes through the point (-4, 0) and the point (0,2). What is the slope of the line?
    a. 2

    b. 4

    c. $\frac{3}{2}$

    d. $\frac{1}{2}$

8. The sequence $\{a_n\}$ is defined by the relation $a_{n+1} = 3a_n - 1, a_1 = 1$. Find $a_3$.
    a. 2
    b. 4
    c. 5
    d. 15

9. What is the volume of a cube with the side equal to 3 inches?
    a. 6 in³
    b. 27 in³
    c. 9 in³
    d. 3 in³

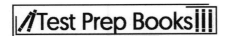

10. What is the 42ⁿᵈ item in the pattern: ▲○○□ ▲○○□ ▲ ...?
    a. ○
    b. ▲
    c. □
    d. None of the above

11. For a group of 20 men, the median weight is 180 pounds and the range is 30 pounds. If each man gains 10 pounds, which of the following would be true?
    a. The median weight will increase, and the range will remain the same.
    b. The median weight and range will both remain the same.
    c. The median weight will stay the same, and the range will increase.
    d. The median weight and range will both increase.

12. What is the volume of a pyramid, with the area of the base measuring 12 inches², and the height measuring 15 inches?
    a. 180 in³
    b. 90 in³
    c. 30 in³
    d. 60 in³

13. What is the volume of a sphere, in terms of $\pi$, with a radius of 3 inches?
    a. 36 $\pi$ in³
    b. 27 $\pi$ in³
    c. 9 $\pi$ in³
    d. 72 $\pi$ in³

14. What is the length of the hypotenuse of a right triangle with one leg equal to 3 centimeters and the other leg equal to 4 centimeters?
    a. 7 cm
    b. 5 cm
    c. 25 cm
    d. 12 cm

15. What is the answer to $(2 + 2i)(2 - 2i)$?
    a. 8
    b. 8$i$
    c. 4
    d. 4$i$

16. If $-3(x + 4) \geq x + 8$, what is the value of $x$?
    a. $x = 4$
    b. $x \geq 2$
    c. $x \geq -5$
    d. $x \leq -5$

17. What is the length of an arc, in terms of $\pi$, that has an angle of 36° and a circle with a 10 centimeter radius?

    a. $\frac{\pi}{2}$ cm

    b. $\pi$ cm

    c. $2\pi$ cm

    d. $4\pi$ cm

18. After a 20% sale discount, Frank purchased a new refrigerator for $850. How much did he save from the original price?

    a. $170

    b. $212.50

    c. $105.75

    d. $200

19. What are the coordinates of the two points marked with dots on this coordinate plane?

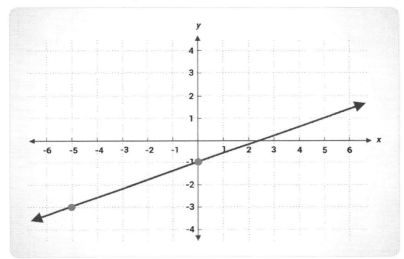

    a. (-3, -5) and (-1, 0)

    b. (5, 3) and (0, 1)

    c. (-5, -3) and (0, -1)

    d. (-3, -5) and (0, -1)

20. What is the value of x for the right triangle shown below?

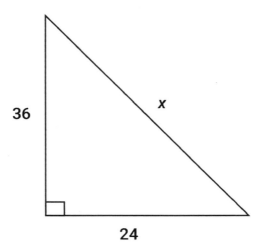

a. 43.3
b. 26.8
c. 42.7
d. 44.1

21. What is the value of *b* in this equation?

$$5b - 4 = 2b + 17$$

a. 13
b. 24
c. 7
d. 21

22. For which of the following are $x = 4$ and $x = -4$ solutions?
   a. $x^2 + 16 = 0$
   b. $x^2 + 4x - 4 = 0$
   c. $x^2 - 2x - 2 = 0$
   d. $x^2 - 16 = 0$

23. Which graph will be a line parallel to the graph of $y = 3x - 2$?
   a. $2y - 6x = 2$
   b. $y - 4x = 4$
   c. $3y = x - 2$
   d. $2x - 2y = 2$

24. Which is closest to $17.8 \times 9.9$?
   a. 140
   b. 180
   c. 200
   d. 350

25. $3\frac{2}{3} - 1\frac{4}{5} =$

    a. $1\frac{13}{15}$

    b. $\frac{14}{15}$

    c. $2\frac{2}{3}$

    d. $\frac{4}{5}$

26. $4\frac{1}{3} + 3\frac{3}{4} =$

    a. $6\frac{5}{12}$

    b. $8\frac{1}{12}$

    c. $8\frac{2}{3}$

    d. $7\frac{7}{12}$

27. A school has 15 teachers and 20 teaching assistants. They have 200 students. What is the ratio of faculty to students?

    a. 3:20
    b. 4:17
    c. 3:2
    d. 7:40

28. Express the solution to the following problem in decimal form:

$$\frac{3}{5} \times \frac{7}{10} \div \frac{1}{2}$$

    a. 0.042
    b. 84%
    c. 0.84
    d. 0.42

29. Alan currently weighs 200 pounds, but he wants to lose weight to get down to 175 pounds. What is this difference in kilograms? (1 pound is approximately equal to 0.45 kilograms.)

    a. 9 kg
    b. 11.25 kg
    c. 78.75 kg
    d. 90 kg

30. $(2x - 4y)^2 =$

    a. $4x^2 - 16xy + 16y^2$
    b. $4x^2 - 8xy + 16y^2$
    c. $4x^2 - 16xy - 16y^2$
    d. $2x^2 - 8xy + 8y^2$

31. What is the volume of a cube with the side equal to 5 centimeters?
   a. 10 cm³
   b. 15 cm³
   c. 50 cm³
   d. 125 cm³

32. When rounding 245.2678 to the nearest thousandth, which place value would be used to decide whether to round up or round down?
   a. Ten-thousandth
   b. Thousandth
   c. Hundredth
   d. Thousand

33. If $x > 3$, then $\frac{x^2-6x+9}{x^2-x-6} =$

   a. $\frac{x+2}{x-3}$

   b. $\frac{x-2}{x-3}$

   c. $\frac{x-3}{x+3}$

   d. $\frac{x-3}{x+2}$

34. What is the volume of a pyramid, with a square base whose side is 6 inches, and the height is 9 inches?
   a. 324 in³
   b. 72 in³
   c. 108 in³
   d. 18 in³

35. What is the volume of a sphere, in terms of $\pi$, with a radius of 6 centimeters?
   a. 144 $\pi$ cm³
   b. 200 $\pi$ cm³
   c. 288 $\pi$ cm³
   d. 120 $\pi$ cm³

36. What is the length of the other leg of a right triangle with a hypotenuse of 10 inches and a leg of 8 inches?
   a. 6 in
   b. 18 in
   c. 80 in
   d. 13 in

37. Write the expression for three times the sum of twice a number and one minus 6.
   a. $2x + 1 - 6$
   b. $3x + 1 - 6$
   c. $3(x + 1) - 6$
   d. $3(2x + 1) - 6$

38. On Monday, Robert mopped the floor in 4 hours. On Tuesday, he did it in 3 hours. If on Monday, his average rate of mopping was $p$ sq. ft. per hour, what was his average rate on Tuesday?

a. $\frac{4}{3}p$ sq. ft. per hour

b. $\frac{3}{4}p$ sq. ft. per hour

c. $\frac{5}{4}p$ sq. ft. per hour

d. $p + 1$ sq. ft. per hour

39. If $a \neq b$, solve for x if $\frac{1}{x} + \frac{2}{a} = \frac{2}{b}$

a. $\frac{a-b}{ab}$

b. $\frac{ab}{2(a-b)}$

c. $\frac{2(a-b)}{ab}$

d. $\frac{a-b}{2ab}$

40. If $x^2 + x - 3 = 0$, then $\left(x + \frac{1}{2}\right)^2 =$

a. $\frac{13}{2}$

b. $\frac{13}{4}$

c. 11

d. $\frac{121}{4}$

# *Reasoning Through Language Arts*

*Questions 1–4 are based on the following passage:*

Three years ago, I think there were not many bird-lovers in the United States who believed it possible to prevent the total extinction of both egrets from our fauna. All the known rookeries accessible to plume-hunters had been totally destroyed. Two years ago, the secret discovery of several small, hidden colonies prompted William Dutcher, President of the National Association of Audubon Societies, and Mr. T. Gilbert Pearson, Secretary, to attempt the protection of those colonies. With a fund contributed for the purpose, wardens were hired and duly commissioned. As previously stated, one of those wardens was shot dead in cold blood by a plume hunter. The task of guarding swamp rookeries from the attacks of money-hungry desperadoes to whom the accursed plumes were worth their weight in gold, is a very chancy proceeding. There is now one warden in Florida who says that "before they get my rookery they will first have to get me."

Thus far the protective work of the Audubon Association has been successful. Now there are twenty colonies, which contain all told, about 5,000 egrets and about 120,000 herons and ibises which are guarded by the Audubon wardens. One of the most

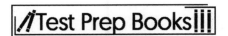 

important is on Bird Island, a mile out in Orange Lake, central Florida, and it is ably defended by Oscar E. Baynard. To-day, the plume hunters who do not dare to raid the guarded rookeries are trying to study out the lines of flight of the birds, to and from their feeding-grounds, and shoot them in transit. Their motto is—"Anything to beat the law, and get the plumes." It is there that the state of Florida should take part in the war.

The success of this campaign is attested by the fact that last year a number of egrets were seen in eastern Massachusetts—for the first time in many years. And so to-day the question is, can the wardens continue to hold the plume-hunters at bay?

from *Our Vanishing Wildlife*, by William T. Hornaday

1. The author's use of first-person pronouns in the following text does NOT have which of the following effects?

Three years ago, I think there were not many bird-lovers in the United States who believed it possible to prevent the total extinction of both egrets from our fauna.

   a. The phrase *I think* acts as a sort of hedging, where the author's tone is less direct and/or absolute.
   b. It allows the reader to more easily connect with the author.
   c. It encourages the reader to empathize with the egrets.
   d. It distances the reader from the text by overemphasizing the story.

2. What purpose does the quote serve at the end of the first paragraph?
   a. The quote shows proof of a hunter threatening one of the wardens.
   b. The quote lightens the mood by illustrating the colloquial language of the region.
   c. The quote provides an example of a warden protecting one of the colonies.
   d. The quote provides much needed comic relief in the form of a joke.

3. What is the meaning of the word *rookeries* in the following sentence from the passage?

To-day, the plume hunters who do not dare to raid the guarded rookeries are trying to study out the lines of flight of the birds, to and from their feeding-grounds, and shoot them in transit.

   a. Houses in a slum area
   b. A place where hunters gather to trade tools
   c. A place where wardens go to trade stories
   d. A colony of breeding birds

4. What is on Bird Island?
   a. Hunters selling plumes
   b. An important bird colony
   c. Bird Island Battle between the hunters and the wardens
   d. An important egret with unique plumes

*Questions 5–9 are based on the following passage:*

"Did you ever come across a protégé of his—one Hyde?" He asked.

"Hyde?" repeated Lanyon. "No. Never heard of him. Since my time."

That was the amount of information that the lawyer carried back with him to the great, dark bed on which he tossed to and fro until the small hours of the morning began to grow large. It was a night of little ease to his toiling mind, toiling in mere darkness and besieged by questions.

Six o'clock struck on the bells of the church that was so conveniently near to Mr. Utterson's dwelling, and still he was digging at the problem. Hitherto it had touched him on the intellectual side alone; but now his imagination also was engaged, or rather enslaved; and as he lay and tossed in the gross darkness of the night in the curtained room, Mr. Enfield's tale went by before his mind in a scroll of lighted pictures. He would be aware of the great field of lamps in a nocturnal city; then of the figure of a man walking swiftly; then of a child running from the doctor's; and then these met, and that human Juggernaut trod the child down and passed on regardless of her screams. Or else he would see a room in a rich house, where his friend lay asleep, dreaming and smiling at his dreams; and then the door of that room would be opened, the curtains of the bed plucked apart, the sleeper recalled, and, lo! There would stand by his side a figure to whom power was given, and even at that dead hour he must rise and do its bidding. The figure in these two phrases haunted the lawyer all night; and if at anytime he dozed over, it was but to see it glide more stealthily through sleeping houses, or move the more swiftly, and still the more smoothly, even to dizziness, through wider labyrinths of lamplighted city, and at every street corner crush a child and leave her screaming. And still the figure had no face by which he might know it; even in his dreams it had no face, or one that baffled him and melted before his eyes; and thus there it was that there sprung up and grew apace in the lawyer's mind a singularly strong, almost an inordinate, curiosity to behold the features of the real Mr. Hyde. If he could but once set eyes on him, he thought the mystery would lighten and perhaps roll altogether away, as was the habit of mysterious things when well examined. He might see a reason for his friend's strange preference or bondage, and even for the startling clauses of the will. And at least it would be a face worth seeing: the face of a man who was without bowels of mercy: a face which had but to show itself to raise up, in the mind of the unimpressionable Enfield, a spirit of enduring hatred.

From that time forward, Mr. Utterson began to haunt the door in the by-street of shops. In the morning before office hours, at noon when business was plenty of time scarce, at night under the face of the full city moon, by all lights and at all hours of solitude or concourse, the lawyer was to be found on his chosen post.

"If he be Mr. Hyde," he had thought, "I should be Mr. Seek."

from Robert Louis Stevenson's *The Strange Case of Dr. Jekyll and Mr. Hyde*

5. What is the purpose of the use of repetition in the following passage?

It was a night of little ease to his toiling mind, toiling in mere darkness and besieged by questions.

    a. It serves as a demonstration of the mental state of Mr. Lanyon.
    b. It is reminiscent of the church bells that are mentioned in the story.
    c. It mimics Mr. Utterson's ambivalence.
    d. It emphasizes Mr. Utterson's anguish in failing to identify Hyde's whereabouts.

6. What is the setting of the story in this passage?
    a. In the city
    b. On the countryside
    c. In a jail
    d. In a mental health facility

7. What can one infer about the meaning of the word "Juggernaut" from the author's use of it in the passage?
    a. It is an apparition that appears at daybreak.
    b. It scares children.
    c. It is associated with space travel.
    d. Mr. Utterson finds it soothing.

8. What is the definition of the word *haunt* in the following selection from the passage?

From that time forward, Mr. Utterson began to haunt the door in the by-street of shops. In the morning before office hours, at noon when business was plenty of time scarce, at night under the face of the full city moon, by all lights and at all hours of solitude or concourse, the lawyer was to be found on his chosen post.

    a. To levitate
    b. To constantly visit
    c. To terrorize
    d. To daunt

9. The phrase *labyrinths of lamplighted city* contains an example of what?
    a. Hyperbole
    b. Simile
    c. Juxtaposition
    d. Alliteration

10. Advertisement: Cigarettes are deadly. Hundreds of thousands of people die every year from smoking-related causes, such as lung cancer or heart disease. The science is clear—smoking a pack per day for years will shorten one's life. Sitting in a room where someone is smoking might as well be a gas chamber in terms of damage to long-term health.

Which one of the following best describes the flaw in the author's reasoning?
    a. The advertisement confuses cause and effect.
    b. The advertisement uses overly broad generalization.
    c. The advertisement draws an unjustified analogy.
    d. The advertisement relies on shoddy science.

11. Mouth guards are increasingly becoming required equipment for contact sports. Besides the obvious benefit of protecting an athlete's teeth, mouth guards also prevent concussions. Youth league referees should penalize teams with players participating without a sanctioned mouth guard.

Which of the following most accurately expresses the argument's main conclusion?
a. Mouth guards protect teeth and prevent concussions.
b. Youth leagues should make mouth guards mandatory.
c. Mouth guards should always be worn during contact sports.
d. It is generally preferable to wear mouth guards while playing contact sports.

*Questions 12–21 are based on the following passage:*

My Good Friends,—When I first imparted to the committee of the projected Institute my particular wish that on one of the evenings of my readings here the main body of my audience should be composed of working men and their families, I was animated by two desires; first, by the wish to have the great pleasure of meeting you face to face at this Christmas time, and accompany you myself through one of my little Christmas books; and second, by the wish to have an opportunity of stating publicly in your presence, and in the presence of the committee, my earnest hope that the Institute will, from the beginning, recognise one great principle—strong in reason and justice—which I believe to be essential to the very life of such an Institution. It is, that the working man shall, from the first unto the last, have a share in the management of an Institution which is designed for his benefit, and which calls itself by his name.

I have no fear here of being misunderstood—of being supposed to mean too much in this. If there ever was a time when any one class could of itself do much for its own good, and for the welfare of society—which I greatly doubt—that time is unquestionably past. It is in the fusion of different classes, without confusion; in the bringing together of employers and employed; in the creating of a better common understanding among those whose interests are identical, who depend upon each other, who are vitally essential to each other, and who never can be in unnatural antagonism without deplorable results, that one of the chief principles of a Mechanics' Institution should consist. In this world, a great deal of the bitterness among us arises from an imperfect understanding of one another. Erect in Birmingham a great Educational Institution, properly educational; educational of the feelings as well as of the reason; to which all orders of Birmingham men contribute; in which all orders of Birmingham men meet; wherein all orders of Birmingham men are faithfully represented—and you will erect a Temple of Concord here which will be a model edifice to the whole of England.

Contemplating as I do the existence of the Artisans' Committee, which not long ago considered the establishment of the Institute so sensibly, and supported it so heartily, I earnestly entreat the gentlemen—earnest I know in the good work, and who are now among us—by all means to avoid the great shortcoming of similar institutions; and in asking the working man for his confidence, to set him the great example and give him theirs in return. You will judge for yourselves if I promise too much for the working man, when I say that he will stand by such an enterprise with the utmost of his patience, his perseverance, sense, and support; that I am sure he will need no charitable aid or condescending patronage; but will readily and cheerfully pay for the advantages which it

confers; that he will prepare himself in individual cases where he feels that the adverse circumstances around him have rendered it necessary; in a word, that he will feel his responsibility like an honest man, and will most honestly and manfully discharge it. I now proceed to the pleasant task to which I assure you I have looked forward for a long time.

*From Charles Dickens' speech in Birmingham in England on December 30, 1853 on behalf of the Birmingham and Midland Institute.*

12. Which word is most closely synonymous with the word *patronage* as it appears in the following statement?

> ...that I am sure he will need no charitable aid or condescending patronage

a. Auspices
b. Aberration
c. Acerbic
d. Adulation

13. Which term is most closely aligned with the definition of the term *working man* as it is defined in the following passage?

> You will judge for yourselves if I promise too much for the working man, when I say that he will stand by such an enterprise with the utmost of his patience, his perseverance, sense, and support...

a. Plebeian
b. Viscount
c. Entrepreneur
d. Bourgeois

14. Which of the following statements most closely correlates with the definition of the term *working man* as it is defined in Question 13?
a. A working man is not someone who works for institutions or corporations, but someone who is well-versed in the workings of the soul.
b. A working man is someone who is probably not involved in social activities because the physical demand for work is too high.
c. A working man is someone who works for wages among the middle class.
d. The working man has historically taken to the field, to the factory, and now to the screen.

15. Based upon the contextual evidence provided in the passage above, what is the meaning of the term *enterprise* in the third paragraph?
a. Company
b. Courage
c. Game
d. Cause

16. The speaker addresses his audience as *My Good Friends.* What kind of credibility does this salutation give to the speaker?
    a. The speaker is an employer addressing his employees, so the salutation is a way for the boss to bridge the gap between himself and his employees.
    b. The speaker's salutation is one from an entertainer to his audience and uses the friendly language to connect to his audience before a serious speech.
    c. The salutation is used ironically to give a somber tone to the serious speech that follows.
    d. The speech is one from a politician to the public, so the salutation is used to grab the audience's attention.

17. According to the passage, what is the speaker's second desire for his time in front of the audience?
    a. To read a Christmas story
    b. For the working man to have a say in his institution, which is designed for his benefit
    c. To have an opportunity to stand in their presence
    d. For the life of the institution to be essential to the audience as a whole

18. The speaker's tone in the passage can be described as:
    a. Happy and gullible
    b. Lazy and entitled
    c. Confident and informed
    d. Angry and frustrated

19. Which of the following is one of the main purposes of the last paragraph?
    a. To persuade the audience to support the Institute no matter what, since it provided so much support to the working class
    b. To market the speaker's new book, while at the same time, supporting the activities of the Institute
    c. To inform the audience that the Institute is corrupt and will not help them out when the time comes to give them compensation
    d. To provide credibility to the working man and share confidence in their ability to take on responsibilities if they are compensated appropriately

20. According to the passage, what does the speaker wish to erect in Birmingham?
    a. An Educational Institution
    b. The Temple of Concord
    c. A Writing Workshop
    d. A VA Hospital

21. As it is used in the second paragraph, the word *antagonism* most nearly means:
    a. Conformity
    b. Opposition
    c. Affluence
    d. Scarcity

*Questions 22–31 are based on the following passage:*

"Mademoiselle Eugénie is pretty—I think I remember that to be her name."

"Very pretty, or rather, very beautiful," replied Albert, "but of that style of beauty which I don't appreciate; I am an ungrateful fellow."

"Really," said Monte Cristo, lowering his voice, "you don't appear to me to be very enthusiastic on the subject of this marriage."

"Mademoiselle Danglars is too rich for me," replied Morcerf, "and that frightens me."

"Bah," exclaimed Monte Cristo, "that's a fine reason to give. Are you not rich yourself?"

"My father's income is about 50,000 francs per annum; and he will give me, perhaps, ten or twelve thousand when I marry."

"That, perhaps, might not be considered a large sum, in Paris especially," said the count; "but everything doesn't depend on wealth, and it's a fine thing to have a good name, and to occupy a high station in society. Your name is celebrated, your position magnificent; and then the Comte de Morcerf is a soldier, and it's pleasing to see the integrity of a Bayard united to the poverty of a Duguesclin; disinterestedness is the brightest ray in which a noble sword can shine. As for me, I consider the union with Mademoiselle Danglars a most suitable one; she will enrich you, and you will ennoble her."

Albert shook his head, and looked thoughtful. "There is still something else," said he.

"I confess," observed Monte Cristo, "that I have some difficulty in comprehending your objection to a young lady who is both rich and beautiful."

"Oh," said Morcerf, "this repugnance, if repugnance it may be called, isn't all on my side."

"Whence can it arise, then? for you told me your father desired the marriage."

"It's my mother who dissents; she has a clear and penetrating judgment, and doesn't smile on the proposed union. I cannot account for it, but she seems to entertain some prejudice against the Danglars."

"Ah," said the count, in a somewhat forced tone, "that may be easily explained; the Comtesse de Morcerf, who is aristocracy and refinement itself, doesn't relish the idea of being allied by your marriage with one of ignoble birth; that is natural enough."

Excerpt from the Count of Monte Cristo by Alexandre Dumas

22. The meaning of the word *repugnance* is closest to:
    a. Strong resemblance
    b. Strong dislike
    c. Extreme shyness
    d. Extreme dissimilarity

23. What can be inferred about Albert's family?
    a. Their finances are uncertain.
    b. Albert is the only son in his family.
    c. Their name is more respected than the Danglars'.
    d. Albert's mother and father both agree on their decisions.

24. What is Albert's attitude towards his impending marriage?
    a. Pragmatic
    b. Romantic
    c. Indifferent
    d. Apprehensive

25. What is the best description of the Count's relationship with Albert?
    a. He's like a strict parent, criticizing Albert's choices.
    b. He's like a wise uncle, giving practical advice to Albert.
    c. He's like a close friend, supporting all of Albert's opinions.
    d. He's like a suspicious investigator, asking many probing questions.

26. Which sentence is true of Albert's mother?
    a. She belongs to a noble family.
    b. She often makes poor choices.
    c. She is primarily occupied with money.
    d. She is unconcerned about her son's future.

27. Based on this passage, what is probably NOT true about French society in the 1800s?
    a. Children often received money from their parents.
    b. Marriages were sometimes arranged between families.
    c. The richest people in society were also the most respected.
    d. People were often expected to marry within their same social class.

28. Why is the Count puzzled by Albert's attitude toward his marriage?
    a. He seems reluctant to marry Eugénie, despite her wealth and beauty.
    b. He is marrying against his father's wishes, despite usually following his advice.
    c. He appears excited to marry someone he doesn't love, despite being a hopeless romantic.
    d. He expresses reverence towards Eugénie, despite being from a higher social class than her.

29. The passage is made up mostly of what kind of text?
    a. Narration
    b. Dialogue
    c. Description
    d. Explanation

30. What does the word *ennoble* mean in the middle of the passage?
    a. To create beauty in another person
    b. To endow someone with wealth
    c. To make someone chaste again
    d. To give someone a noble rank or title

31. Why is the count said to have a "forced tone" in the last paragraph?
    a. Because he is in love with Mademoiselle Eugénie and is trying to keep it a secret.
    b. Because he finally agrees with Albert's point of view but still doesn't understand it.
    c. Because he finally understands Albert's point of view but still doesn't agree with it.
    d. Because he is only pretending that Albert is his friend to get information out of him.

*Questions 32–41 are based on the following passage:*

"MANKIND being originally equals in the order of creation, the equality could only be destroyed by some subsequent circumstance; the distinctions of rich, and poor, may in a great measure be accounted for, and that without having recourse to the harsh ill sounding names of oppression and avarice. Oppression is often the consequence, but seldom or never the means of riches; and though avarice will preserve a man from being necessitously poor, it generally makes him too timorous to be wealthy.

But there is another and greater distinction for which no truly natural or religious reason can be assigned, and that is, the distinction of men into KINGS and SUBJECTS. Male and female are the distinctions of nature, good and bad the distinctions of heaven; but how a race of men came into the world so exalted above the rest, and distinguished like some new species, is worth enquiring into, and whether they are the means of happiness or of misery to mankind.

In the early ages of the world, according to the scripture chronology, there were no kings; the consequence of which was there were no wars; it is the pride of kings which throw mankind into confusion. Holland without a king hath enjoyed more peace for this last century than any of the monarchical governments in Europe. Antiquity favors the same remark; for the quiet and rural lives of the first patriarchs hath a happy something in them, which vanishes away when we come to the history of Jewish royalty.

Government by kings was first introduced into the world by the Heathens, from whom the children of Israel copied the custom. It was the most prosperous invention the Devil ever set on foot for the promotion of idolatry. The Heathens paid divine honors to their deceased kings, and the Christian world hath improved on the plan by doing the same to their living ones. How impious is the title of sacred majesty applied to a worm, who in the midst of his splendor is crumbling into dust!

As the exalting one man so greatly above the rest cannot be justified on the equal rights of nature, so neither can it be defended on the authority of scripture; for the will of the Almighty, as declared by Gideon and the prophet Samuel, expressly disapproves of government by kings. All anti-monarchical parts of scripture have been very smoothly glossed over in monarchical governments, but they undoubtedly merit the attention of countries, which have their governments yet to form. "Render unto Caesar the things which are Caesar's" is the scripture doctrine of courts, yet it is no support of monarchical government, for the Jews at that time were without a king, and in a state of vassalage to the Romans.

Near three thousand years passed away from the Mosaic account of the creation, till the Jews under a national delusion requested a king. Till then their form of government (except in extraordinary cases, where the Almighty interposed) was a kind of republic administered by a judge and the elders of the tribes. Kings they had none, and it was held sinful to acknowledge any being under that title but the Lord of Hosts. And when a man seriously reflects on the idolatrous homage which is paid to the persons of Kings, he need not wonder, that the Almighty ever jealous of his honor, should disapprove of a form of government which so impiously invades the prerogative of heaven.

Excerpt from "Common Sense" by Thomas Paine

32. According to passage, what role does avarice, or greed, play in poverty?
    a. It can make a man very wealthy.
    b. It is the consequence of wealth.
    c. Avarice can prevent a man from being poor, but too fearful to be very wealthy.
    d. Avarice is what drives a person to be very wealthy

33. Of these distinctions, which does the author believe to be beyond natural or religious reason?
    a. Good and bad
    b. Male and female
    c. Human and animal
    d. King and subjects

34. According to the passage, what are the Heathens responsible for?
    a. Government by kings
    b. Quiet and rural lives of patriarchs
    c. Paying divine honors to their living kings
    d. Equal rights of nature

35. Which of the following best states Paine's rationale for the denouncement of monarchy?
    a. It is against the laws of nature.
    b. It is against the equal rights of nature and is denounced in scripture.
    c. Despite scripture, a monarchal government is unlawful.
    d. Neither the law nor scripture denounce monarchy.

36. Based on the passage, what is the best definition of the word *idolatrous*?
    a. Worshipping heroes
    b. Being deceitful
    c. Sinfulness
    d. Engaging in illegal activities

37. What is the essential meaning of the following lines from the passage?

    And when a man seriously reflects on the idolatrous homage which is paid to the persons of Kings, he need not wonder, that the Almighty ever jealous of his honor, should disapprove of a form of government which so impiously invades the prerogative of heaven.

    a. God would disapprove of the irreverence of a monarchical government.
    b. With careful reflection, men should realize that heaven is not promised.
    c. God will punish those that follow a monarchical government.
    d. Belief in a monarchical government cannot coexist with belief in God.

38. Based on the passage, what is the best definition of the word *timorous* in the first paragraph?
    a. Being full of fear
    b. A characteristic of shyness
    c. Being able to see through someone
    d. Being full of anger and hatred

39. The author's attitude toward the subject can best be described as:
    a. Indifferent and fatigued
    b. Impassioned and critical
    c. Awed and enchanted
    d. Enraged and sulky

40. What is the main purpose of the fourth paragraph?
    a. To persuade the audience that heathens were more advanced than Christians
    b. To explain how monarchs came into existence and how Christians adopted the same system
    c. To describe the divination of English monarchs and how it is their birthright to be revered
    d. To counteract the preceding paragraph by giving proof of the damage monarchs can cause

41. In the last paragraph, what does the author mean by the "Mosaic account of creation"?
    a. The author means that creation is based on individuals composed of cells of two genetically different types.
    b. The author implies that the work of God is like a mosaic painting due to the various formations of creation.
    c. The author means that the kings of the past developed a system in which to maintain accounts of creation.
    d. The author implies that the recorded history of creation is a collection, collage, or pattern taken from various accounts of cultures.

42. While scientists aren't entirely certain why tornadoes form, they have some clues into the process. Tornadoes are dangerous funnel clouds that occur during a large thunderstorm. When warm, humid air near the ground meets cold, dry air from above, a column of the warm air can be drawn up into the clouds. Winds at different altitudes blowing at different speeds make the column of air rotate. As the spinning column of air picks up speed, a funnel cloud is formed. This funnel cloud moves rapidly and haphazardly. Rain and hail inside the cloud cause it to touch down, creating a tornado. Tornadoes move in a rapid and unpredictable pattern, making them extremely destructive and dangerous. Scientists continue to study tornadoes to improve radar detection and warning times.

What is the main purpose of this passage?
    a. To show why tornadoes are dangerous
    b. To explain how a tornado forms
    c. To compare thunderstorms to tornadoes
    d. To explain what to do in the event of a tornado

43. There are two major kinds of cameras on the market right now for amateur photographers. Camera enthusiasts can either purchase a digital single-lens reflex camera (DSLR) camera or a compact system camera (CSC). The main difference between a DSLR and a CSC is that the DSLR has a full-sized sensor, which means it fits in a much larger body. The CSC uses a mirrorless system, which makes for a lighter, smaller camera. While both take quality pictures, the DSLR generally has better picture quality due to the larger sensor. CSCs still take very good quality pictures and are more convenient to carry than a DSLR. This makes the CSC an ideal choice for the amateur photographer looking to step up from a point-and-shoot camera.

What is the main difference between the DSLR and CSC?
   a. The picture quality is better in the DSLR.
   b. The CSC is less expensive than the DSLR.
   c. The DSLR is a better choice for amateur photographers.
   d. The DSLR's larger sensor makes it a bigger camera than the CSC.

44. When selecting a career path, it's important to explore the various options available. Many students entering college may shy away from a major because they don't know much about it. For example, many students won't opt for a career as an actuary, because they aren't exactly sure what it entails. They would be missing out on a career that is very lucrative and in high demand. Actuaries work in the insurance field and assess risks and premiums. The average salary of an actuary is $100,000 per year. Another career option students may avoid, due to lack of knowledge of the field, is a hospitalist. This is a physician that specializes in the care of patients in a hospital, as opposed to those seen in private practices. The average salary of a hospitalist is upwards of $200,000. It pays to do some digging and find out more about these lesser-known career fields.

What is an actuary?
   a. A doctor who works in a hospital
   b. The same as a hospitalist
   c. An insurance agent who works in a hospital
   d. A person who assesses insurance risks and premiums

45. Hard water occurs when rainwater mixes with minerals from rock and soil. Hard water has a high mineral count, including calcium and magnesium. The mineral deposits from hard water can stain hard surfaces in bathrooms and kitchens as well as clog pipes. Hard water can stain dishes, ruin clothes, and reduce the life of any appliances it touches, such as hot water heaters, washing machines, and humidifiers.

One solution is to install a water softener to reduce the mineral content of water, but this can be costly. Running vinegar through pipes and appliances and using vinegar to clean hard surfaces can also help with mineral deposits.

Which of the following can be concluded from the passage?
   a. Hard water can cause a lot of problems for homeowners.
   b. Calcium is good for pipes and hard surfaces.
   c. Water softeners are easy to install.
   d. Vinegar is the only solution to hard water problems.

46. Vacationers looking for a perfect experience should opt out of Disney parks and try a trip on Disney Cruise Lines. While a park offers rides, characters, and show experiences, it also includes long lines, often very hot weather, and enormous crowds. A Disney Cruise, on the other hand, is a relaxing,

luxurious vacation that includes many of the same experiences as the parks, minus the crowds and lines. The cruise has top-notch food, maid service, water slides, multiple pools, Broadway-quality shows, and daily character experiences for kids. There are also many activities, such as bingo, trivia contests, and dance parties that can entertain guests of all ages. The cruise even stops at Disney's private island for a beach barbecue with characters, waterslides, and water sports. Those looking for the Disney experience without the hassle should book a Disney cruise.

What is the main purpose of this passage?
- a. To explain how to book a Disney cruise
- b. To show what Disney parks have to offer
- c. To show why Disney parks are expensive
- d. To compare Disney parks to the Disney cruise

# *Extended Response*

There are two passages below. Read both of the passages carefully all the way through. Then, choose which passage you think is better supported by evidence. In your response, be sure to use your own evidence from the passages. You will have forty-five minutes to plan, write, and edit your response. Your essay should be around 500 words.

## Passage I

People who share their lives on social media sites are edging into dangerous territory. Social media sites such as Facebook, Instagram, and Snapchat are black holes for those easily addicted to validation and acceptance. Society should be wary of allowing their kids to have open access to social media sites.

So many people feel a sense of joy at being "liked" or having a certain amount of friends or comments on their pages. This feeling may lead to a false sense of acceptance by peers, and the feeling that one has accomplished something. Friends post vacations, what they ate for lunch, who they are dating, and pictures of themselves and their families. They say that if it's not on social media, it didn't happen. Sharing so much personal information is an invasion of privacy and could prove dangerous. They think sharing personal pictures and details invites predators, cyberbullying, and identity theft.

People should take care to stay away from social media and get their validation and acceptance from entities that truly matter, like from themselves or a higher being. Being outside and getting exercise is a good alternative to staring at a screen all day. Those who get out and expand their worlds will definitely experience happier lives.

## Passage II

Although there are many negative side effects to social media, such as predatory accounts, cyberbullying, and identity theft, there are many positive sides to social media as well. Carrying around information 24/7 has its perks and can't be all bad—in fact, we are a society thriving on technology and connection. Social media can be seen as a good thing due to its connecting us with family and peers, its possibilities for political support, and its support for at-home businesses and marketers.

Social media is great for staying in touch with family and peers. Last year, when I moved to California, I had bouts of loneliness trying to cope without my family and friends. This is where Skype and Facebook came in handy—I could reach out to family and friends anytime I wanted, with just a click of a button!

Social media is also beneficial for giving and receiving political support. In 2011, young persons in the Egyptian Revolution used social media to form protests and request outside help. They used Twitter and YouTube to reach out to the world and let everyone what was going on with their events and the requests they made to their government. Social media was used as a platform for regular citizens to be heard by their government.

Another reason social media is beneficial is because many men and women use it to start and maintain at-home businesses. The platforms of Facebook and YouTube are easy ways to set up shop, to create events, and to create videos to reach out to a particular audience. People can Google certain terms, and those terms will bring them straight to the social media site they are looking for. According to SocialMediaStatsForAtHomeBusiness.org, 75 percent of businesses use social media to supplement their consumer market.

All in all, people should not be afraid of social media when it's able to bring so much opportunity to society. Staying in touch with family and friends, supporting political campaigns, and creating business opportunities are just some of the ways social media is beneficial to the community.

## *Science*

### Passage 1

*Questions 1–5 pertain to Passage 1:*

Scientists use the scientific method to investigate a theory or solve a problem. It includes four steps: observation, hypothesis, experiment, and conclusion. Observation occurs when the scientist uses one of their senses to identify what they want to study. A hypothesis is a conclusive sentence about what the scientist wants to research. It generally includes an explanation for the observations, can be tested experimentally, and predicts the outcome. The experiment includes the parameters for the testing that will occur. The conclusion will state whether or not the hypothesis was supported.

Scientist A would like to know how sunlight affects the growth of a plant. She says that more sunlight will cause the plant to grow faster. She sets up her experimental groups and tests her hypothesis over 11 days.

Figure 1 below shows the experimental data Scientist A collected over 11 days.

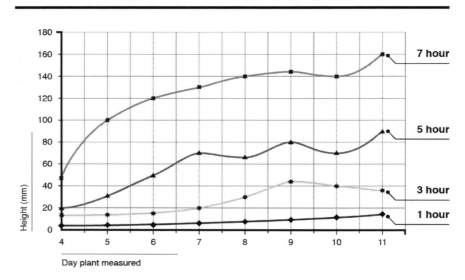

## Length and height of plants in the sunlight

Figure 2 below represents the process of photosynthesis that occurs in plants.

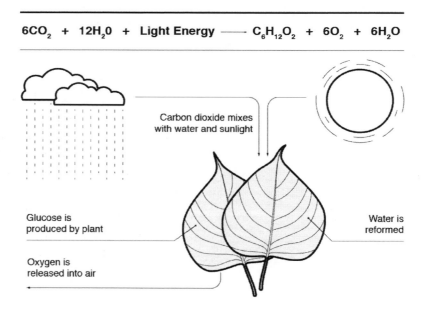

$$6CO_2 \ + \ 12H_2O \ + \ \text{Light Energy} \ \longrightarrow \ C_6H_{12}O_2 \ + \ 6O_2 \ + \ 6H_2O$$

1. What is her hypothesis?
   a. More sunlight will cause the plant to grow faster.
   b. She will test her theory over 11 days.
   c. How sunlight affects plant growth.
   d. Plants do not grow well with one hour of sunlight per day.

2. How many experimental groups does she have?
   a. 1
   b. 3
   c. 4
   d. 11

3. What type of chart is represented in the first figure?
   a. Bar graph
   b. Line graph
   c. Pie chart
   d. Pictogram

4. What part of the photosynthesis reaction is provided directly by sunlight?
   a. Light energy
   b. $H_2O$
   c. $CO_2$
   d. Glucose

5. What should her conclusion be based on her experimental data?
   a. 5 hours of sunlight is optimal for plant growth.
   b. Plants should only be measured for 11 days.
   c. Less sunlight is better for plant growth.
   d. Providing plants with more sunlight makes them grow bigger.

## Passage 2

*Questions 6–10 pertain to Passage 2:*

The periodic table contains all known 118 chemical elements. The first 98 elements are found naturally while the remaining were synthesized by scientists. The elements are ordered according to the number of protons they contain, also known as their atomic number. For example, hydrogen has an atomic number of one and is found in the top left corner of the periodic table, whereas radon has an atomic number of 86 and is found closer on the right side of the periodic table, several rows down. The rows are called periods and the columns are called groups. The elements are arranged by similar chemical properties.

Each chemical element represents an individual atom. When atoms are linked together, they form molecules. The smallest molecule contains just two atoms, but molecules can also be very large and contain hundreds of atoms. In order to find the mass of a molecule, the atomic mass of each individual atom in the molecule must be added together.

Figure 1 below depicts the trends and commonalities between the elements that can be seen in the periodic table.

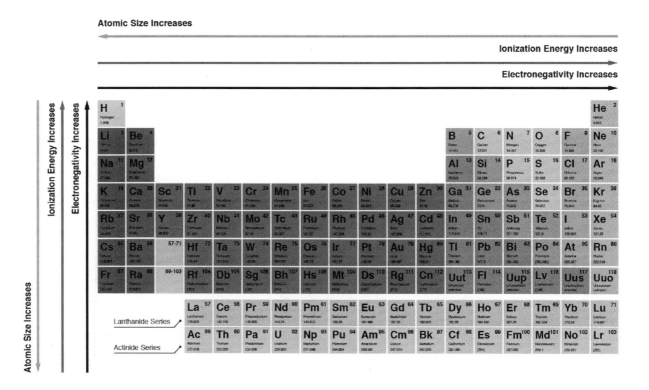

Figure 2 below shows what the information in each element's box represents.

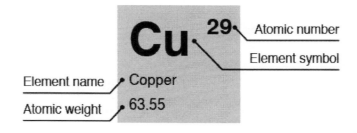

Figure 3 below shows the periodic table.

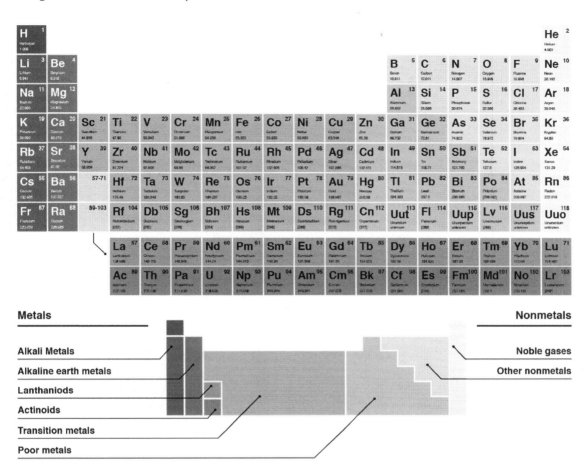

6. What is the atomic mass of NaCl?
    a. 23
    b. 58.5
    c. 35.5
    d. 71

7. Which of the following elements is most electronegative?
    a. Ununoctium (Uuo)
    b. Francium (Fr)
    c. Hydrogen (H)
    d. Helium (He)

8. Which of the following elements has the lowest ionization energy?
    a. Potassium (K)
    b. Gallium (Ga)
    c. Sodium (Na)
    d. Aluminum (Al)

9. Which element has the fewest number of protons?
    a. Radon (Rn)

b. Boron (B)

c. Nitrogen (N)

d. Hydrogen (H)

10. Scientist A needs a noble gas for her experiment. Which of these elements should she consider using?

a. Nitrogen (N)

b. Radon (Rn)

c. Copper (Cu)

d. Boron (B)

## Passage 3

*Questions 11–15 pertain to Passage 3:*

Physical characteristics are controlled by genes. Each gene has two alleles, or variations. Generally, one allele is more dominant than the other allele and when one of each allele is present on the gene, the physical trait of the dominant allele will be expressed. The allele that is not expressed is called the recessive allele. Recessive alleles are expressed only when both alleles present on the gene are the recessive allele.

Punnett squares are diagrams that can predict the outcome of crossing different traits. In these diagrams, dominant alleles are represented by uppercase letters and recessive alleles are represented by lowercase letters.

Scientist A wants to grow white flowered plants and is doing a series of crossbreeding experiments. She had each plant genetically tested so she knows which alleles comprise each plant. The dominant flowers are red (A) and the recessive allele (a) produces white flowers.

Figure 1 below represents the different flowers that underwent crossbreeding during Round #1A

### Round #1A

| Crossbreeding #1A | | | Crossbreeding #2A | | | Crossbreeding #3A | | |
|---|---|---|---|---|---|---|---|---|
| | A | a | | a | a | | a | a |
| A | AA | Aa | A | Aa | Aa | A | Aa | Aa |
| A | AA | Aa | A | Aa | Aa | a | aa | aa |

Figure 2 below represents the number of flowers that were red and white after the first round of crossbreeding experiments.

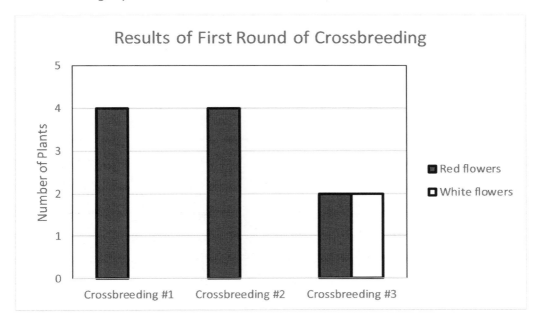

During her second round of crossbreeding, she adds in a plant of unknown genetic makeup with red flowers. She crosses it with a white-flowering plant. The results of her experiment are represented in the next figure.

Figure 3 represents the genetic results from the second round of crossbreeding.

**Round #2**

|   | a | a |
|---|---|---|
| ? | Aa | Aa |
| ? | aa | aa |

Scientist A takes offspring plants from Round #1A and crossbreeds them with each other and calls this Round #1B.

Figure 4 below represents the results of crossbreeding from Round #1B.

## Round #1B

| Crossbreeding #1B | | | Crossbreeding #2B | | | Crossbreeding #3B | | |
|---|---|---|---|---|---|---|---|---|
|   | A | a |   | A | a |   | a | a |
| A | AA | Aa | A | AA | Aa | a | aa | aa |
| A | AA | Aa | a | Aa | aa | a | aa | aa |

11. Crossbreeding which two plants will give her the highest likelihood of obtaining some white plants right away in Round #1A?
    a. AA × Aa
    b. Aa × aa
    c. AA × aa
    d. AA × AA

12. What percentage of plants are white after the first crossbreeding reactions?
    a. 12%
    b. 50%
    c. 16.7%
    d. 25%

13. What is the genetic makeup of the unknown plant from the second round of crossbreeding?
    a. aa
    b. Aa
    c. AA
    d. Cannot be determined

14. From which group of crossbreeding in Round #1B can she obtain 100% white flowers by the second generation?
    a. They are all equal.
    b. 1B
    c. 2B
    d. 3B

15. Which of her five senses did she use for the observation step of the scientific method here?
    a. Sight
    b. Smell
    c. Touch
    d. Hearing

## Passage 4

*Questions 16–20 pertain to Passage 4:*

Rainforests cover approximately 6% of the Earth's surface. Tropical rainforests are found in five major areas of the world: Central America, South America, Central Africa, Asia stretching from India to islands in the Pacific Ocean, and Australia. All of these areas are warm and wet areas within ten degrees of the equator. They do not have a substantial dry season during the year.

Rainforests are large areas of jungle that get an abundance of rain. They comprise four layers, each with unique characteristics. The emergent layer is the highest layer and is made up of the tops of the tall trees. There is very good sunlight in this layer. The canopy layer is the next layer, just under the emergent layer. Here, there is some sun but not as much as the emergent layer. The next layer is the understory layer. This layer does not receive very much sunlight. The plants in this layer need to grow very large leaves to reach the Sun. The bottom-most layer is the forest floor. Sunlight generally does not reach this layer, so plants do not grow here.

Figure 1 below represents the different layers of the rainforest.

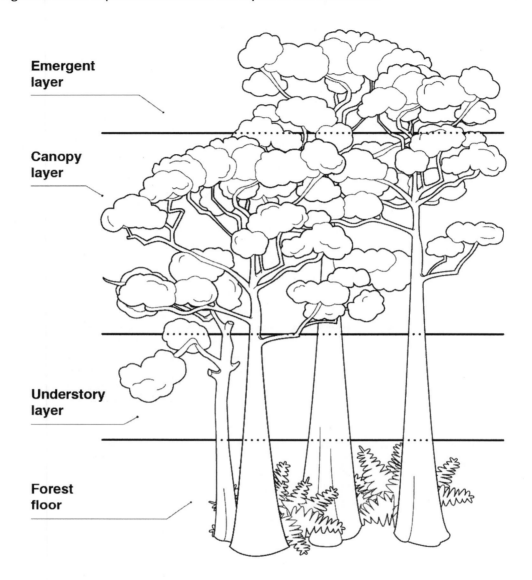

Figure 2 below is a map of the rainforests on Earth and a map of Central America.

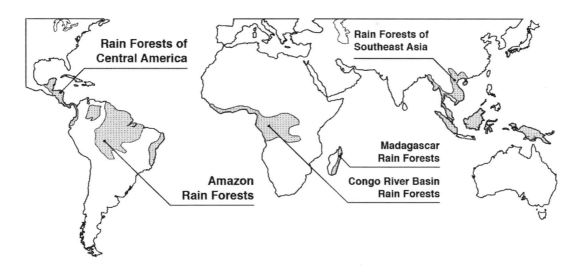

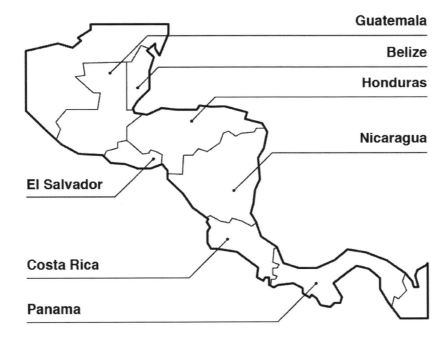

16. What essential part of photosynthesis, which is necessary for plant growth, is lacking on the forest floor and does not allow for plants to grow?

    a. Carbon

    b. Water

    c. Oxygen

    d. Sunlight

17. Which of the following is a country in Central America that contains a rainforest?
    a. India
    b. Panama
    c. Madagascar
    d. Brazil

18. In which layer of the rainforest would birds fly around the most?
    a. Forest floor
    b. Understory layer
    c. Emergent layer
    d. Canopy layer

19. Giant taro plants have the largest leaves in the world that are approximately ten feet in length. In which layer of the rainforest do they reside?
    a. Emergent layer
    b. Canopy layer
    c. Forest floor
    d. Understory layer

20. Which of these plants, based on their listed requirements, would thrive in a rainforest climate?
    a. Giant water lily: warm temperatures, wet environment, has ability to grow large leaves
    b. Cactus: dry environment, long, hot season for growth
    c. Pine tree: dry and sandy soil, lots of sunlight
    d. Black-eyed susan: very hot temperatures, slightly moist soil

## Passage 5

*Questions 21–25 pertain to Passage 5:*

An eclipse occurs when the light from one object in the solar system is completely or partially blocked by another object in the solar system. In 2017, the Earth was a part of two different types of eclipses. One was a solar eclipse, which occurs when the moon passes between the Sun and the Earth and blocks the Sun's light, making it dark during the daytime for several minutes. A total solar eclipse occurs when the moon completely covers the Sun. A partial solar eclipse occurs when the moon only covers part of the Sun. Solar eclipses should not be looked at directly because the Sun's rays can damage a person's eyes even though they appear to be dim while the eclipse is happening. Special viewing devices can be used to look at a solar eclipse indirectly, such as a pinhole camera facing away from the eclipse that allows light from the eclipse to pass through a hole in a piece of cardboard and its image to be reflected on a piece of white paper.

The other type of eclipse that the Earth was a part of was a lunar eclipse. This type of eclipse occurs when the moon passes behind the Earth, into its shadow. The moon is illuminated by the light of the Sun, so when it is in the Earth's shadow, the moon becomes dim for a few hours during the night. This type of eclipse is safe to look at without any protection for your eyes.

Figure 1 below represents a solar eclipse.

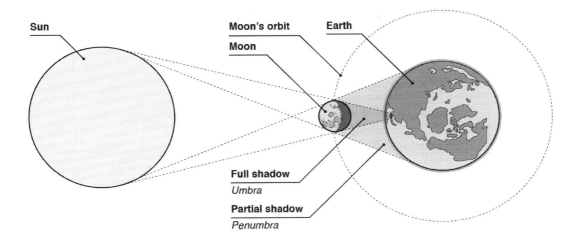

Figure 2 below represents a lunar eclipse.

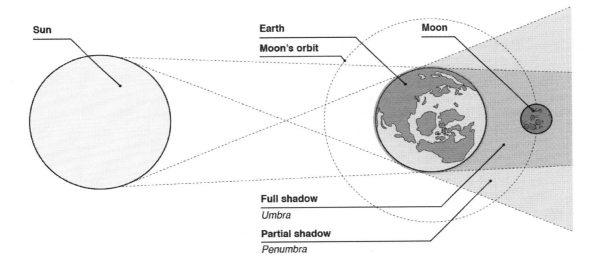

21. Which apparatus would be best to use to look at a solar eclipse?
    a. A telescope facing the eclipse
    b. A pinhole camera facing away from the eclipse
    c. Sunglasses facing the eclipse
    d. Binoculars facing the eclipse

22. What type of eclipse occurs when the moon comes between the Earth and Sun and covers the Sun's light completely?
    a. Total solar eclipse
    b. Partial lunar eclipse
    c. Total lunar eclipse
    d. Partial solar eclipse

23. What object in the solar system becomes dim during a lunar eclipse?
    a. Sun
    b. Earth
    c. Moon
    d. Earth and moon

24. Which type of eclipse could you observe directly using a telescope?
    a. Neither solar nor lunar
    b. Lunar only
    c. Both solar and lunar
    d. Solar only

25. Which type of eclipse is viewed during the daytime?
    a. Both solar and lunar
    b. Solar only
    c. Partial lunar
    d. Total lunar

## Passage 6

*Questions 26–30 pertain to Passage 6:*

Phylogenetic trees are diagrams that map out the proposed evolutionary history of a species. They are branching diagrams that make it easy to see how scientists believe certain species developed from other species. The most recent proposed common ancestor between two species is the one before their lineages branch in the diagram. These diagrams do not attempt to include specific information about physical traits that were thought to be retained or disappeared during the evolutionary process.

Cladograms classify organisms based on their proposed common ancestry but are focused on their common physical traits. Branching points on these diagrams represent when a group of organisms is thought to have developed a new trait. Analogous features are those that have the same function but were not derived from a common ancestor. Homologous features have anatomical similarities, even if the function is no longer the same, due to a proposed common ancestor.

Figure 1 below is a phylogenetic tree of the Carnivora order.

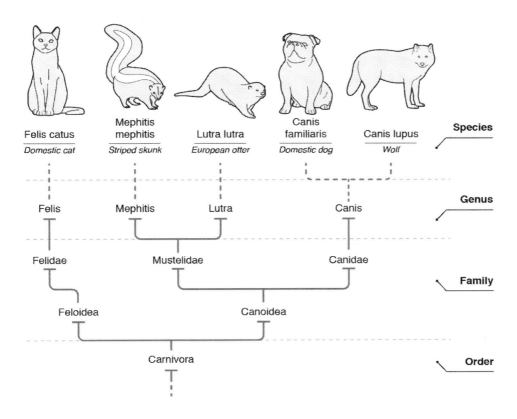

Figure 2 below is a cladogram.

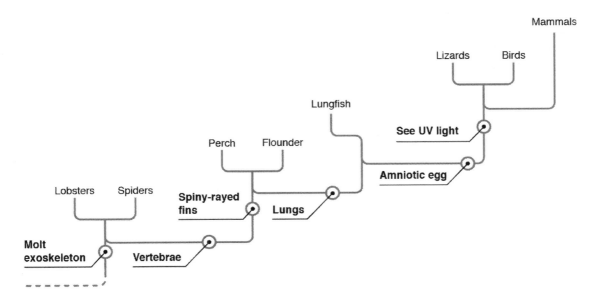

Figure 3 below shows a homologous feature between four different species with a proposed common ancestor.

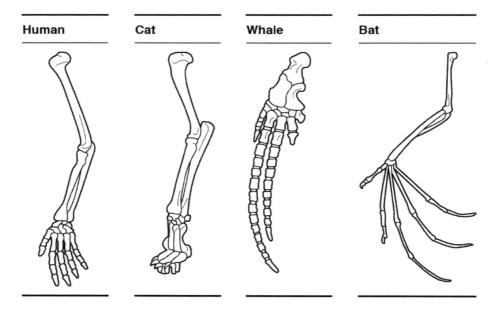

26. Which tool would you use to find out when a common ancestor of two species supposedly developed lungs?
    a. Phylogenetic tree
    b. Cladogram
    c. Punnett square
    d. Photographs

27. According to the earlier details, how are human arms and whale fins related?
    a. They are homologous structures from a common ancestor.
    b. They both have the same number of bones.
    c. They are analogous features.
    d. They are both covered in the same type of skin.

28. According to Figure 1, what common ancestry group do the striped skunk and European otter share?
    a. Mephitis
    b. Felidae
    c. Canidae
    d. Mustelidae

29. What trait do lizards and birds have in common according to Figure 2?
    a. Both see UV light
    b. Both have spiny-rayed fins
    c. Both molt an exoskeleton
    d. They do not have any traits in common.

30. According to Figure 1, at what level of organization are domestic cats and wolves related?
    a. Family
    b. Genus
    c. Order
    d. Species

## Passage 7

*Questions 31–35 pertain to Passage 7:*

Scientists often use an assay called an enzyme-linked immunosorbent assay, or ELISA, to quantify specific substances within a larger sample. An ELISA works based on the specificity of an antibody to an antigen. One type of ELISA is called a sandwich ELISA. In this type of ELISA, a plate is coated with a capture antibody that adheres the antigen in the sample when it is added. Then the primary antibody is added and sticks to any antigen bound to the capture antibody. Next, a secondary antibody is added. Once it attaches to the primary antibody, it releases a colored tag that can be detected by a piece of laboratory equipment. If more color is released, it is indicative of more antigen having been present in the sample.

Figure 1 below describes how a sandwich ELISA works.

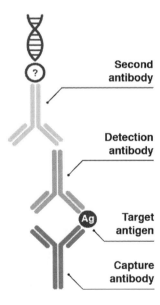

The cytokine protein IL-1β is a marker of inflammation in the body. Scientist A took samples from different locations within the body to find out where there was elevated inflammation in a patient.

Figure 2 below is a picture of the ELISA plate from Scientist A's experiment.

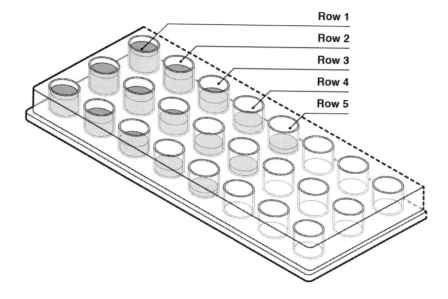

Figure 3 below is a graph of the results of Scientist A's experiment.

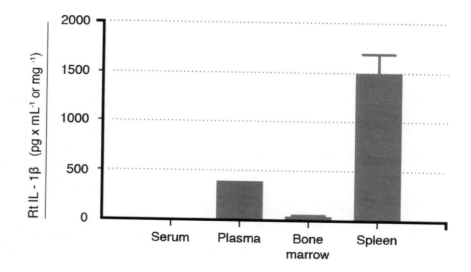

31. Which step of the ELISA allows for the color to be released for detection of the antigen?
    a. Addition of the antigen
    b. Addition of the primary antibody
    c. The presence of the capture antibody
    d. Addition of the secondary antibody

32. According to Figure 2, which row had the largest amount of antigen in the sample?
    a. Row 2
    b. Row 1
    c. Row 5
    d. Row 3

33. According to the ELISA results in Figure 3, which area of the body had the most inflammation?
    a. Serum
    b. Plasma
    c. Spleen
    d. Bone marrow

34. Which two antibodies sandwich the antigen in a sandwich ELISA?
    a. Capture antibody and secondary antibody
    b. Capture antibody and primary antibody
    c. Primary antibody and secondary antibody
    d. Two units of the secondary antibody

35. What is the purpose of an ELISA?
    a. Quantify specific substances within a larger sample
    b. Quantify all substances within a larger sample
    c. To create a colorful pattern with the samples
    d. To develop different antibodies

## Passage 8

*Questions 36–40 pertain to Passage 8:*

Natural selection is the idea that certain traits make an individual have longer survival and higher reproduction rates than other individuals. It is based on the phenotype, or physical appearance, of the individual and not the genotype, or genetic makeup. There are three ways in which a phenotype can change due to natural selection. Directional selection occurs when one extreme of a phenotype is favored. Disruptive selection occurs when both extremes of a phenotype are favored. Stabilizing selection occurs when an intermediate phenotype is favored over either extreme phenotype.

*Scenario 1:* Mice live in an environment that has a mix of light and dark colored rocks. To avoid predators, the mice with intermediate color fur survive longer and produce more offspring.

*Scenario 2:* The Galapagos Islands experienced a drought and large, tough seeds became abundant. Eventually, all finches had large beaks to break up these seeds.

*Scenario 3:* In Cameroon, seeds are either large or small. Finches in Cameroon have either large beaks or small beaks. They are not found with medium-sized beaks.

36. What type of selection is described in Scenario 1?
    a. Stabilizing selection
    b. Directional selection
    c. Disruptive selection
    d. Color selection

37. What type of selection is described in Scenario 2?
   a. Beak-type
   b. Disruptive
   c. Stabilizing
   d. Directional

38. Why would it be hard for small-beaked finches in the Galapagos Island to survive after the drought?
   a. Too much sand got caught in the small beaks
   b. Beaks would not be able to break up large seeds
   c. Large-beaked finches would attack them
   d. Two extreme phenotypes can never be selected by natural selection

39. What type of selection is described in Scenario 3?
   a. Stabilizing
   b. Directional
   c. Disruptive
   d. Beak-type

40. Which statement is true about natural selection?
   a. Individuals are selected based on their genotype.
   b. An extreme phenotype is always selected.
   c. It only occurs after a drought.
   d. Individuals are selected based on phenotypes that are advantageous for survival and reproduction.

# *Social Studies*

1. What is the term for the ability of a ruling body to influence the actions, behavior, and attitude of a person or group of people?
   a. Politics
   b. Power
   c. Authority
   d. Legitimacy

2. Which of the following is NOT a shared characteristic sufficient to form a nation?
   a. Culture and traditions
   b. History
   c. Sovereignty
   d. Beliefs and religion

*Question 3 is based on the following passage:*

Upon this, one has to remark that men ought either to be well treated or crushed, because they can avenge themselves of lighter injuries, of more serious ones they cannot; therefore the injury that is to be done to a man ought to be of such a kind that one does not stand in fear of revenge.

From Niccolo Machiavelli's *The Prince*, 1513

3. What advice is Machiavelli giving to the prince?
   a. Lightly injured enemies will overthrow the prince.
   b. Seek to injure everyone you meet.
   c. Hurting people is always the correct course of action.
   d. If you are going to cause an enemy some injury, ensure the injury is fatal.

*Question 4 is based on the following passage:*

> The creed which accepts as the foundation of morals, Utility, or the Greatest-Happiness Principle, holds that actions are right in proportion as they tend to promote happiness, wrong as they tend to produce the reverse of happiness. By happiness is intended pleasure, and the absence of pain; by unhappiness, pain, and the privation of pleasure.
>
> The utilitarian morality does recognise in human beings the power of sacrificing their own greatest good for the good of others. It only refuses to admit that the sacrifice is itself a good. A sacrifice which does not increase, or tend to increase, the sum total of happiness, it considers as wasted.
>
> From John Stuart Mill's *Utilitarianism*, 1861

4. What is the meaning of the "Utility"?
   a. Actions should be judged based on the net total of pleasure.
   b. Actions requiring sacrifice can never be valuable.
   c. Actions promoting sacrifice that increase happiness are more valuable than actions that only increase happiness.
   d. Actions can be valuable even if the pain outweighs the pleasure.

*Question 5 is based on the following passage:*

> The history of all hitherto existing society is the history of class struggles.
>
> Freeman and slave, patrician and plebeian, lord and serf, guildmaster and journeyman, in a word, oppressor and oppressed, stood in constant opposition to one another, carried on an uninterrupted, now hidden, now open fight, that each time ended, either in the revolutionary reconstitution of society at large, or in the common ruin of the contending classes.
>
> Let the ruling classes tremble at a Communistic revolution. The proletarians have nothing to lose but their chains. They have a world to win.
>
> Workingmen of all countries unite!
>
> Karl Marx and Friedrich Engels, *The Communist Manifesto,* 1848

5. What's the main idea presented in the excerpt?
   a. Working men are morally superior to the ruling class.
   b. Every society will come to an end at some point.
   c. History is defined by class struggle, and working men must now unite and fight the ruling class to gain freedom.
   d. Working men are in the same position as the slave, plebeian, serf, and journeyman.

*Questions 6-7 are based on the following image:*

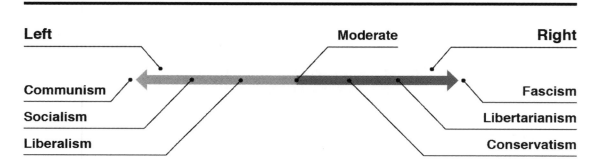

## Spectrum of Political Ideologies

Left                           Moderate          Right

Communism                           Fascism

Socialism                     Libertarianism

Liberalism                    Conservatism

6. Of the following ideologies, which one advocates for the most radical government intervention to achieve social and economic equality?
    a. Socialism
    b. Liberalism
    c. Libertarianism
    d. Fascism

7. Of the following ideologies, which one prioritizes stability and traditional institutions within a culture?
    a. Socialism
    b. Liberalism
    c. Conservatism
    d. Libertarianism

8. The central government established under the Articles of Confederation held which of the following powers?
    a. The power to impose taxes
    b. The power to declare war
    c. The power to regulate trade
    d. The power to enforce laws enacted by Congress

*Question 9 is based on the following diagram:*

## Separation of Powers

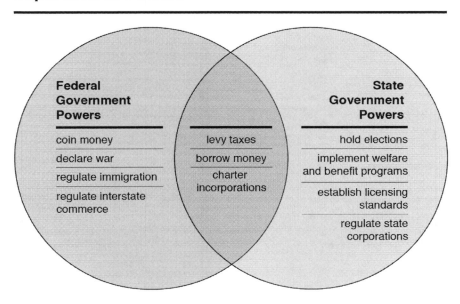

9. Which of the following terms best describes the missing title?
   a. Reserved powers
   b. Implied powers
   c. Delegated powers
   d. Concurrent powers

*Question 10 is based on the following passage:*

Ambition must be made to counteract ambition. The interest of the man must be connected with the constitutional rights of the place. It may be a reflection on human nature, that such devices should be necessary to control the abuses of government. But what is government itself, but the greatest of all reflections on human nature?

If men were angels, no government would be necessary. If angels were to govern men, neither external nor internal controls on government would be necessary. In framing a government which is to be administered by men over men, the great difficulty lies in this: you must first enable the government to control the governed; and in the next place oblige it to control itself.

Alexander Hamilton or James Madison, aka *Publius*, "Federalist No. 50," 1788

10. What is the main idea presented in the excerpt?
    a. Men are inherently immoral and abusive.
    b. The best form of government is the type that angels would construct.
    c. Government reflects human nature.
    d. An effective government requires a separation of powers to regulate itself.

*Question 11 is based on the following diagram:*

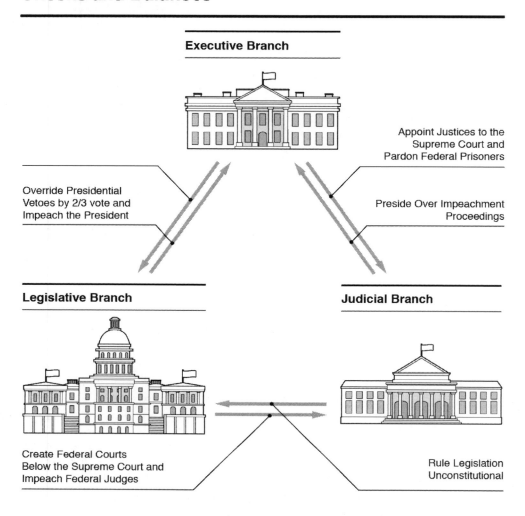

## Checks and Balances

**Executive Branch**

Appoint Justices to the Supreme Court and Pardon Federal Prisoners

Override Presidential Vetoes by 2/3 vote and Impeach the President

Preside Over Impeachment Proceedings

**Legislative Branch**

**Judicial Branch**

Create Federal Courts Below the Supreme Court and Impeach Federal Judges

Rule Legislation Unconstitutional

11. Which of the following answer choices best completes the blank line at the top left section of the diagram by the Executive Branch?
    a. Impeach congressmen and veto legislation
    b. Call special sessions of Congress and refuse to enforce laws
    c. Call special sessions of Congress and veto legislation
    d. Impeach congressmen and refuse to enforce laws

12. What amendment guarantees American citizens the right to keep and bear arms?
    a. First Amendment
    b. Second Amendment
    c. Third Amendment
    d. Fourth Amendment

*Question 13 is based on the following table:*

| Presidential Election of 1824 | | | |
|---|---|---|---|
| **Candidate** | **Electoral Votes** | **Popular Votes** | **State Votes in the House of Representatives** |
| Andrew Jackson | 99 | 153,544 | 7 |
| John Quincy Adams | 84 | 108,740 | 13 |
| William H. Crawford | 41 | 46,618 | 4 |
| Henry Clay | 37 | 47,136 | 0 |

13. Who won the presidential election of 1824?
    a. Andrew Jackson
    b. John Quincy Adams
    c. William H. Crawford
    d. Henry Clay

14. What electoral system can result in a second round of voting, commonly referred to as a runoff?
    a. Majority systems
    b. Plurality systems
    c. Single transferable systems
    d. Party list systems

15. In international relations, which of the following is NOT a basic tenet of realism?
    a. States are the central actors.
    b. States act rationally to advance their self-interest.
    c. States should seek to form international organizations to increase global cooperation and respond to international issues.
    d. All states are interested in maintaining or expanding their power as a means of self-preservation.

16. How did the outcome of the French and Indian War impact the life of American colonists?
    a. The colonies expanded west of the Allegheny Mountains.
    b. Great Britain imposed taxes on the colonies to pay off the British war debt.
    c. A lasting peace developed between the colonists and Native Americans.
    d. The power of self-government increased in the colonies.

*Question 17 is based on the following passage:*

We hold these Truths to be self-evident: that all Men are created equal; that they are endowed by their creator with certain inalienable rights; that among these are life, liberty, and the pursuit of happiness: that to secure these rights, governments are instituted among men, deriving their just powers from the consent of the governed; that whenever any form of government becomes destructive of these ends, it is the right of the people to alter or abolish it, and to institute new government, laying its foundation on such principles, and organizing its powers in such form, as to them shall seem most likely to affect their safety and happiness.

Prudence indeed will dictate that governments long established should not be changed for light and transient causes; and accordingly all experience hath shown that mankind are more disposed to suffer while evils are sufferable, than to right themselves by abolishing the forms to

which they are accustomed. But when a long train of abuses and usurpations begun at a distinguished period and pursuing invariably the same object, evinces a design to reduce them under absolute despotism, it is their right, it is their duty to throw off such government, and to provide new guards for their future security

Declaration of Independence, adopted July 4, 1776

17. What is the main purpose of the excerpt?
   a. Provide a justification for revolution when the government infringes on "certain inalienable rights"
   b. Provide specific evidence of the "train of abuses"
   c. Provide an argument why "all Men are created equal"
   d. Provide an analysis of the importance of "life, liberty, and the pursuit of happiness"

*Question 18 is based on the following map:*

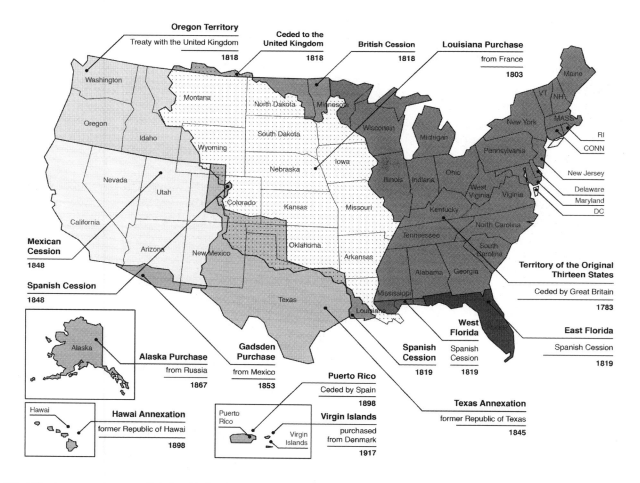

18. What current state did the United States gain through military force with a non-native nation-state?
   a. Nebraska
   b. Missouri
   c. Alaska
   d. Nevada

*Question 19 is based on the following passage:*

> Now, therefore I, Abraham Lincoln, President of the United States, by virtue of the power in me vested as Commander-in-Chief, of the Army and Navy of the United States in time of actual armed rebellion against the authority and government of the United States, and as a fit and necessary war measure for suppressing said rebellion...
>
> And by virtue of the power, and for the purpose aforesaid, I do order and declare that all persons held as slaves within said designated States, and parts of States, are, and henceforward shall be free; and that the Executive government of the United States, including the military and naval authorities thereof, will recognize and maintain the freedom of said persons.
>
> President Abraham Lincoln, Emancipation Proclamation, January 1, 1863

19. How does President Lincoln justify freeing the slaves in designated areas of the South?
    a. Emancipation is necessary since slavery is evil.
    b. Emancipation is necessary to boost the morale of the North.
    c. Emancipation is necessary to punish for the South seceding from the Union.
    d. Emancipation is necessary to strengthen the war effort of the North.

20. What was a consequence of the industrialization that followed the Civil War?
    a. Decreased immigration
    b. Increased urbanization
    c. Decreased socioeconomic inequality
    d. Increased rights for workers

21. Which of the following best describes how the Treaty of Versailles contributed to the outbreak of World War II?
    a. It forced Germany to assume responsibility for all damage incurred.
    b. It failed to adequately end the violence of World War I.
    c. If left large tracts of territory unclaimed by any nation-state.
    d. It created the League of Nations.

*Question 22 is based on the following passage:*

Hand in hand with this we must frankly recognize the overbalance of population in our industrial centers and, by engaging on a national scale in a redistribution, endeavor to provide a better use of the land for those best fitted for the land. The task can be helped by definite efforts to raise the values of agricultural products and with this the power to purchase the output of our cities. It can be helped by preventing realistically the tragedy of the growing loss through foreclosure of our small homes and our farms. It can be helped by insistence that the Federal, State, and local governments act forthwith on the demand that their cost be drastically reduced. It can be helped by the unifying of relief activities which today are often scattered, uneconomical, and unequal. It can be helped by national planning for and supervision of all forms of transportation and of communications and other utilities which have a definitely public character. There are many ways in which it can be helped, but it can never be helped merely by talking about it. We must act and act quickly.

Finally, in our progress toward a resumption of work we require two safeguards against a return of the evils of the old order: there must be a strict supervision of all banking and credits and investments, so that there will be an end to speculation with other people's money; and there must be provision for an adequate but sound currency.

President Franklin D. Roosevelt, Inaugural Address, March 4, 1933

22. Which of the following best describes President Roosevelt's underlying approach to government?
   a. Government must be focused on redistribution of land.
   b. Government must "act and act quickly" to intervene and regulate the economy.
   c. Government must exercise "strict supervision of all banking."
   d. Government must prevent the "growing loss through foreclosure."

*Question 23 is based on the following passage:*

What, to the American slave, is your 4th of July? I answer: a day that reveals to him, more than all other days in the year, the gross injustice and cruelty to which he is the constant victim. To him, your celebration is a sham; your boasted liberty, an unholy license; your national greatness, swelling vanity; your sounds of rejoicing are empty and heartless; your denunciations of tyrants, brass fronted impudence; your shouts of liberty and equality, hollow mockery; your prayers and hymns, your sermons and thanksgivings, with all your religious parade, and solemnity, are, to him, mere bombast, fraud, deception, impiety, and hypocrisy—a thin veil to cover up crimes which would disgrace a nation of savages. There is not a nation on the earth guilty of practices, more shocking and bloody, than are the people of these United States, at this very hour.

Frederick Douglass, "What to the Slave is the 4th of July?" July 5, 1852

23. What is the specific hypocrisy that Douglass repudiates?
   a. The Declaration of Independence declared that all men are created equal, but Thomas Jefferson owned slaves.
   b. Americans are free, but they do not value their freedom.
   c. The Fourth of July is a celebration about freedom, and slavery remained legal in the United States.
   d. The United States is a Christian nation, but American traditions contradict their faith.

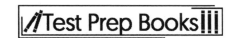

*Question 24 is based on the following passage:*

> May it please your honor, I shall never pay a dollar of your unjust penalty. All the stock in trade I possess is a $10,000 debt, incurred by publishing my paper—The Revolution—four years ago, the sole object of which was to educate all women to do precisely as I have done, rebel against your man-made, unjust, unconstitutional forms of law, that tax, fine, imprison and hang women, while they deny them the right of representation in the government; and I shall work on with might and main to pay every dollar of that honest debt, but not a penny shall go to this unjust claim. And I shall earnestly and persistently continue to urge all women to the practical recognition of the old revolutionary maxim, that "Resistance to tyranny is obedience to God."
>
> *An Account of the Proceedings on the Trial of Susan B. Anthony on the Charge of Illegal Voting,* 1874.

24. What is the main idea presented in the excerpt?
    a. Taxation without representation is tyranny.
    b. Domestic abuse and violence against women is the cause of tyranny.
    c. Anthony cannot pay her fine due to debt accumulated from fighting for women's rights.
    d. Denying women the right to vote is tyranny and must be resisted.

25. Which of the following most accurately describes the platform of Ronald Reagan?
    a. Christianity, optimism, and preserving social safety nets
    b. Increased defense spending, deregulation, and tax cuts
    c. Moral majority, international cooperation, and compromise
    d. Conservatism, opposition to abortion, and organized labor

26. How do market economies differ from planned economies?
    a. Unlike market economies, planned economies have a larger number of both buyers and sellers.
    b. Unlike market economies, planned economies distribute resources more efficiently.
    c. Unlike planned economies, market economies allow demand to set prices.
    d. Unlike planned economies, market economies prioritize public services.

*Question 27 is based on the following passage:*

> Those who are opposed to this proposition tell us that the issue of paper money is a function of the bank and that the government ought to go out of the banking business. I stand with Jefferson rather than with them, and tell them, as he did, that the issue of money is a function of the government and that the banks should go out of the governing business.
>
> If they dare to come out in the open field and defend the gold standard as a good thing, we shall fight them to the uttermost, having behind us the producing masses of the nation and the world. Having behind us the commercial interests and the laboring interests and all the toiling masses, we shall answer their demands for a gold standard by saying to them, you shall not press down upon the brow of labor this crown of thorns. You shall not crucify mankind upon a cross of gold.
>
> William Jennings Bryan, "Cross of Gold" speech, 1896

27. What is the main idea presented in the excerpt?
    a. Banks prefer the gold standard.
    b. Most Americans dislike the gold standard.
    c. Violence is justified when the government oppresses the masses.
    d. The government should set the monetary policy based on the will of the people.

*Question 28 is based on the following graph:*

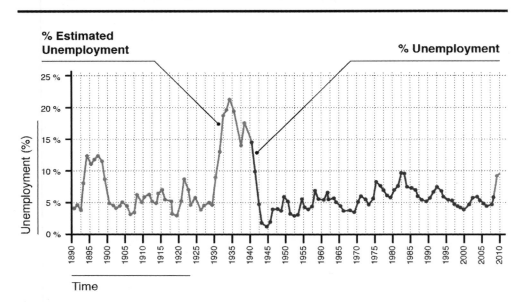

## History of Unemployment in the United States

28. Which event caused the second largest increase in unemployment in American history?
    a. Panic of 1893
    b. Depression of 1920
    c. Depression of 1929
    d. Great Recession of 2007

Question 29 is based on the following diagram:

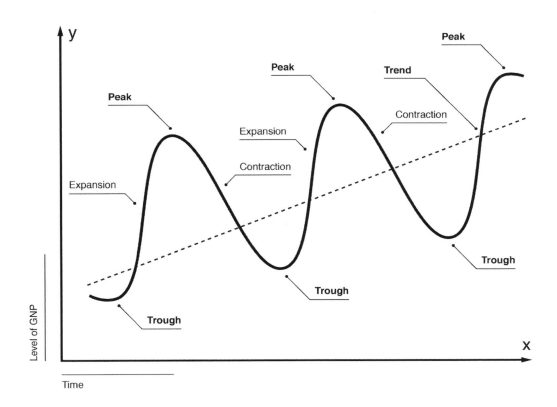

29. Which of the following phases of a business cycle occurs when there is continual growth?
    a. Expansion
    b. Peak
    c. Contraction
    d. Trough

30. Which of the following types of government intervention lowers prices, reassures the supply, and creates opportunity to compete with foreign vendors?
    a. Income redistribution
    b. Price controls
    c. Taxes
    d. Subsidies

31. What type of map would be the most useful for calculating data and differentiating between the characteristics of two places?
    a. Topographic maps
    b. Dot-density maps
    c. Isoline maps
    d. Flow-line maps

*Question 32 is based on the following map:*

# Map of the United States by population density

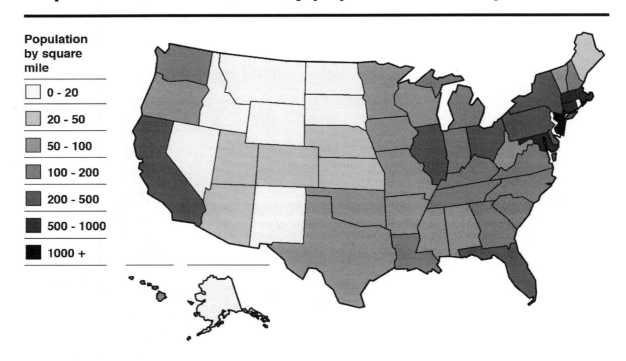

**Population by square mile**

- ☐ 0 - 20
- ☐ 20 - 50
- ☐ 50 - 100
- ☐ 100 - 200
- ☐ 200 - 500
- ☐ 500 - 1000
- ■ 1000 +

32. According to the map, what area of the United States has the highest population density?
    a. Northwest
    b. Northeast
    c. Southwest
    d. Southeast

33. What accounts for different parts of the Earth experiencing different seasons at the same time?
    a. Differences in the rate of Earth's rotation
    b. Ocean currents
    c. Tilt of the Earth's rotational axis
    d. Elevation

34. Which of the following is NOT a reason why nonrenewable energy sources are used more often than renewables?
    a. Nonrenewable energy is currently cheaper.
    b. Infrastructure was built specifically for nonrenewable sources.
    c. Renewable energy is more difficult and expensive to store for long periods.
    d. Renewable energy cannot be converted into a power source.

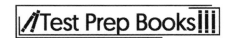

*Question 35 is based on the following map:*

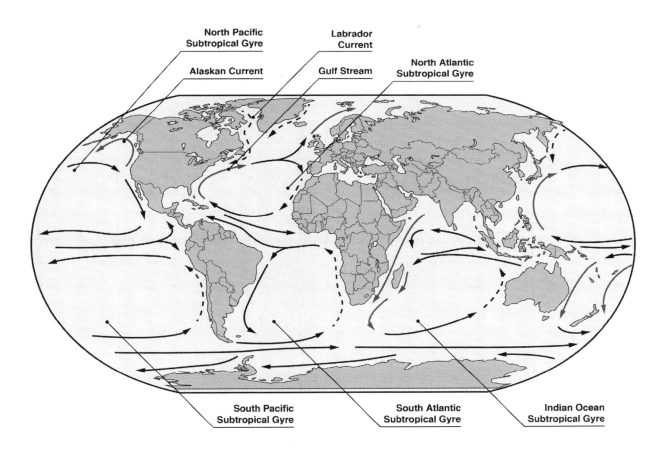

35. Which pair of ocean currents or gyres has the most impact on the weather of the United States?
    a. North Atlantic Subtropical Gyre and South Atlantic Subtropical Gyre
    b. Gulf Stream and North Pacific Subtropical Gyre
    c. North Pacific Subtropical Gyre and South Pacific Subtropical Gyre
    d. Alaskan Current and Indian Ocean Subtropical Gyre

# Answer Explanations for Practice Test #2

## *Mathematical Reasoning*

### No Calculator Questions

**1. C:** We are trying to find $x$, the number of red cans. The equation can be set up like this:

$$x + 2(10 - x) = 16$$

The left $x$ is actually multiplied by $1, the price per red can. Since we know Jessica bought 10 total cans, $10 - x$ is the number blue cans that she bought. We multiply the number of blue cans by $2, the price per blue can.

That should all equal $16, the total amount of money that Jessica spent. Working that out gives us:

$$x + 20 - 2x = 16$$

$$20 - x = 16$$

$$x = 4$$

**2. C:** If $\log_{10} x = 2$, then $10^2 = x$, which equals 100.

**3. D:** In order to solve this problem, the number of feet in a yard must be established. There are 3 feet in every yard. The equation to calculate the minimum number of yards is:

$$79 \div 3 = 26\frac{1}{3}$$

If the material is sold only by whole yards, then Mo would need to round up to the next whole yard in order to cover the extra $\frac{1}{3}$ yard. Therefore, the answer is 27 yards. None of the other choices meets the minimum whole yard requirement.

**4. C:** First, we need to add up the money Taylor had: 2 $1 bills, 5 quarters, 3 dimes, and 1 nickel:

$$(2 \times \$1.00) + (5 \times \$.25) + (3 \times \$.10) + \$.05 = \$3.60$$

Taylor buys 1 brownie, 2 cookies, 1 cupcake, 2 lemon squares, and 1 container of milk. Using the price list, we can write an equation to represent the total cost of his purchases:

$$\$0.50 + (2 \times \$.20) + \$0.75 + (2 \times \$.60) + \$0.35 = \$3.20$$

To calculate this change, we subtract the total cost of his purchases ($3.20) from what he gave the cashier ($3.60) to get $0.40.

**5. C:** In order to calculate the profit, we need to create an equation that models the total income minus the cost of the materials. $60 $\times$ 20 = $1,200 total income. $60 \div 3 = 20$ sets of materials. $20 \times \$12 = \$240$ cost of materials. $\$1,200 - \$240 = \$960$ profit. Choice A is not correct, as it is only

the cost of materials. Choice *B* is not correct, as it is a miscalculation. Choice *D* is not correct, as it is the total income from the sale of the necklaces.

## Calculator Questions

**1. D:** The first field has an area of 1000 feet, so the length of one side is $\sqrt{1000} = 10\sqrt{10}$. Since there are four sides to a square, the total perimeter is $40\sqrt{10}$. The second square has an area of 10 square feet, so the length of one side is $\sqrt{10}$, and the total perimeter is $4\sqrt{10}$. Adding these together gives:

$$40\sqrt{10} + 4\sqrt{10}$$

$$(40 + 4)\sqrt{10}$$

$$44\sqrt{10}$$

**2. A:** 11. To determine the number of houses that can fit on the street, the length of the street is divided by the width of each house: $345 \div 30 = 11.5$. Although the mathematical calculation of 11.5 is correct, this answer is not reasonable. Half of a house cannot be built, so the company will need to either build 11 or 12 houses. Since the width of 12 houses (360 feet) will extend past the length of the street, only 11 houses can be built.

**3. C:** $y = 40x + 300$. In this scenario, the variables are the number of sales and Karen's weekly pay. The weekly pay depends on the number of sales. Therefore, weekly pay is the dependent variable (*y*), and the number of sales is the independent variable (*x*). Each pair of values from the table can be written as an ordered pair (*x*, *y*): (2, 380), (7, 580), (4, 460), (8, 620). The ordered pairs can be substituted into the equations to see which creates true statements (both sides equal) for each pair. Even if one ordered pair produces equal values for a given equation, the other three ordered pairs must be checked.

The only equation which is true for all four ordered pairs is $y = 40x + 300$:

$$380 = 40(2) + 300 \rightarrow 380 = 380$$

$$580 = 40(7) + 300 \rightarrow 580 = 580$$

$$460 = 40(4) + 300 \rightarrow 460 = 460$$

$$620 = 40(8) + 300 \rightarrow 620 = 620$$

**4. A:** The first step is to determine the unknown, which is in terms of the length, *l*.

The second step is to translate the problem into the equation using the perimeter of a rectangle:

$$P = 2l + 2w$$

The width is the length minus 2 centimeters. The resulting equation is:

$$2l + 2(l - 2) = 44$$

The equation can be solved as follows:

| $2l + 2l - 4 = 44$ | Apply the distributive property on the left side of the equation |
|---|---|
| $4l - 4 = 44$ | Combine like terms on the left side of the equation |
| $4l = 48$ | Add 4 to both sides of the equation |
| $l = 12$ | Divide both sides of the equation by 4 |

The length of the rectangle is 12 centimeters. The width is the length minus 2 centimeters, which is 10 centimeters. Checking the answers for length and width forms the following equation:

$$44 = 2(12) + 2(10)$$

The equation can be solved using the order of operations to form a true statement: $44 = 44$.

**5. D:** Because the coefficient of $x^2$ is negative, this function has a graph that is a parabola that opens downward. Therefore, it will be greater than 0 between its real roots, if it has any. Checking the discriminant, the result is:

$$1^2 - 4(-3)(-8) = 1 - 96 = -95$$

Since the discriminant is negative, this equation has no real solutions. Since this has no real roots, it must be always positive or always negative. Its graph opens downward, so it has at least some negative values. That means it is always negative. Thus, it is greater than zero for no real numbers.

**6. D:** Denote the width as $w$ and the length as $l$. Then, $l = 3w + 5$. The perimeter is $2w + 2l = 90$. Substituting the first expression for $l$ into the second equation yields:

$$2(3w + 5) + 2w = 90$$

$$6w + 10 + 2w = 90$$

$$8w = 80$$

$$w = 10$$

Putting this into the first equation, it yields:

$$l = 3(10) + 5 = 35$$

**7. D:** The slope is given by the change in $y$ divided by the change in $x$. The change in $y$ is $2 - 0 = 2$, and the change in $x$ is:

$$0 - (-4) = 4$$

The slope is $\frac{2}{4} = \frac{1}{2}$.

**8. C:** Find:

$$a_2 = 3a_1 - 1$$

$$3 \times 1 - 1 = 2$$

Next, find:

$$a_3 = 3a_2 - 1$$

$$3 \times 2 - 1$$

$$5$$

**9. B:** The volume of a cube is the length of the side cubed, and 3 inches cubed is 27 in³. Choice *A* is not the correct answer because that is 2 × 3 inches. Choice *C* is not the correct answer because that is 3 × 3 inches, and Choice *D* is not the correct answer because there was no operation performed.

**10. A:** ○. The core of the pattern consists of 4 items: ▲○○□. Therefore, the core repeats in multiples of 4, with the pattern starting over on the next step. The closest multiple of 4 to 42 is 40. Step 40 is the end of the core (□), so step 41 will start the core over (▲) and step 42 is ○.

**11. A:** If each man gains 10 pounds, every original data point will increase by 10 pounds. Therefore, the man with the original median will still have the median value, but that value will increase by 10. The smallest value and largest value will also increase by 10 and, therefore, the difference between the two won't change. The range does not change in value and, thus, remains the same.

**12. D:** The volume of a pyramid is ($length \times width \times height$), divided by 3, and (12 × 15), divided by 3 is 60 in³. Choice *A* is not the correct answer because that is 12 × 15. Choice *B* is not the correct answer because that is (12 × 15), divided by 2. Choice *C* is not the correct answer because that is 15 × 2.

**13. A:** The formula for the volume of a sphere is $\frac{4}{3}\pi r^3$, and $\frac{4}{3} \times \pi \times 3^3$ is 36 $\pi$ in³. Choice *B* is not the correct answer because that is only $3^3$. Choice *C* is not the correct answer because that is $3^2$, and Choice *D* is not the correct answer because that is 36 × 2.

**14. B:** This answer is correct because $3^2 + 4^2$ is 9 + 16, which is 25. Taking the square root of 25 is 5.

Choice *A* is not the correct answer because that is 3 + 4.

Choice *C* is not the correct answer because that is stopping at $3^2 + 4^2$ is 9 + 16, which is 25.

Choice *D* is not the correct answer because that is 3 × 4.

**15. A:** This answer is correct because $(2 + 2i)(2 - 2i)$, using the FOIL method and rules for imaginary numbers, is:

$$4 - 4i + 4i - 4i^2 = 8$$

Choice *B* is not the answer because there is no *i* in the final answer, since the *i*'s cancel out in the FOIL. Choice *C*, 4, is not the final answer because we add 4 + 4 in the end to equal 8. Choice *D*, 4*i*, is not the final answer because there is neither a 4 nor an *i* in the final answer.

**16. D:** $x \leq -5$. When solving a linear equation or inequality:

Distribution is performed if necessary:

$$-3(x + 4) \rightarrow -3x - 12 \geq x + 8$$

This means that any like terms on the same side of the equation/inequality are combined.

The equation/inequality is manipulated to get the variable on one side. In this case, subtracting $x$ from both sides produces:

$$-4x - 12 \geq 8$$

The variable is isolated using inverse operations to undo addition/subtraction. Adding 12 to both sides produces $-4x \geq 20$.

The variable is isolated using inverse operations to undo multiplication/division. Remember if dividing by a negative number, the relationship of the inequality reverses, so the sign is flipped. In this case, dividing by -4 on both sides produces $x \leq -5$.

**17. C:** Because the arc is a fraction of a circle, the length of an arc can be found by setting the arc and its central angle in proportion to the circumference of the circle and 360°:

$$\frac{arc\ length}{36°} = \frac{2 \times \pi \times 10\ \text{cm}}{360°}$$

$$arc\ length = \frac{2 \times \pi \times 10\ \text{cm} \times 36°}{360°} = \frac{2 \times \pi \times 10\ \text{cm}}{10} = 2\pi\ \text{cm}$$

Choice *A* is not the answer because the 2 is in the denominator. Choice *B* is not the answer since it was not multiplied by 2. Choice *D* is not the answer because it is double the correct arc length.

**18. B:** Since $850 is the price *after* a 20% discount, $850 represents 80% of the original price. To determine the original price, set up a proportion with the ratio of the sale price (850) to original price (unknown) equal to the ratio of sale percentage (where $x$ represents the unknown original price):

$$\frac{850}{x} = \frac{80}{100}$$

To solve a proportion, cross multiply the numerators and denominators and set the products equal to each other:

$$(850)(100) = (80)(x)$$

Multiplying each side results in the equation $85,000 = 80x$.

To solve for $x$, divide both sides by 80: $\frac{85,000}{80} = \frac{80x}{80}$, resulting in $x = 1062.5$. Remember that $x$ represents the original price. Subtracting the sale price from the original price ($1062.50 - $850) indicates that Frank saved $212.50.

**19: C.** The two points are at -5 and 0 for the x-axis and at -3 and at -1 for y-axis respectively. Therefore, the two points have the coordinates of (-5, -3) and (0, -1).

**20. A:** The Pythagorean theorem states that for right triangles $c^2 = a^2 + b^2$, with $c$ being the side opposite the 90° angle. Substituting 24 as $a$ and 36 as $b$, the equation becomes:

$$c^2 = 24^2 + 36^2$$

$$576 + 1296 = 1872$$

The last step is to square both sides to remove the exponent:

$$c = \sqrt{1872} = 43.3$$

**21. C:** To solve for the value of b, both sides of the equation need to be equalized.

Start by cancelling out the lower value of -4 by adding 4 to both sides:

$$5b - 4 = 2b + 17$$

$$5b - 4 + 4 = 2b + 17 + 4$$

$$5b = 2b + 21$$

The variable $b$ is the same on each side, so subtract the lower 2b from each side:

$$5b = 2b + 21$$

$$5b - 2b = 2b + 21 - 2b$$

$$3b = 21$$

Then divide both sides by 3 to get the value of $b$:

$$3b = 21$$

$$\frac{3b}{3} = \frac{21}{3}$$

$$b = 7$$

**22. D:** There are two ways to approach this problem. Each value can be substituted into each equation. Choice $A$ can be eliminated, since $4^2 + 16 = 32$. Choice $B$ can be eliminated, since:

$$4^2 + 4 \times 4 - 4 = 28$$

Choice $C$ can be eliminated, since:

$$4^2 - 2 \times 4 - 2 = 6$$

However, Choice $D$ does work because plugging in either value into $x^2 - 16$ yields a mathematically true statement:

$$(\pm 4)^2 - 16 = 16 - 16 = 0$$

**23. A:** Parallel lines have the same slope. The slope of the given equation is 3. The slope of Choice $C$ can be seen to be $\frac{1}{3}$ by dividing both sides by 3. The other choice are in standard form $Ax + By = C$, for

which the slope is given by $\frac{-A}{B}$. For Choice *A*, the equation can be written as $-6x + 2y = 2$. Therefore, the slope is:

$$\frac{-A}{B} = \frac{-(-6)}{2} = 3$$

This is the same as the given equation. The slope of Choice *B* is:

$$\frac{-A}{B} = \frac{-(-4)}{1} = 4$$

The slope of Choice *B* is 4. The slope of Choice *D* is:

$$\frac{-A}{B} = \frac{-2}{-2} = 1$$

**24. B:** Instead of multiplying these out, the product can be estimated by using $18 \times 10 = 180$. The error here should be lower than 15, since it is rounded to the nearest integer, and the numbers add to something less than 30.

**25. A:** First, convert the mixed numbers to improper fractions: $\frac{11}{3} - \frac{9}{5}$. Then, use 15 as a common denominator:

$$\frac{11}{3} - \frac{9}{5} = \frac{55}{15} - \frac{27}{15} = \frac{28}{15} = 1\frac{13}{15}$$

**26. B:**

$$4\frac{1}{3} + 3\frac{3}{4}$$

$$4 + 3 + \frac{1}{3} + \frac{3}{4}$$

$$7 + \frac{1}{3} + \frac{3}{4}$$

Adding the fractions gives:

$$\frac{1}{3} + \frac{3}{4}$$

$$\frac{4}{12} + \frac{9}{12}$$

$$\frac{13}{12}$$

$$1 + \frac{1}{12}$$

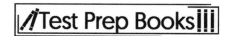

Thus:

$$7 + \frac{1}{3} + \frac{3}{4}$$

$$7 + 1 + \frac{1}{12}$$

$$8\frac{1}{12}$$

**27. D:** The total faculty is $15 + 20 = 35$. So the ratio is 35:200. Then, divide both of these numbers by 5, since 5 is a common factor to both, with a result of 7:40.

**28. C:** The first step in solving this problem is expressing the result in fraction form. Separate this problem first by solving the division operation of the last two fractions. When dividing one fraction by another, invert or flip the second fraction and then multiply the numerator and denominator.

$$\frac{7}{10} \times \frac{2}{1} = \frac{14}{10}$$

Next, multiply the first fraction with this value:

$$\frac{3}{5} \times \frac{14}{10} = \frac{42}{50}$$

In this instance, you can find the decimal form by converting the fraction into $\frac{x}{100}$, where $x$ is the number from which the final decimal is found. Multiply both the numerator and denominator by 2 to get the fraction as an expression of $\frac{x}{100}$.

$$\frac{42}{50} \times \frac{2}{2} = \frac{84}{100}$$

In decimal form, this would be expressed as 0.84.

**29. B:** Using the conversion rate, multiply the projected weight loss of 25 lb by $0.45 \frac{kg}{lb}$ to get the amount in kilograms (11.25 kg).

**30. A:** To expand a squared binomial, it's necessary to use the First, Outer, Inner, Last (FOIL) Method.

$$(2x - 4y)^2$$

$$(2x)(2x) + (2x)(-4y) + (-4y)(2x) + (-4y)(-4y)$$

$$4x^2 - 8xy - 8xy + 16y^2$$

$$4x^2 - 16xy + 16y^2$$

**31. D:** The volume of a cube is the length of the side cubed, and 5 centimeters cubed is 125 cm³. Choice *A* is not the correct answer because that is $2 \times 5$ centimeters. Choice *B* is not the correct answer

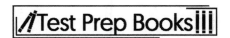 

because that is $3 \times 5$ centimeters. Choice *C* is not the correct answer because that is $5 \times$ 10 centimeters.

**32. A:** The place value to the right of the thousandth place, which would be the ten-thousandth place, is what gets used. The value in the thousandth place is 7. The number in the place value to its right is greater than 4, so the 7 gets bumped up to 8. Everything to its right turns to a zero, to get 245.2680. The zero is dropped because it is part of the decimal.

**33. D:** Factor the numerator into $x^2 - 6x + 9 = (x - 3)^2$, since:

$$-3 - 3 = -6, (-3)(-3) = 9$$

Factor the denominator into $x^2 - x - 6 = (x - 3)(x + 2)$, since:

$$-3 + 2 = -1, (-3)(2) = -6$$

This means the rational function can be rewritten as:

$$\frac{x^2 - 6x + 9}{x^2 - x - 6} = \frac{(x - 3)^2}{(x - 3)(x + 2)}$$

Using the restriction of $x > 3$, do not worry about any of these terms being 0, and cancel an $x - 3$ from the numerator and the denominator, leaving $\frac{x-3}{x+2}$.

**34. C:** The volume of a pyramid is ($length \times width \times height$), divided by 3, and ($6 \times 6 \times 9$), divided by 3 is 108 in³. Choice *A* is incorrect because 324 in³ is ($length \times width \times height$) without dividing by 3. Choice *B* is incorrect because 6 is used for height instead of 9 (($6 \times 6 \times 6$) divided by 3) to get 72 in³. Choice *D* is incorrect because 18 in³ is ($6 \times 9$), divided by 3 and leaving out a 6.

**35. C:** The formula for the volume of a sphere is $\frac{4}{3}\pi r^3$, and $\frac{4}{3} \times \pi \times 6^3$ is $288\,\pi$ in³. Choice *A* is not the correct answer because that is $12^2$. Choice *B* is not the correct answer because that is $10^2$, and Choice *D* is not the correct answer because that is $6 \times 2 \times 10$.

**36. A:** This answer is correct because $100 - 64$ is 36 and taking the square root of 36 is 6. Choice *B* is not the correct answer because that is $10 + 8$. Choice *C* is not the correct answer because that is $8 \times 10$. Choice *D* is also not the correct answer because there is no reason to arrive at that number.

**37. D:** The expression is three times the sum of twice a number and 1, which is $3(2x + 1)$. Then, 6 is subtracted from this expression.

**38. A:** Robert accomplished his task on Tuesday in $\frac{3}{4}$ the time compared to Monday. He must have worked $\frac{4}{3}$ as fast.

**39. B:** $\frac{2}{a}$ must be subtracted from both sides, with a result of $\frac{1}{x} = \frac{2}{b} - \frac{2}{a}$. The reciprocal of both sides needs to be taken, but the right-hand side needs to be written as a single fraction in order to do that. Since the two fractions on the right have denominators that are not equal, a common denominator of $ab$ is needed. This leaves:

$$\frac{1}{x} = \frac{2a}{ab} - \frac{2b}{ab} = \frac{2(a - b)}{ab}$$

Taking the reciprocals, which can be done since $b - a$ is not zero, with a result of:

$$x = \frac{ab}{2(a - b)}$$

**40. B:** The first step is to use the quadratic formula on the first equation ($x^2 + x - 3 = 0$) to solve for $x$. In this case, $a$ is 1, $b$ is 1, and $c$ is -3, yielding:

$$x = \frac{-b \pm \sqrt{b^2 - 4ac}}{2a}$$

$$x = \frac{-1 \pm \sqrt{1 - 4 \times 1(-3)}}{2}$$

$$x = \frac{-1}{2} \pm \frac{\sqrt{13}}{2}$$

Therefore, $x + \frac{1}{2}$, which is in our second equation, equals $\pm \frac{\sqrt{13}}{2}$. We are looking for $\left(x + \frac{1}{2}\right)^2$ though, so we square the $\pm \frac{\sqrt{13}}{2}$. Doing so causes the $\pm$ cancels and left with:

$$\left(\frac{\sqrt{13}}{2}\right)^2 = \frac{13}{4}$$

# *Reasoning Through Language Arts*

**1. D:** The use of "I" could serve to have a "hedging" effect, allow the reader to connect with the author in a more personal way, and cause the reader to empathize more with the egrets. However, it doesn't distance the reader from the text, making Choice *D* the answer to this question.

**2. C:** The quote provides an example of a warden protecting one of the colonies. Choice *A* is incorrect because the speaker of the quote is a warden, not a hunter. Choice *B* is incorrect because the quote does not lighten the mood but shows the danger of the situation between the wardens and the hunters. Choice *D* is incorrect because there is no humor found in the quote.

**3. D:** A *rookery* is a colony of breeding birds. Although *rookery* could mean houses in a slum area, Choice *A*, that does not make sense in this context. Choices *B* and *C* are both incorrect, as this is not a place for hunters to trade tools or for wardens to trade stories.

**4. B:** An important bird colony. The previous sentence is describing "twenty colonies" of birds, so what follows should be a bird colony. Choice *A* may be true, but we have no evidence of this in the text. Choice *C* does touch on the tension between the hunters and wardens, but there is no official "Bird Island Battle" mentioned in the text. Choice *D* does not exist in the text.

**5. D:** It emphasizes Mr. Utterson's anguish in failing to identify Hyde's whereabouts. Context clues indicate that Choice *D* is correct because the passage provides great detail of Mr. Utterson's feelings about locating Hyde. Choice *A* does not fit because there is no mention of Mr. Lanyon's mental state. Choice *B* is incorrect; although the text does make mention of bells, Choice *B* is not the *best* answer

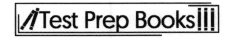 

overall. Choice *C* is incorrect because the passage clearly states that Mr. Utterson was determined, not unsure.

**6. A:** In the city. The word *city* appears in the passage several times, thus establishing the location for the reader.

**7. B:** It scares children. The passage states that the Juggernaut causes the children to scream. Choices *A* and *D* don't apply because the text doesn't mention either of these instances specifically. Choice *C* is incorrect because there is nothing in the text that mentions space travel.

**8. B:** To constantly visit. The mention of *morning*, *noon*, and *night* make it clear that the word *haunt* refers to frequent appearances at various times. Choice *A* doesn't work because the text makes no mention of levitating. Choices *C* and *D* are not correct because the text makes mention of Mr. Utterson's anguish and disheartenment because of his failure to find Hyde but does not make mention of Mr. Utterson's feelings negatively affecting anyone else.

**9. D:** This is an example of alliteration. Choice *D* is the correct answer because of the repetition of the *L*-words. Hyperbole is an exaggeration, so Choice *A* doesn't work. No comparison is being made, so no simile or metaphor is being used, thus eliminating Choices *B* and *C*.

**10. C:** Choice *A* does not identify a flaw in the advertisement's reasoning. The advertisement connects smoking with fatal disease. At no point does the advertisement confuse the cause and effect. Eliminate this choice.

Choice *B* is incorrect. The advertisement does not make any overly broad generalizations. Eliminate this choice.

Choice *C* correctly identifies the argument's flaw. The argument analogizes secondhand smoke with a gas chamber without offering any evidence concerning secondhand smoke's health risk. The advertisement is clearly relying on hyperbole. The advertisement's argument properly justifies smoking with adverse health effects, but it does not do the same for secondhand smoke. This is most likely the correct answer.

Choice *D* is incorrect. Nothing in the argument states that there's real dispute over smoking's effect on health. Eliminate this choice.

**11. C:** Choice *C* encompasses the argument's relevant information—mouth guards protect teeth and prevent concussions—and matches the argument's tone, which advocates penalties for non-compliance. Choice *A* looks promising, but fails to express the argument's main conclusion. This choice merely states reasons why mouth guards provide important protection during contact sports. Eliminate this choice. Choice *B* is a strong answer choice. The author clearly believes this to be true since the argument's last sentence advocates the enforcement of penalties for players who don't wear a mouth guard. However, this is not the main conclusion. Eliminate this choice. Choice *D* is incorrect since it uses weak language. The argument does not think that mouth guards are merely preferable. Rather, it advocates the enforcement of penalties for failing to wear mouth guards. The main conclusion must match the argument's tone and force. Eliminate this choice.

**12. A:** The word *patronage* most nearly means *auspices*, which means *protection* or *support*. Choice *B*, *aberration*, means *deformity* and does not make sense within the context of the sentence. Choice *C*,

*acerbic,* means *bitter* and also does not make sense in the sentence. Choice *D, adulation,* is a positive word meaning *praise,* and thus does not fit with the word *condescending* in the sentence.

**13. D:** *Working man* is most closely aligned with Choice *D, bourgeois.* In the context of the speech, the word *bourgeois* means *working* or *middle class.* Choice *A, Plebeian,* does suggest *common people;* however, this is a term that is specific to ancient Rome. Choice *B, viscount,* is a European title used to describe a specific degree of nobility. Choice *C, entrepreneur,* is a person who operates their own business.

**14. C:** In the context of the speech, the term *working man* most closely correlates with Choice *C,* "A working man is someone who works for wages among the middle class." Choice *A* is not mentioned in the passage and is off-topic. Choice *B* may be true in some cases, but it does not reflect the sentiment described for the term *working man* in the passage. Choice *D* may also be arguably true. However, it is not given as a definition but as *acts* of the working man, and the topics of *field, factory,* and *screen* are not mentioned in the passage.

**15. D:** *Enterprise* most closely means *cause.* Choices *A, B,* and *C* are all related to the term *enterprise.* However, Dickens speaks of a *cause* here, not a company, courage, or a game. "He will stand by such an enterprise" is a call to stand by a cause to enable the working man to have a certain autonomy over his own economic standing. The very first paragraph ends with the statement that the working man "shall . . . have a share in the management of an institution which is designed for his benefit."

**16. B:** The speaker's salutation is one from an entertainer to his audience and uses the friendly language to connect to his audience before a serious speech. Recall in the first paragraph that the speaker is there to "accompany [the audience] . . . through one of my little Christmas books," making him an author there to entertain the crowd with his own writing. The speech preceding the reading is the passage itself, and, as the tone indicates, a serious speech addressing the "working man." Although the passage speaks of employers and employees, the speaker himself is not an employer of the audience, so Choice *A* is incorrect. Choice *C* is also incorrect, as the salutation is not used ironically, but sincerely, as the speech addresses the well-being of the crowd. Choice *D* is incorrect because the speech is not given by a politician, but by a writer.

**17: B:** Choice *A* is incorrect because that is the speaker's *first* desire, not his second. Choices *C* and *D* are tricky because the language of both of these is mentioned after the word *second.* However, the speaker doesn't get to the second wish until the next sentence. Choices *C* and *D* are merely prepositions preparing for the statement of the main clause, Choice *B,* for the working man to have a say in his institution, which is designed for his benefit.

**18. C:** The speaker's tone can best be described as *confident and informed.* The speaker addresses the audience as "My good friends," and says, "I have no fear of being misunderstood," which implies confidence. Additionally, the speaker's knowledge of the proposal and topic can be seen in the text as well, especially in the second paragraph.

**19. D:** To provide credibility to the working man and share confidence in their ability to take on responsibilities if they are compensated appropriately. The speaker provides credibility by saying "he will stand by such an enterprise with the utmost of his patience," and displays their responsibilities by saying "he will feel his responsibility like an honest man."

**20. A:** The speaker says to "Erect in Birmingham a great Education Institution, properly educational." Choice *B* is close, but the speaker uses the name "Temple of Concord" in the passage as a metaphor, so this is incorrect. The other two choices aren't mentioned in the passage.

**21. B:** The word *antagonism* most nearly means opposition. Choice *A*, *conformity*, is the opposite of antagonism. Choice *C*, *affluence*, means abundance. Choice *D*, *scarcity*, means being deficient in something.

**22. B:** Strong dislike. This vocabulary question can be answered using context clues. Based on the rest of the conversation, the reader can gather that Albert isn't looking forward to his marriage. As the Count notes that "you don't appear to me to be very enthusiastic on the subject of this marriage," and also remarks on Albert's "objection to a young lady who is both rich and beautiful," readers can guess Albert's feelings. The answer choice that most closely matches "objection" and "not . . . very enthusiastic" is Choice *B, strong dislike*.

**23. C:** Their name is more respected than the Danglars'. This inference question can be answered by eliminating incorrect answers. Choice *A* is tempting, considering that Albert mentions money as a concern in his marriage. However, although he may not be as rich as his fiancée, his father still has a stable income of 50,000 francs a year. Choice *B* isn't mentioned at all in the passage, so it's impossible to make an inference. Finally, Choice *D* is clearly false because Albert's father arranged his marriage, but his mother doesn't approve of it. Evidence for Choice *C* can be found in the Count's comparison of Albert and Eugénie: "she will enrich you, and you will ennoble her." In other words, the Danglars are wealthier but the Morcerf family has a more noble background.

**24. D:** Apprehensive. There are many clues in the passage that indicate Albert's attitude towards his marriage—far from enthusiastic, he has many reservations. This question requires test takers to understand the vocabulary in the answer choices. *Pragmatic* is closest in meaning to *realistic*, and *indifferent* means *uninterested*. The only word related to feeling worried, uncertain, or unfavorable about the future is *apprehensive*.

**25. B:** He is like a wise uncle, giving practical advice to Albert. Choice *A* is incorrect because the Count's tone is friendly and conversational. Choice *C* is also incorrect because the Count questions why Albert doesn't want to marry a young, beautiful, and rich girl. While the Count asks many questions, he isn't particularly *probing* or *suspicious*—instead, he's asking to find out more about Albert's situation and then give him advice about marriage.

**26. A:** She belongs to a noble family. Though Albert's mother doesn't appear in the scene, there's more than enough information to answer this question. More than once is his family's noble background mentioned (not to mention that Albert's mother is the Comtesse de Morcerf, a noble title). The other answer choices can be eliminated—she is deeply concerned about her son's future; money isn't her highest priority because otherwise she would favor a marriage with the wealthy Danglars; and Albert describes her "clear and penetrating judgment," meaning she makes good decisions.

**27. C:** The richest people in society were also the most respected. The Danglars family is wealthier but the Morcerf family has a more aristocratic name, which gives them a higher social standing. Evidence for the other answer choices can be found throughout the passage: Albert mentioned receiving money from his father's fortune after his marriage; Albert's father has arranged this marriage for him; and the Count speculates that Albert's mother disapproves of this marriage because Eugénie isn't from a noble background like the Morcerf family, implying that she would prefer a match with a girl from aristocratic society.

**28. A:** He seems reluctant to marry Eugénie, despite her wealth and beauty. This is a reading comprehension question, and the answer can be found in the following lines: '"I confess," observed Monte Cristo, "that I have some difficulty in comprehending your objection to a young lady who is both rich and beautiful."' Choice *B* is the opposite (Albert's father is the one who insists on the marriage), Choice *C* incorrectly represents Albert's eagerness to marry, and Choice *D* describes a more positive attitude than Albert actually feels (*repugnance*).

**29. B:** The passage is mostly made up of dialogue. We can see this in the way the two characters communicate with each other, in this case through the use of quotations marks, or dialogue. Narration is when the narrator (not the characters) is explaining things that are happening in the story. Description is when the narrator describes a specific setting and its images. Explanation is when the author is analyzing or defining something for the reader's benefit.

**30. D:** The meaning of the word *ennoble* in the middle of the paragraph means to give someone a noble rank or title. In the passage, we can infer that Albert is noble but not rich, and Mademoiselle Eugénie is rich but not noble.

**31. C:** Because he finally understands Albert's point of view but still doesn't agree with it. The other choices aren't mentioned anywhere in the passage. Remember, although this passage is part of a larger text, the test taker should only pay attention to what's in the passage itself in order to find the correct answer.

**32. C:** In lines 6 and 7, it is stated that avarice can prevent a man from being necessitously poor, but too timorous, or fearful, to achieve real wealth. According to the passage, avarice does not tend to make a person very wealthy. The passage states that oppression, not avarice, is the consequence of wealth. The passage does not state that avarice drives a person's desire to be wealthy.

**33. D:** Paine believes that the distinction that is beyond a natural or religious reason is between king and subjects. He states that the distinction between good and bad is made in heaven. The distinction between male and female is natural. He does not mention anything about the distinction between humans and animals.

**34. A:** The passage states that the Heathens were the first to introduce government by kings into the world. The quiet lives of patriarchs came before the Heathens introduced this type of government. It was Christians, not Heathens, who paid divine honors to living kings. Heathens honored deceased kings. Equal rights of nature are mentioned in the paragraph, but not in relation to the Heathens.

**35. B:** Paine asserts that a monarchy is against the equal rights of nature and cites several parts of scripture that also denounce it. He doesn't say it is against the laws of nature. Because he uses scripture to further his argument, it is not despite scripture that he denounces the monarchy. Paine addresses the law by saying the courts also do not support a monarchical government.

**36. A:** To be *idolatrous* is to worship idols or heroes, in this case, kings. It is not defined as being deceitful. While idolatry is considered a sin, it is an example of a sin, not a synonym for it. Idolatry may have been considered illegal in some cultures, but it is not a definition for the term.

**37. A:** The essential meaning of the passage is that the Almighty, God, would disapprove of this type of government. While heaven is mentioned, it is done so to suggest that the monarchical government is irreverent, not that heaven isn't promised. God's disapproval is mentioned, not his punishment. The passage refers to the Jewish monarchy, which required both belief in God and kings.

**38. A:** The word *timorous* means being full of fear. The author concludes that extreme greed (avarice) makes people too afraid to be prosperous.

**39. B:** The author's attitude is closest to Choice *B*, *impassioned and critical*. Choice *A* is incorrect; the author is not *indifferent or fatigued*—on the contrary, there is a lot of energy and some underlying passion in the writing. Choice *C* is incorrect; the word *enchanted* means delighted, and the author is more critical and concerned of a monarchial government than enchanted with it. Choice *D* is not the best answer; although the author is passionate and critical of a monarchy, there is more logic than anger coming from the words.

**40. B:** To explain how monarchs came into existence and how Christians adapted to this way of government. Choice *A* is incorrect; the author does not agree that heathens were more advanced than Christians in this paragraph, it only explains the catalyst of the monarchial systems. Choice *C* is incorrect; the author would in fact disagree with the divination of the English monarchs. Choice *D* is incorrect; the paragraph *does* believe that monarchs cause damage, but the paragraph does not act as a counterargument to the one preceding it.

**41. D:** The author implies that the recorded history of creation is a collection, collage, or pattern taken from various accounts of cultures. Choice *A* is incorrect; there is no talk of cells or biology in the paragraph. Since "mosaic" modifies the word "account," we know that it is the account of creation that is mosaic, not creation itself, which makes Choice *B* incorrect. Choice *C* is also incorrect; the paragraph does not mention kings developing a system of recording accounts of creation.

**42. B:** The main point of this passage is to explain how a tornado forms. Choice *A* is off base because while the passage does mention that tornadoes are dangerous, this is not the main focus of the passage. While thunderstorms are mentioned, they are not compared to tornadoes, so Choice *C* is incorrect. Choice *D* is incorrect because the passage does not discuss what to do in the event of a tornado.

**43. D:** The passage directly states that the larger sensor is the main difference between the two cameras. Choices *A* and *B* may be true, but these answers do not identify the major difference between the two cameras. Choice *C* states the opposite of what the paragraph suggests is the best option for amateur photographers, so it is incorrect.

**44. D:** An actuary assesses risks and sets insurance premiums. While an actuary does work in insurance, the passage does not suggest that actuaries have any affiliation with hospitalists or working in a hospital, so all other choices are incorrect.

**45. A:** The passage focuses mainly on the problems of hard water. Choice *B* is incorrect because calcium is not good for pipes and hard surfaces. The passage does not say anything about whether water softeners are easy to install, so Choice *C* is incorrect. Choice *D* is also incorrect because the passage does offer other solutions besides vinegar.

46. **D:** The passage compares Disney cruises with Disney parks. It does not discuss how to book a cruise, so Choice *A* is incorrect. Choice *B* is incorrect because though the passage does mention some of the park attractions, it is not the main point. The passage does not mention the cost of either option, so Choice *C* is incorrect.

# Science

1. **A:** The hypothesis is the sentence that describes what the scientist wants to research with a conclusive expected finding. Choice *A* describes how she believes sunlight will affect plant growth. Choice *B* includes details about the experiment. Choice *C* is not a conclusive theory. Choice *D* describes the data that she found after conducting the experiment.

2. **C:** Looking at Figure 1, four experimental groups are shown on the graph for which data were collected: plants that received 1 hour of sunlight, 3 hours of sunlight, 5 hours of sunlight, and 7 hours of sunlight. Choices *A* and *B* could be describing two of the experimental groups and how much sunlight they received. Choice *D* describes how many days' data was collected.

3. **B:** After the data was collected, it was compiled into a line graph. The data points were collected, and then a line was drawn between the points. Data is represented by horizontal or vertical bars in bar graphs, Choice *A*. Pie charts are circular charts, with the data being represented by different wedges of the circle, Choice *C*. Pictograms use pictures to describe their subject, Choice *D*.

4. **A:** Looking at Figure 2, the Sun provides light energy that drives forward the process of photosynthesis, which is how plants make their own source of energy and nutrients. Choices *B* and *C* are found in the environment around the plants. They combine with light energy to make the photosynthesis reaction work. Choice *D* is a product of photosynthesis.

5. **D:** Looking at the Figure 1, the experimental group that received 7 hours of sunlight every day grew taller than any of the other groups that received less sunlight per day. Therefore, it is reasonable to conclude that more sunlight makes plants grow bigger. Choice *A* is not a reasonable conclusion because it did not have the tallest plants. The scientist decided to measure the plants only for 11 days, but that does not describe a conclusion for the experiment, Choice *B*. Choice *C* is the opposite of the correct conclusion and does not have evidence to support it.

6. **B:** The atomic mass of a molecule can be found by adding the atomic mass of each component together. Looking at Figure 3, the atomic mass of each element is found below its symbol. The atomic mass of Na is 23, Choice *A*, and the atomic mass of Cl is 35.5, Choice *C*. The sum of those two components is 58.5, Choice *B*. Choice *D* is equal to two Cl atoms joined together.

7. **D:** Figure 1 shows the trends of the periodic table. Looking at the black arrows representing electronegativity, it is shown that electronegativity increases going towards the top row of the table and also increases going towards the right columns of the table. Therefore, the most electronegative element would be found in the top right corner of the table, which is where the element Helium is found. Choices *A* and *B* are found at the bottom of the table. Choice *D* is found on the left side of the table.

8. **A:** Looking at Figure 1, the ionization energy increases as it goes right and up on the periodic table. Of the choices given, potassium (K) is found in the first column, fourth row. Each of the other choices is found above or to the right of potassium, so they would tend to have higher ionization energy. Since we're looking for the element with the lowest ionization energy, Choice *A*, potassium, is correct.

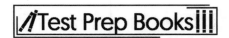 

**9. D:** The atomic number of an element represents the number of protons. The atomic number is located at the top of the box, above the element's symbol. Hydrogen (H) has an atomic number of 1 and has the least number of protons of any other element in the periodic table. Radon (Rn), Choice *A*, has 86 protons. Boron (B), Choice *B*, has 5 protons. Nitrogen (N), Choice *C*, has 7 protons.

**10. B:** Looking at Figure 3, the elements are separated in periods and groups according to their similar properties. Noble gases are located in the right most column of the table. Radon (Rn) is the only one of the element choices marked as a noble gas and would be the right choice for Scientist A. Nitrogen (N) and Boron (B), Choices *A* and *D*, are nonmetals. Copper (Cu), Choice *C*, is a transition metal.

**11. B:** Looking at Figures 1 and 2, crossbreeding experiment #3 in round #1 produces plants that are completely recessive and would have white flowers. Choices *A* and *C*, crossbreeding experiments #1 and 2, respectively, only produce flowers with a dominant allele present, making red flowers. Choice *D* does not have any recessive alleles, so white flowers are not a possibility.

**12. C:** Looking at Figure 2, which represents the number of plants that were produced from each crossbreeding experiment, it can be seen that only 2 plants produced white flowers out of 12 plants total, 4 from each experiment. To find the percentage, divide 2 by 12 and multiply by 100. The result is 16.7%. Choice *A* is the total number of plants that were produced. Choice *B* represents the percentage of white flowers in experiment #3 alone.

**13. B:** In a Punnett Square, each box represents one allele from each of the parent's genes. To find the genetic makeup of the second parent, take out the allele that was contributed from the first parent. Here, the first parent contributed a recessive allele, a, to each offspring. In the top row, that leaves a dominant allele, A, and in the bottom row, that leaves a recessive allele, a. Therefore, the genetic makeup of the second parent is Aa.

**14. D:** Crossbreeding the plants with only recessive alleles will result in 100% white flowering plants. All four offspring have white flowering plants. Choice *B* gives 100% red flowering plants. Choice *C* gives 25%, 1 out of 4 plants, with white flowers.

**15. A:** The observation step of the scientific method involves using your senses to identify the results of the experiment. In this case, the experiment depended on identifying the color of the flowers. This was done using sight. If the experiment had involved different scents produced by the flowers, Choice *B* would have worked. If it has involved different textures of the flowers, Choice *C* would have worked. Flowers generally do not make any noise, so Choice *D* would not have been useful.

**16. D:** The process of photosynthesis requires carbon dioxide and water to combine with sunlight to produce glucose, which is used as an energy source by plants. The forest floor does not get a lot of sunlight since it is shaded by the growth of so many trees and plants in the rainforest. Carbon, Choice *A*, is available through the air. Plants expel carbon dioxide. Water, Choice *B*, is abundant in the humid climate of the rainforest. Oxygen, Choice *C*, is always available in the Earth's atmosphere.

**17. B:** Central America is one of the five major areas of the world that has a rainforest. Looking at Figure 2, it can be seen that the southern countries of Central America contain rainforests. Comparing this map to the map of Central America, it is clear that Panama is a country that shas rainforests. Choices *A*, *C*, and *D* are not found in Central America.

**18. C:** Birds fly above the trees of the rainforest the most. There, they have unobstructed skies, unlike the dense growth of the trees and plants in the other layers of the rainforest.

**19. D:** The understory layer is the third layer from the top of the rainforest. It does not receive much sunlight, so the plants need to grow large leaves to absorb as much sunlight as possible. Giant taro leaves would grow well in this layer since they have large leaves. The emergent layer, Choice *A*, gets plenty of sunlight since it is the topmost layer. The canopy layer, Choice *B*, receives enough sunlight for plants to grow without needing to increase their leaf size. The forest floor, Choice *C*, does not receive sunlight, and plants generally do not grow here.

**20. A:** Rainforests have warm and wet climates. They do not have long dry seasons and tend to have temperate temperatures. The giant water lily is ideal for the rainforest because it can grow large leaves and needs a wet environment to grow in. They grow in the shallow basins of rainforest rivers. Choices *B* and *C* need dry environments. Choice *D* needs a very hot environment, which is not characteristic of rainforests.

**21. B:** Solar eclipses should not be looked at directly. The rays of the Sun do not seem as bright as normal but can still cause damage to the eyes. A pinhole camera facing away from the eclipse allows the viewer to see a reflection of the eclipse instead of the actual eclipse. Choices *A, C,* and *D* all require looking directly at the solar eclipse.

**22. A:** When the moon comes between the Earth and Sun, a solar eclipse occurs. If the sun is far enough away and is completely blocked by the moon, it is a total solar eclipse. If it is only partially blocked by the moon, it is a partial solar eclipse, Choice *D*. A lunar eclipse occurs when the moon is on the opposite side of the Earth as the Sun and the Sun creates a shadow of the Earth on the moon, so that the moon becomes completely dark, Choice *C*, or partially dark, Choice *B*.

**23. C:** During a lunar eclipse, the Sun and moon are on opposite sides of the Earth. They line up so that the Sun's light that normally illuminates the moon is blocked by the Earth. This causes the moon to become dim. Sunlight can still be seen, Choice *A*, and the Earth does not become dark, Choices *B* and *D*.

**24. B:** The moon does not produce harmful light rays that can damage the eyes, so lunar eclipses can be viewed directly. A telescope would allow the lunar eclipse to be magnified and seen more clearly. During a solar eclipse, the Sun's rays appear to be dim and easy to see directly but they are still harmful to the eyes.

**25. B:** Solar eclipses are viewed during the daytime because they involve viewing the Sun while it is out during normal daytime hours. Lunar eclipses, Choices *C* and *D*, are viewed at nighttime when the moon is in the sky during its normal hours. The moon is normally illuminated by the Sun that is on the other side of the Earth. When the Sun is on the other side of the earth, it is nighttime for people looking at the moon.

**26. B:** A cladogram is a diagram that organizes proposed ancestral relations based on the development of physical features. A branching point would be seen on the cladogram where the development of lungs was noted. A phylogenetic tree, Choice *A*, does not note phenotypic features on it. Punnett squares, Choice *C*, are used to determine the possible genetic makeup of offspring and are not related to evolution. Photographs, Choice *D*, may reveal species that look alike but would not reveal if they truly had a common ancestor.

**27. A:** According to Figure 3, human arms and whale fins are homologous structures that were derived from a common ancestor. They have anatomical similarities, although their function is not the same. They have different numbers of bones, so Choice *B* is incorrect. Since they are proposed to be developed

from a common ancestor, they are not analogous features, Choice *C*. Whales have blubber covering their bodies and not layered skin like humans, so Choice *D* is incorrect.

**28. D:** According to the phylogenetic tree in Figure 1, the common ancestor of the striped skunk and European otter is the one that is noted before they branch into separate lineages, which is Mustelidae. Mephitis, Choice *A*, is the genus for only the striped skunk. Felidae, Choice *B*, and Canidae, Choice *C*, are completely different branches of the Carnivora order than the one that leads to the striped skunk and European otter.

**29. A:** According to Figure 2, the common trait that is listed on the branch of the cladogram that leads to lizards and birds is seeing UV light. They also have the common traits listed on the main branch of the cladogram before their lineages are branched off, which are vertebrae, lungs, and amniotic eggs. Perch and flounder branch from the main common ancestor and develop spiny-rayed fins, Choice *B*. Lobsters and spiders branch from the main common ancestor and develop the ability to molt an exoskeleton, Choice *C*.

**30. C:** Domestic cats and wolves are proposed to be related at the point where they share a common line before any branching occurs to separate their lineages. Figure 1 shows this as Carnivora, which is noted as the Order on the left side of the figure.

**31. D:** The color reagent is attached to the secondary antibody. It is released only when the secondary antibody attaches to the activated primary antibody. The antigen, primary antibody, and capture antibody, Choices *A*, *B*, and *C*, do not have any color reagent attached to them, so only the secondary antibody can cause the color reaction.

**32. B:** The color reagent is attached to the secondary antibody. If more antigen is present, more primary and secondary antibody will be attached to it and more color reagent will be released. Row 1 has the darkest green color of all the samples tested in the plate in Figure 2.

**33. C:** Looking at the graph in Figure 3, the highest amount of IL-1β is found in the spleen. IL-1β is a marker of inflammation and indicates that the spleen had the most inflammation of the areas tested. Serum, Choice *A*, had no IL-1β in the sample. Plasma, Choice *B*, had the second highest amount of IL-1β in the sample, and bone marrow, Choice *D*, had the second lowest amount of IL-1β.

**34. B:** Looking at the diagram in Figure 1, the antigen is located between the capture antibody and the primary antibody. The capture antibody keeps the antigen attached to the surface of the plate. The primary antibody recognizes the specific antigen. The secondary antibody generally recognizes the primary antibody is not specific to the antigen.

**35. A:** ELISAs are used to analyze specific substances within a larger sample. The antibodies used in an ELISA are designed specifically for a particular antigen. Sandwich ELISAs are generally used to quantify one antigen and not all substances in a larger sample, making Choice *B* incorrect. When used to quantify an antigen, the antibodies need to already be developed and able to detect the antigen, making Choice *D* incorrect.

**36. A:** Stabilizing selection occurs when an intermediate phenotype is favored over two extreme phenotypes. In Scenario 1, the mice develop an intermediate colored fur so that they can blend in with the rocks in their environment. Developing one or both extremes, Choices *B* and *C*, would make them more visible to predators. Color selection, Choice *D*, is not a type of natural selection.

**37. D:** Directional selection occurs when one extreme of a phenotype is favored. In Scenario 2, large beaks are favored over medium- or small-sized beaks. The large beaks help the finches break up the tough seeds that became abundant after the drought. Finches with medium and small beaks had trouble breaking up the large seeds and did not survive as well as those with large beaks.

**38. B:** Small-beaked finches had trouble breaking up the large seeds after the drought, and therefore could not gain enough nutrition for survival. Natural selection is based on the idea that the individuals most suited for their environment are the ones that have enhanced survival and reproduction. Finches with large beaks were most able to eat the large seeds and continue with their regular feeding schedule. There was no evidence of Choices *A* or *C* in the passage. Two extremes can be selected by natural selection in disruptive selection but that was not the case here, Choice *D*.

**39. C:** Disruptive selection occurs when both extremes of a phenotype are selected. In Cameroon, the finches had both large and small beaks, but did not survive well with medium beaks. If medium beaks were selected, it would have been stabilizing selection, Choice *A*. If only one of the extremes had been favored, it would have been directional selection, Choice *B*.

**40. D:** Natural selection is based on the idea that the individuals most suited for their environment are the ones that have enhanced survival and reproduction. Their phenotypes are advantageous for survival and reproduction over those of other individuals. It is solely based on the phenotype of the individual, not the genotype, Choice *A*. Extreme phenotypes, Choice *B*, may be selected but are not always the most advantageous. It occurs all time, not just in extreme weather conditions, such as a drought, Choice *C*.

# *Social Studies*

**1. B:** Choice *B* is correct, as power is the ability of a ruling body to influence the actions, behavior, and attitude of a person or group of people. Choice *A* is incorrect, as politics is the process of governance typically exercised through the enactment and enforcement of laws over a community, most commonly a state. Although closely related to power, Choice *C* is incorrect, because authority refers to a political entity's justification to exercise power. Legitimacy is synonymous with authority, so Choice *D* is also incorrect.

**2. C:** Choice *C* is correct. There are no definitive requirements to be a nation. Rather, the nation only needs a group bound by some shared characteristic. Examples include language, culture, religion, homeland, ethnicity, and history. Choice *C* isn't a requirement to be a nation, though it is required to be a state.

**3. D:** Choice *D* is correct. Machiavelli was an Italian diplomat, politician, and historian, and *The Prince* is his best-known political treatise. The excerpt instructs the Prince that if he injures a man, then he must ensure the injury is "of such a kind that one does not stand in fear of revenge." Choices *B* and *C* contradict the first sentence of the excerpt, which says that men "ought either to be well treated or crushed." Choice *A* is close, but the selection goes too far, assuming revenge will result in overthrowing the Prince.

**4. A:** Choice *A* is correct. John Stuart Mill was an English philosopher and political economist who advocated for utilitarianism and women's rights. In the excerpt, "utility" is defined as actions that are "right in proportion as they tend to promote happiness, wrong as they tend to produce the reverse of happiness." The excerpt then explains that happiness is measured by pleasure, and the reverse is pain.

Therefore, Mill calls for actions to be evaluated based on the net total of pleasure. Choice *D* contradicts the definition provided in the excerpt. The excerpt doesn't support Choice *C*, as there's no evidence that pleasure-generating sacrifices merit special status. Choice *B* is incorrect because sacrifice can still be valuable if it leads to more pleasure than pain.

**5. C:** Choice *C* is correct. Karl Marx, a philosopher, social scientist, historian, and revolutionary, is considered the father of communism. All the answer choices contain true statements or reasonable assumptions from the passage; however, Choice *C* best articulates the main idea—society is the history of class struggle, and working men must unite and fight a revolutionary battle like their historical ancestors.

**6. A:** Choice *A* is correct. On the political spectrum, ideologies on the left side of the axis emphasize socioeconomic equality and advocate for government intervention, while ideologies on the right axis seek to preserve society's existing institutions and oppose government intervention. Therefore, the answer will be the farthest left on the axis, making Choice *A* correct.

**7. C:** Choice *C* is correct, as it most closely corresponds to the provided definition. Conservatism prioritizes traditional institutions. In general, conservatives oppose modern developments and value stability. Socialism and liberalism both feature the desire to change the government to increase equality. Libertarianism is more concerned with establishing a limited government to maximize personal autonomy.

**8. B:** Choice *B* is correct. The Articles of Confederation were the first form of government adopted in the American colonies. Under the Articles of Confederation, the central government (the Continental Congress) was granted very limited powers, rendering it largely ineffective. Although the choices describe what would appear to be basic functions of government, the central government could only declare war.

**9. D:** Choice *D* is correct. The missing title is in the overlap between federal and state government powers. Concurrent powers are shared between federal and state governments. Reserved powers are the unspecified powers of the states not expressly granted to the federal government or denied to the state by the Constitution and left to the states by the Tenth Amendment. Implied powers are the unstated powers that can be reasonably inferred from the Constitution. Delegated powers are the specific powers granted to the federal government by the Constitution.

**10. D:** Choice *D* is correct. The Federalists supported the expansion of the federal government, and the anti-Federalists feared that a stronger central government would weaken the states. *The Federalist Papers* argued for the ratification of the Constitution to establish a more powerful central government. The main idea of this excerpt is to argue that the Constitution establishes a central government powerful enough to rule, while also providing checks and balances to ensure the government doesn't abuse its power. Separation of powers is the concept behind checks and balances, so Choice *D* is the correct answer. Choices *A* and *C* are true statements, but they don't identify the main idea. Choice *B* references a theoretical assertion from the excerpt, but it's not the main idea.

**11. C:** Choice *C* is the correct answer. Checks and balances refer to the powers granted to ensure other branches don't overstep their authority. The other arrows in the diagram identify checks and balances, so the correct answer is the executive branch's checks and balances on the legislative branch. The executive branch can call special sessions of Congress and veto legislation, so Choice *C* is correct. Unlike the judicial and executive branches, members of the legislative branch cannot be impeached by another

branch, though the legislative branch can expel its own members. The executive branch cannot refuse to enforce laws.

**12. B:** Choice *B* is correct. The Second Amendment states, "A well regulated Militia, being necessary to the security of a free State, the right of the people to keep and bear Arms, shall not be infringed." The First Amendment provides freedom of religion, speech, and the press, the right to assemble, and the right to petition the government. The Third Amendment establishes the right to refuse to house soldiers in times of war. The Fourth Amendment establishes a series of protections for citizens accused and charged with crimes.

**13. B:** Choice *B* is correct. The Electoral College determines the winner of presidential races, but if a candidate doesn't win a majority of electoral votes, the Twelfth Amendment requires the House of Representatives to decide the presidency, with each state delegation voting as a single bloc. The candidate with the most votes in the House wins the election. The table shows that Andrew Jackson won a plurality of electoral and popular votes, but he didn't receive a majority. John Quincy Adams received the most votes in the House of Representatives, so he won the presidency.

**14. A:** Choice *A* is correct. Electoral systems dictate how the members of the ruling body are selected, how votes translate into positions, and how seats are filled in the political offices at each level of government. In a majority system, a candidate must receive a majority of votes in order to be awarded a seat, but if none of the candidates reach a majority, a second round of voting occurs, commonly referred to as a runoff.

**15. C:** Choice *C* is correct. The two major theories of international relations are Realism and Liberalism. Realism analyzes international relations through the interactions of states under the assumption that states act rationally to maintain or expand power as a means of self-preservation, which inevitably leads to conflict in an anarchical system. The question asks for the choice that doesn't adhere to Realism, and the other choices state three of the four basic tenets of Realism. In contrast, Choice *C* states a principle of Liberalism. Realists don't value international organizations or prioritize global cooperation.

**16. B:** Choice *B* is correct. Following the French and Indian War, the British government amassed an enormous war debt, and Great Britain imposed taxes on the colonists to generate more revenue. King George III argued that British resources defended the colonists from French and Native American forces, so the colonists should share in the expenses. The other choices are factually incorrect. The Royal Proclamation of 1763 prevented the colonies from expanding west of the Allegheny Mountains. No lasting peace ever occurred between the colonists and Native Americans. Self-government decreased in the colonies after the French and Indian War.

**17. A:** Choice *A* is correct. Heavily influenced by the Enlightenment, the Declaration of Independence repudiated the colonies' allegiance to Great Britain. The main purpose of the excerpt is to justify the colonists' revolutionary ambitions due to Great Britain's tyranny and the role of consent in government to protect the natural rights of citizens. Although the excerpt alludes to abuses, the purpose isn't to list specific evidence. This occurs later in the Declaration of Independence. Choices *C* and *D* are supporting evidence for the main purpose.

**18. D:** Choice *D* is correct. Any territory gained via purchase is incorrect. Missouri and Nebraska became American territories through the Louisiana Purchase, and the United States purchased Alaska from Russia. In contrast, Mexico ceded Nevada as part of the peace agreement ending the Mexican-American War.

**19. D:** Choice *D* is correct. President Lincoln issued the Emancipation Proclamation to free the slaves in the Confederacy, allowing the institution to continue in states and territories that didn't secede. The excerpt justifies the decision as a "fit and necessary war measure for suppressing said rebellion." Therefore, per the excerpt, emancipation was necessary to strengthen the war effort for the North. Choice *C* is the second-best answer, but the excerpt supports the contention that emancipation was part of an active war effort, rather than merely a punishment. Nothing in the excerpt describes the evil of slavery or the effect of emancipation on morale in the North.

**20. B:** Choice *B* is correct. Industrialization directly caused an increase in urbanization. Factories were located near cities to draw upon a large pool of potential employees. Between 1860 and 1890, the urbanization rate increased from about 20 percent to 35 percent. The other three choices are factually incorrect. Immigration increased during industrialization, as immigrants flooded into America to search for work. Socioeconomic problems plagued the period due to the unequal distribution of wealth and the social ills caused by rapid urbanization. Labor unrest was common as unions advocated for workers' rights and organized national strikes.

**21. A:** Choice *A* is correct. The Treaty of Versailles contained a clause that required Germany to assume responsibility for damages incurred during the conflict. Thus, the Treaty ordered Germany to pay $31.4 billion, the equivalent of $442 billion in 2017. World War I ravaged the German economy, and the country couldn't afford the war debt. The resulting poverty contributed to the rise of the Nazi Party, leading to World War II.

**22. B:** Choice *B* is correct. President Franklin D. Roosevelt introduced the New Deal, a series of executive orders and laws passed by Congress in response to the Great Depression. The excerpt describes how President Roosevelt intended to fight poverty by using the government's power to intervene and regulate the economy. Although the other answer choices correctly identify specific activities referenced in the excerpt, they are examples of the underlying philosophy in action. The underlying philosophy is an active role for government in the nation's economic affairs.

**23. C:** Choice *C* is correct. Frederick Douglass escaped from slavery and worked as an abolitionist for the rest of his life. The excerpt references the hypocrisy of the Fourth of July, as the holiday celebrates freedom in a country with millions of slaves. The other answer choices identify hypocritical aspects surrounding the slavery debate, but Choice *C* directly states the specific hypocrisy attacked in the excerpt.

**24. D:** Choice *D* is correct. Along with Lucy Stone and Elizabeth Cady Stanton, Susan B. Anthony was one of the most outspoken advocates for women's suffrage. Women couldn't vote in the United States until Congress passed the Nineteenth Amendment in 1920. Choice *D* accurately expresses the main idea of the excerpt. Denying women the right to vote is tyranny, so Anthony will not pay a fine for voting illegally. Choice *A* is the second-best answer, but it's too general to be the main idea of an excerpt specifically about women's suffrage.

**25. B:** Choice *B* is correct. Ronald Reagan won the presidential election of 1980 and promised to restore America's military power through defense spending, cutting government regulations, and reducing taxes. Evangelical Christians and the Moral Majority fiercely supported President Reagan's agenda, particularly his opposition to abortion and his conservative approach to social issues. The other answer choices include at least one mischaracterization. Choice *A* is incorrect because President Reagan generally opposed social programs. Choice *C* is incorrect because President Reagan valued American leadership more than international cooperation. In addition, his platform was far more radically

conservative than compromising. Choice *D* is incorrect because President Reagan fought labor unions on several fronts, most notably when he broke a strike organized by an air traffic controllers' union.

**26. C:** Choice *C* is correct. In a market economy, privately owned businesses, groups, or individuals price goods or services and set prices based on demand. In contrast, the government or central authority determines prices and quantity of production in a command economy. Of the two economic systems, the market economy more efficiently uses resources. Choice *C* is the only accurate statement.

**27. D:** Choice *D* is correct. William Jennings Bryan's "Cross of Gold" is one of the most famous speeches in American history, launching his candidacy in the 1896 presidential election. The speech advocates for abolishing the gold standard and adopting a bimetallic system to provide more government control over monetary policy. The excerpt condemns the influence of banks in monetary policy, and without some reform, the masses should act to remove the gold standard. Although the other answer choices accurately state assertions from the excerpt, they aren't the main idea.

**28. A:** Choice *A* is correct. The Depression of 1929, commonly referred to as the Great Depression, is the largest increase to unemployment, but the question stem asks for the second-largest increase. According to the graph, the Panic of 1893 increased unemployment by approximately ten percent; the Depression of 1920 increased unemployment by approximately six percent; the Depression of 1929 increased unemployment by approximately fifteen percent; and the Great Recession of 2007 increased unemployment by approximately four percent. Thus, the Panic of 1893 marks the second-largest increase to unemployment.

**29. A:** Choice *A* is correct. A business cycle is when the gross domestic product (GDP) moves downward and upward over a long-term growth trend, and the four phases are expansion, peak, contraction, and trough. An expansion is the only phase where employment rates and economic growth continually grow. Contraction is the opposite of expansion. The peak and trough are the extreme points on the graph.

**30. D:** Choice *D* is correct. The government can intervene in the economy by imposing taxes, subsidies, and price controls to increase revenue, lower prices of goods and services, ensure product availability for the government, and maintain fair prices for goods and services. Subsidies lower prices, reassure the supply, and create opportunity to compete with foreign vendors, so Choice *D* is correct.

**31. C:** Choice *C* is correct. Isoline maps are used to calculate data and differentiate between the characteristics of two places. In an isoline map, symbols represent values, and lines can be drawn between two points to determine differences. The other answer choices are maps with different purposes. Topographic maps display contour lines, which represent the relative elevation of a particular place. Dot-density maps and flow-line maps are types of thematic maps. Dot-density maps illustrate the volume and density of a characteristic of an area. Flow-line maps use lines to illustrate the movement of goods, people, or even animals between two places.

**32. B:** Choice *B* is correct. The map is a density map illustrating population density by state in the United States. Accordingly, the darker areas have higher population density. The darkest area of the map is the Northeast, so Choice *B* is correct.

**33. C:** Choice *C* is correct. The tilt of the Earth's rotation causes the seasons due to the difference in direct exposure to the Sun. For example, the northern hemisphere is tilted directly toward the Sun from June 22 to September 23, which creates the summer in that part of the world. Conversely, the southern hemisphere is tilted away from the Sun and experiences winter during those months. Choice *A* is

factually incorrect—the rate of Earth's rotation is constant. Choices *B* and *D* are factors in determining climate, but differences in climate don't cause the seasons.

**34. D:** Choice *D* is correct. Nonrenewable energy resources are oil, natural gas, and coal, collectively referred to as fossil fuels. Nonrenewable energy is more widely used due to its abundance and relatively cheap price. In addition, countries have tailored their existing infrastructure to nonrenewable energy. Currently, the technology to store renewable energies for long periods is either nonexistent or expensive. Choice *D* is correct because it's inaccurate. Renewable energy can be converted into a power source, but the issue is scale of use. For example, the United States converts renewable resources to derive ten percent of the country's energy.

**35. B:** Choice *B* is correct. Ocean currents dramatically impact the climate by storing heat from the Sun and transporting the warmth around the globe. The evaporation of ocean water increases the temperature and humidity in the nearby landmasses. A gyre is a system of circulating currents. Countries are most impacted by the currents and gyres closest to their shores. The question stem asks what currents have the most impact on the United States. According to the map, the North Atlantic Gyre, North Pacific Gyre, California Current, Alaskan Current and Gulf Stream impact the United States. Choice *B* is the only answer with a pair of those currents or gyres.

# Index

**Dear GED Test Taker,**

We would like to start by thanking you for purchasing this study guide for your GED exam. We hope that we exceeded your expectations.

Our goal in creating this study guide was to cover all of the topics that you will see on the test. We also strove to make our practice questions as similar as possible to what you will encounter on test day. With that being said, if you found something that you feel was not up to your standards, please send us an email and let us know.

We would also like to let you know about other books in our catalog that may interest you.

| Test Name | Amazon Link |
|---|---|
| HiSET | amazon.com/dp/1628456884 |
| SAT | amazon.com/dp/1628456868 |
| ACT | amazon.com/dp/1637758138 |
| ACCUPLACER | amazon.com/dp/1637758936 |

We have study guides in a wide variety of fields. If the one you are looking for isn't listed above, then try searching for it on Amazon or send us an email.

**Thanks Again and Happy Testing!**
**Product Development Team**
info@studyguideteam.com

# FREE Test Taking Tips DVD Offer

To help us better serve you, we have developed a Test Taking Tips DVD that we would like to give you for FREE. **This DVD covers world-class test taking tips that you can use to be even more successful when you are taking your test.**

All that we ask is that you email us your feedback about your study guide. Please let us know what you thought about it – whether that is good, bad or indifferent.

To get your **FREE Test Taking Tips DVD**, email freedvd@studyguideteam.com with "FREE DVD" in the subject line and the following information in the body of the email:

     a. The title of your study guide.

     b. Your product rating on a scale of 1-5, with 5 being the highest rating.

     c. Your feedback about the study guide. What did you think of it?

     d. Your full name and shipping address to send your free DVD.

If you have any questions or concerns, please don't hesitate to contact us at freedvd@studyguideteam.com.

Thanks again!

Made in the USA
Las Vegas, NV
31 January 2022

42728675R00225